W13

The Creative Spirit

Fifth Edition

The Creative Spirit

An Introduction to Theatre

Stephanie Arnold

Lewis and Clark College

McGraw Hill

Connect
Learn
Succeed™

The McGraw·Hill Companies

Connect
Learn
Succeed™

Published by McGraw-Hill, an imprint of The McGraw-Hill Companies, Inc., 1221 Avenue of the
Americas, New York, NY 10020. Copyright © 2011, 2008, 2004, 2001, 1998. All rights reserved. No
part of this publication may be reproduced or distributed in any form or by any means, or stored in
a database or retrieval system, without the prior written consent of The McGraw-Hill Companies,
Inc., including, but not limited to, in any network or other electronic storage or transmission, or
broadcast for distance learning.

This book is printed on acid-free paper.

1 2 3 4 5 6 7 8 9 0 DOC/DOC 0

ISBN: 978-0-07-338217-3
MHID: 0-07-338217-5

Vice President Editorial: *Michael Ryan*
Publisher: *Chris Freitag*
Sponsoring Editor: *Betty Chen*
Marketing Manager: *Pam Cooper*
Developmental Editor: *Sarah Remington*
Project Manager: *Erika Jordan*
Production Service: *Laserwords Maine*
Manuscript Editor: *Natalia Morgan*
Design Manager: *Allister Fein*
Text and Cover Designer: *Laurie Entringer*
Photo Research Manager: *Nora Agbayani*
Photo Research: *Jessica Holmes, Anna Crandall*
Production Supervisor: *Laura Fuller*
Composition: *9/12 Frutiger Light by Laserwords Private Limited*
Printing: *45# New Era Matte, R. R. Donnelley & Sons*

Cover Image: © *Nancy Keystone*

Credits: The credits section for this book begins on page 497 and is considered an extension of the
copyright page.

Library of Congress Cataloging-in-Publication Data
Arnold, Stephanie.
    The creative spirit : an introduction to theatre/Stephanie Arnold.—5th ed.
        p. cm.
    Includes bibliographical references and index.
    ISBN 978-0-07-338217-3 (alk. paper)
    1. Theater.   2. Drama.   I. Title.
    PN1655.A75 2011
    792—dc22

                                                    2009044365

The Internet addresses listed in the text were accurate at the time of publication. The inclusion of a
Web site does not indicate an endorsement by the authors or McGraw-Hill, and McGraw-Hill does
not guarantee the accuracy of the information presented at these sites.

www.mhhe.com

For Mark and for Daniel

(Brief Contents)

(Contents)

PART 2
The Nature of Performance:
The Theatre Practitioners   45

3   The Playwright's Vision   47

6   The Designers   161

9   Understanding Style: Theatricalism   264

10 Expressing a Worldview through Theatricalism 283

11 The Musical Theatre 348

I wrote *The Creative Spirit* for students like mine, whose interest in live theatre is critical to its future. My goal has been to give students the information they need for an in-depth understanding of the way theatre creates meaning. Rather than using a multitude of examples from plays that students may not have seen, I have chosen to focus on fewer works in greater detail, allowing students to become immersed in the worlds of the plays, the lives of the characters, and the choices involved in bringing these texts to the stage. My teaching has convinced me that students gain the most comprehensive understanding of theatre when plays are presented both in the context of culture and history and in relation to performance.

In order to create this textbook, I turned to my professional colleagues in the theatre and asked for their participation. I selected plays that I thought represented important artistic, philosophical, and social issues and sought out productions of those plays. I sat in on rehearsals and performances. I interviewed playwrights, directors, actors, and designers. I invited theatres to contribute photographs of their productions so that a visual story would accompany a written story. I wove quotes from my interviews through the descriptive material so that the practitioners could be part of a shared dialogue with the students. I tried to create a sense of what it would be like to be in the rehearsal process and what it would be like to be an audience member at the production. I also considered what kind of historical and social background materials would help students understand the plays that they were reading. Building a substantive cultural context meant considering historical, political, and economic background materials as well as

musical and artistic sources. The presentation of the cultural context could then demonstrate for students the place of the theatre in the development of the community and the way the theatre represents a gathering place of knowledge as well as of individuals.

FIVE COMPLETE PLAYSCRIPTS

At the core of the text are five complete plays: *Joe Turner's Come and Gone* by August Wilson, *And the Soul Shall Dance* by Wakako Yamauchi, *Angels in America: Millennium Approaches* by Tony Kushner, *Dog Lady* by Milcha Sanchez-Scott, and *Anna in the Tropics* by Nilo Cruz. Four of the plays are used to illustrate chapter themes: in Chapter 3 *Joe Turner's Come and Gone* illustrates the playwright's vision; Chapter 8 includes *And the Soul Shall Dance* as an example of expressing a worldview through realism; in Chapter 10 *Angels in America: Millennium Approaches* is included as an example of expressing a worldview through theatricalism; and in Chapter 14 *Dog Lady* illustrates the genre of comedy. The final play, *Anna in the Tropics*, is meant for a group project, although it may also be used as an additional or alternative example for other chapters. These five works demonstrate the power of contemporary American theatre to address the questions and concerns of our time.

EXAMPLES FROM A RANGE OF CULTURES AND PERIODS

In addition to the five complete plays, extended examples from classic and contemporary drama are included throughout. Chapter 1, for example, introduces ritual dramas performed by the

Kwakwaka'wakw people of the Pacific Northwest and the Hopi Indians of the Southwestern United States. The chapter also includes an overview of ancient Greek theatre represented through an exploration of Euripides' *Medea*. Medieval mystery cycles, Elizabethan drama, the Beijing Opera of China, European modernism, and American musicals are among the types of drama represented. The primary focus, however, is still the rich diversity of contemporary American theatre. And because the theatre's eloquence depends on visual imagery as well as on language, *The Creative Spirit* is supported by 200 production shots, design sketches, renderings, and drawings that highlight the exciting work of today's theatre artists.

AN INTEGRATED APPROACH: CONTEXT AND PERFORMANCE

I have tried to show students how to explore the text of a play as a theatre practitioner might, and how this exploration also enriches their experiences as audience members. Each of the book's five complete playscripts is accompanied by a discussion of the playwright's other works, his or her sources, and the historical and cultural context that informs the play's plot, setting, and characters. "In Context" boxes provide timelines related to the play; for example, a list of key dates in the African American experience offers some background for *Joe Turner's Come and Gone*. Following each playscript (except the project text *Anna in the Tropics*) is a section on the performance and production of the play at one or more representative American theatres. The theatres range from small, innovative theatres, such as the Eureka Theatre and East West Players, to large regional companies, such as the Oregon Shakespeare Festival and the Mark Taper Forum, to Broadway playhouses. This integrated approach is most apparent in these "case study" chapters, but I have also discussed cultural context and performance choices in the book's ten other chapters.

VOICES OF THEATRE ARTISTS

In writing *The Creative Spirit*, I wanted to bring to the forefront the energy, passion, and commitment of artists working in the theatre today. I wanted students to hear playwrights, actors, designers, and directors explain, in their own words, the choices and methods they use in their work. To obtain this material, I have interviewed more than seventy theatre artists over the course of preparing the five editions of the book. The playwrights Adam Rapp, Milcha Sanchez-Scott and Wakako Yamauchi; directors Nancy Keystone, Libby Appel, Ping Chong, Clinton Turner Davis, Olga Sanchez, and Tony Taccone; actors Sean McNall, Heather Robison, LeWan Alexander, and BW Gonzalez; designers Deborah Dryden, Ming Cho Lee, R. Eric Stone, Randy Tico, and Justin Townsend; dramaturgs Tom Bryant, Oscar Eustis, and Stephen Weeks; and choreographer Shen Wei are among the commentators on plays and productions discussed in the text.

SUPPORTING PEDAGOGICAL FEATURES

Integrated throughout the book are structured assignments that focus on critical thinking, writing, and creative approaches to advance the students' understanding of theatre and to help students develop essential skills applicable in many areas of their education. All chapters include content-specific exercises for discussion, writing, and creative activity. The project chapter at the end of the book provides students with a guided structure for imagining their own productions and engaging creatively with elements of theatre practice. The project also presents the opportunity for historical and period research. The appendix of guided writing assignments builds on the approaches of the dramaturg and critic introduced in Chapter 13. Writing assignments include reviewing productions, preparing research materials for display, and conducting interviews. Together the assignments throughout the book provide students with the foundation for appreciating the complexities of theatremaking and for being insightful and sophisticated audience members. With the expanded Web site and revised testing materials, *The Creative Spirit* includes all of the resources for a complete course.

NEW TO THE FIFTH EDITION

- A new production analysis explores a recent work of theatre performance entitled *Apollo* and complements the four casebook studies based on traditionally scripted plays that are already a central feature of the book. As a work devised by the director, designers, and actors in an improvisational and collaborative process, *Apollo* represents a contemporary trend in the theatre in the creation of new multimedia work. *Apollo* examines key episodes in American history, partly through docudrama and partly through an expressive use of movement, visual imagery, and sound. The presentation of *Apollo* uses a format entirely different from the other production analyses that each has a dedicated chapter. Material from *Apollo* is included in the chapters on acting, directing, and design through a photo essay and commentary from many of the participants. Furthermore, the *Apollo* production analysis is supported by a number of online features on the book's Web site, developed specifically for the instructors and students using this text: a slide show, music, and full interviews with the director, members of the creative staff, and the actors.

- A new play, *Anna in the Tropics*, by Nilo Cruz is now the subject of the project chapter that concludes the book. Winner of the Pulitzer Prize in 2003, *Anna in the Tropics* provides the opportunity for period and historical research in addition to the continuing features that guide students in developing their own production concepts.

- A revision of two key chapters and the reordering of a third offer more effective pacing of course materials. In the first part of the book, Chapter 1 now presents the origins of religious drama through an examination of Native American, Greek, and medieval European performances. Chapter 2 presents the development of the professional theatre through an examination of the Elizabethan theatre and the Chinese opera. These newly configured chapters provide units of study with a sharper focus to enhance student comprehension and more opportunity for teachers to treat important subjects in depth. The chapter on musical theatre (now Chapter 11) has been moved from Part 2 of the book to Part 3 to complement the discussion of theatricalism and to provide more even spacing between the reading of plays, which now are placed in Chapters 3, 8, 10, 14, and 15.

- A new group of actors are introduced in Chapter 4, Acting, through recent production photos and commentary, to illuminate the essential concepts in the chapter from a contemporary perspective.

- Over forty new color photographs provide coverage of many exciting new plays and productions of classics including *Apollo, August: Osage County, Black Watch, Dying City, Endgame, Eurydice, Hamlet, Lydia, Othello, Passing Strange, Richard III, Ruined,* and *Waiting for Godot.*

- Newly developed online materials provide extensive opportunities for student exploration. A number of full text interviews with practitioners introduced in the fifth edition allow students to read further about subjects of interest to them through lively conversations. Actor Sean McNall talks about preparing to play Hamlet in a repertory company. Playwright Adam Rapp discusses directing his own plays. Director Nancy Keystone explains how she develops the material for her productions. Technical director Bradley Thompson (*Fuerzabruta*) discusses the complex process of working with new applications of theatre technology. Producer and artistic director Oskar Eustis speaks about the importance of the Public Theater. In addition to the many interviews conducted specifically for the fifth edition, online features also include a slide show, video, and music from *Apollo*.

SUPPLEMENTS

The following supplements are available through a McGraw-Hill sales representative.

- An **Online Learning Center,** located at www.mhhe.com/creativespirit5e, offers interviews with theatre practitioners, a slide show, video, chapter quizzes, exercises, and more.

- The **Instructor's Manual and Test Bank** (ISBN 0-07-255834-2) offers a variety of resources for instructors, including assignment ideas; chapter summaries; and multiple-choice, short-answer, and essay questions.

ACKNOWLEDGMENTS

As *The Creative Spirit* enters its fifth edition, I am deeply appreciative of the many people who have contributed to its evolution. A large number of theatre artists have given generously of their time in helping to build the case studies of the various productions or in contributing additional interview material. The playwrights, actors, directors, and designers whose insightful commentary is found throughout the text have added immeasurably to the book's specificity and vitality. For the fifth edition, it was my great pleasure to interview a number of remarkable theatre practitioners. At the invitation of Nancy Keystone, I was able to attend a number of rehearsals for *Apollo*, both in Los Angeles and Portland, where I was warmly

welcomed by all involved. Mark Tynan, the production stage manager at Portland Center Stage, and Cynthia Furhman, marketing and communication director, facilitated my interactions with the cast and the creative staff. I thank the following members of the *Apollo* company for their participation in interviews: the director, playwright, and designer Nancy Keystone, composer Randy Tico, dramaturg Tom Bryant, lighting designer Jeff Townsend, projection designer Jeff Teeter, and actors Russell Edge, Ray Ford, Richard Gallegos, Lorne Greene, Christopher Shaw, and Valerie Spencer. And many thanks as well to Nancy Keystone and Randy Tico, for providing photographs and music for the book and the Web site. In New York, I interviewed the director Shep Sobel and actors Sean McNall and Jolly Abraham about their production of *Hamlet* at the Pearl Theatre. The playwright and director Adam Rapp spoke with me about his recent play, *American Sligo*. Bozkurt Karasu, production manager for the Wooster Group's *Hamlet*, and Bradley Thompson, technical director for *Fuerzabruta*, shared with me the challenges of mounting these productions. And Oscar Eustis was most generous in taking time from his demanding schedule as artistic director of the Public Theater to speak with me again about his evolving role in the American theatre. Many years ago I interviewed Oskar Eustis about his work as dramaturg for *Angels in America* for the first edition of *The Creative Spirit*. At the Los Angeles Theater Center, I interviewed the artistic director José Luis Valenzuela and the playwright Evelina Fernandez about the work of that organization and particularly about their production of *La Virgen de Guadalupe, Dios Inantzin*. In the Bay Area the actor Heather Robison talked with me about her preparation process in undertaking a new role. And the actor and director Delroy Lindo discussed his work on *Joe Turner's Come and Gone*. I thank all of these theatre practitioners for sharing their insights about making theatre, and its significance in their lives. The opportunity to speak with leading and emerging theatre and art practitioners is one of the great joys of my continued work on *The Creative Spirit*. I also wish to thank Kimi Kodani Hill and Nori Obata, who graciously arranged for me to use the artwork of their grandfather, Chiura Obata, which is a wonderful addition to the material on the Japanese American experience. And many thanks, as well, to Terence Keene from the Berkeley Repertory Theatre, who assisted us with photos from several Berkeley Repertory Theatre productions.

A growing number of people have reviewed the manuscript at different stages of the project. A fundamental goal of mine in writing *The Creative Spirit* has been to partner effectively with theatre teachers to provide the most meaningful experience for our students. The review process helps to make that goal possible. I wish to thank the following reviewers for their invaluable comments and suggestions for the fifth edition:

Kathy Byrne
University of Florida, Gainesville

Patton Chiles
Washington University in St. Louis

Mike Connor
Livingstone College

Susan Proctor
Rockhurst University

Julien Phillips
North Hennepin Community College

The editorial staff at McGraw-Hill has continued to provide outstanding support for this book. Sarah Remington recently joined the staff as editorial coordinator and it has been a great pleasure to work with her. Thanks also to my sponsoring editors Betty Chen and Chris Freitag. Erika Jordan has expertly managed the manuscript preparation and I am most appreciative of the meticulous work of the copy editor, Natalia Morgan. Over the last year two of my students worked with me as research assistants, Anna Crandall and Jessica Holmes, who also undertook much of the work on the expanded Web site. Their professionalism and enthusiasm made all of my tasks much easier. I also wish to thank Daniel Arnold for reading the chapter revisions.

Once again, I would like to include a few words about my students. I have been most fortunate in my teaching career to have worked closely with many remarkable students. As I have taught them in acting and dramatic literature classes or directed them in plays, we have had the great joy of making discoveries together, learning from each other, and together reaching an understanding of the value of the theatre in our lives. I salute their talent, their openness, their idealism, and their commitment.

Finally, I acknowledge the support of my family, who have never flagged in their enthusiasm for the project or their willingness to undertake all the tasks necessary to make the book possible and to keep my sense of humor intact.

Stephanie Arnold is Professor of Theatre at Lewis and Clark College in Portland, Oregon where she has served in the past as the Chair of the Theatre Department and the Dean of Arts and Humanities. She has also taught at the University of California, Riverside and Mills College. Professor Arnold's B.A. is from Stanford University and she holds M.F.A. and Ph.D. degrees in theatre from the University of Wisconsin, Madison. She teaches acting, directing, and dramatic literature and has directed over forty productions for the theatre, including works by classical and contemporary playwrights, musicals, and opera. Dr. Arnold's research focuses on the American theatre.

PART I

The Nature of Theatre

For thousands of years, in almost all cultures, the theatre has been an essential part of human expression. In his book *The Rainbow of Desire,* the Brazilian theatre director Augusto Boal calls theatre the first human invention because it is through theatre that we step back from ourselves to observe and interpret our own behavior. Through the theatre, we reflect on our experiences and we imagine new possibilities. Making theatre is a way of understanding the world around us and our place in it. We also find this process of projecting ourselves into strange or familiar circumstances immensely entertaining.

In the theatre, the **playwright** and the **actor** together present stories in the form of action. The stage action invites audience members to enter a created, fictional world. The energy of the actors and the energy of the audience fuse to charge the theatre event with an intensity that carries the performance beyond ordinary existence into a magical realm of the human spirit. Into theatre performances we pour our dreams, our myths and stories, our struggles and fears. The conflicts that divide us and the laughter that makes us whole take their place on the stage. We make a journey through space and time that is limited only by our imagination.

Before the electronic age, the theatre provided much or all of a community's dramatic entertainment. Today, drama takes place on small and large screens and over the airwaves as well as in the theatre. But although it has much in common with its electronic relatives, the theatre is distinguished by the very fact that it is a live event dependent on the presence of actor and audience in the same space. The live actor–audience relationship offers countless possibilities for envisioning human experience.

This book presents a study of contemporary American plays and productions as a way of understanding the theatre in our own time. To lay a foundation for this approach, we begin by examining the nature of performance and the way performance responds to deep human needs. We look at the impulse to perform that draws actors onto the stage. We then consider the power of the theatre in society. Just as performance exerts a strong pull on individuals, the theatre generates a forceful presence in the life of a community. By introducing some of the great theatre traditions worldwide, we begin a discussion of the many forms that theatre may take and the complex relationship between theatre and society. ●●●

Chapter 1

The Impulse to Perform: Origins

AS DUSK FALLS, **THE PEOPLE** gather in the ceremonial house for the Winter Dance. All the members of the community are present, from the oldest to the youngest, as well as honored guests who have arrived by boat to the island village located on a remote waterway. A fire burns in the center of the large dark lodge. Beyond the blazing logs stands a screen painted with images of sea animals, whales and otters and eagles, flickering in the firelight. The screen represents the house of the chief of the undersea kingdom.

A loud, commanding whistle sounds, filling the lodge with its notes and announcing the presence of supernatural forces. A rustling is heard from behind the screen and then a large whale swims into view. Swooping and spouting, the whale glides around the fire, bringing with it the authority of the natural world and an ancient story told many times by the community elders about their ancestor, Born-to-Be-Head-of-the-World. A young man from this village was drawn beneath the sea, where he performed feats of heroism in the undersea kingdom. When he returned, he possessed the knowledge and power of the sea.

A dancer wears the enormous whale mask that recalls one of the forms in which Born-to-Be-Head-of-the-World appeared. The mask is animated by this actor through the movement of his own body and the moving parts of the mask, which the master carver has fashioned for this fantastic creature and which the dancer controls by manipulating strings. The enormous, ferocious mouth drops open and snaps shut. The double tail with flukes, curving forward and back, can be lowered to suggest the motion of a diving whale. An eagle rides on the whale's back and even his wings flap as the whale swims on. Paint and mica make the eyes glow in the firelight and glisten as if they carry drops of water from the sea.

The whale mask shown here was collected by the anthropologist George Hunt in 1901 and would have been used to enact the story of Born-to-Be-Head-of-the-World during the nineteenth century in Hopetown, British Columbia. Made from wood, hide, and rope, this heavy piece, measuring about 7½ feet long and 2½ feet wide, would have required skill and practice to maneuver effectively. This mask is in the collection of the American Museum of Natural History in New York City.

The dancer stops and a further pull of the strings causes the entire face of the whale to give way and open to reveal another presence inside, a large bullhead fish (a sculpin), carved and painted to be both fish and man. This transforming mask and the performance itself are nothing less than a display of the supernatural powers of this community's ancestor, Born-to-Be-Head-of-the-World.[1]

This whale performance is part of the **potlatch** ceremonies of the indigenous peoples of the Pacific Northwest Coast of the United States and the Southwest Coast of Canada, and dates from the nineteenth century and perhaps earlier. It is one example of the many ways storytelling and performance function in almost all human societies. Storytelling is central to the formation of human culture. Myth and metaphor are fundamental, imaginative constructs that we employ to distill human experience. But it is not enough for us to tell our stories through words alone. We are compelled to act them out, to perform our understanding of human behavior and the forces that we believe govern our world. This impulse to perform is an essential part of human nature that appears in our daily interactions as well as in the dramas we put on the stage and on film.

PERFORMANCE AND HUMAN BEHAVIOR

If we step back from organized dramas to examine individual behavior, we see that the impulse to perform is part of the way we survive. We adapt to changes in our circumstances by making adjustments in the identity we present to other people. We seek to transform ourselves or to emphasize a compelling characteristic, such as courage or humility, that will carry us safely through danger. The human mind is elastic and imaginative in the construction of identity. Part of growing up depends on observing successful role models and experimenting with identities that make us feel comfortable in the face of changing social pressures or demands. Identity is fluid rather than fixed; we may be one person with our families and quite a different person at work or in public situations. Peer pressure or social conditioning can cause people to adopt various sets of behaviors that make them a recognizable part of a group.

Sometimes we feel that we cannot know certain people until we can break through the masks that they wear to protect themselves or, perhaps, to take us in. Consider on one hand the politician who puts on a different face for every new situation or constituency. We may even doubt that such a person has a core identity at all. On the other hand, we may believe that we cannot really know someone until we recognize that he or she is made up of different identities. Certainly we

The mask shown in these photographs represents the continuation of the ceremonial traditions of the Kwakwaka'wakw people in the present day. The artist George Hunt Jr. has resumed the carving practices that were almost lost when the cultural practices of Native peoples were suppressed. Today Hunt Jr. makes masks and costumes for the potlatch ritual, which is observed by coastal Native peoples of Southwestern Canada and Northwestern United States. At its height in the nineteenth century, the potlatch ceremony lasted for days. It was a major social occasion involving the immediate community and many invited guests, and was also an essential means of expressing changes in the social order. Rites of passage for the young, marriages, and mourning cycles were all observed through the potlatch. Dramatic performances were a highlight of these gatherings and included elaborately carved masks, spectacular costumes, and astonishing special effects. The transformation mask in these photographs changes from a wolf, in the first image, to a killer whale, in the second, when the performer pulls on strings threaded through both sides of the wolf's long face.

understand the great release in letting go of certain "expectations" of behavior and trying out a role that is "nothing like us." In the theatre, actors build on this fundamental human impulse to perform in order to describe and interpret human existence for an audience. As audience members, we take great pleasure in watching the work of actors who have made an art out of an impulse that is part of human nature.

Performance and Role Playing

We begin our study of the theatre by exploring the place of performance in human behavior. What human needs are met through performance? What are the psychological, social, and cultural conditions that motivate performance? Understanding the functions of performance in our lives provides a basis for approaching the professional performance of

These children, living in Iraq, use dramatic play to imitate and interpret the violence that governs their lives.

the actor, whose work is the essence of the theatre.

If we observe children at play, we see that many of them pretend to be the adults who are prominent in their lives. Children often start taking roles by "playing house" or "playing school"—pretending to be parents or teachers. Children living in war zones play out the violence that surrounds them at a very early age. Certainly children's imitation of the behavior they observe is a way of learning about or preparing themselves for roles they expect to assume. But there is more to dramatic play than social conditioning.

Imagine a four-year-old boy going out with his mother. Before leaving the house he insists on putting on his cape and strapping on his sword. Whether he sees himself as Superman, Batman, Spiderman, or the latest incarnation of a superhero, his impersonation is a serious business. At four, he is old enough to know that the world can be a threatening place. He is aware that he is physically small and lacks the skills of older children or adults that would give him more control in a dangerous and confusing environment. So he puts on the costume or "signs" of what he recognizes as power. And through wearing the cape and bearing the sword, he takes on a role that enables him to share in the power of his hero.

We recognize in this small boy's actions a pattern of behavior that occurs in a variety of situations and at different ages. Life is difficult and full of obstacles. In certain situations, we enact roles; we make adjustments in the way we present ourselves, particularly in ways that make us feel more powerful. The small child is not concerned about being obvious as he carts around his sword. He wants threatening forces, whether real or imaginary, to be clear about his new identity. As adults we try to be more subtle as we put on the clothes and accessories of power, assume certain postures, and alter our language or vocal intonation. The actor Bill Irwin, whose work is discussed in Chapter 4, says he approaches many of his characterizations by asking himself two questions: (1) "What am I afraid of right now?" (2) "What are all the mechanisms that I'm putting into play to show that I'm not really afraid of that?"[2]

COMMUNITY PERFORMANCE

The story of the little boy and his superhero battle gear is one of many examples of individual role playing. But humans also engage in forms of collective dramatic expression that are fundamental to the community. Through **dramatic rituals** we reinforce community values and act out community stories that preserve a way of life. The term *ritual* refers to a ceremonial observation that is repeated in a specified way in order to confer certain benefits on the participants. Rituals are highly symbolic events with densely coded meanings. There are sacred rituals, and there are distinctly secular rituals. Indeed, some of the richest forms of ritual dramatic expression take place as part of religious observances such as the enactment of the birth of Jesus in the Christian community

La Carpa del Ausente, the 2007 production for Día de los Muertos at the Miracle Theatre in Portland, Oregon, is shown in this photo. Directed by Philip Cuomo, the production combined vaudeville, acrobatics, and political satire enacted by various skeletal characters. The actors are Daniel Moreno, CarlosAlexis Cruz, Matt Haynes, and Jorge Arredondo.

or the observation of the seder meal at Passover in the Jewish community. The Kwakwaka'wakw whale performance at the beginning of the chapter is part of a traditional religious ritual.

A ritual that is becoming more prevalent in the United States takes place in communities with a Hispanic heritage. *El día de los muertos,* or the Day of the Dead, is observed at the beginning of November as a way of remembering family members who have died and celebrating their lives. The beliefs that underlie the Day of the Dead come first from Aztec worship and embrace a view in which life and death are seen as part of a continuum. Death is accepted rather than abhorred or denied. By tending to family graves and bringing to the cemetery the food and drink enjoyed by those who have died, "the way is prepared for the spirits to return." Far from being a morbid or sad occasion, the day is filled with humor, music, processions, food, and performances. At this time, comic figures of skeletons appear who are engaged in all the activities of life, bright orange marigolds decorate cemeteries, and special breads take over bakeries.

Olga Sanchez is the artistic director of the Miracle Theatre in Portland, Oregon. Each year this theatre celebrates the Day of the Dead with a musical festival or a play that builds on the more personal observations of families. Sanchez sees the Day of the Dead as a "chance to revisit with your ancestors and acknowledge the people who came before us, to hear of their stories, their sacrifices, and their values." The connections to the past help to form more meaningful "personal and community identity."[3]

Weddings and graduations exemplify two types of well-known community rituals. In a traditional wedding, a sacred ritual, the bride, the groom, and the attendants wear elaborate and highly ceremonial clothes, and the couple enact their vows according to the custom of their religious faith. Many believe that such a ceremony strengthens the marriage and subsequently the community, whose members participate as witnesses and join in the celebration; they see the wedding ceremony as essential to the stability of the community. Although rituals tend to change slowly because their form needs to be fixed to be effective, they can also be somewhat flexible. One element of the wedding ritual currently undergoing significant change is giving away the bride. At one time this gesture symbolized shifting authority over a woman from her father to her husband. Today other family members or friends may "give the bride away," or the couple may choose to eliminate this custom altogether.

The secular ritual of the high school graduation is of great significance to towns and cities across the United States. The graduation ceremony is a formal rite of passage for the community's young people, a way for them to be accepted into adulthood. Robes and caps are worn; solemn music is played; the graduates accept their diplomas and congratulations and best wishes for the future from their community leaders. Most students play their parts with an unusual amount of dignity. To complement the formality of the actual graduation ceremony, many graduating classes develop their own more ecstatic, freer ritual festivities to mark the significance of this event.

Other secular rituals include sporting events, particularly college and professional football games. Sports fans wear costumes and makeup as part of their identification with the drama enacted on the playing field. Beauty pageants, too, are community rituals, as are parades, such as the gay-pride parades that occur in a number of communities and involve many dramatic elements of costume and impersonation.

Community rituals bind community members together by reinforcing their common history and shared goals. They help shape the yearly calendar and the many rites of passage in the human life cycle. Because the United States is made up of many religious faiths and cultural groups, our national rituals tend to be secular, which may be one reason sports have become so important to us. Nonetheless, some community rituals in the United States are a form of worship that interpret religious history or values and also allow for intense identification with the most sacred beliefs of the community. For some communities, dramatic religious rituals are central to community life and govern a great deal of community activity throughout the year. It is from such entrenched dramatic ritual that many of the major dramatic traditions worldwide have evolved.

We turn to the dramatic rituals of a small Native American community, the Hopi, as a source for our further examination of the impulse to perform. This community has been chosen for two primary reasons: the richness of its ceremonial performances and the fact that its rituals—as well as other Native American ceremonial dramas—represent one of the earliest dramatic forms indigenous to our continent.

Ritual Performance among the Hopi

In an elaborate sequence of dramatic ceremonies, the Hopi Indians of the southwestern United States represent the *kachinas*, whom they

The performance of the kachina cycle binds the Hopi community together through the preservation of a belief system and a way of life. Kachina dolls like the one shown here are carved by Hopi artists as a sacred representation of the kachina ritual. The preferred Hopi word for kachina is *katsina* and, in the plural form, *katsinam*.

view as their spiritual guardians. According to Dorothy K. Washburn, "Kachinas are the messengers and intermediaries between men and gods."[4] The concept of the kachina is associated with the clouds from which rain falls and with the dead, whom the Hopi believe become part of the clouds and return to earth as rain. The Hopi believe that the intervention of the kachinas will bring rain to the arid landscape of the high desert and ensure the success of their crops.

With their brilliant costumes and **masks** incorporating animal and plant images, the ceremonial dramas make the kachina spirits visible to the Hopi community. Because most elements of the costumes and masks have a symbolic meaning, the Hopi figuratively "wear their world" when they are in their ceremonial dress.[5] For example, different colors represent the different geographic and spiritual directions and the weather and resources represented by those directions. Tortoiseshell rattles refer to the water of the ponds and springs where the tortoises live. Eagle and turkey feathers become the flight of prayers.

Kachina Performances

The kachina ceremonies are central to the Hopi worldview and may have originated as early as the twelfth or thirteenth century. There are more than 300 different kachinas, and kachina rituals are spread over much of the year. From December to July a great epic cycle of kachina performances involves all members of the community in varying responsibilities for the ongoing ritual drama. In fact, the Hopi villages are built around the plazas in which the ceremonial dances take place. The kachina performances are at the center of the community physically as well as spiritually and socially.

Soyal, the first observation of the **kachina cycle,** occurs at the winter solstice, in December, to break the darkness and prepare for the new year. *Niman,* the last ceremony, anticipating a successful harvest, occurs in July. Following this final Home Dance, the kachinas are believed to return to the San Francisco Mountains west of the Hopi villages, where they remain until they rejoin the Hopi at the winter solstice. Between the initiation of the cycle in December and the conclusion in July, the kachinas perform a series of ceremonies in which seeds are planted, children are initiated, community members are taught discipline, and, finally, crops are harvested. Rain, fertility, and maintaining social order are the underlying goals of all kachina activity. The dramatic ritual is a highly complex way of exerting control over the environment—that is, the physical, social, and spiritual world.

The kachina ceremonies are frequently serious and sometimes even frightening. But humor is also an essential part of the ritual; laughter is understood as basic to human survival. Clowns appear among the kachinas, and they offer a critique of negative behavior through **parody** by performing outrageous acts that would be unacceptable outside the ritual observation.

The Hopi Performer

The Hopi man who takes on the persona of a kachina is transformed (women do not participate as performers). He transcends his own being and becomes the kachina spirit that he embodies. He takes on the presence and the power of the kachina and therefore can act for the kachina in the ceremonies. Through the ritual dance, a transaction takes place between the human and the supernatural, a merging of the two levels of existence.

Like personal performance, community performance is very much tied to the quest for power. But in sacred community performance in particular, performers become separated from their status as mere mortal beings. They become elevated. By the nature of their special religious knowledge, their enactment of the ceremony, and their performance skills, they become "magicians" who act on behalf of the other members of the community.

Society and Aesthetic Expression

Throughout the world the impulse to perform, to interpret human existence through the presentation of characters on a stage, has evolved into an astonishing variety of theatre traditions. Just as the human capacity for speech has produced many languages, so the impulse to perform has found expression in many distinct forms. In Indonesia shadow puppets play out complicated stories of kings and battles; in China animal gods fight with demons as actors in highly stylized makeup and costumes perform a combination of sensational gymnastics and martial arts; in India barefoot women with painted faces, hands, and feet perform eloquent dances made up of densely coded, intricate gestures. Sometimes actors speak; sometimes they dance; sometimes they sing. Actors may wear masks or elaborate symbolic costumes, or they may wear the clothes of everyday life. They may inhabit mythical regions, historical locations, or realistic, contemporary environments. They may use elevated speech and gestures or language and actions that correspond with contemporary behavior.

From culture to culture and continent to continent, the theatre responds to the unique worldviews of differing human communities and develops forms of expression that reflect specific community concerns and community aesthetics. By community concerns, we mean the ideas or subjects of theatre performances. By **community aesthetics,** we mean the actual nature of the elements that construct the performance itself, elements that have precise meaning for a particular community and that contribute to the images with which the community describes itself.

For example, the Hopi kachina perfomances emphasize the importance of the harvest and the place of the entire agricultural process in maintaining social order. The relationship between agriculture, the natural environment, and the social order of the community is shaped by the proper regard for a spiritual presence. This complex interaction is the subject of the ritual; it is

Traditional theatre throughout the East uses various forms of dance as the foundation for storytelling and dramatic expression. The Odissi style of classical dance from eastern India shown here uses elaborate symbolic costumes as well as makeup and ornaments to complement the skills of the dancer, which take many years of training to master. Isa Prieto is a student working to learn a revived form of this temple dance that has been handed down for as long as 2,000 years.

what the dramatic cycle is about. The performances themselves are created through certain sequences of dance steps performed by celebrated characters wearing symbolic costumes and carrying iconographic props, all of which form images that express the Hopi view of the world. These characteristics of performance are part of the aesthetic expression of this particular people. Geography, the physical environment, material culture, family structure, social organization,

The Handspring Puppet Company of South Africa produced *Ubu and the Truth Commission* in response to the actual Truth and Reconciliation Commission that held hearings in South Africa on the crimes committed under apartheid. The piece combined puppetry, performance by live actors, music, animation and documentary footage to investigate a charged, contemporary political situation. Busi Zokufa appears as Ma Ubu in this play written by Jane Taylor and directed by William Kentridge in 1998.

history, religion, and philosophy are some of the basic forces that shape artistic expression.

The Collective and Public Nature of Theatre

Sometimes the theatre retells the sacred stories of a community. Sometimes individual playwrights forge the body of work that interprets the life of the social group. Myths, legends, history, contemporary events, and personal experience filtered through the imagination of the playwright may all serve as sources for theatrical expression. Celebrated plays of individual playwrights may come

to function as sacred stories, anchoring community values or providing a measure against which new experience can be tested. But whatever balance is struck between sustaining stories and the innovations of individuals, the formation and evolution of the theatre takes place in a public forum in a collective endeavor. A community of artists gathers to present a performance for a community audience.

Theatre as a Social Force

It is particularly the collective and public nature of the theatre that makes it such a potent social force. The theatre is a gathering place for the public presentation of ideas. Because ideas are expressed through characters caught in difficult or dangerous situations, the theatre creates an intensely emotional experience for the audience. And the impact of the work is then magnified by the number of people present. A collective emotional response is a force of enormous energy and can function in different ways. On one hand, theatre can evoke a collective sigh of relief, an emotional release: Sometimes when a group of people have laughed very hard together or cried together, they feel that they can more easily accept the difficulties of their daily lives or the pressures that face the entire community. On the other hand, theatre can generate and focus collective anger or outrage, which can then take form as a revolutionary force.

The relationship between theatre and society is complex because the theatre has so much potential power. Theatre can be a conservative force that contributes to stability and reinforces the status quo, or it can be part of an experimental process through which a society redefines itself. Theatre can release social tensions, or it can lead to social upheaval. Theatre can be part of social debate, part of the free exchange of ideas, or it can be used for the dissemination of propaganda. Because of its unique power as a collective, public form, theatre has always been of great interest to philosophers and governments.

... THEATRE AND RELIGIOUS FESTIVALS

We now examine the relationship between theatre and society by studying examples of theatres from different nations and different historical periods that have been particularly influential in the development of the modern theatre. We study the subjects and ideas of the particular theatres and the aesthetics of the different styles of performance. As we move from theatre to theatre, we explore some of the issues that have arisen from the volatile relationship between theatre and society: issues of religion and politics, race and gender, social stability and revolution.

Two very different European theatres both developed in conjunction with religious festivals: the Greek theatre of Athens in the fifth century B.C.E. and the medieval mystery cycles, specifically those of England, which reached their high point between 1350 and 1550. Although both of these theatres were associated with community celebrations and ceremonies, the Greek theatre developed into a forum for highly sophisticated philosophical debate about the place of human beings in the universe, whereas the medieval theatre produced a pageant that functioned as a form of devotion, an affirmation of accepted religious beliefs.

THE GREEK THEATRE: ATHENS, FIFTH CENTURY B.C.E.

By the fifth century B.C.E., Athens had become the dominant force in the group of city-states politically, culturally, and geographically linked on the peninsula and islands of Greece. The century produced a dazzling record of the Athenian genius for the arts, for learning, for government, and for the building of an empire. The Athenian theatre and literature of the fifth century B.C.E. has inspired much of the theatre and literature in later eras and throughout the world. The great **tragedies** that came from this period—*Prometheus Bound, Oedipus Rex, Antigone,* and *Medea*—were intricately bound to the religious as well as the political life of the community.

The Origin of Greek Theatre in the Worship of Dionysus

Early on in the development of theatre in Greece, plays were associated with festivals to honor the god **Dionysus.** There is much debate among theatre historians and anthropologists about whether the plays actually evolved out of ritual worship of Dionysus or whether they grew out of the more secular impulses of individual playwrights. Whatever path the evolution of Greek drama followed, the worship of Dionysus was central to the place of theatre in Greek culture.

Dionysus was the Greek god of the life force; he represented new growth for vegetation, new life for herds and flocks, and fertility for human beings. A god of nature, wine, and fertility, Dionysus was honored in the spring with festivals that celebrated regeneration and renewal. These were ecstatic celebrations in which social inhibitions were supplanted by liberated, intoxicated behavior. The worship of Dionysus supposedly began with his followers' tearing apart his body and eating it in order to absorb his power into themselves. In the spring following the dismemberment of the god, Dionysus was miraculously restored to life, resurrected. In its evolution, the worship of Dionysus at first actually involved human sacrifice; later, animals were used for the communion ritual. Stories and songs celebrating the life of Dionysus were added to the ritual observations, which grew into community festivals involving civic and religious activity. Finally, in the sixth century B.C.E., dramas were added to the various activities of the festival of Dionysus, setting the stage for the brilliant Athenian **drama** that would emerge in the fifth century B.C.E.

Although the Greek dramas that came to dominate the festival of Dionysus are profoundly different from the Hopi kachina cycle, certain remarkable similarities are apparent. For both cultures, the drama is central to community observations concerned with renewal and regeneration. The transformation of actors into characters concerned with issues of social and religious order coincides with the transformation of nature to sustain human existence once more. The suffering and rebirth of Dionysus became a model for the theatre, which explores

IN CONTEXT

Origins of the Theatre in Greece

Date	Event
1300–1200 B.C.E.	Worship of Dionysus introduced to Greece from the Middle East
c. 800 B.C.E.	The *Iliad* and the *Odyssey* composed by Homer
534 B.C.E.	Dramatic competition established at City Dionysia
523–456 B.C.E.	Life of Aeschylus
508 B.C.E.	Athenian democracy established
496–406 B.C.E.	Life of Sophocles
490 B.C.E.	Defeat of the Persians by the Greeks at Marathon
480–406 B.C.E.	Life of Euripides
c. 460–430 B.C.E.	Rule of Pericles
458 B.C.E.	*The Oresteia*, by Aeschylus
431 B.C.E.	*Medea*, by Euripides
430 B.C.E.	*Oedipus Rex*, by Sophocles
429–347 B.C.E.	Life of Plato
404 B.C.E.	Athens defeated in Peloponnesian War
384–322 B.C.E.	Life of Aristotle
c. 330 B.C.E.	*The Poetics,* by Aristotle

the suffering and triumph of the human community. This transformative function for the drama would recur in the Christian drama of medieval times, when pageants celebrating the Christian history of the world were performed in conjunction with the Corpus Christi festivals held throughout Europe in the late spring to celebrate the sacraments of the church associated with the body of Christ.

Like the Hopi ritual performances, the Greek theatre was part of the soul of the community, essential to the basic fabric of the life of the city-state. Through plays, the Greeks

The theatre at Epidaurus dates from about 300 B.C.E., which is later than the period we have been studying. However, these well-preserved ruins give a sense of the scale and setting of the theatre of Dionysus in Athens in the fifth century B.C.E. The theatre at Epidaurus seated 14,000 spectators and was known for its excellent acoustics. In spite of the vast size of the theatre, the actors could be heard by everyone present. Our knowledge of Greek theatre practice is based on fragmentary evidence and involves much speculation on the part of theatre historians. We imagine that the actors in the fifth century B.C.E. performed on a circular, unraised playing area, with a wooden building behind, which served as a place to change costumes and masks and from which actors entered and exited the stage. The wooden building might have created the sense of a palace facade. The roof of the scene building also provided a raised level for the appearance of the gods and a crane to facilitate special effects like Medea's final exit in a flying chariot.

examined the relationships necessary to sustain human existence as they understood it. Family relationships, social organization, the relationships and obligations of individuals to the larger society, and the interplay between human action and the actions of the gods dominated the dramas written by playwrights such as Aeschylus (523–456 B.C.E.), Sophocles (496–406 B.C.E.), and Euripides (480–406 B.C.E.). By raising ethical and political questions, the Greek plays helped shape the emergence of democracy in Athens.

There are, however, significant differences between the kachina cycle and the theatre of Greece. The kachina performances evolved over generations of community participation; no single playwright shaped the ideas and images. By contrast, in the Greek theatre the imagination of the individual playwright was celebrated. The presentation of plays, in fact, took the form of a competition, at the festival known as the **City Dionysia,** and prizes were given each year to the outstanding playwright. Further, the kachina performances reinforce an accepted set of religious beliefs, whereas Greek theatre questioned the nature of fate and the very existence of the gods.

The Greek plays were presented each year over a period of several days. Most traditional work stopped, and 15,000 community members or more would gather on a hill outside the city where a rudimentary theatre had been constructed. From wooden benches built into the hillside, the audience would look down on an open-air playing space. At the back of this circular playing area was a plain stone building that provided for the entrances and exits of the actors and served as a place for costume changes and storage for simple stage machinery. Beyond the theatre lay the sea. The audience and the actors gathered in the middle of the geographic features that delineated the external boundaries of the Athenian world as they witnessed or acted the plays that probed the internal nature of that world. From early morning to late afternoon, the playwrights staged dramas to entertain, to illuminate, and to reflect on the concerns of the huge audience. We now examine one of the Greek dramas, *Medea*, to explore the merging of ideas and aesthetics in the Greek theatre. Accompanying our discussion of *Medea* are photos from two of the numerous recent productions of this work, which continues to be compelling for modern producers and audiences. Reviews of these productions are included in Chapter 13.

Medea, by Euripides

Medea was written by Euripides in 438 B.C.E. and is one of eighteen of his plays that have survived into our own times. Euripides is known for his concerns with the complexity of human motivation, the difficulty of negotiating love and desire, and the conflicts between men and women. Human behavior out of control is the subject of both *The Bacchae* and *Hippolytus*. Euripides has also written eloquently about the destructive nature of war in the often-produced *Trojan Women*.

With characters drawn from well-known Greek mythology, *Medea* focuses on the obsessive passion of the title character, Medea, for her husband, Jason. The play is both the intimate and the public telling of the breakdown of a marriage. As a domestic story, the plot is familiar. A married man leaves his wife, the mother of his children, for a younger woman. Euripides' rendering of this material not only portrays the shifting terms of a relationship but also presents a struggle for power and self-preservation. The younger woman Jason hopes to marry, Glauce, is the daughter of the king of Corinth. By marrying her, Jason stands to inherit a throne. Medea faces losing her husband, and as the play begins, she is threatened with banishment. Furthermore, she bears the weight of a complicated history. Early in their relationship, so devoted was Medea to

Jason that she committed murder and alienated her own family in order to help him obtain and then escape with the legendary Golden Fleece. Now, she is regarded as an outsider, a barbarian, among the majority population, the Greeks. For Jason, his alliance with Medea is no longer useful. He sees her as a dangerous and disruptive force. Medea sees the man for whom she sacrificed home and family abandoning her to a life in which she will be alone with neither a country nor friends to support her. The explosive conflict between husband and wife results in the deaths of their children, an outcome that has both personal and symbolic significance. Euripides' *Medea* tells a bloody story of revenge and murder as disturbing as some of today's films. Violence in the drama and in the conduct of human affairs is not a uniquely contemporary phenomenon.

Staging Conventions

Every theatre has its own conventions, which are understood and accepted by performers and audience members alike. **Theatrical conventions** are the unique devices of dramatic construction and performance that facilitate the presentation of stories on the stage. One convention in Greek theatre was that no more than three actors appeared on the stage at any one time; another was that the actors always wore masks. Although we know some of the major conventions followed in Greek performance, many others are unrecorded or are the subject of continuing intense debate. However, using evidence from the plays themselves as well as from other writings, artwork, and archaeological investigation, we can imagine some aspects of a performance.

MALE ACTORS We know that women did not participate in the Greek theatre in any way. All the roles, male and female, were played by men. Therefore, the central role of Medea would have been played by a man, as would the Nurse and

● ● ●   **IN CONTEXT**

Mythological Background

Jason sails on the ship *Argo* to find the Golden Fleece, which is in the possession of King Aeetes of Colchis. Medea is the daughter of Aeetes and the granddaughter of the Sun. With her mixed ancestry, human and divine, she has the powers of a sorcerer. She falls deeply in love with Jason and resolves to become his partner in his quest for the Golden Fleece. To help Jason escape from her father's pursuit, she kills her brother Apsyrtus and cuts his body into pieces, forcing her father to stop to gather the scattered remains of his dead son. Medea then tricks the daughters of Pelias, king of Iolkos, into killing their father, who had promised to restore Jason's inheritance in exchange for the fleece. Medea and Jason must flee once again and travel to Corinth, where Euripides' play takes place.

Character Relationships in the Play

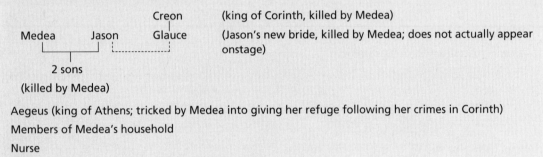

Creon   (king of Corinth, killed by Medea)

Medea   Jason   Glauce   (Jason's new bride, killed by Medea; does not actually appear onstage)

2 sons

(killed by Medea)

Aegeus (king of Athens; tricked by Medea into giving her refuge following her crimes in Corinth)

Members of Medea's household

Nurse

Tutor

the chorus of Corinthian women. We also know that the Greeks used a small number of actors, two or three, to perform all the individual speaking parts in any particular play; so actors usually played more than one role. In imagining a performance of *Medea* in its own time, we must shift our contemporary perspective to envision two or three men onstage at a time, wearing masks and costumes to indicate the roles they are assuming. One of the actors would probably have played only Medea because this character is onstage throughout most of the play. All the other roles—Nurse, Tutor, Creon, Jason, and Aegeus—would have been divided between two additional actors. After an actor finished one scene or section of the play, he would exit to change his costume and mask so that he could appear as another character. *Medea* is clearly structured with two-person

scenes in order to allow the third actor to exit and prepare to reenter in another role. In general, the same actor could play a man, a woman, and a god all within a few scenes. This particular staging convention reveals a great deal about Greek society. In a story about marriage and betrayal, jealousy and infanticide, the central character, who is held up as a psychological study of a woman in extreme circumstances, was written by a man to be played by a man. Furthermore, the audience would have been composed largely or completely of men.

OFFSTAGE VIOLENCE   The murders in *Medea* bring us to a particularly noteworthy convention of Greek theatre. All the violence was performed offstage. Frequently, dead bodies were wheeled onstage on a special wagon called the **ekkyklema.**

The audience heard in gory detail from messengers about the violent encounters that resulted in the loss of life, and they saw the reactions of the other characters. But the Greek audience did not witness the fight scenes, the murders, and the dismemberments that played a prominent part in their dramas and that have essentially taken center stage in contemporary plays and films.

During the course of this play, Medea commits two atrocious crimes. First she sends a gift to Jason's new wife, Glauce: a beautiful dress and crown infused with poisonous chemicals that bring the girl to a fiery death when she puts them on. The poison also envelops Glauce's father, Creon, when he tries to rescue her. Following the murders of Glauce and Creon, Medea kills her own sons by Jason. In the play, as it is written by Euripides, none of this violence takes place onstage. The episode of the poisonous dress is described in graphic detail by the Messenger in a speech of over two pages which he delivers to Medea:

> Blood mingled with fire dripped from the
> top of her head, her flesh melted from her
> bones like teardrops of resin as your poisons
> gnawed invisibly.[6]

The cries for help of Medea's children are heard from offstage, and then their dead bodies are revealed in the chariot in which Medea makes her exit at the end of the play, pulled through the sky by dragons.

THE MASK   Another convention of the Greek theatre that sharply contrasts with contemporary theatre practice is the use of the mask. The mask has been a vital element of theatrical expression in a variety of cultures and had a number of significant functions in the Greek theatre. For the Greeks the mask had practical implications as well as aesthetic ones. As our discussion of *Medea* demonstrates, masks allowed one actor to play a number of roles. The same actor may have played Creon and Jason or the Nurse and Aegeus. Masks also enabled male actors to play female roles. And masks allowed mortals to play the roles of

Fiona Shaw plays Medea and Jonathan Cake plays Jason in a production of *Medea* directed by Deborah Warner for the Abbey Theatre of Ireland in 2002. This production emphasizes Medea's obsession with her husband and the intensity of their sexual relationship. The play is placed in a contemporary setting and the chorus speeches are divided between individuals rather than spoken in unison. The realism of the domestic conflict takes precedence over the mythical dimensions of the story. Note the children's toys in Medea's left hand.

the gods, projecting the power and authority of Olympian deities. Because the Greek plays took place in huge outdoor theatres, the mask also increased the visibility of the actor, who would have been at a considerable distance from many of those in the audience. And in the case of the Greeks, the mask put yet more emphasis on the importance of the voice in conveying the meaning of the text and holding the audience's attention.

The mask also significantly affected the nature of acting. Whereas contemporary performance is frequently dominated by the personality and appearance of the actor, the use of masks in the Greek theatre put the emphasis in performance on the character rather than on the actor. The mask allowed the character to emerge as an entity separate from the actor who wore it. The mask shifted the actor's focus to his voice and gestures, although the positioning of the head would have been eloquent in the absence of changing facial expression. In the Greek theatre, the gestures and body positions would have had to be large and striking to communicate across the vast space of the amphitheatre. The most sharply drawn contrast with performance today would be to the close-up of the actor in a film where the most subtle and natural expressions of the face suggest great depth of feeling. The eyes that turn inward, the mouth that trembles slightly—these can convey significant meaning. The Greek actor had to work with an entirely different apparatus and on a much larger scale to make his meaning clear.

Any actor who wears a mask experiences some degree of transcendence as he or she identifies with the spirit of the mask. For actors such as the Hopi or the Kwakwaka'wakw engaged in a religious ceremony, the mask is an essential intermediary that transports the actor into the spirit world. In more secular performances, masks can still have the effect of lifting the actors out of themselves to identify with the essence of what the masks represent. Finally, for the audience, masks transform the stage or playing space into a magical world inhabited by larger-than-life characters who prompt a shift in the audience's consciousness. The audience members feel that they are in the presence of powerful, archetypal figures who bring a cosmic drama onto the stage.

THE CHORUS The **chorus,** like the mask, was another convention of the Greek theatre. Although audiences today are familiar with singing choruses of all kinds, they might find a speaking or chanting chorus on the contemporary stage

Medea, played here by April Yvette Thompson, clings to her children, played by Brian Gilbert and Laron Griffin, in the production of *Medea* staged by the Classical Theatre of Harlem in 2005. The director Alfred Preisser incorporated dance and music throughout the performance, using the movement and chanting of the chorus to provide a rhythmic underscoring and strong visual images to accompany the actions of the main characters, reinforcing the mythological background.

somewhat strange. A group of twelve to fifteen characters dressed alike and speaking in unison would not seem to represent the world as we see it. But for the Greek audience, the chorus was an expected part of the theatre experience. The chorus first appeared in early religious festivals, when groups of fifty would sing choral hymns in honor of Dionysus. Some theatre historians believe tragedy had its beginning when one of the chorus members initiated a dialogue between himself—as a single speaker or character—and the rest of the chorus. This legendary first speaker, Thespis, is the source of the word **thespian,** meaning actor.

Sometimes the Greek chorus spoke in **dialogue** and sometimes in longer poetic passages. In the sections of dialogue, the chorus played opposite major characters, asking questions and then listening, serving as a confidant who allowed the central characters to explain themselves. The chorus in *Medea* is made up of Corinthian women who remain sympathetic to Medea throughout the play, relating the painful history of Medea and Jason's relationship and then, as the action progresses, pleading with Medea not to kill her children.

Choral passages also contained many references to other mythological situations, and these allowed the playwright to expand on the significance of the immediate dramatic conflict. He built a complex background through the choral commentary.

In addition to functioning as both a character and a storyteller, the chorus had rhythmic and visual functions. The choral sections were accompanied by music and had their own meter, which contrasted with the dialogue episodes and heightened the growing tensions. The staging of the choruses involved intricate choreography and were an important part of the visual spectacle.

In *Medea*, a tormented woman kills her enemies and kills her own children. But performed in its own time, the horror of the play was contained by the formal nature of the presentation. The masked male actor portraying Medea was surrounded by the masked members of the chorus who chanted their responses, while the violent actions took place offstage.

The Greek theatre of Athens in the fifth century B.C.E. reinforced the existing social structure and celebrated Athenian democracy. But it was also a theatre of questions. The playwrights recognized that life is full of contradictions and that the future can be neither predicted nor controlled. The dramas that have come down to us call the community to account for its actions and charge individuals with responsibility for their choices. Characters struggle toward

self-knowledge, but their view is frequently distorted by arrogance and passion. Wisdom follows only from catastrophic suffering.

THE MEDIEVAL MYSTERY CYCLE

Medieval society was organized largely around the Catholic Church, and it was as part of religious observation that the theatre developed in medieval Europe. The great medieval **mystery cycles** that were staged across western Europe from the thirteenth century to the sixteenth are a fascinating example of a religious theatre tradition that depended on the same kind of broad community participation found in the Hopi kachina cycle.

Initiated by the Catholic Church in the tenth century to make Christian teachings more accessible to a largely illiterate population, the mystery cycles dramatizing the Christian history of the world grew into elaborate pageants associated with the late spring festivals of Corpus Christi. Towns in England, France, Germany, Italy, and Spain all staged similar variations of these performances, which focused on biblical events from the creation of the world to the birth and crucifixion of Jesus to the last judgment. The number of episodes presented ranged from forty to as many as hundred. Not only did the normal work of the communities cease during the time the plays were performed—as it did during the City Dionysia in Athens and as it continues to do during the kachina cycle in Hopi communities— the entire town was responsible for the presentation of the elaborate sequence of plays.

Staging and Production: A Community Endeavor

In England, production of the plays was organized through the business community and specifically through workers' unions known as guilds. Different guilds were responsible for the production of the different plays. In fact, the work of a particular guild would sometimes relate to the subject of its assigned play: The

A group of American and Italian actors under the direction of Karin Coonrod developed a modern presentation of a medieval mystery cycle entitled *Laude in Urbis: Mystery Plays in the 21st Century.* The performance was presented as a procession moving through the streets of Orvieto, Italy in June of 2006 at the time of the Corpus Christi observation. *Laude in Urbis* combines text from the English mystery plays with excerpts from modern music, poetry, and fiction. The episode represented in this photograph is entitled "The angels create the wall of Paradise" and took place on the steps of the Duomo (the main church) of Orvieto.

boatwrights produced *Noah's Ark*, and the bakers were responsible for *The Last Supper*.

The individual playlets of the English cycles were staged on **pageant wagon,** or carts that were drawn through the town by horses, each wagon essentially a miniature traveling stage. In the town of York, for example, forty plays were presented beginning at the earliest morning light and continuing far into the night. Each play was performed at twelve different sites throughout the town. People would gather at the designated locations along the "parade" route, and the plays would come to them. Food and music added to the air of great festivity and celebration.

The involvement of the guilds in the production of the plays is not unlike the corporate sponsorship of contemporary entertainments, including parades. The huge nationally televised parades, such as the Tournament of Roses parade on New Year's Day in Pasadena, California, with its flower-covered floats, and the Macy's Thanksgiving Day parade in New York, with its gigantic balloon characters, are supported by both commercial enterprises and city and state governments.

The Los Angeles Theatre Center has created a contemporary performance honoring the Virgin of Guadalupe, entitled *La Virgen de Guadalupe: Dios Inantzin,* that draws on traditions tied to the Catholic mystery or miracle plays in combination with Aztec performance traditions that pre-date the arrival of Europeans in the Americas. Presented annually in the Cathedral of Our Lady of the Angels, a church seating 3,000 people, the play is performed in both Spanish and Nahuatl, the Aztec language, and is a Christmas celebration for Los Angeles area residents of Hispanic heritage. The Director Jose Luis Valenzuela says, "the intent of this piece has been that every year we can come together and have a performance of a play that is ours and is built by us together as a community."[7] The goal of the performance is to empower the community in addition to reinforcing culture and faith.

However, perhaps closer in spirit to the community involvement in the medieval mystery cycles is the small-town parade on the Fourth of July or another day dear to the heart of a local community. The high school bands, groups of riders on horseback, veterans, civic dignitaries, Shriners, and floats sponsored by local businesses—all represent community institutions and community values. The people who line the parade route recognize their friends and neighbors in the parade, and they clearly understand the significance of the celebration.

The kind of community effort that was required to produce the medieval mystery cycles is hard for us to imagine, because most of our elaborate entertainments are put on by professionals and involve a variety of commercial considerations. Over a hundred male actors, and sometimes several hundred, were involved in the mystery plays, as were dozens of men to build scenery and arrange the stage or pageant wagons. Numerous musicians played during or between episodes. And a director and technicians in charge of special effects coordinated the many participants. The undertaking was so complex and demanding of community resources that productions took place only every few years rather than annually.

AESTHETIC EXPRESSION: A SHARED, SACRED LANGUAGE We have seen that the Greek theatre of the fifth century B.C.E. developed a distinct life of its own in part because of the brilliant playwrights who shaped the ideas in the plays and the conventions of performance. In fact, the Greek playwrights directed their own plays, thereby exercising virtually complete control over the material. The medieval theatre, in contrast, was guided by no such original thinking. Rather, it can be seen as one element in an overall pattern of aesthetic expression influenced by the Catholic Church. Because artwork was done for the glory of God, the artists, including visual artists, were all anonymous. We know neither the names of the playwrights nor the identity of the artisans who made the glorious stained glass windows of the great medieval cathedrals. Art was seen as a collective effort of devotion rather than as something done for personal aggrandizement. Instead of focusing on individual innovation or style, artists used the same system of signs and symbols that had evolved within the church and that functioned as a kind of sacred language or writing understood by the entire community. The theatre and the various forms of visual art all used the same subjects, the same ideas of organization, the same details of character, and the same symbols of religious significance.

STORY AND SYMMETRY We have already observed that the mystery cycles were organized in an **episodic,** or processional, manner, constituting a number of separate incidents all related to one epic story. The visual art forms of the time, such as stained glass windows and paintings, were also structured as a group of individual panels with episodes or story incidents all related to one larger theme. Within each panel the figures were organized in a symmetrical and hierarchical manner. For example, three angels at the top of a panel might be balanced by three devils at the bottom, or a certain number of virtuous characters might be depicted to the right of Jesus, with a comparable number of sinners to the left. Functioning as a background in many of these visual images was often a small building or emblematic structure that indicated the location of the scene. The same small buildings became the scenic units placed on the pageant wagons. The arrangement and spacing of the characters probably drew on the same principles of symmetry and hierarchy.

PERFORMANCE AND SPECIAL EFFECTS The simplicity and order of the staging, however, did not restrict the exuberance of the performances, which were far from stiff religious exercises. The point of the performances was to give the audience a chance to identify with Christ's suffering, to feel the power of the miracles and the degradation of the devils and those who had sinned. The central subject of the entire pageant was salvation itself. To have a powerful and useful effect on the audience, the staging had to be clever, magical, lively, and humorous.

Much effort went into the staging of special effects, such as fire, flying angels, ascensions, flowing water, and the bouncing head of St. John the Baptist. One of the most popular parts of the spectacle was the hell mouth, a gaping, monstrous structure emitting smoke and fire and discharging devils in fantastic costumes out into the audience. And the small plays themselves all had compelling details of human interest that connected the situations of the characters to the immediate hardships and joys experienced by those in the audience.

The Role of the Mystery Cycles in Medieval Society

There are several ways to view the relationship of the Christian mystery cycles to society. On one level they must be seen as a celebration that gave people a break from their routine tasks and a chance to work together to re-create primary community stories. Participants had the double satisfaction of contributing their own skills to the performances and enjoying the results of their neighbors' contributions. Although the mystery plays quickly grew beyond the walls of the church buildings themselves, they served to tie the church and community together. The plays reinforced people's faith by allowing community members to identify with Christ's suffering and triumph and to act on their devotion through the production of the plays.

At the same time, the plays served the interests of the ruling classes and the Catholic Church. They reinforced the social organization of the time, which held people in rigidly structured hierarchical positions with almost no possibility of upward mobility. The plays were full of lessons based on accepting one's position in society no matter what the degree of poverty or deprivation; the true rewards of human existence, the plays taught, were to be received in the hereafter.

The mystery cycles were performed in a holiday atmosphere. Music, food, large crowds, and the interruption of work contributed to the audience's anticipation of the performance. Fire, smoke, and the appearance of devils who interacted with the audience all made for very lively entertainment.

The relationship of the mystery cycles to society can be seen clearly in the changes that occurred in England in the sixteenth century. In medieval times the mystery cycles benefited both church and state, but after the Protestant Reformation (beginning in 1511), the religious theatre became embroiled in the political upheavals of the day. In England, Henry VIII broke with the pope in 1534 over issues of autonomy in general and divorce in particular. His daughter, Elizabeth I, governed a nation with an expanding sense of national identity and power and a newly established Church of England, which allowed Christian worship without papal interference. Up to this time, the performance of the mystery cycles had reinforced a strong Catholic presence in England. Worried that continued performances would provide a rallying ground for supporters of the pope and Catholicism, the English government set about eliminating the mystery cycles. Manuscripts recording the plays were destroyed, regulations against religious performances onstage were enforced, and plays expressing Catholic views were not licensed. The mystery cycles, long considered a fundamental part of English society, were suppressed when they no longer served the interests of the state.

Summary

Performance is a vital part of human expression that may involve playing roles in daily life, participating in community rituals, or working as a professional actor. Performance is an essential human activity that relates to successful personal adaptation. Children use performance to test new roles; adults use performance to adjust to changes in their circumstances. Much of the shifting of roles in daily life relates to our attempts to become more powerful.

Through dramatic rituals, communities reach out to supernatural forces to secure control over their environment. Ceremonial performances, such as the kachina cycle of the Hopi, are central to the social and religious organization of the community. The individual who takes on a ceremonial role goes through a process of transformation.

The power of the theatre derives from its collective public nature, from the combined energies of the community of artists and the community audience. Theatre addresses issues of religion and politics, gender and race, social stability and revolution. It functions as a mirror to society, reflecting the themes and subjects that concern the people and the forms of aesthetic expression deemed appropriate and acceptable in that community.

Some theatre traditions developed in association with religious festivals. The theatre of Athens in the fifth century B.C.E. arose from festivals celebrating the transformative powers of Dionysus, god of the life force. Performed outdoors in natural amphitheatres overlooking the sea, the Greek dramas provided the occasion for thousands of Athenians to gather for a few days every year to experience community myths and legends in the form of drama. Greek theatre employed certain well-understood conventions of performance, including the mask and the chorus. Through drama, the Greeks explored difficult questions about human existence. *Medea*, by Euripides, explores troubled relationships between individuals and the chaos generated by unchecked passion and relentless ambition.

Like Greek theatre, the medieval mystery cycles were religious in origin and purpose. Every few years, community members, working through their guilds, re-created the story of Christianity in a series of playlets presented during the late spring festival of Corpus Christi. Plays were staged on pageant wagons that moved from place to place in the town. The conventions of the medieval theatre were derived from the shared, sacred language of signs and symbols used to evoke and represent Christianity. Stories were simple and told in episodic fashion, both in the plays and in medieval visual art forms such as stained glass windows; the works of playwrights and artists were anonymous and emphasized order and symmetry. In the medieval cycles, religious meaning merged with the humorous and exuberant performances to create an event that was highly entertaining as well as deeply moving. The plays reinforced the hierarchical structure of medieval society with stories that encouraged obedience and humility.

Topics for Discussion and Writing

1. The purpose of this exercise is to examine the way "personal performance" is used in everyday life. Choose "nonactors" for your observations. Where do you see people performing in daily life? That is, under what circumstances do people make some kind of switch in how they present themselves, taking on a different role, putting on a mask, or dramatically aggrandizing their behavior? What is the purpose of the "performance"? Observe people in five different situations. Write approximately one-half page for each observation.

2. Discuss the ways in which the Hopi kachina cycle benefits the Hopi community.

   Do you know of any dramatic ceremonial performances that are part of your community?

3. Greek tragedies involved a great deal of violence. However, all the violent incidents took place offstage and were then described in detail to the audience by messengers who had witnessed the violence. The dead bodies were also frequently brought onstage as a display of what had happened. What reasons might the Greeks have had to place the violence offstage? What do you think the effect would have been on the audience? What would happen to contemporary drama and films if the violence occurred offstage? What is the effect of onstage and onscreen violence on audiences today?

Chapter 2

Theatre as a Mirror of Society

••• THE PROFESSIONAL THEATRE

THE GREEK THEATRE OF THE FIFTH CENTURY B.C.E. and the medieval mystery cycles were both associated with religious festivals and appeared only seasonally. The plays in both cases were community endeavors involving large numbers of community members and resources. The production of plays was considered a civic and religious responsibility and brought together religious leaders, civic leaders, business interests, and community members. The participants in the performances themselves consisted of a few semiprofessional theatre practitioners, but the majority were nonprofessionals.

We turn now to two professional theatres with different aesthetics and different conditions of performance: the theatre of Shakespeare and the **Beijing Opera** (also called the Chinese opera). Unlike the Greek and medieval theatres, both of these theatres involved professional practitioners engaged full-time in the production of plays. Commercial considerations were vital to the financial well-being of each theatre. Attracting a regular and substantial paying audience and securing the patronage of the aristocracy were equally important. Although the theatres of Shakespeare and the Beijing Opera represent extremely different cultural traditions, they share staging conventions that focus on the abilities of actors working on a bare stage to engage the imagination of the audience.

Tudor and Jacobean England

Date	Event
1455–1485	Wars of the Roses
1485	Battle of Bosworth in which Richard III is defeated by the first Tudor king, Henry VII
1509–1547	Reign of Henry VIII (father of Elizabeth I)
1534	Henry VIII breaks with the pope and founds the Church of England
1547–1553	Reign of Edward VI
1553–1558	Reign of Mary I
1558–1603	Reign of Elizabeth I
1588	Defeat of the Spanish Armada by the English navy
1564–1623	Life of Shakespeare
c. 1590–1610	Shakespeare's theatre career in London
1603–1625	Reign of James I (referred to as the Jacobean period)

THE ELIZABETHAN THEATRE

Elizabeth I, the daughter of Henry VIII by Ann Boleyn, came to the English throne in 1558. She inherited the English crown when England was entering an era of adventure and expansion, when the spirit of the Renaissance was firing the English imagination. But her reign began in the shadow of English civil wars, the Wars of the Roses, that had bled the nation during the preceding century. And Elizabeth faced an ongoing religious struggle between Protestants and Catholics, initiated when her father, Henry VIII, broke with the pope in 1534 and established himself as head of the Church of England. Elizabeth reigned for almost fifty years, until 1603, and she did much to stabilize the nation, creating an atmosphere conducive to spectacular achievements in science, exploration, and the arts. But she held together a contentious society that would return to civil war some years following her death, and there was a price to be paid for the peace that she maintained.

The Theatre in Society

The Elizabethan theatre inherited much both from the Greek theatre and from the medieval theatre that immediately preceded it, but its place in the English society of the late sixteenth century and early seventeenth century was quite different from the place of those theatres in their societies. The production of Greek and medieval plays merged religious observation with performances that entertained as they reinforced community values. Regular citizens were involved at every level of the productions, so productions were community-based and amateur in nature. In both Greece and medieval Europe, theatre festivals were held at special times of the year when the normal life of the community stopped to allow the presentation of plays.

In contrast, Elizabethan theatre was a secular theatre operated by professional actors and playwrights who supported themselves with their theatre activities year-round. This secular theatre interpreted the ambitions and the tremendous changes in worldview of the age. Elizabethan theatre was fascinated by the power struggles of kings and the inner turmoil provoked by such struggles. But in spite of seizing on the political maneuverings of the human community as one of its principal subjects, the theatre was cautious in keeping its distance from the political debates that swirled around the throne of Elizabeth I.

The film *Elizabeth* (1999), with Cate Blanchett in the title role, chronicled the evolution of Elizabeth I into a monarch with an iron will, strong enough to withstand the threats to her throne and the power struggles surrounding her. In a remarkable performance, Blanchett begins as a lively and emotional girl and gradually builds up her defenses until she withdraws behind the mask of the invulnerable queen. Elizabeth I brought considerable stability to England, allowing the theatre, including the work of William Shakespeare, to flourish.

The unique circumstances of the late sixteenth century in England afforded the opportunity for a national theatre. The intellectual and artistic curiosity of the Renaissance prepared the way for sophisticated plays such as those of Shakespeare. The stability of the long reign of Elizabeth I allowed the economy to prosper, and with it the theatre. The patronage of the nobility protected playwrights and actors and allowed them to continue to work, even when some religious and civic leaders saw the theatre as either a moral danger or an actual physical danger through the spread of the plague. The growth of London—with a population of 200,000, the largest city in Europe—provided a lively audience eager for frequent theatre performances. And the English language, already rich in expressive words and rhythmic possibilities, was open to the playwright's inventive vocabulary and phrasing, unfettered by rigid rules or academic restrictions.

The Nature of Elizabethan Drama

Elizabethan drama focused on the complexity of human motivation. The human mind and human action were placed center stage. Human action was played out against a background of religious and political concerns, but it was the internal struggles of the characters that became the major subject of the drama. The most compelling characters from Elizabethan drama were those whose vision for themselves outreached their abilities to live the lives they imagined. It was the drama of an age of human possibility, full of startling opportunities for the expansion of human understanding, underscored by the expansion of the European nations on the high seas and on vast, distant continents. The unknowns were enormous, but the possibilities were exhilarating. A new view of human existence was emerging from Renaissance philosophy and science; at the same time, however, medieval thinking still persisted.

A play that offered an illuminating prologue for the Elizabethan dramas to follow, particularly the plays of William Shakespeare, was *Doctor Faustus,* by Christopher Marlowe. *Doctor Faustus* explores the mind of a man with a consuming ambition to understand the nature of the world and the universe. But his science proves to be no more than a magician's tricks. Faustus's hope for the mind of man shatters his faith in God. He dies in despair, unable to achieve the heights of human understanding that he envisions but also unable to repent for his desire to know. In his quest for knowledge, he is damned by his own conscience as well as the prevailing morality of his society. Faustus has lost the comfort of the medieval worldview, a view that he has yet to escape.

Doubts and questions also torment Shakespearean characters whose burning ambitions lead them to ill-conceived courses of action. Macbeth pursues a course of murder to gain the crown but cannot silence his conscience. King Lear divides up his kingdom in order to receive the adulation of his daughters and is driven mad by the consequences of his actions. In his greatest play, Shakespeare creates a character, Hamlet, who is forced to deal with the murderous ambition of his uncle Claudius. The play explores the questioning mind of a character who cannot make sense of the political and philosophical issues confronting him.

William Shakespeare

As we examine Elizabethan theatre, we focus on William Shakespeare, the playwright whose soaring achievements became synonymous with the age. A number of other playwrights, such as Christopher Marlowe and Ben Jonson, contributed to the vitality and brilliance of this remarkable period of theatre, but as the theatre became central to Elizabethan and Jacobean England, so Shakespeare became central to the theatre.

Although images of Shakespeare exist, he continues to be an elusive historical figure, known through the eloquence of his plays but not through substantial biographical materials. We can only imagine the life he led in London as a member of the Lord Chamberlain's Men who sometimes wrote as many as three plays a year to keep up with the demands of his company and his audience.

SHAKESPEARE'S CAREER   Shakespeare's career in the theatre illuminates the characteristics of the professional London stage of the late sixteenth century and the early seventeenth. Between approximately 1590 and 1610 Shakespeare wrote thirty-seven plays that together are considered the greatest achievement of any playwright in the history of world theatre.

Shakespeare emerged from an obscure background in Stratford to become one of the important members of the Lord Chamberlain's Men, a small but prominent professional theatre company in London. As part of this company, Shakespeare was an actor, a shareholder, a part owner

of the Globe Theatre, and, most significantly, a playwright. Shakespeare's membership and participation in the Lord Chamberlain's Men greatly facilitated his career as a playwright. He worked with a company that had a continuing need for new material, and he knew the strengths and weaknesses of the company, the specialized skills of individual members, and the range of the different actors. In fact, he knew who would play the roles as he wrote them—which actor excelled at comedy, which actor had a good singing voice, which boy actor was available to play a woman's role, and how many lines he could be expected to handle. There was a continuous

Michael Cumpsty plays Richard III in this 2007 production at the Classic Stage Company, directed jointly by Cumpsty and Brian Kulick. Cumpsty plays Richard as a seductive villain who successfully overcomes his opposition with charm before he turns to murder. The play was performed on an open stage with the only scenic element large crystal chandeliers that were raised or lowered by the actors to create a throne room, a forest, or even an undersea environment. The use of the chandeliers was a modern variation of the flexible staging employed in Shakespeare's time.

interplay between the playwright and the company as he crafted his work to take advantage of the gifts of his fellow company members.

THE SOURCES OF SHAKESPEARE'S PLAYS
Shakespeare was not an original story maker. Rather, he was a genius at taking materials from other sources—historical chronicles, romances, and even other plays—and dramatizing them for his company, his theatre, and his lively audience, which consisted of royalty, aristocrats, merchants, and laborers. Written histories of the dynastic struggles that led to the triumph of the House of Tudor provided the material for his chronicling

of the English kings. His comedies were modeled on the Latin comedies of Plautus and on Italian romances; his tragedies were derived from violent stories and plays of revenge. But no matter how indebted he may have been to his sources, Shakespeare's particular genius—his brilliant language, his facility with plot and action, and his deep understanding of human nature expressed through his unparalleled array of characters—allowed him to bring a series of dramas to the stage that made his company the most successful in London.

Although the struggle for political power was a prominent subject of his plays, Shakespeare generally managed to focus on character rather than on political analysis, which might have been seen as commentary on the national debate over succession. One of the most striking of his history plays, *The Tragedy of Richard III*, however, reveals the manipulation of history in the drama. Drawing on the distortions in Thomas More's biography of Richard III, also repeated in the Holinshed *Chronicles* (histories of England, Scotland, and Ireland), Shakespeare created a portrait of a monstrous, misshapen villain who murders the two boys who are the true heirs to the throne and slashes his way across England to revenge himself for his bitter life. As a study of evil, *Richard III* conveniently justifies the killing of Richard by Henry VII and Henry's subsequent usurpation of the throne. Henry VII was the grandfather of Shakespeare's sovereign, Elizabeth I. The portrait of Richard III immortalized by Shakespeare obviously justifies the presence of Elizabeth on the throne. That Richard was actually far different from Shakespeare's character has generally been lost to history, so vivid was Shakespeare's rendering of his villain.

Elizabethan Staging

THE GLOBE AND OTHER THEATRES   A cluster of professional theatres was built across the River Thames from the city of London, just beyond the jurisdictional reach of a city government that was dubious about the wisdom of a growing theatrical presence. But theatre owners saw profit to be made from theatrical entertainments that drew 3,000 spectators at a time to their large, round, wooden theatres. The most famous of these public commercial theatres, the Globe, was the home of Shakespeare's company, the Lord Chamberlain's Men, from 1599 to 1609. The name of the Globe not only reflected the circular shape of the theatre but also described the way the physical structure of the theatre contained the universe as the Elizabethans saw it. And this point of view, encompassed by the theatre building, echoed the

same combination of medieval and Renaissance thinking as did the structure of the plays.

Because the theatre was partly open to the sky, the stage was protected by a canopy that might have had stars painted on it to represent the heavens. The stage platform itself was the world, the level of human endeavor; and the area below the stage, accessible through trapdoors, suggested hell, with its ghosts and spirits. This hierarchical representation was similar to the understanding of the universe expressed by the medieval stage. The difference was the expansion of the human arena, where most of the action took place.

Of the three theatres discussed so far, the medieval theatre had the most elaborate scenic effects. The Elizabethan stage—like the stage of the Beijing Opera discussed later in this chapter—was an empty space with minimal stage properties: a table, a chair, banners. It was through the playwright's eloquent language that the Elizabethan actor defined the space.

LANGUAGE AS AN ELEMENT OF STAGING   Like the Greek theatre, the Elizabethan stage relied on vivid, energetic, and evocative **language** to fill the stage space and shape the **action**. In scene after scene, the playwright framed the action with only a few poetic words to create setting or time of day. In *Hamlet*, the sunrise is created with the following memorable lines:

> But, look, the morn, in russet mantle clad,
> Walks o'er the dew of yon high eastern hill.[1]

In *King Lear*, a storm is created when Lear pours out a description of the weather that also describes the breaking of his heart:

LEAR: Blow, winds, and crack your cheeks! Rage! Blow!
You cataracts and hurricanoes, spout
Till you have drench'd our steeples, drown'd the cocks!
You sulph'rous and thought-executing fires,
Vaunt-couriers of oak-cleaving thunderbolts,

The Globe Theatre was built for the Lord Chamberlain's Men and was the site of the premiere performances of some of Shakespeare's most famous plays. This photo shows a reconstruction of the Globe, built on the south bank of the Thames River, that is now used for theatre performances in London. In Elizabethan times the Thames served as a boundary between the city of London and the theatres that by law were kept outside the city limits. This photo shows a production of *Coriolanus* with Jonathan Cake in the title role under the direction of Dominic Dromgoole, performed at the Globe Theatre in 2006.

Singe my white head! And thou, all-shaking
    thunder,
Strike flat the thick rotundity o' th' world!
Crack nature's moulds, all germens spill at once
That makes ingrateful man![2]

The entering or exiting of characters indicated a change of scene, and frequently characters referred to their next destination as they went. All the information needed by the audience to follow the action was contained in the language. The importance of the language points to an audience prepared to listen closely to the words and rapidly process verbal cues, although there were certainly visual cues as well.

The performance of Shakespeare depended on the imagination of the audience. *Henry V* opens with a prologue in which a character called Chorus asks the audience to fill in the images suggested by the actors so that the stage might become a battlefield where a few actors become armies led by kings:

Piece out our imperfections with your thoughts;
Into a thousand parts divide one man,
And make imaginary puissance;

Think, when we talk of horses, that you
    see them
Printing their proud hoofs i' th' receiving earth.
For 'tis your thoughts that now must deck our
    kings,
Carry them here and there, jumping o'er times,
Turning the accomplishment of many years
Into an hour-glass.[3]

As suggested in these lines, Elizabethan plays involved numerous characters acting out complicated events in rapidly shifting locations over extended periods of time. This expansiveness of space and time was a direct inheritance from the medieval stage, which told the entire history of the Christian world in a single production. The Greek drama, in contrast, generally offered a concentrated representation of human experience, portrayed by only a few characters in one location in a very compressed passage of time: human action reduced to its essence. Shakespeare and his contemporaries looked to show the variations of human action by writing complex plays with multiple plots or subplots. To accomplish this sweeping presentation of action, the Elizabethan stage depended on the alertness of its audience and the language of the playwright.

Acting in Elizabethan Dramas

The professional English actor was a master of speech. In discussions of Elizabethan acting, the most famous acting teacher was Shakespeare himself, who through the character of Hamlet instructs a group of traveling actors on their craft:

Speak the speech, I pray you, as I pronounced it to you, trippingly on the tongue; but if you mouth it, as many of your players do, I had as lief the town-crier had spoke my lines.[4]

Hamlet goes on to emphasize a natural acting style, performed with moderation rather than exaggeration.

Nor do not saw the air too much with your hand, thus, but use all gently; for the very torrent, tempest, and, as I may say, the

whirlwind of passion, you must acquire and beget a temperance that may give it smoothness. . . . Suit the action to the word, the word to the action; with this special observance, that you o'erstep not the modesty of nature. For anything so overdone is from the purpose of playing, whose end, both at the first and now, was and is, to hold, as 'twere, the mirror up to nature; to show virtue her own feature, scorn her own image, and the very age and body of the time his form and pressure.[5]

In fact, the actor would frequently perform very close to the audience, again more like the medieval theatre than the Greek. The platform stage extended into the audience space, and audience members would have stood on three sides of the stage pressing close against it. The actor playing at the edge of the stage would have been able to address the audience easily and intimately in his soliloquies and asides. Even the audience seated in boxes placed around the walls of the audience space would have been close enough to the stage to observe the details of character action. The proximity of the audience to the actors suggests that broad gestures and exaggerated speech were unnecessary. Furthermore, the indication is that the speech was delivered with considerably more speed than it would be today, making a broad style of delivery impossible to maintain.

THE BEIJING OPERA OF CHINA

China is a nation with ancient origins that date back to around 4000 B.C.E. The theatre has played a significant part in the rich Chinese cultural heritage for more than 3,000 years and has taken many forms over that remarkable span of time. The relatively recent form that we examine here, the Beijing Opera, draws on many earlier theatre movements or styles but is usually recognized as being established in 1790. It was at the eightieth birthday party of the reigning emperor in that year that new forms of performance were introduced to Beijing, the capital of China.

A Formal Society

The teachings of Confucius, who lived in the fifth century B.C.E., at the same time as the major Greek playwrights, provided the foundation for the organization of Chinese society. Confucian ideas of family, respect for and deference to elders, acceptance of one's place in the hierarchy, and the importance of formal codes of conduct evolved over a period of centuries into a society governed officially by a vast bureaucracy and internally by a complex and pervasive network of rules and obligations. Although Confucius adhered to ideals that included democracy, what resulted from the modifications of his principles led to a society committed to conformity as a way of maintaining social stability.

At the center of Chinese society was the extended family. The effective functioning of the family as the basic social and political unit depended on the observation of intricate rules that governed relationships and the demonstration of appropriate regard for the elders who headed the family and the ancestors who had preceded them. The dramas of the Beijing Opera took this organization of the family as one of its major subjects. The theatre developed its own precise rules of style and detailed codes for the presentation of character types in response to the formal organization of Chinese society.

Playwrights and Plays

Like the Greek dramatists and Shakespeare, the playwrights for the Beijing Opera drew on earlier sources, such as historical novels, myths, and legends. But the goal of the Chinese dramatist was not to create a work that would stand on its own philosophical or poetic merit but to provide a vehicle for the actor. The Chinese playwright was an anonymous arranger of a text, bringing together functional passages that would support the actor's creation. And the audience members who gathered in large restaurant-like theatres, drinking tea and eating during the performances,

did not hang on every word but paused in their noisy activity to pay close attention only to the most exciting or clever parts.

The plays were loosely divided into two areas of focus: civil plays that dealt with domestic and social situations and military plays that maximized the opportunity for the action of warriors, outlaws, and demons. Plays were constructed around a set of instantly recognizable stock characters: four categories—male, female, painted-face, and comic—were divided into representative types whose characteristics were predetermined through generations of performances. A male character could be the hero, the official, the warrior, or the patriarch. A female character could be the virtuous and demure woman, the lively but untrustworthy woman, the warrior woman, or the matriarch. As in the Greek, medieval, and Elizabethan theatres, men played the women's roles, and because these were professional actors, female impersonation became a highly refined art. The gender issues related to female impersonation were complicated further by the social and sexual position of the male actors who undertook these roles in Chinese society. We return to the issue of female impersonation later in the chapter.

The painted-face characters brought the fantastic, the grotesque, and the supernatural into the world constructed by the Chinese theatre. Animal gods, outlaws, and warriors were given a larger-than-life appearance with bold and colorful makeup applied in such strong patterns that it functioned much like a mask. Finally, the comic roles included characters who contradicted expectations: the elderly soldier who was foolish rather than wise, the peasant who was cunning rather than simple.

A Language of Gesture

Although the form of the Beijing Opera is absolutely distinct from the other major forms of theatre in Asia, such as the **kabuki** theatre of

••• IN CONTEXT

The Beijing Opera and Chinese History

Date	Event
1644	Manchus conquer China. China is ruled by Manchu dynasties until 1911.
1790	Beijing Opera introduced at the eightieth birthday celebration of Emperor Ch'ien Lung.
1911	Revolution breaks out against dynastic rule. After 1911, women slowly begin to appear on the stage in traditional plays as well as more Westernized drama.
1912	China becomes a republic. A period of great instability begins, involving continuous military and political struggles over the next thirty-seven years, including feuding warlords, Japanese invasion, and civil war between Chiang Kai-shek and the communists.
1921	Creation of the Communist Party.
1930/1935	The actor Mei Lan-Fang tours Japan, the United States, and Russia, where he is seen by Bertolt Brecht.
1937	War with Japan.
1942	Talks at Yan'an Forum on Art and Literature, during which Mao Zedong presents his theories of art and theatre serving the political cause.
1949	Communist takeover of China.
1966	Cultural Revolution. Harshest period of censorship of the arts under supervision of Mao's wife, Jiang Qing. Substitution of model plays for traditional Chinese theatre.
1976	Death of Mao. Overthrow of the "gang of four." Revival of traditional theatre forms.
1978	New openness.
1989	Massacre at Tiananmen Square. Crackdown against democracy movement.
1990s	Acceleration of social change.
2008	Summer Olympics in Beijing.

Japan, the **kathakali** theatre of India, and the dance drama of Bali, certain basic principles guide all the traditional theatres of Asia. Just as text is the dominating force in the Western theatre, so gesture is the language of the actor in the Eastern theatre. In the West, the scripts of famous playwrights have been handed down through the centuries, and theatre is largely a verbal, language-based art. In Asian theatre, the gestures, stylized and intricate, convey codes of meaning that can be "read" by an audience just as plainly as we in the West can interpret the actor's speech.

The text of the Beijing Opera may lack the power of the finest writing for the Western stage; similarly, the use of character types may have precluded the development of highly individualized, psychologically developed characters such as Oedipus and Hamlet, whose struggles have made them central to Western culture. But

The heroine prepares for battle in this scene from *The Peony Pavilion,* which demonstrates the way the intensity of the gestural acting style combined with brilliant costumes and elaborate makeup provides the visual expression of Chinese opera without the use of any scenic background.

the Beijing Opera developed a poetry of theatrical expression that we cannot yet approximate. And the speech of Asian theatre, which is totally unlike Western conversational stage speech, is as stylized and removed from the everyday world as the actor's movement patterns.

Acting and Staging

The movement and the speech or singing of the Asian theatre demand a technical proficiency achievable only after years of the most disciplined training, which begins when the actors are children. It is through such rigorous training that the physical interpretation of a role can be passed from generation to generation, even over centuries.

With the conventions of the Chinese theatre in mind, we can imagine a performance of the Beijing Opera in the mid-nineteenth century. The actor stood alone on a bare platform stage. Although elaborate scenery was in use throughout European and American theatres at this time, in the Beijing Opera there were no clever scenic elements to capture the audience's imagination, no special lighting effects to focus their attention. The actor had to use his own resources to create everything that the audience would see. And for this, the actor was singularly well prepared. With a few steps he crossed an invisible threshold and entered a new room or building. With a flick of his whip he rode

The Peony Pavilion represents a form of Chinese opera called kungku, which is less acrobatic and more lyrical than the Beijing Opera. *The Peony Pavilion,* written in 1598, tells the story of a scholar, Liu Mengmei, who rescues his beloved, Du Liniang, from the underworld. Told in fifty-five episodes, which take nineteen hours to perform, *The Peony Pavilion* was revived in 1999 with performances at Lincoln Center in New York City and in Shanghai, China.

a nonexistent horse; with a swaying motion he was carried down the river in an imaginary boat. Dressed in sumptuously embroidered robes and wearing an elaborate wig and headdress, the Chinese actor created a compelling presence.

Later in the performance the subtle pantomime that created both environment and action gave way to more spectacular choreography. A battle scene took place, and the combatants seemed to come flying across the stage. With enormous swords in hand, the actors performed acrobatic feats that had the audience shouting approval. Bodies hurtled about the stage at unbelievable speeds, performing multiple flips and somersaults in the air, akin to the flights of Olympic gymnasts. All the

action, the entrances and exits, the pantomimed sequences, and the acrobatic choreography were accompanied by musicians seated in view of the audience playing drums, gongs, cymbals, flutes, and traditional Chinese string instruments. The actors' lines, which had their own stylistic patterns, were sung and chanted rather than spoken.

A few basic pieces of furniture were all that helped designate location. A table and two chairs in different configurations changed the scene from a palace to a law court to a bedroom or indicated a wall, a bridge, or a mountain. A stagehand whose invisibility was an accepted convention of the Chinese theatre appeared as needed to reposition the furniture or to add or remove the few additional props that gave further definition to the changing space. The flexible approach to staging meant that performances could easily accommodate multiple locations and shifting conditions, such as time of day and weather. This style of performance emphasized the bond between the actor's skill and the audience's imagination. It also depended heavily, as so many performance traditions do, on a body of theatrical conventions accepted and understood by all participants in the dramatic event.

The Beijing Opera and the Communist Revolution

The history of the Beijing Opera in the twentieth century was closely intertwined with the rise of the Communist Party to power and its subsequent cultural policies. In the first part of the twentieth century approximately 3,000 opera companies performed the traditional repertoire throughout China. A typical company was a private commercial endeavor organized around one or more star performers that played regular engagements in a theatre and also was hired to perform for various festivals, both public and private.

The most famous company was headed by the actor Mei Lan-Fang, who was revered throughout China for his brilliant performances and for the innovations he brought to the traditional theatre form. Mei Lan-Fang also achieved an international reputation by undertaking a series of tours with his company in the 1920s and the 1930s to Japan, the United States, and Russia. He made an enormous impression on Western theatre practitioners, particularly the German director and playwright Bertolt Brecht, who would become one of the defining forces in twentieth-century theatre.

The Chinese communists saw the arts as essential to their goals for transforming Chinese society. From the early days of communist activity in China, Mao Zedong and his followers encouraged the development of a political theatre that would serve the revolutionary cause. In 1942, seven years before the communists came to power in China,

Mao officially articulated his theories about the relationship between politics and art and literature at the Yan'an Forum on Art and Literature. According to his view, the only acceptable function for art was to celebrate and serve the proletariat:

> If everyone agrees on the fundamental policy of art serving the workers, peasants, and soldiers and on how to serve them, such should be adhered to by all our workers, our schools, publications, and organizations in the field of literature and art and in all our literary and artistic activities. It is wrong to depart from this policy. Anything at variance with it must be duly corrected.

The implications of this policy would be as wrenching for the Beijing Opera as the upheaval and strife generated by Mao and his wife, Jiang Qing, would be for the Chinese nation as they reformed what they perceived to be the corruptions of the past. Jiang Qing, who had been an actor before she became a communist leader, brought both personal and ideological concerns into her drive to dominate the arts in China. Because of its enormous popularity, the Beijing Opera was targeted as a major vehicle for communist propaganda. During the **Cultural Revolution** (1966 to 1976), the traditional Beijing Opera was almost completely suppressed and replaced with eight model plays that dealt with contemporary themes and emphasized heroic, sacrificial actions on behalf of the revolution and the workers. Enormous sums of money and human resources were lavished on the development of the model productions. Productions such as *The Red Lantern* and *The White-Haired Girl* demonstrated the class struggle at the heart of the Chinese revolution and clearly identified the corrupt, capitalist enemies of the people.

Although these plays are not without strong characters and rising tension, they are extremely didactic. And although the model productions held the attention of audiences during this intense period of upheaval in China, they undermined the ability of the opera form to sustain itself when the political winds changed. The old actors and stories were gone. Audiences became wary of overtly political theatre. The model productions had laid no groundwork for the development of new material, and the companies had no other plays available with which to attract audiences.

The manipulation of the Beijing Opera to present communist propaganda had the long-term effect of practically destroying the theatre form itself; this development was not unlike the elimination of the mystery cycles in Elizabethan England as part of the government's policy to create a nation removed from the pope's influence. In China, the Beijing Opera was appropriated to promote the social change envisioned by Mao Zedong and his wife, Jiang Qing.

These examples are far from unique. Many societies, past and present, have sought to manipulate the theatre for political ends. Some societies have persecuted and even murdered actors and playwrights, and some cultures have worshiped them, sometimes simultaneously. Actors and playwrights have been slaves and they have been military leaders and heads of state. They have been social outcasts and the confidantes of kings.

For example, in the United States in the mid-twentieth century, fear of communism prompted the United States Congress to call playwrights and screenwriters, actors and directors before the House Committee on Un-American Activities (HUAC) to answer questions about their political affiliations. Without due process or proof of laws being broken, theatre and film practitioners were sent to jail or were blacklisted. They were blocked from further participation in film or play making until this committee was discredited for its attempts to control the free expression of ideas, an overt contradiction of one of our nation's founding principles.

••• THE THEATRICAL MIRROR

The Chinese opera, like the Elizabethan theatre, the Greek theatre, and the medieval theatre, was at the center of its society. All four of these theatres functioned as the mirror that, in Hamlet's words, revealed the "form and pressure" of "the very age and body of the time." The performance traditions and the subjects of the plays reflected the concerns of the community and the way the community understood and expressed itself.

Thus far we have observed the way the theatre has reflected religious beliefs, political organization, and social relationships. As we try to understand what the theatre has to tell us about the past, we are struck particularly by one theatrical convention shared by all of these theatres from vastly different periods and with extremely different political and religious points of view: Although women characters appeared on the stage, all the female roles were written and played by men.

In the theatres that we have studied in the first two chapters, women did not participate in any way except as audience members. The exclusion of women from participation in the theatre reflected a significant aspect of a social organization that excluded women from the public discourse. Just as women did not vote, hold office, or participate in the educational system or the government—with the exception of Elizabeth I—so they were not allowed to be part of the theatre as playwrights or actors. Women characters were presented, but women did not represent themselves through writing or acting. The female behavior constructed onstage was considered appropriate or even ideal. But men created all the images that represented women, both physically and psychologically.

Today, some theatre historians and social critics see this representation of women by men as an absence. That is, any actual sense of women was completely missing. The female characters were part of a man's world but not part of a woman's world. The female characters may have become erotic objects for the male characters or they may have reflected male attitudes toward women, but they did not genuinely represent the actual nature and concerns of women themselves.

In the Greek theatre, masks and costumes designated the gender of the characters, and because three actors played all the individual roles, actors moved back and forth between male and female characters. In the unmasked Elizabethan theatre, boys or young men played the female roles. In the Beijing Opera, elaborate makeup, costuming, and wigs were used to complete the illusion. In the Asian theatre, actors were designated at an early age to take female roles, and their whole training focused on techniques of impersonation. These actors, called *dan* in the Beijing Opera, then played female roles throughout their careers. In the Chinese theatre, female-character actors had to wear and master special blocked shoes that gave the impression that the character had bound feet. Later, beginning in 1911, when women began to appear onstage and bound feet had been outlawed in China, the women had to learn from the male actors how to create the accepted stage impression of a woman's bound foot.[6]

The exclusion of women from the theatre has had a number of significant consequences. The theatre has always been a central institution for the exchange of ideas and the evolution of culture. By being excluded from the early forms of theatre, women lost a valuable opportunity to participate in the life of the community. Their voices were not heard, and so there was a serious distortion of what both women and men in a given society saw as "believable" female behavior. Because the theatre functions as a major source of culturally accepted gender identity, ideas or models of behavior were generated that defined women's roles and their nature, even though women had no part in their creation. As a result, women may have shaped or distorted their own behavior or adopted styles of dress or attitude in response to what had been represented in the theatre. This distortion resulted both from the selection of character qualities to be represented—that is, what was chosen and what was left out—and from the context in which the female characters were placed.

In a solo show, **Heather Raffo** plays nine different Iraqi women characters. Raffo developed the text for the play by drawing on her interviews with ordinary Iraqi citizens over a period of ten years. The play creates a social document about life in Iraq before and after American military intervention through the characters' different perspectives on the upheavals that defines their lives. Raffo has been performing *9 Parts of Desire* in a variety of theatres since 2004.

THEATRE AND SOCIAL CHANGE

In the United States today, society is vitally concerned with issues of gender and race. These concerns are reflected in legislation, education, economic initiatives, public debate, and theatre. The theatre not only mirrors the roles human beings take in their respective societies but also plays an important part in changing

The play *Black Watch* uses explosive and startling staging to draw the audience into life in a combat zone. In the words of reviewer Ben Brantley, "every moment seems to bleed from the previous one in an uninterrupted river of sensations."[7] Written by Gregory Burke, with direction by John Tiffany, movement direction by Steven Hogget, and music direction by Davey Anderson, *Black Watch* shocks the audience into a new awareness of the war in Iraq that so many have seen only from a distance.

the way we see ourselves. Many contemporary plays, including those represented in this book, directly address questions of race and gender and challenge us to rethink issues of equity and citizenship. In such recent plays as *Joe Turner's Come and Gone*, *And the Soul Shall Dance*, *Angels in America*, and *Dog Lady*, identity is considered in connection to the individual psychology of the characters, but it is also explored in

terms of the way social expectations condition human behavior.

Plays and theatrical movements have frequently been a significant factor in challenging prevailing points of view and bringing about social change. We must always remember that although the theatre is vulnerable to government intervention, it is the power of theatre that provokes government scrutiny. For example, in the 1960s in the United States, a protest movement aimed at ending U.S. participation in the war in Vietnam eventually gathered such strength that the U.S. government ended its military involvement there. An important part of that protest movement was theatre. Theatre performances in the streets, on college campuses, and in traditional professional and community theatres were a powerful way of bringing people together and expressing the suffering and the futility of war.

More recently, plays have begun to appear addressing the consequences of the military action led by the United States in Iraq. A play by Heather Raffo, *9 Part of Desire*, explores the violence governing the lives of Iraqi women, both under the dictatorship of Saddam Hussein and afterward since the American invasion. A new play from the National Theatre of Scotland has been performed around the world since its premiere in 2006. Drawing on interviews with members of the three-hundred-year-old Black Watch Regiment of Scotland, this play explores the consequences of the soldiers' deployment to Iraq as a turning point in the regiment's proud, long history. The soldiers who contributed their histories were surviving members of a squad that backed up the U.S. assault on Fallouja. The play documents the soldiers' experiences through realistic scenes, television clips, email messages, combat sequences, and songs and dances using the bagpipe music of the Scottish military tradition.

In considering the relationship between theatre and social change we turn to further

The Nature of Performance
The Theatre Practitioners

In Chapters 1 and 2 we considered the centrality of theatre for societies earlier than our own, societies in which dramas could only be presented live, not through the film media prevalent today. We now shift our attention to the significance of the theatre in modern society, particularly the American theatre, and the work that must be done to realize theatre productions on the contemporary stage. As we expand our references to American playwrights and productions, we quickly see that no one playwright speaks for the nation as Shakespeare did in Elizabethan England; nor do we have a national theatre like the Greek and medieval theatres, with a set of myths and signs recognized by everyone. Furthermore, the American theatre is not dominated by a particular place or group of producers. For many decades the center of the American theatre was considered to be New York City. The acceptance of any new play depended on a production in one of the prestigious theatres clustered on and around **Broadway.** Other parts of the nation would see what Broadway had sanctioned through touring productions or the gradual passage of successful plays to smaller theatres around the country. But the energy of the American theatre is no longer focused in one geographic area. Although New York is certainly still a leader in the development of plays and performance styles, large and small theatres play a vital part in communities throughout the country and collectively help to form an evolving idea of the American theatre.

Producing theatre depends on a collaborative process, usually begun by a playwright who is joined by actors, a director, and designers. In this section of the book, we turn our attention to the work of these theatre practitioners. First we examine the way the contributions of the different participants come together to develop ideas, images, dramatic action, and characters. Through a study of the play *Joe Turner's Come and Gone* by August Wilson in a production at the Oregon Shakespeare Festival, we explore the playwright's creation and then the collective effort of producing the play for an audience. We see the play as a work of art and an exploration of historical and social issues.

Following the discussion of the play in production, we take a closer look at the unique arts of the actor, the director, and the designers. We separate and examine the special abilities and skills required of each theatre artist and the kinds of training necessary to prepare for the intense demands of theatre work. Whether a playwright, a performer, a director, or a visual artist, every theatre practitioner shares the need to merge creativity and discipline, intuition and analysis, imagination and technique. Only through years of training does the skilled artist emerge. •••

Chapter 3

The Playwright's Vision

Looking at *Joe Turner's Come
and Gone*
by August Wilson

WHEN AUGUST WILSON WAS a fifteen-year-old high school student living in Pittsburgh with his mother, he wrote a paper on Napoleon for his history class. The quality of the paper was so high that the teacher had two responses: He gave the paper an A+, and he told the young African American student that he would have to prove that the work in the paper was really his. Wilson pointed to the bibliography and footnotes but otherwise refused to plead his case. The teacher then changed the grade to an F. On that day, August Wilson quit school and never went back.

He turned instead to the public library and began to educate himself through the books he found there. And at age twenty he began his writing career, first as a poet and then as a writer of short stories. As a young man who had been rejected by the institutions of white culture, he began "remaking the world in his own image through the act of writing."[1] But while he responded to his own experiences, he also started listening to the stories and experiences of the people he met on the street, people such as the elderly black men who hung around the cigar store, "swapping tales, discussing the day's headlines, arguing and needling."[2] Their lives and memories were long, going back to the postslavery days in the South and the great migration to the North.

Eventually Wilson would prove that he had a rich and unique way of presenting history: the history of African Americans, too frequently left out of American history books. Wilson ultimately turned to playwriting in order to present this history on the stage, where his characters could come to life and share their revelations with audiences across the country.

In the early 1980s Wilson began writing a cycle of plays chronicling African American life in the United States. These plays interpret periods of history through the stories of ordinary people rather than the powerful or famous individuals who are usually considered historical figures. For each decade of the twentieth century, Wilson focused on a representative group of characters whose struggles and dreams reflect the events and attitudes of the larger society. Just before his death in 2005, Wilson completed the tenth and final play of this ambitious cycle. In his first play, *Ma Rainey's Black Bottom*, originally produced in 1984 and set in the 1920s, Wilson explores the world of black jazz musicians who seek recognition for themselves and ownership of the music that they are making. *Ma Rainey's Black Bottom* takes place in Chicago; it is the only one of the ten plays not set in Pittsburgh's Hill District, where Wilson grew up. *Fences* looks at life in the America of the 1950s. A former baseball player, forced by racial circumstances to become a garbage hauler, battles with his son to justify his own life.

In *The Piano Lesson*, representing the 1930s, a brother and sister fight over the fate of the old family piano. Carved on the piano's legs are the faces of relatives who were slaves. By selling the piano, the brother hopes to make enough money to buy land and secure a place for himself in America. For the sister, the piano symbolizes the presence of their ancestors, a presence that she cannot part with.

In *Two Trains Running*, the characters gather in Memphis Lee's diner, where they find the determination in each other's company to take their places with dignity in the hostile urban environment of Pittsburgh in 1969. *Seven Guitars*, set in 1940s Pittsburgh, returns to the struggles of a musician, this time the singer and guitar player Floyd Barton, and the events that led up to his death.

King Hedley II looks at the struggles of an ex-convict trying to make a life for himself in the 1980s. *Jitney*, written in 1979, was recently revised and given a new series of productions beginning in 1996. Set in the 1970s, *Jitney* reflects the tensions of inner-city life through the world of unlicensed cab drivers who drive their "jitneys" through the decaying streets of Pittsburgh, beyond the boundaries of the legal taxi trade. The last two plays written by Wilson, *Gem of the Ocean* and *Radio Golf*, provide the beginning and the ending for the ten-play, 100-year cycle. *Gem of the Ocean*, placed at the opening of the twentieth century in 1904, features a mystical 300-year-old character, Aunt Ester, who lives at 1839 Wylie Avenue and has the power to cleanse people's souls. *Radio Golf,*

THE AUTHOR SPEAKS

August Wilson

To write is to fix language, to get it down and fix it to a spot and have it have meaning and be fat with substance. It is in many ways a remaking of the self in which all of the parts have been realigned, redistributed, and reassembled into a new being of sense and harmony. You have wrought something into being, and what you have wrought is what you have learned about life, and what you have learned is always pointed toward moving the harborless parts of your being closer to home. To write is to forever circle the maps, marking it all down, the latitude and longitude of each specific bearing, giving new meaning to something very old and very sacred—life itself.[3]

—*August Wilson*

BERTHA: Well, watch him, then. He's gonna dig a little hole and bury that pigeon. Then he's gonna pray over that blood . . . pour it on top . . . mark out his circle and come on into the house.

SETH: That's what he doing . . . he pouring that blood on top.

BERTHA: When they gonna put you back working daytime? Told me two months ago he was gonna put you back working daytime.

SETH: That's what Mr. Olowski told me. I got to wait till he say when. He tell me what to do. I don't tell him. Drive me crazy to speculate on the man's wishes when he don't know what he want to do himself.

BERTHA: Well, I wish he go ahead and put you back working daytime. This working all hours of the night don't make no sense.

SETH: It don't make no sense for that boy to run out of here and get drunk so they lock him up either.

BERTHA: Who? Who they got locked up for being drunk?

SETH: That boy that's staying upstairs . . . Jeremy. I stopped down there on Logan Street on my way home from work and one of the fellows told me about it. Say he seen it when they arrested him.

BERTHA: I was wondering why I ain't seen him this morning.

SETH: You know I don't put up with that. I told him when he came . . .

(BYNUM enters from the yard carrying some plants. He is a short, round man in his early sixties. A conjure man, or rootworker, he gives the impression of always being in control of everything. Nothing ever bothers him. He seems to be lost in a world of his own making and to swallow any adversity or interference with his grand design.)

What you doing bringing them weeds in my house? Out there stepping on my vegetables and now wanna carry them weeds in my house.

BYNUM: Morning, Seth. Morning, Sister Bertha.

SETH: Messing up my garden growing them things out there. I ought to go out there and pull up all them weeds.

BERTHA: Some gal was by here to see you this morning, Bynum. You was out there in the yard . . . I told her to come back later.

BYNUM: (To SETH.) You look sick. What's the matter, you ain't eating right?

SETH: What if I was sick? You ain't getting near me with none of that stuff.

(BERTHA sets a plate of biscuits on the table.)

BYNUM: My . . . my . . . Bertha, your biscuits getting fatter and fatter.

(BYNUM takes a biscuit and begins to eat.)

Where Jeremy? I don't see him around this morning. He usually be around riffing and raffing on Saturday morning.

SETH: I know where he at. I know just where he at. They got him down there in the jail. Getting drunk and acting a fool. He down there where he belong with all that foolishness.

BYNUM: Mr. Piney's boys got him, huh? They ain't gonna do nothing but hold on to him for a little while. He's gonna be back here hungrier than a mule directly.

SETH: I don't go for all that carrying on and such. This is a respectable house. I don't have no drunkards or fools around here.

BYNUM: That boy got a lot of country in him. He ain't been up here but two weeks. It's gonna take a while before he can work that country out of him.

SETH: These niggers coming up here with that old backward country style of living. It's hard enough now without all that ignorant kind of acting. Ever since slavery got over with there ain't been nothing but foolish-acting niggers. Word get out they need men to work in the mill and put in these roads . . . and niggers drop everything and head North looking for freedom. They don't know the white fellows looking too. White fellows

61

coming from all over the world. White fellow come over and in six months got more than what I got. But these niggers keep on coming. Walking . . . riding . . . carrying their Bibles. That boy done carried a guitar all the way from North Carolina. What he gonna find out? What he gonna do with that guitar? This the city.

(There is a knock on the door.)

Niggers coming up here from the backwoods . . . coming up here from the country carrying Bibles and guitars looking for freedom. They got a rude awakening.

(SETH goes to answer the door. RUTHERFORD SELIG enters. About SETH's age, he is a thin white man with greasy hair. A peddler, he supplies SETH with the raw materials to make pots and pans which he then peddles door to door in the mill towns along the river. He keeps a list of his customers as they move about and is known in the various communities as the People finder. He carries squares of sheet metal under his arm.)

Ho! Forgot you was coming today. Come on in.

BYNUM: If it ain't Rutherford Selig . . . the People finder himself.

SELIG: What say there, Bynum?

BYNUM: I say about my shiny man. You got to tell me something. I done give you my dollar . . . I'm looking to get a report.

SELIG: I got eight here, Seth.

SETH: (Taking the sheet metal.) What is this? What you giving me here? What I'm gonna do with this?

SELIG: I need some dustpans. Everybody asking me about dustpans.

SETH: Gonna cost you fifteen cents apiece. And ten cents to put a handle on them.

SELIG: I'll give you twenty cents apiece with the handles.

SETH: All right. But I ain't gonna give you but fifteen cents for the sheet metal.

SELIG: It's twenty-five cents apiece for the metal. That's what we agreed on.

SETH: This low-grade sheet metal. They ain't worth but a dime. I'm doing you a favor giving you fifteen cents. You know this metal ain't worth no twenty-five cents. Don't come talking that twenty-five cent stuff to me over no low-grade sheet metal.

SELIG: All right, fifteen cents apiece. Just make me some dustpans out of them.

(SETH exits with the sheet metal out the back door.)

BERTHA: Sit on down there, Selig. Get you a cup of coffee and a biscuit.

BYNUM: Where you coming from this time?

SELIG: I been upriver. All along the Monongahela. Past Rankin and all up around Little Washington.

BYNUM: Did you find anybody?

SELIG: I found Sadie Jackson up in Braddock. Her mother's staying down there in Scotchbottom say she hadn't heard from her and she didn't know where she was at. I found her up in Braddock on Enoch Street. She bought a frying pan from me.

BYNUM: You around here finding everybody how come you ain't found my shiny man?

SELIG: The only shiny man I saw was the Nigras working on the road gang with the sweat glistening on them.

BYNUM: Naw, you'd be able to tell this fellow. He shine like new money.

SELIG: Well, I done told you I can't find nobody without a name.

BERTHA: Here go one of these hot biscuits, Selig.

BYNUM: This fellow don't have no name. I call him John 'cause it was up around Johnstown where I seen him. I ain't even so sure he's one special fellow. That shine could pass on to anybody. He could be anybody shining.

SELIG: Well, what's he look like besides being shiny? There's lots of shiny Nigras.

BYNUM: He's just a man I seen out on the road. He ain't had no special look. Just a man walking toward me on the road. He come up and asked me which way the road went. I told him everything I knew about the road, where it went and all, and he asked me did I have anything to eat 'cause he was hungry. Say he ain't had nothing to eat in three days. Well, I never be out there on the road without a piece of dried meat. Or an orange or an apple. So I give this fellow an orange. He take and eat that orange and told me to come and go along the road a little ways with him, that he had something he wanted to show me. He had a look about him made me wanna go with him, see what he gonna show me.

We walked on a bit and it's getting kind of far from where I met him when it come up on me all of a sudden, we wasn't going the way he had come from, we was going back my way. Since he said he ain't knew nothing about the road, I asked him about this. He say he had a voice inside him telling him which way to go and if I come and go along with him he was gonna show me the Secret of Life. Quite naturally I followed him. A fellow that's gonna show you the Secret of Life ain't to be taken lightly. We get near this bend in the road . . .

(SETH enters with an assortment of pots.)

SETH: I got six here, Selig.

SELIG: Wait a minute, Seth. Bynum's telling me about the secret of life. Go ahead, Bynum. I wanna hear this.

(SETH sets the pots down and exits out the back.)

BYNUM: We get near this bend in the road and he told me to hold out my hands. Then he rubbed them together with his and I looked down and see they got blood on them. Told me to take and rub it all over me . . . say that was a way of cleaning myself. Then we went around the bend in that road. Got around that bend and it seem like all of a sudden we ain't in the same place. Turn around that bend and everything look like it was twice as big as it was. The trees and everything bigger than life! Sparrows big as eagles! I turned around to look at this fellow and he had this light coming out of him. I had to cover up my eyes to keep from being blinded. He shining like new money with that light. He shined until all the light seemed like it seeped out of him and then he was gone and I was by myself in this strange place where everything was bigger than life.

I wandered around there looking for that road, trying to find my way back from this big place . . . and I looked over and seen my daddy standing there. He was the same size he always was, except for his hands and his mouth. He had a great big old mouth that look like it took up his whole face and his hands were as big as hams. Look like they was too big to carry around. My daddy called me to him. Said he had been thinking about me and it grieved him to see me in the world carrying other people's songs and not having one of my own. Told me he was gonna show me how to find my song. Then he carried me further into this big place until we come to this ocean. Then he showed me something I ain't got words to tell you. But if you stand to witness it, you done seen something there. I stayed in that place awhile and my daddy taught me the meaning of this thing that I had seen and showed me how to find my song. I asked him about the shiny man and he told me he was the One Who Goes Before and Shows the Way. Said there was lots of shiny men and if I ever saw one again before I died then I would know that my song had been accepted and worked its full power in the world and I could lay down and die a happy man. A man who done left his mark on life. On the way people cling to each other out of the truth they find in themselves. Then he showed me how to get back to the road. I came out to where everything was its own size and I had my song. I had the Binding Song. I choose that song because that's what I seen most when I was traveling . . . people walking away and leaving one another. So I takes the power of my song and binds them together.

(SETH enters from the yard carrying cabbages and tomatoes.)

Been binding people ever since. That's why they call me Bynum. Just like glue I sticks people together.

SETH: Maybe they ain't supposed to be stuck sometimes. You ever think of that?

BYNUM: Oh, I don't do it lightly. It cost me a piece of myself every time I do. I'm a Binder of What Clings. You got to find out if they cling first. You can't bind what don't cling.

SELIG: Well, how is that the Secret of Life? I thought you said he was gonna show you the secret of life. That's what I'm waiting to find out.

BYNUM: Oh, he showed me alright. But you still got to figure it out. Can't nobody figure it out for you. You got to come to it on your own. That's why I'm looking for the shiny man.

SELIG: Well, I'll keep my eye out for him. What you got there, Seth?

SETH: Here go some cabbage and tomatoes. I got some green beans coming in real nice. I'm gonna take and start me a grapevine out there next year. Butera says he gonna give me a piece of his vine and I'm gonna start that out there.

SELIG: How many of them pots you got?

SETH: I got six. That's six dollars minus eight on top of fifteen for the sheet metal come to a dollar twenty out the six dollars leave me four dollars and eighty cents.

SELIG: (Counting out the money.) There's four dollars . . . and . . . eighty cents.

SETH: How many of them dustpans you want?

SELIG: As many as you can make out them sheets.

SETH: You can use that many? I get to cutting on them sheets figuring how to make them dustpans . . . ain't no telling how many I'm liable to come up with.

SELIG: I can use them and you can make me some more next time.

SETH: Alright, I'm gonna hold you to that, now.

SELIG: Thanks for the biscuit, Bertha.

BERTHA: You know you welcome anytime, Selig.

SETH: Which way you heading?

SELIG: Going down to Wheeling. All through West Virginia there. I'll be back Saturday. They putting in new roads down that way. Makes traveling easier.

SETH: That's what I hear. All up around here too. Got a fellow staying here working on that road by the Brady Street Bridge.

SELIG: Yeah, it's gonna make traveling real nice. Thanks for the cabbage, Seth. I'll see you on Saturday.

(SELIG exits.)

SETH: (To BYNUM.) Why you wanna start all that nonsense talk with that man? All that shiny man nonsense.

BYNUM: You known it ain't no nonsense. Bertha know it ain't no nonsense. I don't know if Selig know or not.

BERTHA: Seth, when you get to making them dustpans make me a coffeepot.

SETH: What's the matter with your coffee? Ain't nothing wrong with your coffee. Don't she make some good coffee, Bynum?

BYNUM: I ain't worried about the coffee. I know she makes some good biscuits.

SETH: I ain't studying no coffeepot, woman. You heard me tell the man I was gonna cut as many dustpans as them sheets will make . . . and all of a sudden you want a coffeepot.

BERTHA: Man, hush up and go on and make me that coffeepot.

(JEREMY enters the front door. About twenty-five, he gives the impression that he has the world in his hand, that he can meet life's challenges head on. He smiles a lot. He is a proficient guitar player, though his spirit has yet to be molded into song.)

BYNUM: I hear Mr. Piney's boys had you.

JEREMY: Fined me two dollars for nothing! Ain't done nothing.

SETH: I told you when you come on here everybody know my house. Know these is respectable quarters. I don't put up with no foolishness. Everybody know Seth Holly keep a good house. Was my daddy's house. This house been a decent house for a long time.

JEREMY: I ain't done nothing, Mr. Seth. I stopped by the Workmen's Club and got me a bottle. Me and Roper Lee from Alabama. Had us a half pint. We was fixing to cut that half in two when they came up on us. Asked us if we was working. We told them we was putting in the road over yonder and that it was our payday. They snatched hold of us to get that two dollars. Me and Roper Lee ain't even had a chance to take a drink when they grabbed us.

SETH: I don't go for all that kind of carrying on.

BERTHA: Leave the boy alone, Seth. You know the police do that. Figure there's too many people out on the street they take some of them off. You know that.

SETH: I ain't gonna have folks talking.

BERTHA: Ain't nobody talking nothing. That's all in your head. You want some grits and biscuits, Jeremy?

JEREMY: Thank you, Miss Bertha. They didn't give us a thing to eat last night. I'll take one of them big bowls if you don't mind.

(There is a knock at the door. SETH goes to answer it. Enter HERALD LOOMIS and his eleven-year-old daughter, ZONIA. HERALD LOOMIS is thirty-two years old. He is at times possessed. A man driven not by the hellhounds that seemingly bay at his heels, but by his search for a world that speaks to something about himself. He is unable to harmonize the forces that swirl around him, and seeks to recreate the world into one that contains his image. He wears a hat and a long wool coat.)

LOOMIS: Me and my daughter looking for a place to stay, mister. You got a sign say you got rooms.

(SETH stares at LOOMIS, sizing him up.)

Mister, if you ain't got no rooms we can go somewhere else.

SETH: How long you plan on staying?

LOOMIS: Don't know. Two weeks or more maybe.

SETH: It's two dollars a week for the room. We serve meals twice a day. It's two dollars for room and board. Pay up in advance.

(LOOMIS reaches into his pocket.)

It's a dollar extra for the girl.

LOOMIS: The girl sleep in the same room.

SETH: Well, do she eat off the same plate? We serve meals twice a day. That's a dollar extra for food.

LOOMIS: Ain't got no extra dollar. I was planning on asking your missus if she could help out with the cooking and cleaning and whatnot.

SETH: Her helping out don't put no food on the table. I need that dollar to buy some food.

LOOMIS: I'll give you fifty cents extra. She don't eat much.

SETH: Okay . . . but fifty cents don't buy but half a portion.

BERTHA: Seth, she can help me out. Let her help me out. I can use some help.

SETH: Well, that's two dollars for the week. Pay up in advance. Saturday to Saturday. You wanna stay on then it's two more come Saturday.

(LOOMIS pays SETH the money.)

BERTHA: My name's Bertha. This my husband, Seth. You got Bynum and Jeremy over there.

LOOMIS: Ain't nobody else live here?

BERTHA: They the only ones live here now. People come and go. They the only ones here now. You want a cup of coffee and a biscuit?

LOOMIS: We done ate this morning.

BYNUM: Where you coming from, Mister . . . I didn't get your name.

LOOMIS: Name's Herald Loomis. This my daughter, Zonia.

BYNUM: Where you coming from?

LOOMIS: Come from all over. Whicheverway the road take us that's the way we go.

JEREMY: If you looking for a job, I'm working putting in that road down there by the bridge. They can't get enough mens. Always looking to take somebody on.

LOOMIS: I'm looking for a woman named Martha Loomis. That's my wife. Got married legal with the papers and all.

SETH: I don't know nobody named Loomis. I know some Marthas but I don't know no Loomis.

BYNUM: You got to see Rutherford Selig if you wanna find somebody. Selig's the People finder. Rutherford Selig's a first-class People finder.

JEREMY: What she look like? Maybe I seen her.

LOOMIS: She a brownskin woman. Got long pretty hair. About five feet from the ground.

JEREMY: I don't know. I might have seen her.

BYNUM: You got to see Rutherford Selig. You give him one dollar to get her name on his list . . . and after she get her name on his list Rutherford Selig will go right on out there and find her. I got him looking for somebody for me.

LOOMIS: You say he find people. How you find him?

BYNUM: You just missed him. He's gone downriver now. You got to wait till Saturday. He's gone downriver with his pots and pans. He come to see Seth on Saturdays. You got to wait till then.

SETH: Come on, I'll show you to your room.

(SETH, LOOMIS, and ZONIA exit up the stairs.)

JEREMY: Miss Bertha, I'll take that biscuit you was gonna give that fellow, if you don't mind. Say, Mr. Bynum, they got somebody like that around here sure enough? Somebody that find people?

BYNUM: Rutherford Selig. He go around selling pots and pans and every house he come to he write down the name and address of whoever lives there. So if you looking for somebody, quite naturally you go and see

him . . . 'cause he's the only one who know where everybody live at.

JEREMY: I ought to have him look for this old gal I used to know. It be nice to see her again.

BERTHA: (Giving JEREMY a biscuit.) Jeremy, today's the day for you to pull them sheets off the bed and set them outside your door. I'll set you out some clean ones.

BYNUM: Mr. Piney's boys done ruined your good time last night, Jeremy . . . what you planning for tonight?

JEREMY: They got me scared to go out, Mr. Bynum. They might grab me again.

BYNUM: You ought to take your guitar and go down to Seefus. Seefus got a gambling place down there on Wylie Avenue. You ought to take your guitar and go down there. They got a guitar contest down there.

JEREMY: I don't play no contest, Mr. Bynum. Had one of them white fellows cure me of that. I ain't been nowhere near a contest since.

BYNUM: White fellow beat you playing guitar?

JEREMY: Naw, he ain't beat me. I was sitting at home just fixing to sit down and eat when somebody come up to my house and got me. Told me there's a white fellow say he was gonna give a prize to the best guitar player he could find. I take up my guitar and go down there and somebody had gone up and got Bobo Smith and brought him down there. Him and another fellow called Hooter. Old Hooter couldn't play no guitar, he do more hollering than playing, but Bobo could go at it awhile.

This fellow standing there say he the one that was gonna give the prize and me and Bobo started playing for him. Bobo play something and then I'd try to play something better than what he played. Old Hooter, he just holler and bang at the guitar. Man was the worst guitar player I ever seen. So me and Bobo played and after a while I seen where he was getting the attention of this white fellow. He'd play something and while he was playing it he be slapping on the side of the guitar, and that made it sound like he was playing more than he was. So I started doing it too. White fellow ain't knew no difference. He ain't knew as much about guitar playing as Hooter did. After we play awhile, the white fellow called us to him and said he couldn't make up his mind, say all three of us was the best guitar player and we'd have to split the prize between us. Then he give us twenty-five cents. That's eight cents apiece and a penny on the side. That cured me of playing contest to this day.

BYNUM: Seefus ain't like that. Seefus give a whole dollar and a drink of whiskey.

JEREMY: What night they be down there?

BYNUM: Be down there every night. Music don't know no certain night.

BERTHA: You go down to Seefus with them people and you liable to end up in a raid and go to jail sure enough. I don't know why Bynum tell you that.

BYNUM: That's where the music at. That's where the people at. The people down there making music and enjoying themselves. Some things is worth taking the chance going to jail about.

BERTHA: Jeremy ain't got no business going down there.

JEREMY: They got some women down there, Mr. Bynum?

BYNUM: Oh, they got women down there, sure. They got women everywhere. Women be where the men is so they can find each other.

JEREMY: Some of them old gals come out there where we be putting in that road. Hanging around there trying to snatch somebody.

BYNUM: How come some of them ain't snatched hold of you?

JEREMY: I don't want them kind. Them desperate kind. Ain't nothing worse than a desperate woman. Tell them you gonna leave them and they get to crying and carrying on. That just make you want to get away quicker. They

get to cutting up your clothes and things trying to keep you staying. Desperate women ain't nothing but trouble for a man.

(SETH enters from the stairs.)

SETH: Something ain't setting right with that fellow.

BERTHA: What's wrong with him? What he say?

SETH: I take him up there and try to talk to him and he ain't for no talking. Say he been traveling . . . coming over from Ohio. Say he a deacon in the church. Say he looking for Martha Pentecost. Talking about that's his wife.

BERTHA: How you know it's the same Martha? Could be talking about anybody. Lots of people named Martha.

SETH: You see that little girl? I didn't hook it up till he said it, but that little girl look just like her. Ask Bynum.

(To BYNUM.) Bynum. Don't that little girl look just like Martha Pentecost?

BERTHA: I still say he could be talking about anybody.

SETH: The way he described her wasn't no doubt about who he was talking about. Described her right down to her toes.

BERTHA: What did you tell him?

SETH: I ain't told him nothing. The way that fellow look I wasn't gonna tell him nothing. I don't know what he looking for her for.

BERTHA: What else he have to say?

SETH: I told you he wasn't for no talking. I told him where the outhouse was and to keep that gal off the front porch and out of my garden. He asked if you'd mind setting a hot tub for the gal and that was about the gist of it.

BERTHA: Well, I wouldn't let it worry me if I was you. Come on get your sleep.

BYNUM: He says he looking for Martha and he a deacon in the church.

SETH: That's what he say. Do he look like a deacon to you?

BERTHA: He might be, you don't know. Bynum ain't got no special say on whether he a deacon or not.

SETH: Well, if he the deacon I'd sure like to see the preacher.

BERTHA: Come on get your sleep. Jeremy, don't forget to set them sheets outside the door like I told you.

(BERTHA exits into the bedroom.)

SETH: Something ain't setting right with that fellow, Bynum. He's one of them mean-looking niggers look like he done killed somebody gambling over a quarter.

BYNUM: He ain't no gambler. Gamblers wear nice shoes. This fellow got on clodhoppers. He been out there walking up and down them roads.

(ZONIA enters from the stairs and looks around.)

BYNUM: You looking for the back door, sugar? There it is. You can go out there and play. It's alright.

SETH: (Showing her the door.) You can go out there and play. Just don't get in my garden. And don't go messing around in my workshed.

(SETH exits into the bedroom. There is a knock on the door.)

JEREMY: Somebody at the door.

(JEREMY goes to answer the door. Enter MATTIE CAMPBELL. She is a young woman of twenty-six whose attractiveness is hidden under the weight and concerns of a dissatisfied life. She is a woman in an honest search for love and companionship. She has suffered many defeats in her search, and though not always uncompromising, still believes in the possibility of love.)

MATTIE: I'm looking for a man named Bynum. Lady told me to come back later.

JEREMY: Sure, he here. Mr. Bynum, somebody here to see you.

BYNUM: Come to see me, huh?

MATTIE: Are you the man they call Bynum? The man folks say can fix things?

BYNUM: Depend on what need fixing. I can't make no promises. But I got a powerful song in some matters.

MATTIE: Can you fix it so my man come back to me?

BYNUM: Come on in . . . have a sit down.

MATTIE: You got to help me. I don't know what else to do.

BYNUM: Depend on how all the circumstances of the thing come together. How all the pieces fit.

MATTIE: I done everything I knowed how to do. You got to make him come back to me.

BYNUM: It ain't nothing to make somebody come back. I can fix it so he can't stand to be away from you. I got my roots and powders, I can fix it so wherever he's at this thing will come up on him and he won't be able to sleep for seeing your face. Won't be able to eat for thinking of you.

MATTIE: That's what I want. Make him come back.

BYNUM: The roots is a powerful thing. I can fix it so one day he'll walk out his front door . . . won't be thinking of nothing. He won't know what it is. All he knows is that a powerful dissatisfaction done set in his bones and can't nothing he do make him feel satisfied. He'll set his foot down on the road and the wind in the trees be talking to him and everywhere he step on the road, that road'll give back your name and something will pull him right up to your doorstep. Now, I can do that. I can take my roots and fix that easy. But maybe he ain't supposed to come back. And if he ain't supposed to come back . . . then he'll be in your bed one morning and it'll come up on him that he's in the wrong place. That he's lost outside of time from his place that he's supposed to be in. Then both of you be lost and trapped outside of life and ain't no way for you to get back into it. 'Cause you lost from yourselves and where the places come together, where you're supposed to be alive, your heart kicking in your chest with a song worth singing.

MATTIE: Make him come back to me. Make his feet say my name on the road. I don't care what happens. Make him come back.

BYNUM: What's your man's name?

MATTIE: He go by Jack Carper. He was born in Alabama then he come to West Texas and find me and we come here. Been here three years before he left. Say I had a curse prayer on me and he started walking down the road and ain't never come back. Somebody told me, say you can fix things like that.

BYNUM: He just got up one day, set his feet on the road, and walked away?

MATTIE: You got to make him come back, mister.

BYNUM: Did he say goodbye?

MATTIE: Ain't said nothing. Just started walking. I could see where he disappeared. Didn't look back. Just keep walking. Can't you fix it so he come back? I ain't got no curse prayer on me. I know I ain't.

BYNUM: What made him say you had a curse prayer on you?

MATTIE: 'Cause the babies died. Me and Jack had two babies. Two little babies that ain't lived two months before they died. He say it's because somebody cursed me not to have babies.

BYNUM: He ain't bound to you if the babies died. Look like somebody trying to keep you from being bound up and he's gone on back to whoever it is 'cause he's already bound up to her. Ain't nothing to be done. Somebody else done got a powerful hand in it and ain't nothing to be done to break it. You got to let him go find where he's supposed to be in the world.

MATTIE: Jack done gone off and you telling me to forget about him. All my life I been looking for somebody to stop and stay with me. I done already got too many things to forget about. I take Jack Carper's hand and it feel so rough and strong. Seem like he's the strongest man in the world the way he hold me. Like he's bigger than the whole world and can't nothing bad get to me. Even when he act mean sometimes he still make everything seem okay with the world. Like there's part of it that belongs just to you. Now you telling me to forget about him?

BYNUM: Jack Carper gone off to where he belong. There's somebody searching for your doorstep right now. Ain't no need you fretting over Jack Carper. Right now he's a strong thought in your mind. But every time you catch yourself fretting over Jack Carper you push that thought away. You push it out your mind and that thought will get weaker and weaker till you wake up one morning and you won't even be able to call him up on your mind.

(BYNUM gives her a small cloth packet.)

Take this and sleep with it under your pillow and it'll bring good luck to you. Draw it to you like a magnet. It won't be long before you forget all about Jack Carper.

MATTIE: How much . . . do I owe you?

BYNUM: Whatever you got there . . . that'll be alright.

(MATTIE hands BYNUM two quarters. She crosses to the door.)

You sleep with that under your pillow and you'll be alright.

(MATTIE opens the door to exit and JEREMY crosses over to her. BYNUM overhears the first part of their conversation, then exits out the back.)

JEREMY: I overheard what you told Mr. Bynum. Had me an old gal did that to me. Woke up one morning and she was gone. Just took off to parts unknown. I woke up that morning and the only thing I could do was look around for my shoes. I woke up and got out of there. Found my shoes and took off. That's the only thing I could think of to do.

MATTIE: She ain't said nothing?

JEREMY: I just looked around for my shoes and got out of there.

MATTIE: Jack ain't said nothing either. He just walked off.

JEREMY: Some mens do that. Womens too. I ain't gone off looking for her. I just let her go. Figure she had a time to come to herself. Wasn't no use of me standing in the way. Where you from?

MATTIE: Texas. I was born in Georgia but I went to Texas with my mama. She dead now. Was picking peaches and fell dead away. I come up here with Jack Carper.

JEREMY: I'm from North Carolina. Down around Raleigh where they got all that tobacco. Been up here about two weeks. I likes it fine except I still got to find me a woman. You got a nice look to you. Look like you have mens standing in your door. Is you got mens standing in your door to get a look at you?

MATTIE: I ain't got nobody since Jack left.

JEREMY: A woman like you need a man. Maybe you let me be your man. I got a nice way with the women. That's what they tell me.

MATTIE: I don't know. Maybe Jack's coming back.

JEREMY: I'll be your man till he come. A woman can't be by her lonesome. Let me be your man till he come.

MATTIE: I just can't go through life piecing myself out to different mens. I need a man who wants to stay with me.

JEREMY: I can't say what's gonna happen. Maybe I'll be the man. I don't know. You wanna go along the road a little ways with me?

MATTIE: I don't know. Seem like life say it's gonna be one thing and end up being another. I'm tired of going from man to man.

JEREMY: Life is like you got to take a chance. Everybody got to take a chance. Can't nobody say what's gonna be. Come on . . . take a chance with me and see what the year bring. Maybe you let me come and see you. Where you staying?

MATTIE: I got me a room up on Bedford. Me and Jack had a room together.

JEREMY: What's the address? I'll come by and get you tonight and we can go down to Seefus. I'm going down there and play my guitar.

MATTIE: You play guitar?

JEREMY: I play guitar like I'm born to it.

MATTIE: I live at 1727 Bedford Avenue. I'm gonna find out if you can play guitar like you say.

JEREMY: I plays it sugar, and that ain't all I do. I got a ten-pound hammer and I knows how to drive it down. Good god . . . you ought to hear my hammer ring!

MATTIE: Go on with that kind of talk, now. If you gonna come by and get me I got to get home and straighten up for you.

JEREMY: I'll be by at eight o'clock. How's eight o'clock? I'm gonna make you forget all about Jack Carper.

MATTIE: Go on, now. I got to get home and fix up for you.

JEREMY: Eight o'clock, sugar.

(The lights go down in the parlor and come up on the yard outside. ZONIA is singing and playing a game.)

ZONIA:

I went downtown
To get my grip
I came back home
Just a pullin' the skiff

I went upstairs
To make my bed
I made a mistake
And I bumped my head
Just a pullin' the skiff

I went downstairs
To milk the cow
I made a mistake
And I milked the sow
Just a pullin' the skiff

Tomorrow, tomorrow
Tomorrow never comes
The marrow the marrow
The marrow in the bone.

(REUBEN enters.)

REUBEN: Hi.

ZONIA: Hi.

REUBEN: What's your name?

ZONIA: Zonia.

REUBEN: What kind of name is that?

ZONIA: It's what my daddy named me.

REUBEN: My name's Reuben. You staying in Mr. Seth's house?

ZONIA: Yeah.

REUBEN: That your daddy I seen you with this morning?

ZONIA: I don't know. Who you see me with?

REUBEN: I saw you with some man had on a great big old coat. And you was walking up to Mr. Seth's house. Had on a hat too.

ZONIA: Yeah, that's my daddy.

REUBEN: You like Mr. Seth?

ZONIA: I ain't see him much.

REUBEN: My grandpap say he a great big old windbag. How come you living in Mr. Seth's house? Don't you have no house?

ZONIA: We going to find my mother.

REUBEN: Where she at?

ZONIA: I don't know. We got to find her. We just go all over.

REUBEN: Why you got to find her? What happened to her?

ZONIA: She ran away.

REUBEN: Why she run away?

ZONIA: I don't know. My daddy say some man named Joe Turner did something bad to him once and that made her run away.

REUBEN: Maybe she coming back and you don't have to go looking for her.

ZONIA: We ain't there no more.

REUBEN: She could have come back when you wasn't there.

ZONIA: My daddy said she ran off and left us so we going looking for her.

REUBEN: What he gonna do when he find her?

ZONIA: He didn't say. He just say he got to find her.

REUBEN: Your daddy say how long you staying in Mr. Seth's house?

ZONIA: He don't say much. But we never stay too long nowhere. He say we got to keep moving till we find her.

REUBEN: Ain't no kids hardly live around here. I had me a friend but he died. He was the best friend I ever had. Me and Eugene used to keep secrets. I still got his pigeons. He told me to let them go when he died. He say, "Reuben, promise me when I die you'll let my pigeons go." But I keep them to remember him by. I ain't never gonna let them go. Even when I get to be grown up. I'm just always gonna have Eugene's pigeons.

(Pause.)

Mr. Bynum a conjure man. My grandpap scared of him. He don't like me to come over here too much. I'm scared of him too. My grandpap told me not to let him get close enough to where he can reach out his hand and touch me.

ZONIA: He don't seem scary to me.

REUBEN: He buys pigeons from me . . . and if you get up early in the morning you can see him out in the yard doing something with them pigeons. My grandpap say he kill them. I sold him one yesterday. I don't know what he do with it. I just hope he don't spook me up.

ZONIA: Why you sell him pigeons if he's gonna spook you up?

REUBEN: I just do like Eugene do. He used to sell Mr. Bynum pigeons. That's how he got to collecting them to sell to Mr. Bynum. Sometime he give me a nickel and sometime he give me a whole dime.

(LOOMIS enters from the house.)

LOOMIS: Zonia!

ZONIA: Sir?

LOOMIS: What you doing?

ZONIA: Nothing.

LOOMIS: You stay around this house, you hear? I don't want you wandering off nowhere.

ZONIA: I ain't wandering off nowhere.

LOOMIS: Miss Bertha set that hot tub and you getting a good scrubbing. Get scrubbed up good. You ain't been scrubbing.

ZONIA: I been scrubbing.

LOOMIS: Look at you. You growing too fast. Your bones getting bigger everyday. I don't want you getting grown on me. Don't you get grown on me too soon. We gonna find your mamma. She around here somewhere. I can smell her. You stay on around this house now. Don't you go nowhere.

ZONIA: Yes, sir.

(LOOMIS exits into the house.)

REUBEN: Wow, your daddy's scary!

ZONIA: He is not! I don't know what you talking about.

REUBEN: He got them mean-looking eyes!

ZONIA: My daddy ain't got no mean-looking eyes!

REUBEN: Aw, girl, I was just messing with you. You wanna go see Eugene's pigeons? Got a great big coop out the back of my house. Come on, I'll show you.

(REUBEN and ZONIA exit as the lights go down.)

Scene Two

It is Saturday morning, one week later. The lights come up on the kitchen. BERTHA is at the stove preparing breakfast while SETH sits at the table.

SETH: Something ain't right about that fellow. I been watching him all week. Something ain't right, I'm telling you.

BERTHA: Seth Holly, why don't you hush up about that man this morning?

SETH: I don't like the way he stare at everybody. Don't look at you natural like. He just be staring at you. Like he trying to figure out something about you. Did you see him when he come back in here?

BERTHA: That man ain't thinking about you.

SETH: He don't work nowhere. Just go out and come back. Go out and come back.

BERTHA: As long as you get your boarding money it ain't your cause about what he do. He don't bother nobody.

SETH: Just go out and come back. Going around asking everybody about Martha. Like Henry Allen seen him down at the church last night.

BERTHA: The man's allowed to go to church if he want. He say he a deacon. Ain't nothing wrong about him going to church.

SETH: I ain't talking about him going to church. I'm talking about him hanging around outside the church.

BERTHA: Henry Allen say that?

SETH: Say he be standing around outside the church. Like he be watching it.

BERTHA: What on earth he wanna be watching the church for, I wonder?

SETH: That's what I'm trying to figure out. Looks like he fixing to rob it.

BERTHA: Seth, now do he look like the kind that would rob the church?

SETH: I ain't saying that. I ain't saying how he look. It's how he do. Anybody liable to do anything as far as I'm concerned. I ain't never thought about how no church robbers look . . . but now that you mention it, I don't see where they look no different than how he look.

BERTHA: Herald Loomis ain't the kind of man who would rob no church.

SETH: I ain't even so sure that's his name.

BERTHA: Why the man got to lie about his name?

SETH: Anybody can tell anybody anything about what their name is. That's what you call him . . . Herald Loomis. His name is liable to be anything.

BERTHA: Well, until he tell me different that's what I'm gonna call him. You just getting yourself all worked up about the man for nothing.

SETH: Talking about Loomis: Martha's name wasn't no Loomis nothing. Martha's name is Pentecost.

BERTHA: How you so sure that's her right name? Maybe she changed it.

SETH: Martha's a good Christian woman. This fellow here look like he owe the devil a day's work and he's trying to figure out how he gonna pay him. Martha ain't had a speck of distrust about her the whole time she was living here. They moved the church out there to Rankin and I was sorry to see her go.

BERTHA: That's why he be hanging around the church. He looking for her.

SETH: If he looking for her, why don't he go inside and ask? What he doing hanging around outside the church acting sneaky like?

(BYNUM enters from the yard.)

BYNUM: Morning, Seth. Morning, Sister Bertha.

(BYNUM continues through the kitchen and exits up the stairs.)

BERTHA: That's who you should be asking the questions. He been out there in that yard all morning. He was out there before the sun come up. He didn't even come in for breakfast. I don't know what he's doing. He had three of them pigeons line up out there. He dance around till he get tired. He sit down awhile then get up and dance some more. He come through here a little while ago looking like he was mad at the world.

SETH: I don't pay Bynum no mind. He don't spook me up with all that stuff.

BERTHA: That's how Martha come to be living here. She come to see Bynum. She come to see him when she first left from down South.

SETH: Martha was living here before Bynum. She ain't come on here when she first left from down there. She come on here after she went back to get her little girl. That's when she come on here.

BERTHA: Well, where was Bynum? He was here when she came.

SETH: Bynum ain't come till after her. That boy Hiram was staying up there in Bynum's room.

BERTHA: Well, how long Bynum been here?

SETH: Bynum ain't been here no longer than three years. That's what I'm trying to tell you. Martha was staying up there and sewing and cleaning for Doc Goldblum when Bynum came. This the longest he ever been in one place.

BERTHA: How you know how long the man been in one place?

SETH: I know Bynum. Bynum ain't no mystery to me. I done seen a hundred niggers like him. He's one of them fellows never could stay in one place. He was wandering all around the country till he got old and settled here. The only thing different about Bynum is he bring all this heebie-jeebie stuff with him.

BERTHA: I still say he was staying here when she came. That's why she came . . . to see him.

SETH: You can say what you want. I know the fact of it. She come on here four years ago all heartbroken 'cause she couldn't find her little girl. And Bynum wasn't nowhere around. She got mixed up in that old heebie-jeebie nonsense with him after he came.

BERTHA: Well, if she came on before Bynum I don't know where she stayed. 'Cause she stayed up there in Hiram's room. Hiram couldn't get along with Bynum and left out of here owing you two dollars. Now, I know you ain't forgot about that!

SETH: Sure did! You know Hiram ain't paid me that two dollars yet. So that's why he be ducking and hiding when he see me down on Logan Street. You right. Martha did come on after Bynum. I forgot that's why Hiram left.

BERTHA: Him and Bynum never could see eye to eye. They always rubbed each other the wrong way. Hiram got to thinking that Bynum was trying to put a fix on him and he moved out. Martha came to see Bynum and ended up taking Hiram's room. Now, I know what I'm talking about. She stayed on here three years till they moved the church.

SETH: She out there in Rankin now. I know where she at. I know where they moved the church to. She right out there in Rankin in that place used to be a shoe store. Used to be Wolf's shoe store. They moved to a bigger place and they put that church in there. I know where she at. I know just where she at.

BERTHA: Why don't you tell the man? You see he looking for her.

SETH: I ain't gonna tell that man where that woman is! What I wanna do that for? I don't know nothing about that man. I don't know why he looking for her. He might wanna do her a harm. I ain't gonna carry that on my hands. He looking for her, he gonna have to find her for himself. I ain't gonna help him. Now, if he had come and presented himself as a gentleman—the way Martha Pentecost's husband would have done—then I would have told him. But I ain't gonna tell this old wild-eyed mean-looking nigger nothing!

BERTHA: Well, why don't you get a ride with Selig and go up there and tell her where he is? See if she wanna see him. If that's her little girl . . . you say Martha was looking for her.

SETH: You know me, Bertha. I don't get mixed up in nobody's business.

(BYNUM enters from the stairs.)

BYNUM: Morning, Seth. Morning, Bertha. Can I still get some breakfast? Mr. Loomis been down here this morning?

SETH: He done gone out and come back. He up there now. Left out of here early this morning wearing that coat. Hot as it is, the man wanna walk around wearing a big old heavy coat. He come back in here paid me for another week, sat down there waiting on Selig. Got tired of waiting and went on back upstairs.

BYNUM: Where's the little girl?

SETH: She out there in the front. Had to chase her and that Reuben off the front porch. She out there somewhere.

BYNUM: Look like if Martha was around here he would have found her by now. My guess is she ain't in the city.

SETH: She ain't! I know where she at. I know just where she at. But I ain't gonna tell him. Not the way he look.

BERTHA: Here go your coffee, Bynum.

BYNUM: He says he gonna get Selig to find her for him.

SETH: Selig can't find her. He talk all that . . . but unless he get lucky and knock on her door he can't find her. That's the only way he find anybody. He got to get lucky. But I know just where she at.

BERTHA: Here go some biscuits, Bynum.

BYNUM: What else you got over there, Sister Bertha? You got some grits and gravy over there? I could go for some of that this morning.

BERTHA: (Sets a bowl on the table.) Seth, come on and help me turn this mattress over. Come on.

SETH: Something ain't right with that fellow, Bynum. I don't like the way he stare at everybody.

BYNUM: Mr. Loomis alright, Seth. He just a man got something on his mind. He just got a straightforward mind, that's all.

SETH: What's that fellow that they had around here? Moses, that's Moses Houser. Man went crazy and jumped off the Brady Street Bridge. I told you when I seen him something wasn't right about him. And I'm telling you about this fellow now.

(There is a knock on the door. SETH goes to answer it. Enter RUTHERFORD SELIG.)

Ho! Come on in, Selig.

BYNUM: If it ain't the People finder himself.

SELIG: Bynum, before you start . . . I ain't seen no shiny man now.

BYNUM: Who said anything about that? I ain't said nothing about that. I just called you a first-class People finder.

SELIG: How many dustpans you get out of that sheet metal, Seth?

SETH: You walked by them on your way in. They sitting out there on the porch. Got twenty-eight. Got four out of each sheet and made Bertha a coffeepot out the other one. They a little small but they got nice handles.

SELIG: That was twenty cents apiece, right? That's what we agreed on.

SETH: That's five dollars and sixty cents. Twenty on top of twenty-eight. How many sheets you bring me?

SELIG: I got eight out there. That's a dollar twenty makes me owe you . . .

SETH: Four dollars and forty cents.

SELIG: (Paying him.) Go on and make me some dustpans. I can use all you can make.

(LOOMIS enters from the stairs.)

LOOMIS: I been watching for you. He say you find people.

BYNUM: Mr. Loomis here wants you to find his wife.

LOOMIS: He say you find people. find her for me.

SELIG: Well, let see here . . . find somebody, is it?

(SELIG rummages through his pockets. He has several notebooks and he is searching for the right one.)

Alright now . . . what's the name?

LOOMIS: Martha Loomis. She my wife. Got married legal with the paper and all.

SELIG: (Writing.) Martha . . . Loomis. How tall is she?

LOOMIS: She five feet from the ground.

SELIG: Five feet . . . tall. Young or old?

LOOMIS: She a young woman. Got long pretty hair.

SELIG: Young . . . long . . . pretty . . . hair. Where did you last see her?

LOOMIS: Tennessee. Nearby Memphis.

SELIG: When was that?

LOOMIS: Nineteen hundred and one.

SELIG: Nineteen . . . hundred and one. I'll tell you, mister . . . you better off without them. Now you take me . . . old Rutherford Selig could tell you a thing or two about these women. I ain't met one yet I could understand. Now, you take Sally out there. That's all a man needs is a good horse. I say giddup and she go. Say whoa and she stop. I feed her some oats and she carry me wherever I want to go. Ain't a speck of trouble out of her since I had her. Now, I been married. A long time ago down in Kentucky. I got up one morning and I saw this look on my wife's face. Like way down deep inside her she was wishing I was dead. I walked around that morning and every time I looked at her she had that look on her face. It seem like she knew I could see it on her. Every time I looked at her I got smaller and smaller. Well, I wasn't gonna stay around there and just shrink away. I walked out on the porch and closed the door behind me. When I closed the door she locked it. I went out and bought me a horse. And I ain't been without one since! Martha Loomis, huh? Well, now I'll do the best I can do. That's one dollar.

LOOMIS: (Holding out dollar suspiciously.) How you find her?

SELIG: Well now, it ain't no easy job like you think. You can't just go out there and find them like that. There's a lot of little tricks to it. It's not an easy job keeping up with you Nigras the way you move about so. Now you take this woman you looking for . . . this Martha Loomis. She could be anywhere. Time I find her, if you don't keep your eye on her, she'll be gone off someplace else. You'll be thinking she over here and she'll be over there. But like I say there's a lot of little tricks to it.

LOOMIS: You say you find her.

SELIG: I can't promise anything but we been finders in my family for a long time. Bringers and finders. My great-granddaddy used to bring Nigras across the ocean on ships. That's wasn't no easy job either. Sometimes the winds would blow so hard you'd think the hand of God was set against the sails. But it set him well in pay and he settled in this new land and found him a wife of good Christian charity with a mind for kids and the like and well . . . here I am, Rutherford Selig. You're in good hands, mister. Me and my daddy have found plenty Nigras. My daddy, rest his soul, used to find runaway slaves for the plantation bosses. He was the best there was at it. Jonas B. Selig. Had him a reputation stretched clean across the country. After Abraham Lincoln give you all Nigras your freedom papers and with you all looking all over for each other . . . we started finding Nigras for Nigras. Of course, it don't pay as much. But the People finding business ain't so bad.

Loomis: (Hands him the dollar.) Find her. Martha Loomis. Find her for me.

Selig: Like I say, I can't promise you anything. I'm going back upriver, and if she's around in them parts I'll find her for you. But I can't promise you anything.

Loomis: When you coming back?

Selig: I'll be back on Saturday. I come and see Seth to pick up my order on Saturday.

Bynum: You going upriver, huh? You going up around my way. I used to go all up through there. Blawknox . . . Clairton. Used to go up to Rankin and take that first righthand road. I wore many a pair of shoes out walking around that way. You'd have thought I was a missionary spreading the gospel the way I wandered all around them parts.

Selig: Okay, Bynum. See you on Saturday.

Seth: Here, let me walk out with you. Help you with them dustpans.

(SETH and SELIG exit out the back. BERTHA enters from the stairs carrying a bundle of sheets.)

Bynum: Herald Loomis got the People finder looking for Martha.

Bertha: You can call him a People finder if you want to. I know Rutherford Selig carries people away too. He done carried a whole bunch of them away from here. Folks plan on leaving plan by Selig's timing. They wait till he get ready to go, then they hitch a ride on his wagon. Then he charge folks a dollar to tell them where he took them. Now, that's the truth of Rutherford Selig. This old People finding business is for the birds. He ain't never found nobody he ain't took away. Herald Loomis, you just wasted your dollar.

(BERTHA exits into the bedroom.)

Loomis: He say he find her. He say he find her by Saturday. -I'm gonna wait till Saturday.

(The lights fade to black.)

Scene Three

It is Sunday morning, the next day. The lights come up on the kitchen. SETH sits talking to BYNUM. The breakfast dishes have been cleared away.

Seth: They can't see that. Neither one of them can see that. Now, how much sense it take to see that? All you got to do is be able to count. One man making ten pots is five men making fifty pots. But they can't see that. Asked where I'm gonna get my five men. Hell, I can teach anybody how to make a pot. I can teach you. I can take you out there and get you started right now. Inside of two weeks you'd know how to make a pot. All you got to do is want to do it. I can get five men. I ain't worried about getting no five men.

Bertha: (Calls from the bedroom.) Seth. Come on and get ready now. Reverend Gates ain't gonna be holding up his sermon 'cause you sitting out there talking.

Seth: Now, you take the boy, Jeremy. What he gonna do after he put in that road? He can't do nothing but go put in another one somewhere. Now, if he let me show him how to make some pots and pans . . . then he'd have something can't nobody take away from him. After a while he could get his own tools and go off somewhere and make his own pots and pans. find him somebody to sell them to.

BYNUM: Then what happened, Herald Loomis?

LOOMIS: They ain't moved or nothing. They just laying there.

BYNUM: You just laying there. What you waiting on, Herald Loomis?

LOOMIS: I'm laying there . . . waiting.

BYNUM: What you waiting on, Herald Loomis?

LOOMIS: I'm waiting on the breath to get into my body.

BYNUM: The breath coming into you, Herald Loomis. What you gonna do now?

LOOMIS: The wind's blowing the breath into my body. I can feel it. I'm starting to breathe again.

BYNUM: What you gonna do, Herald Loomis?

LOOMIS: I'm gonna stand up. I got to stand up. I can't lay here no more. All the breath coming into my body and I got to stand up.

BYNUM: Everybody's standing up at the same time.

LOOMIS: The ground's starting to shake. There's a great shaking. The world's busting half in two. The sky's splitting open. I got to stand up.

(LOOMIS attempts to stand up.)

My legs . . . my legs won't stand up!

BYNUM: Everybody's standing and walking toward the road. What you gonna do, Herald Loomis?

LOOMIS: My legs won't stand up.

BYNUM: They shaking hands and saying goodbye to each other and walking every which-away down the road.

LOOMIS: I got to stand up!

BYNUM: They walking around here now. Mens. Just like you and me. Come right up out the water.

LOOMIS: Got to stand up.

BYNUM: They walking, Herald Loomis. They walking around here now.

LOOMIS: I got to stand up. Get up on the road.

BYNUM: Come on, Herald Loomis.

(LOOMIS tries to stand up.)

LOOMIS: My legs won't stand up! My legs won't stand up!

(LOOMIS collapses on the floor as the lights go down to black.)

ACT TWO

Scene One

The lights come up on the kitchen. BERTHA busies herself with breakfast preparations. SETH sits at the table.

SETH: I don't care what his problem is! He's leaving here!

BERTHA: You can't put the man out and he got that little girl. Where they gonna go then?

SETH: I don't care where he go. Let him go back where he was before he come here. I ain't asked him to come here. I knew when I first looked at him something wasn't right with him. Dragging that little girl around with him. Looking like he be sleeping in the woods somewhere. I knew all along he wasn't right.

BERTHA: A fellow get a little drunk he's liable to say or do anything. He ain't done no big harm.

SETH: I just don't have all that carrying on in my house. When he come down here I'm gonna tell him. He got to leave here. My daddy wouldn't stand for it and I ain't gonna stand for it either.

BERTHA: Well, if you put him out you have to put Bynum out too. Bynum right there with him.

SETH: If it wasn't for Bynum ain't no telling what would have happened. Bynum talked to that fellow just as nice and calmed him down. If he wasn't here ain't no telling what would have happened. Bynum ain't done nothing but talk to him and kept him calm. Man acting all crazy with that foolishness. Naw, he's leaving here.

BERTHA: What you gonna tell him? How you gonna tell him to leave?

SETH: I'm gonna tell him straight out. Keep it nice and simple. Mister, you got to leave here!

(MOLLY enters from the stairs.)

MOLLY: Morning.

BERTHA: Did you sleep alright in that bed?

MOLLY: Tired as I was I could have slept anywhere. It's a real nice room, though. This is a nice place.

SETH: I'm sorry you had to put up with all that carrying on last night.

MOLLY: It don't bother me none. I done seen that kind of stuff before.

SETH: You won't have to see it around here no more.

(BYNUM is heard singing offstage.)

I don't put up with all that stuff. When that fellow come down here I'm gonna tell him.

BYNUM: (singing)

Soon my work will all be done
Soon my work will all be done
Soon my work will all be done
I'm going to see the king.

BYNUM: (Enters.) Morning, Seth. Morning, Sister Bertha. I see we got Molly Cunningham down here at breakfast.

SETH: Bynum, I wanna thank you for talking to that fellow last night and calming him down. If you hadn't been here ain't no telling what might have happened.

BYNUM: Mr. Loomis alright, Seth. He just got a little excited.

SETH: Well, he can get excited somewhere else 'cause he leaving here.

(MATTIE enters from the stairs.)

BYNUM: Well, there's Mattie Campbell.

MATTIE: Good morning.

BERTHA: Sit on down there, Mattie. I got some biscuits be ready in a minute. The coffee's hot.

MATTIE: Jeremy gone already?

BYNUM: Yeah, he leave out of here early. He got to be there when the sun come up. Most working men got to be there when the sun come up. Everybody but Seth. Seth work at

night. Mr. Olowski so busy in his shop he got fellows working at night.

(LOOMIS enters from the stairs.)

SETH: Mr. Loomis, now . . . I don't want no trouble. I keeps me a respectable house here. I don't have no carrying on like what went on last night. This has been a respectable house for a long time. I'm gonna have to ask you to leave.

LOOMIS: You got my two dollars. That two dollars say we stay till Saturday.

(LOOMIS and SETH glare at each other.)

SETH: Alright. Fair enough. You stay till Saturday. But come Saturday you got to leave here.

LOOMIS: (Continues to glare at SETH. He goes to the door and calls.) Zonia. You stay around this house, you hear? Don't you go anywhere.

(LOOMIS exits out the front door.)

SETH: I knew it when I first seen him. I knew something wasn't right with him.

BERTHA: Seth, leave the people alone to eat their breakfast. They don't want to hear that. Go on out there and make some pots and pans. That's the only time you satisfied is when you out there. Go on out there and make some pots and pans and leave them people alone.

SETH: I ain't bothering anybody. I'm just stating the facts. I told you, Bynum.

(BERTHA shoos SETH out the back door and exits into the bedroom.)

MOLLY: (To BYNUM.) You one of them voodoo people?

BYNUM: I got a power to bind folks if that what you talking about.

MOLLY: I thought so. The way you talked to that man when he started all that spooky stuff. What you say you had the power to do to people? You ain't the cause of him acting like that, is you?

BYNUM: I binds them together. Sometimes I help them find each other.

MOLLY: How do you do that?

BYNUM: With a song. My daddy taught me how to do it.

MOLLY: That's what they say. Most folks be what they daddy is. I wouldn't want to be like my daddy. Nothing ever set right with him. He tried to make the world over. Carry it around with him everywhere he go. I don't want to be like that. I just take life as it come. I don't be trying to make it over.

(Pause.)

Your daddy used to do that too, huh? Make people stay together?

BYNUM: My daddy used to heal people. He had the Healing Song. I got the Binding Song.

MOLLY: My mama used to believe in all that stuff. If she got sick she would have gone and saw your daddy. As long as he didn't make her drink nothing. She wouldn't drink nothing nobody give her. She was always afraid somebody was gonna poison her. How your daddy heal people?

BYNUM: With a song. He healed people by singing over them. I seen him do it. He sung over this little white girl when she was sick. They made a big to-do about it. They carried the girl's bed out in the yard and had all her kinfolk standing around. The little girl laying up there in the bed. Doctors standing around can't do nothing to help her. And they had my daddy come up and sing his song. It didn't sound no different than any other song. It was just somebody singing. But the song was its own thing and it come out and took upon this little girl with its power and it healed her.

MOLLY: That's sure something else. I don't understand that kind of thing. I guess if the doctor couldn't make me well I'd try it. But otherwise I don't wanna be bothered with that kind of thing. It's too spooky.

BYNUM: Well, let me get on out here and get to work.

(BYNUM gets up and heads out the back door.)

MOLLY: I ain't meant to offend you or nothing. What's your name . . . Bynum? I ain't meant to say nothing to make you feel bad now.

(BYNUM exits out the back door.)

(To MATTIE.) I hope he don't feel bad. He's a nice man. I don't wanna hurt nobody's feelings or nothing.

MATTIE: I got to go on up to Doc Goldblum's and finish his ironing.

MOLLY: Now, that's something I don't ever wanna do. Iron no clothes. Especially somebody else's. That's what I believe killed my mama. Always ironing and working, doing somebody's else's work. Not Molly Cunningham.

MATTIE: It's the only job I got. I got to make it someway to fend for myself.

MOLLY: I thought Jeremy was your man. Ain't he working?

MATTIE: We just be keeping company till maybe Jack come back.

MOLLY: I don't trust none of these men. Jack or nobody else. These men liable to do anything. They wait just until they get one woman tied and locked up with them . . . then they look around to see if they can get another one. Molly don't pay them no mind. One's just as good as the other if you ask me. I ain't never met one that meant nobody no good. You got any babies?

MATTIE: I had two for my man, Jack Carper. But they both died.

MOLLY: That be the best. These men make all these babies, then run off and leave you to take care of them. Talking about they wanna see what's on the other side of the hill. I make sure I don't get no babies. My mama taught me how to do that.

MATTIE: Don't make me no mind. That be nice to be a mother.

MOLLY: Yeah? Well, you go on, then. Molly Cunningham ain't gonna be tied down with no babies. Had me a man one time who I thought had some love in him. Come home one day and he was packing his trunk. Told me the time come when even the best of friends must part. Say he was gonna send me a Special Delivery some old day. I watched him out the window when he carried that trunk out and down to the train station. Said if he was gonna send me a Special Delivery I wasn't gonna be there to get it. I done found out the harder you try to hold onto them, the easier it is for some gal to pull them away. Molly done learned that. That's why I don't trust nobody but the good Lord above, and I don't love nobody but my mama.

MATTIE: I got to get on. Doc Goldblum gonna be waiting.

(MATTIE exits out the front door. SETH enters from his workshop with his apron, gloves, goggles, etc. He carries a bucket and crosses to the sink for water.)

SETH: Everybody gone but you, huh?

MOLLY: That little shack out there by the outhouse . . . that's where you make them pots and pans and stuff?

SETH: Yeah, that's my workshed. I go out there . . . take these hands and make something out of nothing. Take that metal and bend and twist it whatever way I want. My daddy taught me that. He used to make pots and pans. That's how I learned it.

MOLLY: I never knew nobody made no pots and pans. My uncle used to shoe horses.

(JEREMY enters at the front door.)

SETH: I thought you was working? Ain't you working today?

JEREMY: Naw, they fired me. White fellow come by told me to give him fifty cents if I wanted to keep working. Going around to all the colored making them give him fifty cents to keep hold to their jobs. Them other fellows, they was giving it to him. I kept hold to mine and they fired me.

SETH: Boy, what kind of sense that make? What kind of sense it make to get fired from a job where you making eight dollars a week and all it cost you is fifty cents. That's seven dollars and fifty cents profit! This way you ain't got nothing.

JEREMY: It didn't make no sense to me. I don't make but eight dollars. Why I got to give him fifty cents of it? He go around to all the colored and he got ten dollars extra. That's more than I make for a whole week.

SETH: I see you gonna learn the hard way. You just looking at the facts of it. See, right now, without the job, you ain't got nothing. What you gonna do when you can't keep a roof over your head? Right now, come Saturday, unless you come up with another two dollars, you gonna be out there in the streets. Down up under one of them bridges trying to put some food in your belly and wishing you had given that fellow that fifty cents.

JEREMY: Don't make me no difference. There's a big road out there. I can get my guitar and always find me another place to stay. I ain't planning on staying in one place for too long noway.

SETH: We gonna see if you feel like that come Saturday!

(SETH exits out the back. JEREMY sees MOLLY.)

JEREMY: Molly Cunningham. How you doing today, sugar?

MOLLY: You can go on back down there tomorrow and go back to work if you want. They won't even know who you is. Won't even know it's you. I had me a fellow did that one time. They just went ahead and signed him up like they never seen him before.

JEREMY: I'm tired of working anyway. I'm glad they fired me. You sure look pretty today.

MOLLY: Don't come telling me all that pretty stuff. Beauty wanna come in and sit down at your table asking to be fed. I ain't hardly got enough for me.

JEREMY: You know you pretty. Ain't no sense in you saying nothing about that. Why don't you come on and go away with me?

MOLLY: You tied up with that Mattie Campbell. Now you talking about running away with me.

JEREMY: I was just keeping her company 'cause she lonely. You ain't the lonely kind. You the kind that know what she want and how to get it. I need a woman like you to travel around with. Don't you wanna travel around and look at some places with Jeremy? With a woman like you beside him, a man can make it nice in the world.

MOLLY: Molly can make it nice by herself too. Molly don't need nobody leave her cold in hand. The world rough enough as it is.

JEREMY: We can make it better together. I got my guitar and I can play. Won me another dollar last night playing guitar. We can go around and I can play at the dances and we can just enjoy life. You can make it by yourself alright, I agrees with that. A woman like you can make it anywhere she go. But you can make it better if you got a man to protect you.

MOLLY: What places you wanna go around and look at?

JEREMY: All of them! I don't want to miss nothing. I wanna go everywhere and do everything there is to be got out of life. With a woman like you it's like having water and berries. A man got everything he need.

MOLLY: You got to be doing more than playing that guitar. A dollar a day ain't hardly what Molly got in mind.

JEREMY: I gambles real good. I got a hand for it.

MOLLY: Molly don't work. And Molly ain't up for sale.

JEREMY: Sure, baby. You ain't got to work with Jeremy.

MOLLY: There's one more thing.

JEREMY: What's that, sugar?

MOLLY: Molly ain't going South.

(The lights go down on the scene.)

Scene Two

The lights come up on the parlor. SETH and BYNUM sit playing a game of dominoes. BYNUM sings to himself.

BYNUM: (Singing.)

> *They tell me Joe Turner's come and gone*
> *Ohhh Lordy*
> *They tell me Joe Turner's come and gone*
> *Ohhh Lordy*
> *Got my man and gone*
>
> *Come with forty links of chain*
> *Ohhh Lordy*
> *Come with forty links of chain*
> *Ohhh Lordy*
> *Got my man and gone*

SETH: Come on and play if you gonna play.

BYNUM: I'm gonna play. Soon as I figure out what to do.

SETH: You can't figure out if you wanna play or you wanna sing.

BYNUM: Well sir, I'm gonna do a little bit of both.

(Playing.)

> There. What you gonna do now?

(Singing.)

> *They tell me Joe Turner's come and gone*
> *Ohhh Lordy*
> *They tell me Joe Turner's come and gone*
> *Ohhh Lordy*

SETH: Why don't you hush up that noise.

BYNUM: That's a song the women sing down around Memphis. The women down there made up that song. I picked it up down there about fifteen years ago.

(LOOMIS enters from the front door.)

BYNUM: Evening, Mr. Loomis.

SETH: Today's Monday, Mr. Loomis. Come Saturday your time is up. We done ate already. My wife roasted up some yams. She got your plate sitting in there on the table.

(To BYNUM.) Whose play is it?

BYNUM: Ain't you keeping up with the game? I thought you was a domino player. I just played so it got to be your turn.

(LOOMIS goes into the kitchen, where a plate of yams is covered and set on the table. He sits down and begins to eat with his hands.)

SETH: (Plays.) Twenty! Give me twenty! You didn't know I had that ace five. You was trying to play around that. You didn't know I had that lying there for you.

BYNUM: You ain't done nothing. I let you have that to get mine.

SETH: Come on and play. You ain't doing nothing but talking. I got a hundred and forty points to your eighty. You ain't doing nothing but talking. Come on and play.

BYNUM: (Singing.)

They tell me Joe Turner's come and gone
Ohhh Lordy
They tell me Joe Turner's come and gone
Ohhh Lordy
Got my man and gone
He come with forty links of chain
Ohhh Lordy

LOOMIS: Why you singing that song? Why you singing about Joe Turner?

BYNUM: I'm just singing to entertain myself.

SETH: You trying to distract me. That's what you trying to do.

BYNUM: (Singing.)

Come with forty links of chain
Ohhh Lordy
Come with forty links of chain
Ohhh Lordy

LOOMIS: I don't like you singing that song, mister!

SETH: Now, I ain't gonna have no more disturbance around here, Herald Loomis. You start any more disturbance and you leavin' here, Saturday or no Saturday.

BYNUM: The man ain't causing no disturbance, Seth. He just say he don't like the song.

SETH: Well, we all friendly folk. All neighborly like. Don't have no squabbling around here. Don't have no disturbance. You gonna have to take that someplace else.

BYNUM: He just say he don't like the song. I done sung a whole lot of songs people don't like. I respect everybody. He here in the house too. If he don't like the song, I'll sing something

else. I know lots of songs. You got "I Belong to the Band," "Don't You Leave Me Here." You got "Praying on the Old Campground," "Keep your Lamp Trimmed and Burning" . . . I know lots of songs.

(Sings.)

Boys, I'll be so glad when payday come
Captain, Captain, when payday comes
Gonna catch that Illinois Central
Going to Kankakee

SETH: Why don't you hush up that hollering and come on and play dominoes.

BYNUM: You ever been to Johnstown, Herald Loomis? You look like a fellow I seen around there.

LOOMIS: I don't know no place with that name.

BYNUM: That's around where I seen my shiny man. See, you looking for this woman. I'm looking for a shiny man. Seem like everybody looking for something.

SETH: I'm looking for you to come and play these dominoes. That's what I'm looking for.

BYNUM: You a farming man, Herald Loomis? You look like you done some farming.

LOOMIS: Same as everybody. I done farmed some, yeah.

BYNUM: I used to work at farming . . . picking cotton. I reckon everybody done picked some cotton.

SETH: I ain't! I ain't never picked no cotton. I was born up here in the North. My daddy was a freedman. I ain't never even seen no cotton!

BYNUM: Mr. Loomis done picked some cotton. Ain't you, Herald Loomis? You done picked a bunch of cotton.

LOOMIS: How you know so much about me? How you know what I done? How much cotton I picked?

BYNUM: I can tell from looking at you. My daddy taught me how to do that. Say when you look at a fellow, if you taught yourself to look for it, you can see his song written on him. Tell you what kind of man he is in the world. Now, I can look at you, Mr. Loomis, and see you a man who done forgot his song. Forgot how to sing it. A fellow forget that and he forget who he is. Forget how he's supposed to mark down life. Now, I used to travel all up and down this road and that . . . looking here and there. Searching. Just like you, Mr. Loomis. I didn't know what I was searching for. The only thing I knew was something was keeping me dissatisfied. Something wasn't making my heart smooth and easy. Then one day my daddy gave me a song. That song had a weight to it that was hard to handle. That song was hard to carry. I fought against it. Didn't want to accept that song. I tried to find my daddy to give him back the song. But I found out it wasn't his song. It was my song. It had come from way deep inside me. I looked long back in memory and gathered up pieces and snatches of things to make that song. I was making it up out of myself. And that song helped me on the road. Made it smooth to where my footsteps didn't bite back at me. All the time that song getting bigger and bigger. That song growing with each step of the road. It got so I used all of myself up in the making of that song. Then I was the song in search of itself. That song rattling in my throat and I'm looking for it. See, Mr. Loomis, when a man forgets his song he goes off in search of it . . . till he find out he's got it with him all the time. That's why I can tell you one of Joe Turner's niggers. 'Cause you forgot how to sing your song.

LOOMIS: You lie! How you see that? I got a mark on me? Joe Turner done marked me to where you can see it? You telling me I'm a marked man. What kind of mark you got on you?

(BYNUM begins singing.)

BYNUM:

> They tell me Joe Turner's come and gone
> Ohhh Lordy
> They tell me Joe Turner's come and gone
> Ohhh Lordy
> Got my man and gone

LOOMIS: Had a whole mess of men he catched. Just go out hunting regular like you go out hunting possum. He catch you and go home to his wife and family. Ain't thought about you going home to yours. Joe Turner catched me when my little girl was just born. Wasn't nothing but a little baby sucking on her mama's titty when he catched me. Joe Turner catched me in nineteen hundred and one. Kept me seven years until nineteen hundred and eight. Kept everybody seven years. He'd go out hunting and bring back forty men at a time. And keep them seven years.

I was walking down this road in this little town outside of Memphis. Come up on these fellows gambling. I was a deacon in the Abundant Life Church. I stopped to preach to these fellows to see if maybe I could turn some of them from their sinning when Joe Turner, brother of the Governor of the great sovereign state of Tennessee, swooped down on us and grabbed everybody there. Kept us all seven years.

My wife Martha gone from me after Joe Turner catched me. Got out from under Joe Turner on his birthday. Me and forty other men put in our seven years and he let us go on his birthday. I made it back to Henry Thompson's place where me and Martha was sharecropping and Martha's gone. She taken my little girl and left her with her mama and took off North. We been looking for her ever since. That's been going on four years now we been looking. That's the only thing I know to do. I just wanna see her face so I can get me a starting place in the world. The world got to start somewhere. That's what I been looking for. I been wandering a long time in somebody else's world. When I find my wife that be the making of my own.

BYNUM: Joe Turner tell why he caught you? You ever asked him that?

LOOMIS: I ain't never seen Joe Turner. Seen him to where I could touch him. I asked one of them fellows one time why he catch niggers. Asked him what I got he want? Why don't he keep on to himself? Why he got to catch me going down the road by my lonesome? He told me I was worthless. Worthless is something you throw away. Something you don't bother with. I ain't seen him throw me away. Wouldn't even let me stay away when I was by my lonesome. I ain't tried to catch him when he going down the road. So I must got something he want. What I got?

SETH: He just want you to do his work for him. That's all.

LOOMIS: I can look at him and see where he big and strong enough to do his own work. So it can't be that. He must want something he ain't got.

BYNUM: That ain't hard to figure out. What he wanted was your song. He wanted to have that song to be his. He thought by catching you he could learn that song. Every nigger he catch he's looking for the one he can learn that song from. Now he's got you bound up to where you can't sing your own song. Couldn't sing it them seven years 'cause you was afraid he would snatch it from under you. But you still got it. You just forgot how to sing it.

LOOMIS: (To BYNUM.) I know who you are. You one of them bones people.

(The lights go down to black.)

Scene Three

The lights come up on the kitchen. It is the following morning. MATTIE and BYNUM sit at the table. BERTHA busies herself at the stove.

BYNUM: Good luck don't know no special time to come. You sleep with that up under your pillow and good luck can't help but come to you. Sometimes it come and go and you don't even know it's been there.

BERTHA: Bynum, why don't you leave that gal alone? She don't wanna be hearing all that. Why don't you go on and get out the way and leave her alone?

BYNUM: (Getting up.) Alright, alright. But you mark what I'm saying. It'll draw it to you just like a magnet.

(BYNUM exits up the stairs as LOOMIS enters.)

BERTHA: I got some grits here, Mr. Loomis.

(BERTHA sets a bowl on the table.)

If I was you, Mattie, I wouldn't go getting all tied up with Bynum in that stuff. That kind of stuff, even if it do work for a while, it don't last. That just get people more mixed up than they is already. And I wouldn't waste my time fretting over Jeremy either. I seen it coming. I seen it when she first come here. She that kind of woman run off with the first man got a dollar to spend on her. Jeremy just young. He don't know what he getting into. That gal don't mean him no good. She's just using him to keep from being by herself. That's the worst use of a man you can have. You ought to be glad to wash him out of your hair. I done seen all kind of men. I done seen them come and go through here. Jeremy ain't had enough to him for you. You need a man who's got some understanding and who willing to work with that understanding to come to the best he can. You got your time coming. You just tries too hard and can't understand why it don't work for you. Trying to figure it out don't do nothing but give you a troubled mind. Don't no man want a woman with a troubled mind.

You get all that trouble off your mind and just when it look like you ain't never gonna find what you want . . . you look up and it's standing right there. That's how I met my Seth. You gonna look up one day and find everything you want standing right in front of you. Been twenty-seven years now since that happened to me. But life ain't no happy-go-lucky time where everything be just like you want it. You got your time coming. You watch what Bertha's saying.

(SETH enters.)

SETH: Ho!

BERTHA: What you doing come in here so late?

SETH: I was standing down there on Logan Street talking with the fellows. Henry Allen tried to sell me that old piece of horse he got.

(He sees LOOMIS.)

Today's Tuesday, Mr. Loomis.

BERTHA: (Pulling him toward the bedroom.) Come on in here and leave that man alone to eat his breakfast.

SETH: I ain't bothering nobody. I'm just reminding him what day it is.

(SETH and BERTHA exit into the bedroom.)

LOOMIS: That dress got a color to it.

MATTIE: Did you really see them things like you said? Them people come up out the ocean?

LOOMIS: It happened just like that, yeah.

MATTIE: I hope you find your wife. It be good for your little girl for you to find her.

LOOMIS: Got to find her for myself. Find my starting place in the world. Find me a world I can fit in.

MATTIE: I ain't never found no place for me to fit. Seem like all I do is start over. It ain't nothing to find no starting place in the world. You just start from where you find yourself.

LOOMIS: Got to find my wife. That be my starting place.

MATTIE: What if you don't find her? What you gonna do then if you don't find her?

LOOMIS: She out there somewhere. Ain't no such thing as not finding her.

MATTIE: How she got lost from you? Jack just walked away from me.

LOOMIS: Joe Turner split us up. Joe Turner turned the world upside-down. He bound me on to him for seven years.

MATTIE: I hope you find her. It be good for you to find her.

LOOMIS: I been watching you. I been watching you watch me.

MATTIE: I was just trying to figure out if you seen things like you said.

LOOMIS: (Getting up.) Come here and let me touch you. I been watching you. You a full woman. A man needs a full woman. Come on and be with me.

MATTIE: I ain't got enough for you. You'd use me up too fast.

LOOMIS: Herald Loomis got a mind seem like you a part of it since I first seen you. It's been a long time since I seen a full woman. I can smell you from here. I know you got Herald Loomis on your mind, can't keep him apart from it. Come on and be with Herald Loomis.

(LOOMIS has crossed to MATTIE. He touches her awkwardly, gently, tenderly. Inside he howls like a lost wolf pup whose hunger is deep. He goes to touch her but finds he cannot.)

I done forgot how to touch.

(The lights fade to black.)

Scene Four

It is early the next morning. The lights come up on ZONIA and REUBEN in the yard.

REUBEN: Something spookly going on around here. Last night Mr. Bynum was out in the yard singing and talking to the wind . . . and the wind it just be talking back to him. Did you hear it?

ZONIA: I heard it. I was scared to get up and look. I thought it was a storm.

REUBEN: That wasn't no storm. That was Mr. Bynum. First he say something . . . and the wind it say back to him.

ZONIA: I heard it. Was you scared? I was scared.

REUBEN: And then this morning . . . I seen Miss Mabel!

ZONIA: Who Miss Mabel?

REUBEN: Mr. Seth's mother. He got her picture hanging up in the house. She been dead.

ZONIA: How you seen her if she been dead?

REUBEN: Zonia . . . if I tell you something you promise you won't tell anybody?

ZONIA: I promise.

REUBEN: It was early this morning . . . I went out to the coop to feed the pigeons. I was down on the ground like this to open up the door to the coop . . . when all of a sudden I seen some feets in front of me. I look up . . . and there was Miss Mabel standing there.

ZONIA: Reuben, you better stop telling that! You ain't seen nobody!

REUBEN: Naw, it's the truth. I swear! I seen her just like I see you. Look . . . you can see where she hit me with her cane.

ZONIA: Hit you? What she hit you for?

REUBEN: She says, "Didn't you promise Eugene something?" Then she hit me with her cane. She say, "Let them pigeons go." Then she hit me again. That's what made them marks.

ZONIA: Jeez man . . . get away from me. You done see a haunt!

REUBEN: Shhhh. You promised, Zonia!

ZONIA: You sure it wasn't Miss Bertha come over there and hit you with her hoe?

REUBEN: It wasn't no Miss Bertha. I told you it was Miss Mabel. She was standing right there by the coop. She had this light coming out of her and then she just melted away.

ZONIA: What she had on?

REUBEN: A white dress. Ain't even had no shoes or nothing. Just had on that white dress and them big hands . . . and that cane she hit me with.

ZONIA: How you reckon she knew about the pigeons? You reckon Eugene told her?

REUBEN: I don't know. I sure ain't asked her none. She say Eugene was waiting on them pigeons. Say he couldn't go back home till I let them go. I couldn't get the door to the coop open fast enough.

ZONIA: Maybe she an angel? From the way you say she look with that white dress. Maybe she an angel.

REUBEN: Mean as she was . . . how she gonna be an angel? She used to chase us out her yard and frown up and look evil all the time.

ZONIA: That don't mean she can't be no angel 'cause of how she looked and 'cause she wouldn't let no kids play in her yard. It go by if you got any spots on your heart and if you pray and go to church.

REUBEN: What about she hit me with her cane? An angel wouldn't hit me with her cane.

ZONIA: I don't know. She might. I still say she was an angel.

REUBEN: You reckon Eugene the one who sent old Miss Mabel?

ZONIA: Why he send her? Why he don't come himself?

REUBEN: Figured if he send her maybe that'll make me listen. 'Cause she old.

ZONIA: What you think it feel like?

REUBEN: What?

ZONIA: Being dead.

REUBEN: Like being sleep only you don't know nothing and can't move no more.

ZONIA: If Miss Mabel can come back . . . then maybe Eugene can come back too.

REUBEN: We can go down to the hideout like we used to! He could come back everyday! It be just like he ain't dead.

ZONIA: Maybe that ain't right for him to come back. Feel kinda funny to be playing games with a haunt.

REUBEN: Yeah . . . what if everybody came back? What if Miss Mabel came back just like she ain't dead? Where you and your daddy gonna sleep then?

ZONIA: Maybe they go back at night and don't need no place to sleep.

REUBEN: It still don't seem right. I'm sure gonna miss Eugene. He's the bestest friend anybody ever had.

ZONIA: My daddy say if you miss somebody too much it can kill you. Say he missed me till it liked to killed him.

REUBEN: What if your mama's already dead and all the time you looking for her?

ZONIA: Naw, she ain't dead. My daddy say he can smell her.

REUBEN: You can't smell nobody that ain't here. Maybe he smelling old Miss Bertha. Maybe Miss Bertha your mama?

ZONIA: Naw, she ain't. My mamma got long pretty hair and she five feet from the ground!

REUBEN: Your daddy say when you leaving?

(ZONIA doesn't respond.)

Maybe you gonna stay in Mr. Seth's house and don't go looking for your mama no more.

ZONIA: He say we got to leave on Saturday.

REUBEN: Dag! You just only been here for a little while. Don't seem like nothing ever stay the same.

ZONIA: He say he got to find her. Find him a place in the world.

REUBEN: He could find him a place in Mr. Seth's house.

ZONIA: It don't look like we never gonna find her.

REUBEN: Maybe he find her by Saturday then you don't have to go.

ZONIA: I don't know.

REUBEN: You look like a spider!

ZONIA: I ain't no spider!

REUBEN: Got them long skinny arms and legs. You look like one of them Black Widows.

ZONIA: I ain't no Black Widow nothing! My name is Zonia!

REUBEN: That's what I'm gonna call you . . . Spider.

ZONIA: You can call me that, but I don't have to answer.

REUBEN: You know what? I think maybe I be your husband when I grow up.

ZONIA: How you know?

REUBEN: I ask my grandpap how you know and he say when the moon falls into a girl's eyes that how you know.

ZONIA: Did it fall into my eyes?

REUBEN: Not that I can tell. Maybe I ain't old enough. Maybe you ain't old enough.

ZONIA: So there! I don't know why you telling me that lie!

REUBEN: That don't mean nothing 'cause I can't see it. I know it's there. Just the way you look at me sometimes look like the moon might have been in your eyes.

ZONIA: That don't mean nothing if you can't see it. You supposed to see it.

REUBEN: Shucks, I see it good enough for me. You ever let anybody kiss you?

ZONIA: Just my daddy. He kiss me on the cheek.

REUBEN: It's better on the lips. Can I kiss you on the lips?

ZONIA: I don't know. You ever kiss anybody before?

REUBEN: I had a cousin let me kiss her on the lips one time. Can I kiss you?

ZONIA: Okay.

(REUBEN kisses her and lays his head against her chest.)

What you doing?

REUBEN: Listening. Your heart singing!

ZONIA: It is not.

REUBEN: Just beating like a drum. Let's kiss again.

(They kiss again.)

Now you mine, Spider. You my girl, okay?

ZONIA: Okay.

REUBEN: When I get grown, I come looking for you.

ZONIA: Okay.

(The lights fade to black.)

Scene Five

The lights come up on the kitchen. It is Saturday. BYNUM, LOOMIS, and ZONIA sit at the table. BERTHA prepares breakfast. ZONIA has on a white dress.

BYNUM: With all this rain we been having he might have ran into some washed-out roads. If that wagon got stuck in the mud he's liable to be still upriver somewhere. If he's upriver then he ain't coming until tomorrow.

LOOMIS: Today's Saturday. He say he be here on Saturday.

BERTHA: Zonia, you gonna eat your breakfast this morning.

ZONIA: Yes, ma'am.

BERTHA: I don't know how you expect to get any bigger if you don't eat. I ain't never seen a child that didn't eat. You about as skinny as a bean pole.

(Pause.)

Mr. Loomis, there's a place down on Wylie. Zeke Mayweather got a house down there. You ought to see if he got any rooms.

(LOOMIS doesn't respond.)

Well, you're welcome to some breakfast before you move on.

(MATTIE enters from the stairs.)

MATTIE: Good morning.

BERTHA: Morning, Mattie. Sit on down there and get you some breakfast.

BYNUM: Well, Mattie Campbell, you been sleeping with that up under your pillow like I told you?

BERTHA: Bynum, I done told you to leave that gal alone with all that stuff. You around here meddling in other people's lives. She don't want to hear all that. You ain't doing nothing but confusing her with that stuff.

MATTIE: (To LOOMIS.) You all fixing to move on?

LOOMIS: Today's Saturday. I'm paid up till Saturday.

MATTIE: Where you going to?

LOOMIS: Gonna find my wife.

MATTIE: You going off to another city?

LOOMIS: We gonna see where the road take us. Ain't no telling where we wind up.

MATTIE: Eleven years is a long time. Your wife . . . she might have taken up with someone else. People do that when they get lost from each other.

LOOMIS: Zonia. Come on, we gonna find your mama.

(LOOMIS and ZONIA cross to the door.)

MATTIE: (To ZONIA.) Zonia, Mattie got a ribbon here match your dress. Want Mattie to fix your hair with her ribbon?

(ZONIA nods. MATTIE ties the ribbon in her hair.)

There . . . it got a color just like your dress.
(To LOOMIS.) I hope you find her. I hope you be happy.

LOOMIS: A man looking for a woman be lucky to find you. You a good woman, Mattie. Keep a good heart.

(LOOMIS and ZONIA exit.)

BERTHA: I been watching that man for two weeks . . . and that's the closest I come to seeing him act civilized. I don't know what's between you all, Mattie . . . but the only thing that man needs is somebody to make him laugh. That's all you need in the world is love and laughter. That's all anybody needs. To have love in one hand and laughter in the other.

(BERTHA moves about the kitchen as though blessing it and chasing away the huge sadness that seems to envelop it. It is a dance and demonstration of her own magic, her own remedy that is centuries old and to which she is connected by the muscles of her heart and the blood's memory.)

You hear me, Mattie? I'm talking about laughing. The kind of laugh that comes from way deep inside. To just stand and laugh and let life flow right through you. Just laugh to let yourself know you're alive.

(She begins to laugh. It is a near-hysterical laughter that is a celebration of life, both its pain and its blessing. MATTIE and BYNUM join in the laughter. SETH enters from the front door.)

SETH: Well, I see you all having fun.

(SETH begins to laugh with them.)

That Loomis fellow standing up there on the corner watching the house. He standing right up there on Manila Street.

BERTHA: Don't you get started on him. The man done left out of here and that's the last I wanna hear of it. You about to drive me crazy with that man.

SETH: I just say he standing up there on the corner. Acting sneaky like he always do. He can stand up there all he want. As long as he don't come back in here.

(There is a knock on the door. SETH goes to answer it. Enter MARTHA LOOMIS [PENTECOST]. She is a young woman about twenty-eight. She is dressed as befitting a member of an Evangelist church. RUTHERFORD SELIG follows.)

SETH: Look here, Bertha. It's Martha Pentecost. Come on in, Martha. Who that with you? Oh . . . that's Selig. Come on in, Selig.

BERTHA: Come on in, Martha. It's sure good to see you.

BYNUM: Rutherford Selig, you a sure enough first-class People finder!

SELIG: She was right out there in Rankin. You take that first righthand road . . . right there at that church on Wooster Street. I started to go right past and something told me to stop at the church and see if they needed any dustpans.

SETH: Don't she look good, Bertha.

BERTHA: Look all nice and healthy.

MARTHA: Mr. Bynum . . . Selig told me my little girl was here.

SETH: There's some fellow around here say he your husband. Say his name is Loomis. Say you his wife.

MARTHA: Is my little girl with him?

SETH: Yeah, he got a little girl with him. I wasn't gonna tell him where you was. Not the way this fellow look. So he got Selig to find you.

MARTHA: Where they at? They upstairs?

SETH: He was standing right up there on Manila Street. I had to ask him to leave 'cause of how he was carrying on. He come in here one night—

(The door opens and LOOMIS and ZONIA enter. MARTHA and LOOMIS stare at each other.)

LOOMIS: Hello, Martha.

MARTHA: Herald . . . Zonia?

LOOMIS: You ain't waited for me, Martha. I got out the place looking to see your face. Seven years I waited to see your face.

MARTHA: Herald, I been looking for you. I wasn't but two months behind you when you went to my mama's and got Zonia. I been looking for you ever since.

LOOMIS: Joe Turner let me loose and I felt all turned around inside. I just wanted to see your face to know that the world was still there. Make sure everything still in its place so I could reconnect myself together. I got there and you was gone, Martha.

MARTHA: Herald . . .

LOOMIS: Left my little girl motherless in the world.

MARTHA: I didn't leave her motherless, Herald. Reverend Tolliver wanted to move the church up North 'cause of all the trouble the colored folks was having down there. Nobody knew what was gonna happen traveling them roads. We didn't even know if we was gonna make it up here or not. I left her with my mama so she be safe. That was better than dragging her out on the road having to duck and hide from people. Wasn't no telling what was gonna happen to us. I didn't leave her motherless in the world. I been looking for you.

LOOMIS: I come up on Henry Thompson's place after seven years of living in hell, and all I'm looking to do is see your face.

MARTHA: Herald, I didn't know if you was ever coming back. They told me Joe Turner had you and my whole world split half in two. My whole life shattered. It was like I had poured it in a cracked jar and it all leaked out the bottom. When it go like that there ain't nothing you can do put it back together. You talking about Henry Thompson's place like I'm still gonna be working the land by myself. How I'm gonna do that? You wasn't gone but two months and Henry Thompson kicked me off his land and I ain't had no place to go but to my mama's. I stayed and waited there for five years before I woke up one morning and decided that you was dead. Even if you weren't, you was dead to me. I wasn't gonna carry you with me no more. So I killed you in my heart. I buried you. I mourned you. And then I picked up what was left and went on to make life without you. I was a young woman with life at my beckon. I couldn't drag you behind me like a sack of cotton.

LOOMIS: I just been waiting to look on your face to say my goodbye. That goodbye got so big at times, seem like it was gonna swallow me up. Like Jonah in the whale's belly I sat up in that goodbye for three years. That goodbye kept me out on the road searching. Not looking on women in their houses. It kept me bound up to the road. All the time that goodbye swelling up in my chest till I'm about to bust. Now that I see your face I can say my goodbye and make my own world.

(LOOMIS takes ZONIA's hand and presents her to MARTHA.)

Martha . . . here go your daughter. I tried to take care of her. See that she had something to eat. See that she was out of the elements. Whatever I know I tried to teach her. Now she need to learn from her mother whatever you got to teach her. That way she won't be no one-sided person.

(LOOMIS stoops to ZONIA.)

Zonia, you go live with your mama. She a good woman. You go on with her and listen to her good. You my daughter and I love you like a daughter. I hope to see you again in the world somewhere. I'll never forget you.

ZONIA: (Throws her arms around LOOMIS in a panic.) I won't get no bigger! My bones won't get no bigger! They won't! I promise! Take me with you till we keep searching and never finding. I won't get no bigger! I promise!

LOOMIS: Go on and do what I told you now.

MARTHA: (Goes to ZONIA and comforts her.) It's alright, baby. Mama's here. Mama's here. Don't worry. Don't cry.

(MARTHA turns to BYNUM.)

Mr. Bynum, I don't know how to thank you. God bless you.

LOOMIS: It was you! All the time it was you that bind me up! You bound me to the road!

BYNUM: I ain't bind you, Herald Loomis. You can't bind what don't cling.

LOOMIS: Everywhere I go people wanna bind me up. Joe Turner wanna bind me up! Reverend Tolliver wanna bind me up. You wanna bind me up. Everybody wanna bind me up. Well, Joe Turner's come and gone and Herald Loomis ain't for no binding. I ain't gonna let nobody bind me up!

(LOOMIS pulls out a knife.)

BYNUM: It wasn't you, Herald Loomis. I ain't bound you. I bound the little girl to her mother. That's who I bound. You binding yourself. You bound onto your song. All you got to do is stand up and sing it, Herald Loomis. It's right there kicking at your throat. All you got to do is sing it. Then you be free.

MARTHA: Herald . . . look at yourself! Standing there with a knife in your hand. You done gone over to the devil. Come on . . . put down the knife. You got to look to Jesus. Even if you done fell away from the church you can be saved again. The Bible say, "The Lord is my shepherd I shall not want. He maketh me to lie down in green pastures. He leads me beside the still water. He restoreth my soul. He leads me in the path of righteousness for His name's sake. Even though I walk through the shadow of death—"

LOOMIS: That's just where I be walking!

MARTHA: "I shall fear no evil. For Thou art with me. Thy rod and thy staff, they comfort me."

LOOMIS: You can't tell me nothing about no valleys. I done been all across the valleys and the hills and the mountains and the oceans.

MARTHA: "Thou preparest a table for me in the presence of my enemies."

LOOMIS: And all I seen was a bunch of niggers dazed out of their woolly heads. And Mr. Jesus Christ standing there in the middle of them, grinning.

MARTHA: "Thou annointest my head with oil, my cup runneth over."

LOOMIS: He grin that big old grin . . . and niggers wallowing at his feet.

MARTHA: "Surely goodness and mercy shall follow me all the days of my life, and I shall dwell in the house of the Lord forever."

LOOMIS: Great big old white man . . . your Mr. Jesus Christ. Standing there with a whip in one hand and tote board in another, and them niggers swimming in a sea of cotton. And he counting. He tallying up the cotton. "Well, Jeremiah . . . what's the matter, you ain't picked but two hundred pounds of cotton today? Got to put you on half rations." And Jeremiah go back and lay up there on his half rations and talk about what a nice man Mr. Jesus Christ is 'cause he give him salvation after he die. Something wrong here. Something don't fit right!

MARTHA: You got to open up your heart and have faith, Herald. This world is just a trial for the next. Jesus offers you salvation.

LOOMIS: I been wading in the water. I been walking all over the River Jordan. But what it get me, huh? I done been baptized with blood of the lamb and the fire of the Holy Ghost. But what I got, huh? I got salvation? My enemies all around me picking the flesh from my bones. I'm choking on my own blood and all you got to give me is salvation?

MARTHA: You got to be clean, Herald. You got to be washed with the blood of the lamb.

LOOMIS: Blood make you clean? You clean with blood?

MARTHA: Jesus bled for you. He's the Lamb of God who takest away the sins of the world.

LOOMIS: I don't need nobody to bleed for me! I can bleed for myself.

MARTHA: You got to be something, Herald. You just can't be alive. Life don't mean nothing unless it got a meaning.

LOOMIS: What kind of meaning you got? What kind of clean you got, woman? You want blood? Blood make you clean? You clean with blood?

(LOOMIS slashes himself across the chest. He rubs the blood over his face and comes to a realization.)

I'm standing! I'm standing. My legs stood up! I'm standing now!

(Having found his song, the song of self-sufficiency, fully resurrected, cleansed and given breath, free from any encumbrance other than the workings of his own heart and the bonds of the flesh, having accepted the responsibility for his own presence in the world, he is free to soar above the environs that weighed and pushed his spirit into terrifying contractions.)

Goodbye, Martha.

(LOOMIS turns and exits, the knife still in his hands. MATTIE looks about the room and rushes out after him.)

BYNUM: Herald Loomis, you shining! You shining like new money!

The lights go down to BLACK.

••• PRODUCING *JOE TURNER'S COME AND GONE*

THE CONSTRUCTION OF MEANING THROUGH COLLABORATION

Theatre production is a unique process that is unlike the creation of visual art, music, or literature. The creation of a stage production is an **interpretive art** and a **collaborative art.** The beginning point is the playwright's **script.** But a script is not a blueprint with all the details precisely recorded. The playscript essentially expresses a drama through dialogue.

In the case of *Joe Turner's Come and Gone,* in addition to the dialogue, Wilson's script outlines basic stage directions, the characters' entrances and exits and other important movements, and the nature of the physical space. It also provides hints of character description. For example, Wilson tells us that Seth is in his early fifties, a skilled craftsman, and that he has a certain "stability." We also learn from the script that Bertha is slightly younger than Seth and that "she has learned to negotiate around Seth's apparent orneriness." Wilson gives us no details of their appearance or their dress.

The script identifies a boardinghouse as the setting and details the layout of the downstairs rooms and the placement of the doors. Most of the play takes place in the kitchen and the parlor, with two short scenes for the children in the garden. There is no specific description of the architectural style of the house, no indication of painting or wall decor, no discussion of the style or the quantity of furniture, and, perhaps most important, no description of the atmosphere created by the combination of the physical details of place.

The playwright begins a process that must be joined by a director, actors, and designers. Together they will interpret the playwright's work by filling in details of character, action, scenery, costumes, lighting, and sound. All are creative artists in their own right. But in the theatre, no one person's work stands alone. Only when the play is fully realized on the stage with an audience present does theatre actually exist.

Working closely with the **director,** who guides the process, the designers and actors give physical shape, a concrete reality, to the playwright's vision. They study the text closely to grasp the playwright's intentions. And then they use their particular talents as a group to create a theatrical event that expresses their understanding of the truth in the playwright's text. This is an enormously complex task, with many people responsible for different parts of the production, all working under the strictest of deadlines. The curtain must go up on the scheduled day, at the scheduled hour.

In the following pages we explore the process of staging *Joe Turner's Come and Gone* at the Oregon Shakespeare Festival in Ashland, Oregon. We begin to analyze the nature of the work done by the director, the actors, and the designers. We look at the collaborative process, the ways in which people work together; and also at the process of interpretation, how expressive choices are made. An examination of the production process will also give us further insights into the meaning of *Joe Turner's Come and Gone.*

THE OREGON SHAKESPEARE FESTIVAL

Ashland, Oregon, is a small, picturesque town of 30,000 people located in the mountains of southern Oregon. Much of the life of the community revolves around the Oregon Shakespeare Festival, located in the center of the town. The Shakespeare Festival is the largest not-for-profit theatre of its kind in the United States. Other theatres that we examine in this book are in the heart of large cities such as New York, Los Angeles, or Seattle. Attending the theatre in Ashland, however, is a quieter, more reflective experience than going to the theatre in a fast-paced city at the end of a workday or as part of one's daily activities. The actors who perform *Joe Turner's Come and Gone* will have the full attention of their audience as they give life to the world that August Wilson has created.

Although the festival, which began in 1935, was originally dedicated to the plays of Shakespeare, it now presents the works of many other playwrights as well. Recent seasons have offered a total of eleven plays, with about one-third by Shakespeare. For eight months of the year, from late February to October, plays are performed on the festival's three stages.

Many of the audience members at the festival are residents of Ashland or Oregonians from Portland (about four hours away) and closer, smaller communities. But the entire population of Oregon, 2.5 million, would fit into New York City or Los Angeles many times over. It is the out-of-state and even international visitors who enable this large, complex organization to maintain its many enterprises. People come to Ashland from all over the world specifically to go to the theatre. Most people will spend several days and see more than one play. This is why the festival produces plays in **repertory**—that is, a number of plays are produced at once and then performed in rotation. During the same week, theatre-goers might be able to attend performances of *Joe Turner's Come and Gone*, a Shakespearian tragedy, a nineteenth-century French farce, and another new American play. In 1993 the festival's 600-seat Angus Bowmer Theatre opened the season with *Joe Turner's Come and Gone*.

THE ACTORS AT WORK
Understanding the Play

The actors sit around a large table quietly reading the play to one another. Some of them know each other well. They have worked together for years in this small Oregon town. A few of the actors are new. They have come to Ashland for the first time as part of the *Joe Turner* cast, although they will stay in Ashland to take part in other plays. The director, Clinton Turner Davis, who leads the discussion, has come from New York just to direct this play. Most of the actors are working with Davis for the first time.

During this first phase of the **rehearsal** process, called **table work,** the actors do not get up and start to move around the stage until the director, Davis, feels that they have asked enough questions and explored enough possible answers about the history and motivation of each character. Why does each character make certain choices? What is behind the words the characters speak? The answers may change a number of times, and more questions will certainly arise. But each actor must have a starting point for the thread that leads him or her from moment to moment during the course of the play.

The discussion shifts to the character of Herald Loomis, and Davis leans toward Derrick Lee Weedon, the actor who is playing Loomis.

CLINTON TURNER DAVIS: What did you feel, what was going through your mind when you went back, when you were released from the chain gang and you went back home and Martha wasn't there? All right now, think of that moment, and nonverbally say the first thing that comes into your mind, nonverbally.[14]

THEATRE TALENTS AND SKILLS •••

Starting Points in the Rehearsal Process

1. Careful reading of the play and research into the historical time period
2. Joint reading of the play and discussion of the characters' history and motivation
3. Repetition of and response to the language
4. Physicalization
5. Music

J. P. Phillips portrays Seth, "just a regular American guy trying to be decent."

Weedon pauses and then an anguished, choking sound comes from his throat. Davis says softly, "Remember that sound. We'll use that later." What begins as a sound, an inarticulate expression of loss and rage, becomes a point of departure for the passion that drives Herald Loomis through the course of the play.

J. P. Phillips, playing Seth, is intrigued by the connection of Seth to Booker T. Washington, an African American educator who during the 1910s advocated separating the races and focusing on vocational education for African Americans. Phillips strongly believes that Seth is simply a man "searching for the American dream and trying to prove his decency. He's just a regular American guy trying to be decent." Davis is eager for the actors to begin the process

of building the inner life of their characters as he poses a variety of questions to open up the discussion. But he also welcomes the answer "I don't know."

> **CLINTON TURNER DAVIS:** "I don't know" is sometimes the most empowering answer because it frees the air. And likewise if the actors ask me a question and I don't have an answer, I'll tell them, "I don't know." We have to reveal ourselves to each other and build trust in that revelation.

As they approach Wilson's characters and the world of the play, Davis and the cast also discuss significant events of the times and background source materials. Sitting around that large table, in the quiet, empty rehearsal hall, the actors spread out pictures of Pittsburgh from the early 1900s. They look at photographs of houses, the clothing of the period, and people at work. They share readings from W. E. B. Dubois's essential work *The Souls of Black Folk*, which explores the political and economic structures of the time and their consequences for black Americans. They read from the work of Zora Neale Hurston to expand their awareness of the language spoken by Wilson's characters and for information on traditional religious practice. Davis shares his studies of the Yoruban culture of western Nigeria, which he feels is the appropriate source for the Juba and for Bynum's incantations. After three days of questions and discussion and reading and rereading the play, the actors know enough about the inside of their characters to get the play "up on its legs." They also know most of their lines.

The Rehearsal Process

The next week and a half is spent working on the **blocking**—that is, all of the actors' movements around the stage that make up the physical action of the performance. Not all directors have lengthy discussions with the actors before they start the blocking rehearsals; some have individual discussions with actors, and some have no discussions at all. But for Davis, it is crucial that the actors arrive at an understanding of the play together and that their understanding be informed by the history and the texture of the times as well as their own emotional and intellectual responses to their characters.

The continuing discussion about the play is one of the ways that the director and the actors collaborate to create meaning. The discussion is also a way of building trust between the members of the company. This way of working depends on shared responsibility rather than on competition or a hierarchical structure. Ultimately, the director must make certain decisions and keep examining the performance to ensure that the playwright's ideas are being communicated. But Davis encourages the actors to take risks, to try out new ideas, to contribute their own thoughts.

CLINTON TURNER DAVIS: When you work with an ensemble, it is essential to have a high degree of trust, and the earlier you can create that, the stronger the working environment will be. I try not to impose my views too early on because I think too often the actors feel that they are just the instrument of the director. An autocratic director will tell the actor what to do, when to do it, where, why, and how. And so the actors spend more time trying to contort and mold themselves into his concept of the characters without totally understanding why. It can be frightening.

An atmosphere of trust and receptivity gives the actors a freedom that many believe allows them to do their best work.

LEWAN ALEXANDER (BYNUM): The collaborative way that he worked—he encouraged, really demanded, input, not only in what we were doing with our own characters but the shape of the play, how we saw certain scenes develop. It was really a collaborative effort, and that's very rare.

TAMU GRAY (BERTHA): I was given an opportunity to really concentrate on the craft, to concentrate on the art, to be empowered as an actor in the rehearsal hall. We worked in a respectful and truly collective and community-based way. We walked into the rehearsal hall with a sense of play and a desire to play and a willingness to play that I've not seen anywhere else.

Sometimes when the actors enter the rehearsal room, Davis has music playing.

CLINTON TURNER DAVIS: We listened to gospel tapes, down-home revival, really backwoods revivals where you just had a cappella singing started by the traditional starter of the church. They would wail into it and ultimately discover the communal harmony. And since we had started rehearsal right after Christmas, we had Quincy Jones's interpretation of Handel's Messiah—A Soulful Celebration. Through that recording Quincy has given a complete history of African American music. Other times we listened to jazz or blues. Sometimes we'd have the music playing to set the mood when the actors would come in in the morning or when we would take a break. This would keep us in a specific context.

Davis sees music as part of the texture of the play, the connection to the oral tradition discussed in the first part of this chapter. But he also recognizes a musical structure in the language itself, a poetry in the rhythm of the speeches and the telling of the stories. For J. P. Phillips, who plays Seth, the music has to start with the language:

J. P. PHILLIPS: I'm looking for words and minding the language. You take the playwright's words and you add breath and bring the words to life and reveal what the playwright is trying to say.

Bynum (LeWan Alexander) tells Mattie Campbell (BW Gonzalez) to push thoughts of Jack Carper out of her mind.

BW Gonzalez, who portrays Mattie, also sees the language as the starting point for building character:

BW GONZALEZ: What I feel I do as an actor is like painting. I paint the portrait through the words. The words create the images that I need to paint the portrait of the character.

Physical Characterization

The actors also work to create a specific physical presence for their characters. Although there are many different approaches to the physicalization of a character, we look at the problems faced by the young actor LeWan Alexander in approaching the much older character of Bynum. In 1993 Alexander was in his early thirties. The script gives Bynum's age as early sixties. That presents the actor not only with a large span of years to bridge physically, but also with a significant gap in experience to bridge emotionally.

LEWAN ALEXANDER (BYNUM): Everyone in the play was already cast before Christmas of last year, and they were to start rehearsals at the beginning of January, except for me. I knew I wasn't in the play. I wasn't cast. They were still looking for Bynum, and I got a call about a week before Christmas to see if I wanted to play Bynum. And I said to Henry Woronicz, the artistic director of the Festival, "Oh, thanks, Hank, but I can't do that role. That's just way out of my range." He said, "Well, it's either you or someone that we're going to find, so why don't you give yourself a couple of days to think about it?" Well, I didn't sleep that night, and I called him ten hours later and said, "Yeah, I'd like to do it." The main reason that I balked, which is also the reason that I decided to accept, was the fact that not only is he thirty years my senior, but the nature of the man and what he's connected to was very far from my own personal experience. Just the thought of a conjure man, a rootworker, is very foreign to me. It was quite a challenge. I started in the rehearsal process with three things, three physical things. My grandfather died when I was very young, but I remember how he used to sit in a chair. I remember that and the way he used to slump and the way he used to eat, particularly bread. I picked those things up from him. There was a homeless man in Milwaukee that I used to observe a lot. He would never pick up his feet when he walked, and he always walked with his head very low, shoulders slumped. And he had a beard that was very gray, and it was kind of curly around him. The script says that Bynum is very connected to the earth, and

I wanted his center of gravity to be very low so that it's easy for him to get down to the ground if he needs to.[15]

The director and the actors work together to create an atmosphere that makes the world of the play gradually come alive for them. They study the play and its times. They explore the specific nature of each character, and his or her personal history, objectives, or goals. They begin with individual moments in the stage life of each character and work to build a coherent whole that makes sense of everything the characters say and do. For example, the actor playing Loomis may start with what he has lost and the search for his wife, but ultimately it is himself that he seeks. They focus on the language and the way the rhythms of speech shape character. They listen to music that feeds the work on rhythm and creates a certain atmosphere. They create a physical presence. All of the director's and the actors' preparations are aimed at refining their understanding of the playwright's text and making imaginative choices that will make this understanding clear to an audience.

STAGING THE JUBA

Our summary of the rehearsal process for *Joe Turner's Come and Gone* is far from a complete description of the actors' work. In later chapters we expand our discussion of the nature of acting as we examine other productions and study other actors' work. At this point we pursue the way the director and actors work together to interpret the playwright's text for the audience through staging. We examine the director's blocking of a crucial section of the play to see how the action combines with speech to create meaningful images. For Davis, the Juba is at the center of the play and leads directly to Herald Loomis's first major revelation: his vision of bones rising up out of the water at the end of act 1. The interruption of the Juba by Loomis's entrance sharply escalates the conflict between the characters and exposes the depth of Loomis's

despair. We see in physical terms the crippling of his soul by slavery.

The Juba begins after Sunday dinner with all the boardinghouse characters present except Loomis. Together Seth and Bynum organize the other characters.

SETH: . . . Come on, Bertha, leave them dishes be for a while. We gonna Juba.

BYNUM: Alright. Let's Juba down! (act 1, scene 4)

The stage directions describe the Juba as

reminiscent of the Ring Shouts of the African slaves. It is a call and response dance. BYNUM sits at the table and drums. He calls the dance as others clap hands, shuffle and stomp around the table. It should be as African as possible, with the performers working themselves up into a near frenzy. The words can be improvised, but should include some mention of the Holy Ghost. (act 1, scene 4)

Drumming and Dancing

In staging the Juba, Davis begins with the drum. He explains that drumming is at the heart of African communication and language. According to Davis, one of the greatest deprivations in slavery was the loss of the drum. Drumming was forbidden by slaveowners, who couldn't understand but sensed the power of the drum to speak across the distances and carry the voices, the language, of the African captives from plantation to plantation. For Davis, then, the drumming in the Juba is part of reestablishing communication after the end of slavery, a way of developing community.

The stage directions suggest that Bynum use the dining table as his "drum." After discussing with the cast various possibilities for household items that could be used as drums, Davis settles on the table as the "gbedu," a big, deep-timbred royal drum. The table is the hearth, the center of nurturing and community, and is therefore appropriate to serve as the instrument of communication. Davis establishes that Bynum will sit at the table and drum on the tabletop while

Loomis (Derrick Lee Weedon) destroys the Juba celebration with his vision of the "bones people," which is a symbolic telling of both his personal history and the larger history of a people brought across the sea into slavery.

the others dance in a processional circle around him. The circle is suggested by the descriptions of Bynum's ceremonies at the beginning of the play:

SETH: He done drew a big circle with that stick and now he's dancing around. (act 1, scene 1)

Davis sees power and completeness in the many symbolic associations of the circle that spatially and visually contribute to the harmony he is trying to develop rhythmically.

Once the basic image is established for the cast, Davis works with the actors on African rhythms to be clapped and dance steps that they may use, some of which have African origins and some of which are associated with religious observation in the United States, such as

Pentecostal worship. The ceremony represents a merging of African and Christian worship. After Bynum begins his drumming, Davis asks each actor to enter the Juba in order of the age and importance of his or her character to the household. Seth is first as the owner of the house, and Zonia is last as a visiting child. The actors are free to improvise off the basic rhythm and off the basic dance steps to increase the density of sound and movement.

Text and Verbal Improvisation

In addition to the drumming and dancing of the Juba, there is also a whole verbal score to be improvised. Davis asks the cast to approach their words for the Juba section as a kind of personal prayer, a

Herald Loomis (Derrick Lee Weedon) describes his paralyzing vision of bones rising from the water to Bynum (LeWan Alexander) in the Oregon Shakespeare Festival production of *Joe Turner's Come and Gone.*

statement of their needs at that particular point in the play. Through a combination of improvised speech, chanting, and song, they call upon the "Spirit" to provide guidance in their lives. Once the actors have begun to develop this verbal text or score for the Juba, Davis adds one more element: He translates some of the actors' improvised words into Dutch, French, Spanish, German, and Portuguese, all languages of the slave traders who carried African people on their ships. The words come out as a kind of genetic memory of the experience of slavery.

The Meaning of the Juba

In this particular production, then, the Juba has a number of structural and thematic functions. In terms of the **plot,** it is an activity that brings the characters together following their Sunday dinner. Even though they come from widely different backgrounds and have very different goals for themselves, they all know the Juba. It is an informal household religious observation, a ceremony that celebrates an African heritage fused with Christianity and allows for an emotional release following the daily struggle for survival. For the characters it is also a way of focusing their particular search during the course of the play. In addition, the Juba is a symbolic representation of the obstacles the characters have overcome to arrive at this point in their journeys. The languages of the slave traders and the recovery of the drum introduce references to slavery that will become explosive after Herald Loomis's entrance.

The Juba builds a sense of community and harmony that will be broken by Herald Loomis. It also builds all the tensions of act 1 to a high level of intensity, a "frenzy" that essentially launches Herald Loomis into his soul-searing vision. Loomis, who has collapsed to the floor, sees a vision of bones that sink into the ocean and then are washed ashore as black people. Bynum, trying to get Loomis to his feet, tells him that the "bones people" have risen and taken to the road. But Loomis is crushed by the vision and cannot rise. Loomis is reexperiencing the Middle Passage, the holocaustic journey of Africans crossing the ocean to become slaves. The Juba establishes a memory of the passage into slavery that sets the context for Loomis's breakdown.

The many levels of meaning that emerge from a piece of staging that lasts only a few minutes demonstrate one of the fundamental aspects of theatrical communication: stage images are constantly built with many layers of expression, some visual, some verbal, some rhythmic, some psychological or emotional. The audience receives complex information from these images that are so much more than a mere sequence in the storytelling process.

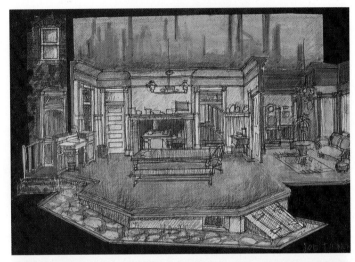

The rendering of the scene design by Mike Fish for *Joe Turner's Come and Gone* communicates the feeling and atmosphere of the set as well as the definition of the space, the placement of the furniture, and the details of place. After the designer creates the scenic images, the scene shop constructs the actual set from technical drawings.

The scene design is transformed into the actual setting for *Joe Turner's Come and Gone*. The warmth of the kitchen is placed against the smokestacks of industrial Pittsburgh. The table offers a gathering place for the characters and becomes the center of the play's action.

Bynum and Loomis and finally only Loomis. The consequences of slavery come crashing down on us as we see the torment for Herald Loomis when he says, "I got to stand up" and then, "My legs won't stand up! My legs won't stand up!" The primary focus is on the actors, but the work of the designers is essential in supporting and completing the images the actors create.

EXPANDING THE STAGE IMAGE: THE WORK OF THE DESIGNERS

The intensity of the actors' movement and language should be riveting for the audience in the sequence that we have been discussing at the end of act 1. All of the actors' skills are engaged at a high level to create a spellbinding moment of revelation. In the Juba the actors create a sense of community, using the whole stage. Then the harmony of the stage picture is destroyed by Herald Loomis's entrance, and the focus narrows until we see only

The Set Design

In the **rendering** of the set designed by Mike Fish, we can see the placement of the table center stage and get some idea of its relative size. In developing a **ground plan** for the set (the placement of the furniture, doors, and walls), Fish as **scene designer** and Davis as director need to create a space that (1) allows the characters a sense of intimacy produced by being in the warmth of

Bertha's kitchen and (2) provides a space that is big enough and spacious enough for the characters to eat together at the dining table and then to be able to dance around it in the Juba sequence. The placement of the table center stage makes it the primary visual focus and also allows for the action described in the previous section. The set design must first support the characters' actions and movements required by the play. It must provide spaces that allow the appropriate physical relationships between characters.

As the characters eat their Sunday dinner and then begin the Juba, we in the audience sense the comfort provided by the boardinghouse kitchen. The set helps create an atmosphere that is warm and inviting. There is a large fireplace; there is also a stove. The colors are reds and browns and antique rose. And precise attention is paid to detail.

MIKE FISH: It was a very large house but at the same time it had to be very, very intimate because this is Bertha's house and it had all her little knick-knacks. When I furnished the house I was very careful to put details: the Civil War, little precious mementos, little porcelain figures, a sign above the mantel, "God Bless This Home."

The set design also reveals the time and place. Fish shapes the space with nineteenth-century architectural details and furnishes it with period antiques that are purchased or are reproduced in the scene shop. The time and place are also strongly reinforced by the use of a painted backdrop that rises above the three-dimensional structure of the house. Behind the house we see the smokestacks of the Pittsburgh steel mills. The backdrop places us in an industrial setting and reminds us that the boardinghouse must protect its occupants against

---

THEATRE TALENTS AND SKILLS •••

Summary of Basic Design Functions

A. Set
1. Reflects time period
2. Gives sense of place
3. Creates appropriate atmosphere
4. Creates space that provides for necessary character action and movement
5. Creates space that allows the appropriate physical relationships between characters

B. Costuming
1. Reflects time period
2. Reveals class and background of characters
3. Demonstrates individuality of characters
4. Highlights contrasts between characters

C. Lighting
1. Creates visibility
2. Creates atmosphere
3. Works with pacing and rhythms of actors to establish overall rhythm of the play

All build visual metaphors.

---

the urban factory world. Even as we see the family gathering and ritual observation, with its African origins, held in the safety of the kitchen, the reality of Pittsburgh in 1911 looms behind. We see that the characters face an enormous task of integrating experiences and realities.

The Costume Design

The costumes play a very important part in creating a sense of the time period and in defining the class and individuality of the characters. As the characters gather for their Sunday dinner and then the Juba, we see them in their "good" clothes, which are nicer but well-worn versions of their work clothes. These are proud people who have to work extremely hard for everything

JOE TURNER'S COME AND GONE

MATTIE CAMPBELL
BW Gonzales

The costume design for Mattie Campbell by Candice Cain shows the contrast with Herald Loomis.

they have. The goal of the **costume designer,** Candice Cain, is to create the effect of real clothing.

CANDICE CAIN: I didn't want them to be "costumes." I called them clothes the whole time. There was a lot of work to do after the clothing was built and fit. We even ill-fitted some of the clothing, so it didn't look perfect. We worked with sandpaper, we worked with paint, we worked with washing and dyeing. You know when they washed their clothes, they used washboards. A lot of the petticoats were actually real petticoats from the period. And I chose some style lines earlier than when the play is set because these people had these clothes for a long period of time.

One of the major design issues for the costume designer in *Joe Turner's Come and Gone* is establishing a strong contrast between Herald Loomis and all the other characters. He destroys the harmony of the Juba with his entrance, just as he has unbalanced the household since his first appearance. The character is in a fury, and his visual presence is a critical part of his disruptive force.

CANDICE CAIN: When Loomis walked into that room, I wanted him to suck up everybody's energy, every bit of energy that was in there. The playwright says he comes in a black coat, but you have to find out why that is. All those layers that he wears. There's almost an ecclesiastical feel, and his coat is so solid and so dark and so mysterious. And then that hat with the five-inch brim.

Loomis is the only character in black; the other characters wear a variety of lighter and brighter colors—blues, greens, and browns. Loomis is wearing large, heavy pieces of clothing that hide the outline of his body. His shape is that of the huge coat and the broad hat. The clothing of the other characters is much more formfitting, suggesting that these are ordinary human beings. They also have much more visible details on their clothes—ruffles, buttons, suspenders—giving them a smaller-scale presence. Nothing breaks the line of Loomis's silhouette. Visually, when Loomis is not onstage, all the other characters emerge as individuals. When Loomis enters, the other characters become a group.

The Lighting Design

The **lighting designer,** Jim Sale, had much to do with creating the atmosphere for the Juba sequence. Slowly, as the characters start to dance and shout, the lights change from the warm, realistic light of the kitchen to a strange, moody light, casting strong shadows. The lights for the Juba build gradually so that the audience becomes aware of the shifting mood but not the

JOE TURNER'S COME AND GONE

JOE TURNER'S COME AND GONE

The costume designer **Candice Cain** begins her work by sketching ideas for the costumes of the characters. The silhouette of each character emerges from the sketches. The top costume sketches are for Jeremy Furlow *(left)* and Herald Loomis *(right)*. Following discussions with the director and the other designers, sketches are developed into detailed color renderings, accompanied by fabric swatches that indicate the texture and pattern of the different fabrics that will make up each costume.

mechanics. But then, on Loomis's entrance, the lights shift instantly to the bright, realistic light.

> **JIM SALE:** It's almost like he came in and flipped on a light switch, his energy came in so strong.

The designers work continuously with the director and the actors to create a coherent interpretation of the playwright's work. They create images in space, using materials that add layers of meaning to the images created by the actors. Their work goes far beyond illustrating time and place. All the design areas contribute to visual metaphors that define the world of the play. The warmth of Bertha's kitchen juxtaposed

with the imposing Pittsburgh skyline of factory smokestacks sets the stage for the struggles of the characters to find a place for themselves. Shadows contrast with the light as Herald Loomis emerges from the dark clothes—in which he hides himself and which weigh him down—to embrace a reborn, expansive sense of himself.

CONCLUSION: HISTORY AND MEANING IN *JOE TURNER'S COME AND GONE*

At the beginning of the chapter we introduced August Wilson as a dramatic historian. In examining Wilson's sources, we outlined the history of African Americans that forms the background for

This photograph of the first entrance of Herald Loomis demonstrates the way the heavy, severe costume contributes to the power of the character's appearance.

the play, a history that includes forced labor and migration. Within the play itself, however, Wilson presents an understanding of history that goes beyond the facts of the chain gang and the movement of African Americans to the urban areas of the North. That history is built from the actions of all the characters, as each searches for what is most precious in life and what has been lost. Multiple stories are told, and so what we might call a multidimensional view of history emerges from the play. This multidimensional vision of history begun in the text by Wilson is given physical shape in production by the imaginative work of the actors, director, and designers.

The Quest for Self

The central action of the play is Herald Loomis's search for himself, which is connected to Bynum's search for the "shiny man." In fact, what they seek is the same. By the end of the play, Loomis becomes what his name suggests. He becomes the "luminous," shiny man of Bynum's vision from act 1. Together, the quests of Loomis and Bynum can be seen to represent a large movement from slavery to freedom that suggests both the hundreds of years of American slavery and the internal journey of the individual. Herald Loomis cannot begin his life until he finds a way to cut the ties that bind him, to cleanse himself of the pollution of slavery. This he does symbolically by cutting himself with a knife at the end of the play and bleeding for himself. He has regained the song of himself, a "song of self-sufficiency."

Bynum cannot die "a happy man, a man who done left his mark on life" until he helps bring about the liberation of Herald Loomis that transforms him into the shiny man. A celebration of freedom echoes in the final line of the play, which is spoken by Bynum: "Herald Loomis, you shining! You shining like new money!"

Family and Inheritance: The Way from the Past to the Future

This movement toward freedom and affirmation is the overarching history that the play expresses. But this history of the journey out of slavery is framed by the views of Seth, the northern African American born in freedom; and of the People Finder, Rutherford Selig, who is the descendant of slave traders. The house where the play takes place belongs to Seth, a man born free, unburdened by the baggage of slavery. His history is tied to a father who could leave him the inheritance of a house and a strong sense of himself, in spite of the fact that he is still unable to start his own business.

Seth fears the decency of his house, his history, will be compromised by the turmoil that Loomis brings with him. He rejects Loomis even though

in exploratory theatre forms, sees the actor-audience relationship as a matter of trust:

> If I as an actor invest myself to the best of my ability in the work I have chosen to present—if I give it my best energy—then there's a chance that the audience can trust what is going on on stage. If I hold back, if I sit in judgment on myself or the material or the audience, then there is less chance that the audience is going to be justified in trusting and therefore joining the experience. If the actor is willing to go through some kind of transmutation, then the audience can, too.[2]

Frequently the actor's presence is described as a kind of double or triple existence. On the stage the actor is always present in his or her own person. In addition to this elemental self, the actor creates a character who has his or her own boundaries separate from those of the actor's own person. The performer projects a double representation of self and character. A third layer of the actor's presence might be considered a critical facility that the actor uses to step back from the performance and view it from the audience's perspective, making adjustments and modifications as necessary. BW Gonzalez, who played Mattie Campbell in *Joe Turner's Come and Gone*, describes the actor's state of mind as one of "hyperawareness."[3] Stephen Spinella, who played Prior in *Angels in America* at the Eureka Theatre, at the Mark Taper Forum, and on Broadway, discussed in Chapter 10, says that he is always aware of his own presence on the stage and the presence of the audience:

> I am absolutely, completely conscious of the audience. I feel what they are doing. I'm completely conscious of what's going on in my body. It's the height of reality. I actually feel as though I'm suspended above myself

When Anna Deavere Smith performs, she brings a whole community of people with her: people who find themselves divided by crisis. Here she performs one of the characters from *Twilight: Los Angeles,* which presents the upheaval of the 1992 Los Angeles riots in response to police brutality. Although only Smith is actually present on the stage, the people of Los Angeles speak through her. Smith plays as many as thirty different characters, based on people she has interviewed, simply by changing a costume piece and her attitude. She portrays old and young, female and male, black and white. She finds the essence of her characters in what she calls their "speech rhythms." "The sections of the interviews I repeat onstage, word for word, are those where people have come into a greater understanding of themselves. I'm not just repeating the words, I'm re-enacting a slight lift in consciousness. My re-enactment, slightly, ever so slightly, lifts my own consciousness. That's the only way I know how to learn."[4]

or in back of myself and my body. Everything is moving and doing exactly what it should be doing. And I'm saying to myself, "Now do this," making little tiny artistic choices.[5]

The actor commands the attention of the audience by bringing concentrated and explosive energy onto the stage. The actor brings the stage space to life and sweeps the audience up

Summary of the Actor's Responsibilities

- To study the text
- To memorize lines and blocking quickly
- To bring new ideas to the rehearsal process on a daily basis
- To work openly with the director and other actors
- To be creative in rehearsal
- To constantly refine and adjust character development
- To work with consistent high energy
- To maintain health and flexibility of voice and body
- To sustain freshness in performance and execute repeated performances at a consistent level of quality

in the vitality of the performance. This energy is part of the actor's charisma. In this respect, the actor is like an athlete or a rock star. For the actor, the energy may be less overtly displayed than for a football receiver leaping to make a catch or a popular singer dancing in front of the microphone. But high-voltage energy is present nonetheless, and the audience senses the electricity generated by the actor's presence.

Because of the unique nature of live performance—with the very real connection between performer and audience—the actor receives energy from the audience just as the audience is energized by the actor's presence. For BW Gonzalez, the energy generated by the audience contributes directly to her readiness to begin the play.

> Before I say my first line, once I feel the energy of the audience, I feel perfectly at home on the stage.[6]

Sean McNall, who recently played Hamlet, believes Shakespeare intended a personal relationship between Hamlet and the audience to be an essential part of the play, particularly in the soliloquies such as the one presented in the photograph on page 117:

> In *Hamlet* you reach out to the audience and you cast the audience in a certain way so you know to whom you are speaking and the reason why you need to address them at this moment. With this particular part, the audience became a kind of conscience, a touchstone. Having the audience on my side was of great importance. But I had to assume that they weren't simply on my side. So when I had the opportunity to reach out to them, I was always making a case. Suddenly, I had all this different energy coming at me.[7]

Stephen Spinella sees the audience energy as a major catalyst for his performance:

> The theatrical event requires the overwhelming focus of the audience. The actors, who have acquired that attention through control of the space and the moment, have power, and if the muse is with them, that power makes them soar.[8]

The actor Heather Robison, whose photograph appears on page 124, sees the audience as the final defining factor in the theatre event:

> The play doesn't work without the audience. That's when the play first lives. The audience is the last character of the play and you live and breathe with them.[9]

James Earl Jones also uses the analogy of flight to describe the propulsion that the audience brings to the performance:

> All acting, at its best, is about entering the stage and, spiritually, going to the edge of that cliff that is the proscenium, acknowledging there is an energy there, and like a sky-diver, pushing yourself off. You trust the thermal waves of energy that the audience is and you soar.[10]

THE ACTOR'S CRAFT

The vitality and talent of the actor are contained and shaped through the development of technique. We expect musicians to study and practice for many years to perfect skills on the piano, the cello, or the saxophone and to acquire subtleties of musicianship. Dancers, too, commit themselves to a training schedule of many hours a day to develop their physical abilities and artistry. In the same way, technique is essential to the actor working on the stage.

We can easily summarize the skills that most actors work to achieve and maintain. The vocal technique of the actor involves the ability to control and project the voice, to speak with richness of tone and nuance of expression, to enunciate with clarity at all times, to use dialects and accents with authenticity, to maintain a healthy voice that doesn't succumb to overuse, to give the language of Shakespeare or August Wilson its own style and rhythm, to speak for the characters and the playwright with authority and imagination. Physical technique allows the actor to move with grace; to command the stage space; to change posture, gestures, and body rhythms to create a range of characters; to present a sense of period style; to perform at a high level of intensity every day; to achieve the appropriate degree of relaxation and freedom from tension; to dance or juggle or walk on stilts.

However, performance skills alone do not make an actor. The words *alchemy* and *magic* are frequently used to describe the way the actor animates the skills of performance and gives life to a dramatic text or situation. Analogy is often used to describe acting because it is difficult to define the actor's process with precision. First, many forces intervene: the text, the director, the other actors, the rehearsal structure and duration, the playing space. Second, acting is such a personal and individual endeavor that it can be impossible to identify with certainty what has taken place internally to produce the result that the audience sees. Some choices are conscious; some are the result of intuitive responses to the text or the rehearsal situation. To investigate the components of the actor's work, we begin with the phases the actor goes through before arriving at a performance in front of an audience: the audition, individual preparation for the role, and the rehearsal.

THE WORK OF THE ACTOR
Competing for Roles: The Audition

One of the harshest and must grueling aspects of the actor's profession is the **audition.** Acting is a highly competitive business. There are many more actors and aspiring actors than there are acting opportunities at every level of theatre and film

The actors warm up in rehearsal for a production of *Apollo* directed by Nancy Keystone at Portland Center Stage in 2009. The actors perform a complex sequence of exercises that build stamina and flexibility and also provide a way for them to connect to the images in the play and physically and emotionally to one another. One of the cast members, Richard Gallegos, explains: "The warm-up brings us into the rehearsal room, into a collective energy, and it establishes a common vocabulary. It encompasses the body, the breath, and the psyche. It completely makes us a unit."[11]

The professional actor is a kind of magician who can do what we, the audience, cannot. Bill Irwin has an extensive background in mime and dance that also includes studying at the Clown College of Ringling Brothers Barnum and Bailey Circus. In fact, he began his acting career as a clown with the Pickle Family Circus. He then began to develop his own magical "new vaudeville" pieces, such as *Largely New York* (1989) shown here, that have no spoken text and depend on the broad, comic physicality of the actor to communicate.

production, in part because of the passion that actors feel about their work and in part because of the large rewards for the few "stars." To enter the competition for roles or places in training programs, actors must participate in auditions.

The audition allows directors and casting directors to see how different actors may fill a certain role or to see which actors complement each other as a group to make an **ensemble.** Because auditions are usually set up to screen a large number of people, the actors are allotted very little time to convince those making the casting decisions of their "rightness" for the part and the depth of their talent. For example, the Yale School of Drama auditions 900 aspiring actors for its graduate training program. Of those 900, only 16 students are offered places. Likewise, hundreds of dancers and singers may audition for the roles in the chorus of a Broadway musical, and smaller theatres attract scores of actors to their auditions.

Furthermore, auditions may call for unique combinations of talents. Susan Stroman auditioned actors for both the recent revival of *Oklahoma!* (1999) and the new production of *The Producers* (2001). For *Oklahoma!* the actors had to sing and dance and then do monologue. For *The Producers* they also had to be able to tell jokes. Richard Gallegos, who appears as the Ghost of the Prisoner of

Sean McNall is a young actor who won an Obie (Off Broadway) award in 2008 for sustained excellence in performance. He is shown here playing Hamlet in the Pearl Theatre's 2007 production directed by Shep Sobel. McNall has been a member of the Pearl Theatre's resident acting company since 2003, which reflects his goal of being an actor in an ongoing repertory company rather than participating in a continuous sequence of auditions. "What I don't like about the way the business of theatre works is that every production and every performance, particularly in New York, is an audition for the next performance. Some people are able to be creative with the thrill of that. But I think that is a detriment to the creative spirit because that's where people find out what they're good at and then they craft and hone exactly what they're good at, in much the same way that we try to make the best "product." We turn ourselves into a product and we sell that product. This is the model that many of us work with and I'm just not attracted to that. So being in a company gives me this opportunity to be bad, to fail, to do something radically different for a change. Time and time again, that is rewarding."[12]

Camp Dora in the photograph of *Apollo* on page 131, recalls a memorable audition experience:

> For six years I did the *Wild Wild Wild West Stunt Show* at Universal Studios. When I auditioned, I didn't know what I was getting myself into. I thought they wanted me to tumble and do a couple of cartwheels. They took us into this big warehouse at Universal Studios. There were about 300 of us. They unveiled this huge platform that was about twenty feet high and there was a big fall pad. They wanted us to climb up there and do a forward fall. I was scared out of my mind. The majority of them were actual stunt men. Somehow I weaseled myself into this audition and made the cut. I was there and I just had to breathe in. I remember climbing the ladder and saying to myself, "waiting tables, stunt show, waiting tables . . ." and the next thing I knew, my body was in the air and I did it and I got the job. It was crazy.[13]

Directors pride themselves on being able to recognize almost instantly the qualities that they seek for a certain role. Gordon Davidson, artistic director of the Mark Taper Forum, says, "I have a feeling within a minute of the audition that you know whether you're in the presence of talent or not."[14] The composer and lyricist Stephen Sondheim can judge singing ability in sixteen measures, or even in eight or four bars of a song.[15] This tendency toward immediate judgment puts enormous pressure on the actor in the audition to deliver a knockout performance. Actors, in fact, study auditioning techniques as part of their career preparation and constantly work to hone their auditioning skills.

Some auditions may involve the presentation of set pieces that the actors have had a chance to study and prepare in detail in advance of the audition. Actors perform monologues or songs of their own choosing for graduate training programs, repertory theatre, or summer stock opportunities—all situations that require actors to take multiple roles. Actors try to choose

Sage Howard and Brandon Zerr-Smith audition for a production of *Anna in the Tropics* at Lewis and Clark College with scripts in hand. They receive feedback from the director before reading the scene again. Actors are strongly encouraged to study the full text before auditioning for a play.

one of the most important factors that directors try to ascertain in the audition:

> Directors want to come away from an audition knowing that they're going to be able to work with the actor, and that the actor is imaginative enough and well-trained enough to handle different directions. They also need to get a feel for what the actor will be like to work with for an extended period of time.[16]

material from well-respected plays and musicals, but also material that directors may not have already seen hundreds of times. The pieces also need to be well suited to the actor and show the range of the actor's abilities.

A dramatic audition consisting of two contrasting monologues is frequently limited to four minutes. A singing audition may be limited to thirty-two measures of music. In that scant time, actors must show their understanding of the text, their speech or singing skills, their energy, and their ability to reach an audience. The actor must jump into the heart of the character and the play and deliver the lines or the song with all the passion and intensity of a performance, usually without the help of a supporting cast, set, or costumes. The audition also reveals how much training the actors have, their stage presence, and their openness. Jack Bowdan, who casts for Broadway and television, emphasizes that the ability to take direction is

Some auditions focus on cold readings of scenes from the play that is going into production. In this situation, with minimal preparation, actors must read from the script, often with a stage manager or some other member of the production staff who is not an actor as their scene partner. The producer Stuart Ostrow believes that although the cold reading is "the best of a worst lot," its benefits outweigh the drawbacks:

> What it does first and foremost is tell you about the intelligence quotient of the actor. And I would always opt for an intelligent actor, even though he may be wrong for the part. In the creation of a play, that cold reading leads to an understanding about the actor's capacity for imagination and creativity.[17]

If the actor gets through the initial phase of the audition and is called back for further readings, then the process opens up in interesting ways,

James Earl Jones transformed his physical appearance to play the boxer Jack Jefferson in *The Great White Hope* (1967) at the Arena Stage in Washington, D.C. The physical training involved in preparing for the role of a boxer also provided psychological insight into the character. James Earl Jones and Jane Alexander, shown here, also re-created their stage roles for the film version of Howard Sackler's play.

depending on the type of production and the producing company. Interviews, group improvisations, and extended readings with other potential cast members may all be part of the "callback." But first, actors must show that they have enough talent, skill, flexibility, and commitment to stand out from the crowd. No matter how stressful or disappointing the audition process may be, all actors must struggle through the ordeal of auditioning if they are to work. Tamu Gray, who played Bertha in *Joe Turner's Come and Gone*, summarizes the feelings of many actors when she says, "You must raise an amazing amount of courage to go out and audition, but that makes you even stronger because you do it."[18]

Preparing for the Role

When a part has been secured, actors may go to extraordinary lengths to prepare for their roles. They might read histories and biographies or study real-life situations, or they might immerse themselves in the actual circumstances of characters' lives before they try to re-create or interpret those circumstances on the stage or in front of the camera. Sometimes actors transform themselves physically, losing or gaining weight or participating in intense physical training to reshape their bodies or learn difficult physical skills.

James Earl Jones is an actor known for his distinguished performances in the plays of Shakespeare, the South African Athol Fugard,

ARTISTIC FOUNDATIONS •••

The Necessary Skills and Talents of the Actor

- Interest in human nature
- Keen observation
- A good memory
- Concentration
- Imagination
- The drive to appear on the stage in front of an audience
- The ability to create characters and interpret dramatic situations
- A strong, expressive voice
- An expressive face and body
- High energy and physical stamina
- The ability to work openly as part of a group process
- Discipline

and August Wilson, as well as for his film work, including the famous voice of Darth Vader in *Star Wars*. To play the role of Jack Jefferson, a boxer, in *The Great White Hope*, by Howard Sackler, Jones undertook the training of a fighter:

> I didn't have the bulk of a fighter but I had the sinewiness, the flexibility. In Washington D.C., when we were at the Arena Stage, I had a trainer named Bill Terry who was a former fighter. He took me through the life of a boxer-in-training. Every morning you get up, you run a certain number of miles, you go to the gymnasium, you consume certain kinds of liquids and foods that are good for strength and endurance.

Jones then shaved his beard and his head as part of his mental and physical preparation:

> At this point the physical training I had been doing came into focus and I was a different person. By then I had learned, with

the director Ed Sherin's encouragement, to walk and behave physically, unconsciously like an athlete, which I'm not. By the time I finished the run of the play and the film, I hated the training. I was not good at diets and I wanted to be free to eat what I thought my body was crying out for in terms of sustenance.[19]

The Rehearsal Process

In Chapter 3, we reviewed the work of the actors as they rehearsed *Joe Turner's Come and Gone*. We saw them studying the text, memorizing lines, seeking the characters' motivation, developing the characters' relationships, rehearsing blocking patterns, and finding the speech rhythms that would give authenticity to their characters and bring passion and eloquence to the playwright's words.

What happens in rehearsal is a very intricate process of give-and-take between the actors and the director. For a production to have vitality and originality, the rehearsal must be a time of exploration. Discoveries must be made about the characters and their relationships. Staging ideas are tested and discarded. Rhythms and pacing are built and adjusted.

THE ACTOR'S COMMITMENT   Acting is extraordinarily hard work. It is a physical and mental process that requires great physical stamina and high energy. Actors must be able to remember their lines, work creatively, and be open and receptive to one another and the director. They must come to rehearsal well rested and fully alert, able to concentrate intensely on the work at hand, whether it is repeating a sword fight many times or discovering the intimate rhythms of a love scene. At each rehearsal, actors must be prepared to try out new approaches to line readings and blocking or to refine choices that have already been made. Rehearsals demand at least as much from the actors as performances; and, for some, rehearsals are the most satisfying part of the production process.

In *Hamlet,* the actor playing Ophelia must find a way to express the character's desperation resulting from the death of her father and her rejection by Hamlet. But the reactions of the other characters are essential to building the belief that she is, as Claudius, says "divided from herself," and in her brother Laertes's words, "a document in madness." In this photo, Laertes reacts with dismay as he tries to comprehend his sister Ophelia's incoherent speeches. Laertes is played by David L. Townsend and Ophelia by Jolly Abraham in the 2007 Pearl Theatre production of *Hamlet* directed by Shep Sobel.

Kathleen Chalfant, who played multiple roles in *Angels in America,* including the part of Ethel Rosenberg, describes rehearsals as a way of pulling a role or a text apart in order to put it back together again:

> In order to learn to act you must take apart something that happens faster than thought, break it into its component parts, and then put it back together. That's also what rehearsal is, breaking down a speech or a reaction, and then getting it close to the speed at which a human being actually does it. Quite often, plays are just a little slower than life because you've

added a step, the breaking down. The trick is to act as quickly as you think, which is not necessarily a function of speed. When you're doing it properly, it often feels as though you have all the time in the world. Then you can allow yourself to be entirely taken, with no conscious control. That's what being in the moment means. In order to be prepared to give yourself over to the moment, you have to have done all the work beforehand: knowing the words backwards and forwards, knowing where you're supposed to stand, and more importantly, knowing what the character is doing at every turn and why she does it.[20]

ACTION AND REACTION   In rehearsal, actors discover their actions and their reactions. Much of their work depends on playing actions that communicate a passionate expression of life's defining moments. The action may be contained in a speech such as Hamlet's "To be, or not to be, that is the question," or Bynum's story of the "shiny man." The action may be physicalized through gesture—for example, when the actor playing Herald Loomis cuts himself with the knife or when the actor playing Juliet drinks the sleeping potion.

But as important as the actors' actions are the actors' reactions. Much of what actors create comes through reaction, through response, through seeing and believing. Actors bring a sense of the environment onto the stage; they feel the weather—the cold wind blowing through the cracks of a dilapidated house or the stifling heat of an urban summer. They experience the weariness of the passing of time, see the opulence of a ballroom or the emptiness of a Beckett landscape. Most of all, through reaction, actors give reality to the characters of the other actors onstage. They make these characters believable for the audience by the way that they watch and register the truth of what they have seen. They recognize loss, and they recognize triumph. They feel a threat and respond to an invitation. The art of acting has to do with creative expression and with the construction of belief.

IMPROVISATION   **Improvisation** is a useful rehearsal method for enhancing belief and creating imaginative actions. It is used with increasing frequency in many different kinds of production situations. Improvisation can be defined as spontaneous invention that goes beyond the scripted material to explore aspects of character or situation. Actors may do group improvisations at the beginning of rehearsals as a warm-up. They may also use improvisation to solve acting problems or to generate staging ideas. Improvisation is also an important method for establishing creative rapport between actors. Most acting students now have considerable exposure to improvisation as a fundamental part of their training.

One of the most common improvisations involves playing a scene in the actors' own words instead of the playwright's scripted words. This technique allows actors to work through scene content and to explore areas of the characters' relationships. For example, there may be an argument between two characters that lasts two minutes or less in the actual play. The two actors involved might then improvise a much longer argument to explore the sources of the tension between their characters. Their improvisation might even involve extreme physical interactions to help shape the verbal exchange. The scripted

In the South African playwright Athol Fugard's play, *Sorrows and Rejoicings*, Cynthia Martells and John Glover re-create their characters' love for each other, even though the character played by Glover has recently died. The actors must create a sense of the present and the past simultaneously. They must bring the intimacy of their relationship to life for the audience, which for one character is a memory and for the other the reason for his presence. *Sorrows and Rejoicings* was directed by Athol Fugard for the Mark Taper Forum in 2002.

argument might be set at a dining room table or in a court of law, where restrained behavior is expected, but to get to the strong feelings underlying the situation, the two actors might improvise some physical interaction while saying their lines. They might begin a tug-of-war or shoving match to heighten their responses to each other. The actors then use the intensity generated by the physicalization of the conflict in their verbal exchanges when they play the argument as scripted in the more confined situation.

Improvisation can also take the form of a game. Actors often invent situations in which, for example, the weather, the age of the characters, or the nature of the relationships keeps changing. Actors also improvise stories in which one person begins with a single word or a sentence and then the other actors add pieces to the developing narration. Improvisation can also involve invented languages in which the actors communicate for long periods of time through made-up words. Susan Stroman, whose work as a director and choreographer is discussed in Chapter 11, on musical theatre, has dancers who have no lines to speak create "back stories" to give each of them more character detail and a sense of individual development when they dance their roles.

Improvisation is a liberating technique for actors that encourages spontaneity and quickness and can deepen relationships with the other actors in a production. Most of all, by immersing themselves completely in the given circumstances, actors use improvisation to increase their commitment to the truth of the situation.

THE REHEARSAL SCHEDULE In **equity theatres** (theatres with more than 100 seats in which all actors are paid according to a union contract), rehearsals last eight hours a day. At the Oregon Shakespeare Festival, which must rehearse several plays at once because actors perform in repertory, rehearsals are held in four-hour units. Actors may rehearse two different plays in one day or rehearse for one play during the day and perform a different play during the evening. In **equity waiver theatres** (theatres with fewer than 100 seats that are not governed by union regulations), rehearsals may last several hours each evening after actors finish their other jobs.

The standard rehearsal process for a play begins with the reading aloud of the script by the company. Sometimes the actors read their parts; sometimes the director reads to the actors. The objective of the reading is for all the actors to hear the words as a starting point for their work. The actors are neither expected nor encouraged to have defined their characters at the first reading. Decisions made too early in the process may impede the work to be done. First readings are not meant to be performances and can sometimes seem very flat.

The work done after the first reading is usually referred to as "table work." It involves the kind of discussion, questioning, and rereading of the play that we observed in the early rehearsals of *Joe Turner's Come and Gone*. During the table work, the director might present the actors with background materials as well as establish the directorial concept or interpretation of the play that will be pursued.

COLLABORATION WITH THE DESIGNERS Sometimes the designers participate during this phase by showing the actors a model of the set and costume sketches, or "renderings." The participation of the designers helps the actors to imagine the world of the play being constructed and contributes to their own work on their characters. The costume designer's interpretation of a character in terms of silhouette, color, weight and texture of fabric, and accessories has enormous implications for the actors' own work in defining character. The presentation of the designers' work gives the actors a sense of the visual style of the production and makes clear the physical realities and practical requirements of the set and costumes: how many steps they will have to navigate, how long a skirt will be, what colors their character will wear. Joe Mantello, who played the role of Louis

For *The Belle's Strategem* produced in 2005 at the Oregon Shakespeare Festival under the direction of Davis McCallum, Heather Robison played a character that she says "asked her to be three different people." The play originally written by Hannah Cowley in 1780 is about views of love and marriage and involves the central character disguising herself to test the heart of the man she hopes to marry. Robison says the role "pulled on every bit of training I've ever had, from movement and speech and text analysis to dance and all of my circus training." Robison collaborated closely with the costume designer Deborah Dryden and found the costume designs were essential to the shift in her character from a proper member of society to a "gauche, country bumpkin," appearing in a petticoat, "with all of her formality and the preconceived ideas of what a lady should be in that time period stripped away. I found it very freeing to wear something so risqué and dangerous. Then she has permission to do anything."[21]

in *Angels in America*, found costume choices to be an important part of the foundation for his character work:

> Louis is always looking to be judged. Tony Kushner, the playwright, and I always saw Louis wearing oversized boy clothes that he could disappear into when things got hard, when he was being judged. . . . Louis is swimming in his clothes. They make him look like he just wouldn't grow up. . . . In rehearsal I always wore an overcoat or a scarf that I made sure was too big for me.[22]

Early on in the rehearsal process, the actors will start wearing **rehearsal costumes.** Doing so allows them to practice with the limitations created by their particular costume pieces

Some actor training programs teach forms of Asian martial arts in combination with a movement vocabulary influenced by the kabuki or nō theatres of Japan, the Beijing Opera, or Indian kathakali. Eastern approaches to performance may be combined with Western dramatic literature—for example, in kabuki productions of Shakespeare.

Acting in *Apollo*

Drawing on new directions in actor training and theatre production, the director Nancy Keystone and a group of actors have formed a theatre company, Critical Mass, to develop theatre pieces in which movement is as important to the performance as the text. Nancy Keystone explains her goals for the staging of *Apollo*, their most recent production:

> Theatre is a very physical medium. But most of the time what we see is people acting from the neck up. The body is forgotten. Actors as living beings in front of a living audience have great potential for physical expression. One of the goals of *Apollo* was to create a piece in which movement told as much of the story as anything else, to present information—narrative, aesthetic, thematic information—nonverbally. A life lived onstage is a full and extreme life. An actor will do extraordinary things as a character living the events of the play. When we are creating and developing the piece, what I do to prepare, since there is no script, is to write a foundation for the play through exercises. The exercises explore physical states and psychic states which we believe are at the core of the story we're trying to tell.[25]

For this 2009 production, the actors used their bodies to convey actions such as astronauts floating weightless in space, living characters haunted by the dead, or confrontations over civil rights. Gestures combined with simple props constructed themes through their repetition from character to character, such as the use of handkerchiefs to wipe hands and consciences clean or the wrapping and unwrapping of bundles of ashes to recall lives lost to violence. Sometimes the actors played characters exchanging dialogue; sometimes they were part of an abstracted choreographic sequence. Some scenes were emotionally charged; some were parody. Each of the twelve actors played multiple roles and they needed to shift instantly between characters and between different uses of their acting skills. In order to develop their approach for *Apollo*, Keystone and the actors spent eight years studying research materials and exploring ideas through exercises and improvisations that were distilled and refined to become the scenes of the play.

Space flight is celebrated in Part 1 of *Apollo* as the characters imagine a rocket trip to the moon. The weightlessness of the astronauts is created only through the actors balancing upside down on plain metal chairs with their floating arms and legs magnified by the light in this 2009 production at Portland Center Stage, directed by Nancy Keystone. The actors are Richard Gallegos, Andy Hirsch, Jeffrey Johnson, Nick Santoro, and Christopher Shaw.

••• IN CONTEXT

Apollo: Thematic Development

Apollo, an epic theatre piece composed in three parts, develops themes rather than building a tightly knit plot. The themes are connected to key aspirations in American history: the desire to conquer space and the struggle for civil rights. Geographically, the production moves between Germany in the 1930s and 1940s and the United States in the 1950s and 1960s. But ultimately the focus is on Hunts-ville, Alabama, where German scientists and engineers were brought following World War II to help develop the American space program and where African Americans were engaged in attempts to integrate public institutions and secure voting rights. The desire to glorify human ingenuity through sending rockets to the moon is seen against the desire to honor human dignity through fighting for equal rights. A consuming quest for power is seen against a consuming quest for freedom. The text for *Apollo* is drawn from historical documents, as well as the improvisation of the actors and the scripting of the director. The production depends on elaborate uses of sound and music, projected slides and film, and choreographed stage movement, in addition to spoken text and character action.

Part 1: *Lebensraum*

Part 1 celebrates a fantasy view of rocket history with glimpses of the development of German tech-nology before and during World War II and America's love affair with space flight. Werner von Braun, a key character, appears with both Hitler and Walt Disney as he sells first Germany and then the United States on his vision to reach the moon.

Part 2: *Gravity*

The mood of the play shifts, as Part 2 uncovers the history of the slave labor used by the Germans to build their V-2 rockets and the war crimes of Germans brought to the United States to satisfy America's desire to win the space race and put a man on the moon. U.S. prosecutor Eli Rosenbaum confronts German engineer Arthur Rudolph about his past, as they examine the contents of some of the 3,000 file boxes that form the set for Part 2 of the play. The revelations bring to light the way the U.S. government put its determination to succeed in space ahead of the nation's laws.

Part 3: *Liberation*

The Nazi "rocketeers" begin their work in Huntsville, Alabama at the same time that the momentum of the civil rights struggle is increasing, with attempts to integrate lunch counters and then the Uni-versity of Alabama. Although many historical figures appear in the play, such as Werner Von Braun, Governor George Wallace, Robert Kennedy, and the Reverend Ralph Abernathy, the play focuses, in the end, on a fictional character, David McCadden. He becomes one of the first black students to integrate the University of Alabama and eventually joins NASA to work on the Apollo space program.

One of the characters played by Richard Gallegos in *Apollo,* the Ghost of the Prisoner from Camp Dora, is seen kneeling on the table in the photograph on page 131. This charac-ter represents the many people who worked at forced labor building rockets for the Nazis dur-ing World War II. In *Apollo* the "Prisoner" has returned from the dead to personify the past of a German rocket scientist, Arthur Rudolph, who faces deportation from the United States for war

An American prosecutor, Eli Rosenbaum, one of the characters played by Andy Hirsch, interrogates Arthur Rudolph, one of the characters played by Christopher Shaw, about his past as director of an underground factory in Germany which built V-2 rockets in *Apollo* (2009). The Ghost of the Prisoner of Camp Dora, Richard Gallegos, represents the atrocities of the past, which have been evaded while Rudolph was a leader in the American space program.

crimes. Richard Gallegos describes the external process involved in developing the presentation of his character:

> In the beginning Nancy Keystone told me, "you're not reliving these moments; you are now of the other world. You are drifting by. You are here for a purpose and then you leave. You are simply telling, so you can't have too much emotional connection."
>
> I found the physicality of the character first, the master gesture, the voice. The center of him is the core of my body, just above the pelvis. I wanted to find a gliding quality for him physically. So when he's walking, it's almost like he's moving through space without even touching the ground. He's just an energy that is hovering and not really quite in time movement-wise with everybody else.[26]

A synopsis of *Apollo* is included in this chapter for reference, since we discuss this production here and in chapters to come.

Whatever the style of the play, the actor's process is both highly individual and subject to fluctuation. Actors usually combine various techniques in their work, and there may be many

subtle shifts in the degree of actual emotional engagement in the role at various stages of the rehearsal and performance process. Actors constantly integrate various sources of information and inspiration into their creation of a role. All the work focuses on the creation of stage life that is original and truthful and that the actor can play with maximum conviction. No matter what the approach, good actors achieve complete concentration on the moment being played. As Valerie Spencer, a member of the *Apollo* cast, says:

> For me, I have to be completely in the now. Completely in the present, just in my body, on the stage, or backstage doing what I'm doing. I can't start thinking, "what if, what if, what if," or it will be a train wreck. If I'm changing my clothes, I'm listening to what's going on onstage. I can't be thinking ahead or daydreaming. I can't let my mind wander. I have to be completely focused on the task. It requires absolute concentration and focus and determination. A complete giving myself over to the ride.[27]

THE PERFORMANCE

The purpose of all the actor's training and all the work in rehearsal is to provide the foundation for performance. A well-rehearsed play provides the actor with the control and confidence to give a fully energized and completely detailed performance, to be open to audience responses

Mary-Louise Parker, seen here in *Dead Man's Cell Phone* by Sarah Ruhl (2007). Parker emphasizes that process is the way actors sustain the freshness of their work when doing a long run. "The idea that I've got a role completely doesn't fit in with my philosophy. It's never something to be fully arrived at. It's just something to experience, to keep flexing and testing and to grow with, rather than to fully find."[28]

and to make adjustments for the unexpected that always occurs with live performance. Sometimes the run of a play lasts a few weeks or a few months. Sometimes an actor may appear in the same play for years. The final, crucial element of the actor's work is finding ways to sustain the performance over the entire run no matter how long that may be.

THEATRE AND FILM

Far more than other theatre practitioners, actors working in the United States today frequently alternate between the theatre and film work. Bill Irwin and Anna Deavere Smith focus most of their energies on the theatre. But both have made a

number of films and, most recently, they appeared together in *Rachel, Getting Married*. Other prominent actors who appear in both theatre and film include Cate Blanchett, Billy Crudup, Charles Dutton, Laura Linney, Liam Neeson, Mary Louise Parker, Kevin Spacey, and Meryl Streep.

The difference between acting in the theatre and acting on film is usually described in terms of scale. In film acting, the camera comes to the actor. Actors then work to open their responses but not to enlarge them. In the theatre, the actor crosses a distance to reach the audience. The size of the performance must respond to the size of the stage and the auditorium. Stage actors need to contain their instincts to be expansive when they are working on a film, and film actors must increase their energy and the breadth of their response when they appear on the stage. Ray Ford, who appeared in *Apollo*, trained as a stage actor and then found he needed to acquire new techniques to act in film and television:

> For the theatre, my intensity needs to land at the back of the house. In a TV show, my intensity just needs to make it a few inches away from my face. So it's the same work, the same preparation, but the delivery is different. It took me two years in L.A. to learn how to do that.[29]

The film actor is aware at all times of the camera lens, both the width of the shot and the focus. Acting must be concentrated in the body parts seen by the camera—the face or a hand, for example, in a close-up. Film actors compose their actions and reactions in synchronization with the size and movement of the lens. Like so many other aspects of the actor's craft, working with the camera is a technical skill to be learned and practiced.

VALERIE SPENCER: In film you're playing to a lens and are always conscious of being watched and photographed; of how your image is being picked up; how you look and the angle of your head. You have to be considerate of that stuff because it's splayed on a huge wall.[30]

The director Lisa Peterson has set this 2008 production of Shakespeare's *A Midsummer Night's Dream*, produced by Hartford Stage, in the 1950s. In this scene, a group of local amateurs, "the mechanicals," are rehearsing a play to be presented for the court. The characters' professions have been re-interpreted through costuming to place them in modern times.

one knows is that he wrote a chain of words that have in them the possibility of giving birth to forms that are constantly renewed. There is no limit to the virtual forms that are present in a great text.[4]

time frame, or in the future. A production can follow Elizabethan staging practice that frankly acknowledges the presence of the audience, or it can use the convention of the "fourth wall" (an imaginary barrier between the actors and the audience across the front of the stage) to seal the characters in their own world. A director can choose to emphasize the central character's philosophical questioning or the struggles of power politics. In the words of Brook:

> Many years ago it used to be claimed that one must "perform the play as Shakespeare wrote it." Today the absurdity of this is more or less recognized: nobody knows what scenic form he had in mind. All that

And the plays of Anton Chekhov, for whom Stanislavsky created intricately realistic productions full of detailed properties and sound effects, could be interpreted with abstract settings that emphasize the symbolic content of the plays. Although some, including the playwright himself, have disagreed with Stanislavsky's interpretations of Chekhov's plays, Stanislavsky defined the position of the director as one who interprets the playwright's creation. Other directors have moved beyond the idea of collaboration with a playwright to view themselves as the primary creators of the theatrical event.

Peter Brook has done his own adaptation of *Hamlet,* in collaboration with Marie-Helene Estienne, in which he cut and rearranged the text. The entire play was performed by only eight actors, without intermission. In the Brook production, the play became even more tightly focused on Hamlet himself, played by Adrian Lester. The stage was defined only by an orange carpet with a few large stools and cushions moved around by the actors to provide a sense of the change of scenes.

Andrei Serban directed *The Cherry Orchard* in 1977 at Lincoln Center, New York. Although the actors are dressed in period costumes, Serban and the designer Santo Loquasto dispensed with the walls and most of the furnishings of realism that are evident in Stanislavsky's late-nineteenth-century production of another Chekhov play, *The Seagull,* shown on page 136. The house in which the characters live is suggested by a white rug and only a few pieces of furniture. Serban creates the idea that the characters' lives are suspended. The cherry orchard that defines the history of the family estate becomes a symbolic environment for the play's action.

The Visionary Director: Jerzy Grotowski

In 1959, sixty years after Stanislavsky began his work on *The Seagull,* Jerzy Grotowski, a Polish director, began an experimental theatre in Opole, Poland. Six years later, in 1965, Grotowski's Laboratory Theatre moved to the larger city of Wroclaw, Poland. Throughout its existence, the experimental Laboratory Theatre would be subsidized through state and city resources. Although the subsidy was hardly lavish, it did provide a level of basic support that

such an experimental company could not expect in the United States. The following discussion of Grotowski's theatre practice is based on his career in Poland, before he shifted the site of his work to the United States and then to Italy.

Like Stanislavsky, Grotowski was devoted to reforming actor training. But instead of employing Stanislavsky's internal acting system, aimed at producing the most naturalistic performance, Grotowski sought an approach to acting that would maximize the expressive power of the actor's total instrument. Grotowski wanted to

Adam Rapp directed the premiere production of his play, *American Sligo*, at the Rattlestick Playwrights Theater in New York in 2007. The play examines the family of a wrestler, "Crazy Train," at the end of his career. The cast includes actors Paul Sparks, Michael Chernus, and Guy Boyd with whom Rapp frequently works because of their continuing rapport.

that the actors know what they are doing, which is very different from telling them to stand or sit.[10]

The director Bertolt Brecht was outspoken about his theories of epic theatre as they applied to acting methods and scenic presentation. But in rehearsal he was famous for sitting quietly while the actors worked and making only brief suggestions when they had finished.

Describing the process the director uses is even more difficult than pinning down the process and methods that actors use to create roles and give performances. Directing is studied and discussed less than acting is. Far fewer people are involved as directors than as actors, and the path of the director is a highly individual one. We can identify only the kinds of tasks that a director must accomplish, and we can form an overview of the directing process by describing the approaches used by some prominent directors. Frequently, the views and the methods used by one director contradict those of another director.

There are four models of directorial approach that summarize the current status of the directing profession. The first two refer to approaches we have already discussed. The first model, the director who works in partnership with the playwright and the actors, was established by the duke of Saxe-Meiningen and Stanislavsky and is exemplified by the production of *Joe Turner's Come and Gone* studied in Chapter 3. Directors who follow the second model, using or creating a text to support their own visions, include Grotowski, Ping Chong, and Robert Wilson.

Two additional models demonstrate further possibilities for the director. In the third model, the director guides the work of a theatre collective. For example, Elizabeth LeCompte is a founding member and director of the Wooster Group, an experimental theatre company. The performances of the Wooster Group interweave materials from many sources, including play texts, autobiographies, poetry, letters, personal biographical contributions from the actors, and group improvisation. This theatre company creates its own material, but through a group process rather than through the view of a single director. This approach is often referred to as devised work. Although the material is generated collectively, LeCompte exerts authority in shaping the performance:

I like to run a tight ship. I like to have the final say, not so much because I want the power of it, but because otherwise I lose my way. These workers bring this material to me, and I sift and siphon through it. It isn't that some material is "better than other material." I use it when it links up to something very particular with me, when it extends my vision.[11]

The fourth model is a return to the earliest tradition of the theatre: playwrights who direct their own works. Adam Rapp is a playwright who believes his work on a play is not finished until he has directed the first production:

> I started writing in 1994, and I had a hunger to direct right away. I did the New York production of *Blackbird* (see page 169) and it was one of the few times I've ever felt that alive in my life. What I've found is, for me, directing is an extension of authorship. It's about preserving the play and illuminating what is on the page with the actors. I usually stay away from large concepts. It's about actors connecting and finding moments together, and finding the speed of the play. I find that when I'm a director, my plays improve because I've become a really rigorous audience advocate. I want them to be involved in every moment. Before, when I was simply the playwright in the room, I was like a 14-year-old misfit in the corner who was daydreaming about other things. I wasn't as good a re-writer. I wasn't as engaged. Now I find that when I'm in my third week of rehearsal, the work that we've done to rewrite or to tweak the work jumps up to another level. I look at the text that we take into the first day of rehearsal as a point of departure. Plays will find radically new shapes. I'm adventurous with discovering new things. I have great trust in the actors that I work with. They're some of the smartest people I've ever known. These wonderful actors are like detectives. When something is not working for them, they will tell me.[12]

For a production of *Iphigeneia* (1997) at the Court Theatre, the director JoAnne Akalaitis reset this Greek tragedy in contemporary times with the use of modern dress and the character of Iphigeneia telling her story over a hand held microphone. In the background, the chorus cleans the blood from the temple stairs.

THE DIRECTOR AT WORK
Choosing the Play

Directors usually have some choice about what they are going to direct, and they tend to choose plays they care deeply about. They choose plays that connect to their understanding of the world, plays that make sense to them. A play that is a good choice for one director may not work for another. A director may admire and enjoy a particular play and yet lack an inner understanding of the work that would lead to a successful production. Although some directors are hired for a theatre season for which the plays have already been selected, most theatre practitioners and producers recognize the importance of the connection between the director and the script. If the director is to interpret the world of the play for an audience, then the playwright's vision must appeal to the director's imagination and understanding of human nature.

JoAnne Akalaitis, a member of the experimental Mabou Mines for many years and a director in regional theatres, looks for an imagistic response to new material:

> If I don't see a picture in my mind when I read a script, I know that play is not for me. The first images are the most important. When I first read *Leonce and Lena*, I saw a road, a colored sky, the sun and I heard Terry Allen's

Summary of the Director's Responsibilities

- To choose the play
- To study the play and the historical context, possibly in collaboration with a dramaturg
- To develop a "concept" for the production in collaboration with the designers
- To audition and cast the actors
- To guide the work of the actors:

  To establish an acting style

  To block the play

  To clarify character development and the characters' relationships

  To build the play's rhythm in order to maximize audience involvement

- To maintain an atmosphere that is conducive to the creative work of all involved
- To guide the work of all participants to a timely and coherent readiness for performance

music. As far as content goes, I'm interested in history and social and political issues. I feel I have a responsibility to work in these areas.[13]

Peter Sellars, who moves back and forth between directing theatre and directing opera, is concerned about the opportunity for discovery:

It seems to me that drama is about the search for the unknown. . . . If somebody sends me a play and I understand it, I will never do it. Why spend six weeks in rehearsal? I can understand it just reading it. You need a play that you can't figure out and have to rehearse in order to discover it. I only embark on material that I feel is wide open at the end, when I don't know where the journey will end, don't know what the final production will look or feel like.[14]

Lloyd Richards, who directed the original productions of many of August Wilson's plays,

found that the beliefs articulated by Wilson's characters coincided with his own understanding of human nature. Richards says of reading the plays for the first time:

There were characters in the play that were well delineated. And the things that they were talking about, I believed. So the playwright, in a sense, was speaking for me as well as to me.[15]

Richards was drawn to Wilson's artistry in expressing a moral position: "He has a very deep sense of social responsibility. He is a repository of unlimited stories which reveal human experience."[16] And the rhythmic structure of the plays inspired Richards's directorial approach: "August Wilson is music. I directed all of his pieces as if they were music."[17]

When directors have a feel for certain material, they sometimes direct a play more than once. Libby Appel, who first directed *Macbeth* in 1987, felt compelled to return to it at the Oregon Shakespeare Festival in 2002 because she had come to a new understanding of this work.

I've always wanted to do it differently, in a way that would focus on the psychology of the event. I wanted to take it out of the spectacular epic and put it in a smaller space to concentrate on the thought processes of the characters.[18]

Since directing *Joe Turner's Come and Gone* at the Oregon Shakespeare Festival, Clinton Turner Davis has directed Wilson's play for the Milwaukee Repertory Theatre and the New Federal Theatre in New York City. Tisa Chang, the artistic director of the Pan Asian Repertory Theatre in New York, directed *And the Soul Shall Dance*, discussed in Chapter 8, twice and produced a third production over a period of fifteen years. She says that she is drawn to Yamauchi's work because of the truth she recognizes in the characters:

And the Soul Shall Dance is so special because it has very strong women's roles. Emiko is a woman who is utterly unfulfilled, unsatisfied,

In Part 2 of *Apollo* at Portland Center Stage in 2009, the actors search in the file boxes for evidence about the past of Arthur Rudolph. Three thousand boxes filled the stage and were moved by the actors to create the stage environment. All of the props used by the actors were discovered in the boxes. Andy Hirsch, standing center, plays the prosecutor, Eli Rosenbaum. Chris Shaw, seated with the magnifying glass, plays Arthur Rudolph. Valerie Spencer, holding the bundle of handkerchiefs, plays the daughter of Arthur Rudolph, and Jeffrey Johnson, standing with his back to the audience, plays the ghost of Werner von Braun. The director Nancy Keystone was also the scene designer for *Apollo;* the metaphoric use of the boxes informed both her work with the actors and her shaping of the space.

but has great yearnings, intellectual yearnings, artistic yearnings, and very deep feelings, emotional and sensual. There's nothing false, the sexuality, the brutality. Yamauchi really is the central figure and she was writing about issues that were very daring. *And the Soul Shall Dance* is also remarkable because it seems to speak to so many different people at once. We've had audiences, Italian, Jewish, all say, "This is my story."

The play is an actor's paradise. These roles are so meaty. And until then most of the roles for Asian actors on the American stage were abysmally stereotypical images.[19]

The Director's Initial Response to the Play

Just as actors go through a process of discovering the essence or inner life of the characters they will play, so directors go through their own process of discovering the essence or inner life of the play. They build their own understanding of the world of the play before they attempt to communicate their responses to other members of the production team. Directors use many approaches for exploring a play's images, textures, rhythms, characters, and possible meanings. Directors analyze characters' motivation, but they also listen to music and look at paintings. They study thematic developments, and they also read history. They travel to cities and even foreign countries in search of landscapes or ways of life or performance traditions that may serve the needs of the production. The directorial process is analytical, but it is also intuitive and imaginative.

Creating Metaphors

As a director approaches a play, he or she begins a process of discovering a metaphor, or image, that will translate the ideas of the play into a stage language. The metaphor is a way of expressing the most compelling ideas of the play in a concentrated form that will become a guide for the work of all the theatre artists involved in the production. A metaphor is an analogy, or comparison, a symbolic way of expressing the action of the play. The founding director of the American Conservatory Theatre in San Francisco, William Ball, emphasizes the need for a single, strong metaphor to guide the work on the production:

> I have learned from my own experiences and from my observations of the work of other directors that the more clear and striking the metaphor, the more unified and powerful the production.[20]

Building metaphors was central to the director Nancy Keystone's work on the production of *Apollo* that was introduced in Chapter 4. One of the subjects of this play was the history of the German scientists who were brought to the United States to work on the American space program after World War II.

> When I'm thinking about a play, metaphor is one of the key ways of developing the work. An example would be Part 2 of *Apollo*. When we first developed Part 2, we were dealing a lot with history, with the Holocaust, and with concentration camp victims, and crimes of the Third Reich. Approximately 20,000 people died in the V-2 rocket factory where some of the German engineers worked. This

> was the key ethical issue of the story. My first thought was could we have 20,000 of something onstage? What would that be? And then, also, what's the main action of this piece? The main action is the search for the truth. When we started, there were two characters who were researchers, who were searchers. It felt to me like they were digging through archives, digging through the past. So I thought, what if we have a bunch of file boxes onstage, and the file boxes create the environment and everything comes out of the file boxes. That thought is what led to this design. The first time that we performed this part of the play was a workshop in a very small theatre. We had 200 file boxes, and they really filled up the space. Justin Townsend, who is the lighting designer, is also a very close collaborator. He had the idea of creating a wall with these boxes at the front of the stage. The piece would start with this wall and the actors would then remove the boxes. We found that just thrilling to contemplate. The actors then become manipulators of the environment. That's how it started. I think now we have almost 3,000 file boxes. That's an example of how the conception of the set and the ideas of the piece intersect.[21]

The formulation of a metaphor is a process initiated by the director but very much dependent on the collaboration between the director and the designers. Exactly who will define the nature of the stage imagery, and at what point in the process a central metaphor can be determined, varies from production to production and depends on the working dynamics of the production team.

For a new production, the process of formulating a metaphor, involving the director and the designers, is usually begun well in advance of the work involving the actors. However, in certain situations when the production process takes months or even years, the designers may work in rehearsal with the actors and make design decisions and changes as the production evolves. Theatrical metaphors must be strong enough to provide a physical shape to a production and

Robert Wilson creates a vivid and horrifying image of violence using the actor's body position and the light to convey the intensity of the moment in his 2002 production of *Wozyeck,* produced in collaboration with the Betty Nansen Teatret of Demark, with music by Kathleen Brennan and Tom Waits. Wilson is known for his use of visual metaphor as a central expressive device in his productions.

open-ended enough that they will engage the imaginations of the theatre artists and the audience members.

Directorial images have a visual component that is crucial to the designers, and the images usually include a sense of the stage action as well that will guide the director in the blocking of the actors. At the Oregon Shakespeare Festival in 2002, the director and designers for the production of *Macbeth* looked for a simple, concentrated image around which to build their work. Shakespeare's *Macbeth* is about the ambition of the title character to become king and then to keep the crown at any cost. This ambition transforms Macbeth from a heroic soldier into a bloody murderer

who strikes king and servant, friend and foe, woman and child in a desperate course of spiraling violence. The first key decision made by the director, Libby Appel, was to do the play in the round with the audience surrounding the stage (see page 168).

> I knew that I wanted an empty space and that it was just about the actors telling the story. I wanted the audience to be as "cabined, cribbed, confined" as Macbeth is—so that they would feel the claustrophobia of the small space with Macbeth. There's no escape.

Aware that only minimal visual effects would be possible, the director and the designers turned to the language of the play, the many references to blood, summed up in the following lines spoken by Macbeth, as the source for the production's guiding metaphor:

Will all great Neptune's ocean wash this blood
Clean from my hand? No. This my hand will rather
The multitudinous seas incarnadine,
Making the green one red.[22]

First they decided that a bucket or pool of blood would be placed center stage, and all the action would revolve around it.

> It grew into this pool of blood that became the cauldron, "fire burn and cauldron bubble." And the whole of the round, the theatre, is the cauldron. And we're all in this cauldron together.

Once the idea of placing a pool of blood onstage was established, the costume designer, Deborah Dryden, concluded that the costumes should be white in order to show the blood. This decision then evolved into the idea that the "blood should be accumulated all the way through the play with every bloody deed multiplied." The costumes became a canvas that would be painted with the murderous actions of the characters. Finally, the movement director, John Sipes, responsible for staging the fight sequences, saw that the pool of blood onstage should govern the fight choreography. Rather than using swords, the fighting was stylized, with the characters dipping into the pool and marking each other with blood where a blow would have opened a wound.

WORKING WITH THE ACTORS
Casting

The first crucial contact the director has with the actors comes during the auditions. Choosing actors wisely is essential to the success of the entire enterprise. Sometimes actors will be chosen at the kind of open auditions discussed in

BW Gonzalez is seen here as Lady Macbeth in the sleepwalking scene wearing the white costume designed by Deborah Dryden to show the bloody misdeeds committed by the Macbeths during the course of the play. The production was directed by Libby Appel at the Oregon Shakespeare Festival in 2002.

Chapter 4. Sometimes actors are invited to read for a play, and sometimes actors whom the director has worked with before are simply asked to take a part. Actors in a repertory situation such as the Oregon Shakespeare Festival are cast in several parts for different plays, all at the beginning of the season.

The director must choose actors who are suited to the roles in the play, who have good work habits, and who will work well in the particular configuration of the cast. The right balance and chemistry among the cast members are as important as the talents of individual actors. **Typecasting,** the selection of certain actors because they have a certain physical appearance and personality, is still entrenched in some areas of the American theatre, particularly in musicals and summer stock. Although a presence that makes the character believable is essential, more and more directors seek actors who will bring insight and creativity to a role rather than a preconceived physical appearance.

Nontraditional Casting

A recent development in the American theatre involves a rethinking of approaches to casting in terms of race. This shift has resulted in part from the increased participation in the theatre of actors and directors from diverse ethnic groups as well as increased social awareness on the part of theatre producers and directors.

Contemporary productions frequently combine actors from different racial backgrounds—even when they are playing members of the same family. Such casting is currently referred to as "nontraditional" or "color-blind casting." The director assumes in this kind of casting that the best actor should be cast for the role and that the audience will respond to the group of characters, not to the racial difference of the actors. In some productions, characters are cast specifically with race in mind to bring out certain ideas in the text. As we reevaluate where we are as a nation in terms of race, casting in the theatre will serve as a way of expressing and addressing the diversity of the U.S. population.

The Work Environment

At the heart of the director's responsibilities in the production of a play is his or her work with the actors. This process begins with the audition and continues through the rehearsal period and the first performances. From the beginning of the auditions, the director is responsible for creating an atmosphere that is conducive to the creative work of all involved, that ensures respectful consideration of the actors' efforts, and that recognizes the vulnerability inherent in the acting process. Because the actors' progress during the rehearsal period depends on their making open and honest responses, the director must be protective of the working environment. Rehearsals are usually closed to outside observers, who might make inappropriate commentary or inhibit the actors' work by making them feel that they are "performing" before they have completed their foundation work. The actors must trust the director; otherwise the process is imperiled. The director who shouts or humiliates an actor immediately shuts down the lines of communication.

The rehearsal should be a time when risks are taken and discoveries are made about the characters' deepest feelings and most compelling motivations. Hidden desires, buried secrets, burdens of the past, and ambitions for the future must be teased out during the rehearsal process. The actors must be open not only to the director and themselves but also, perhaps most of all, to each other. The connections between the actors drive a play forward and create a sense of an imagined world come to life. And it is the responsibility of the director to encourage the bonding of the actors and to guide them in making sense of the characters' relationships.

We have already looked at a number of directorial approaches in our discussion of the production process at different theatres and in the chapter on acting. Although the director usually has a planned structure for the rehearsal process, involving table work, blocking, and character development, the creativity and spontaneity of the director in rehearsals are as important as the creativity of the actors. The director must respond in the moment to the contributions and questions of the actors and the progress of the work. The director may stop a scene that is problematic to set up an improvisation in an attempt to get at deeper, more committed responses from the actors. Or the director may make suggestions for stage business that will physicalize a character's motivation.

The director always functions as the actor's audience to confirm what is being clearly communicated and to help clarify moments when the

The lunch counter scene in *Apollo* directed by Nancy Keystone was developed through improvisation. In this violent encounter, played out in slow motion, the man standing repeatedly mimes hitting the seated characters, who, each time they are hit, fall forward. The stage picture makes clear the relationship between the characters and the shift in who is occupying the space and the price to be paid to take a seat at the table. The actors include Ray Ford, J. Karen Thomas, Richard Gallegos, Nick Santoro, Angie Browne, Valerie Spencer, Lorne Green, Brandon Ford Green, and Russell Edge.

actor's intention is unclear. The director must maintain the company's focus and do whatever is necessary to inspire a continuous high level of energy and creativity. Although the director may be watching the action quietly, in fact she or he must match and encompass the energy of everyone on the stage.

Improvisation

Nancy Keystone, the director of *Apollo*, used improvisation to generate both the text and staging for many of the scenes in this production. The photograph on this page shows a moment from a

scene in Part 3 of *Apollo*, representing the attempt to integrate lunch counters in Alabama during the civil rights movement. The finished scene was performed with no words and structured through the precise repetition of the gestures of a group of archetypal white characters used to eating in a segregated restaurant. The characters repeat the motions of entering the diner, eating, and exiting, all in speeded up time, until the rhythm and pace of their movements is broken by the entrance of an African American character. The pace then shifts to extreme slow motion as more African American characters take seats at the lunch counter in spite of the hostile responses with which they are met. The actor Ray Ford, who appears seated at the table on the left in the front, describes the development of the scene:

> The lunch counter sequence was born as an improv. Nancy came in and said, "Ok, here's two tables, it's a lunch counter. You be the chef, you be the cook, you be the waitress, and everyone else be the customers." So we did that improv for a couple of hours. It starts off just as an acting exercise, but there comes a moment where your reality sort of drops away and you're really there. When you're doing an improv for two hours, your defenses are down, and it completely shifts the energy, not just in the actor, but in the entire room. I remember leaving that night and we were all just completely wiped out and exhausted. But you just go there. You completely go there. It's just about that action of walking into this diner where you're not welcome, and what that feels like on both sides. That was all we had to work with for a long time. There still are no words in that scene, you know, it wasn't like we were playing it out. And we would flip roles, blacks played whites, whites played blacks, to see what that felt like. It's all about the feeling underneath all of that.[24]

Early in the rehearsals for his production of *The Cherry Orchard* (see page 140), the director Andrei Serban had the actors, who included Irene Worth, play their roles in silence while others read their lines to enable them to investigate character interactions unimpeded by holding a script or searching for lines. Serban also had them do animal improvisations. Irene Worth chose a swan for her character, Madame Ranevskaya, a graceful and elegant woman who has made disastrous choices in her personal life: "I felt that Ranevskaya was a swan. She's very beautiful and she just sails the water in this rather enigmatic, not neurotic way."[25] Serban observed that through the improvisation Worth discovered a ferocious side to the character, "vicious, very fierce, that she could bite."[26] Late in the play, the character loses her usual control

ARTISTIC FOUNDATIONS •••

The Necessary Skills and Talents of the Director

- A visual sense
- A rhythmic sense
- The ability to analyze dramatic structure
- The ability to interpret through image and metaphor
- The ability to work with actors
- The ability to compose stage action
- Strong managerial skills
- Physical stamina
- Discipline

and has a brief but intense quarrel with another character. In that quarrel, Worth used the material generated by the improvisation and, in fact, even made a sharp hissing sound that viscerally communicated the character's deep distress.

STAGING THE PLAY

The director's own particular eloquence is expressed through the staging of the play. The director must arrange the actors in the theatrical space and develop sequences of actions that account for the necessary actions required by the script. But this staging of action through spatial relationships goes far beyond serving the practical needs of the script. Like designers, directors should be spatial artists. They compose in space and time with the actors and the scenic elements to interpret the ideas of the play.

The director arranges what is called the **stage picture,** the arrangements of actors onstage to communicate character relationships. But unlike a photograph, the stage picture cannot remain static and still hold the audience's attention. Characters cannot appear like posed statues. The stage picture must be dynamic, ever-changing.

And the composition of the stage picture must direct the audience's attention to the important character or characters while also making clear the relationships among the group of characters. Blocking a play is far more complicated and subtle than merely getting the actors on and off the stage and getting them to do interesting things.

Focus

One of the most important components of directorial composition is focus. By the arrangement of the actors' bodies in the theatrical space the director must guide the audience's attention to a specific actor or to the point on the stage where key actions, reactions, or line deliveries will take place. A film director uses the camera to focus the spectator's attention. With a close-up shot, the camera singles out the significant actor and makes sure that the slightest response is registered clearly for the audience's appreciation. A long shot is used to give a view of the whole scene and then, through editing, the film cuts from actor to actor as the director wishes the spectator's attention to shift from character to character.

Stage directors, however, cannot employ such editing techniques. The audience views the

Focus is achieved in this scene from *Sorrows and Rejoicings* through the placement of the actors and the direction of their attention to the daughter, Rebecca, played by Brienin Nequa Bryant. The three older characters hope that she will accept her father *(to her right),* but she refuses to do so. The play, written and directed by Athol Fugard, explores the difficulties of race relations in South Africa. Rebecca, who is the interracial child of a white father and a black mother, now denies the father whom she was not allowed to acknowledge when she was a child. The production from the Mark Taper Forum also features John Glover, Cynthia Martells, and Judith Light.

full stage space continuously and remains at a constant distance from the stage. The director achieves focus through the placement of characters in relation to one another on the stage. Contrast in the visual presentation of the characters is one of the director's most important compositional tools. A character dressed differently from all the other characters and placed prominently attracts focus. A character separated from a group of characters becomes the focal point. Contrast can also be achieved by elevating or lowering the position of the actors onstage. A character who stands while everyone else sits receives focus; and as long as the character is plainly visible, a character who sits or even falls to the floor while everyone else stands receives the focus. A character raised up higher yet on stairs or an elevated platform will receive the focus if the other characters onstage are on a lower level. The focus of the actors will also direct the focus of the audience. If all the actors are looking at one character, the audience's attention will follow. Actors may also lean their bodies toward a particular character, or they may hold objects that direct the audience to look in a particular direction. The photograph of Herald Loomis on the floor at the end of act 1 of *Joe Turner's Come and Gone* demonstrates several of the principles of stage focus (see page 102).

Spatial Composition and Character Development

In addition to focus, another major function of directorial composition is the communication of character relationships and character development. William Ball compares his spatial work with actors to choreography:

> Picturization is similar to choreography in that the body positions reveal the relationships, independent of the words. My productions usually bear a slight resemblance to ballets, because I tend to picturize as intensely as possible. For example in my production, when the script calls for two people

seated on opposite sides of a table, the one who is winning is usually climbing over the table, and the one who is losing is sliding under the other side.[27]

By expressing the essence of character relationships and individual character development spatially, the director provides a visual telling of a play's story or a visual score just as the playwright's script provides a verbal score. The audience reads the nature of relationships or changes in relationships by the placement of the characters in space and their physical interactions. How close together or far apart are the characters? Do they face each other, or do they face away? Do they touch each other or avoid physical contact? Do the play's events bring the characters together, or do they push the characters apart? Does one character dominate the space while the other shrinks into a less important or a restricted part of the space? Does one character move freely through the space while the other is hesitant? Does one character lead while the other follows? *The progression*, the evolution of the spatial placements, is crucial in defining the progression of the character relationships or character development. Does an independent character who has kept herself apart come to depend on the character she has avoided? Does a character who has moved aggressively through the whole stage space come to occupy a smaller and smaller part of the stage as his power is stripped away?

Plays frequently have strong spatial implications built into their structure that give directors the starting point for their work. A battle for the stage space occurs in a number of plays. The confrontation between the Angel and Prior in act 2, scene 2 of *Perestroika* is a fight for Prior's soul that is realized in physical terms. In *Joe Turner's Come and Gone*, Seth wants to force Loomis out of his house while Loomis is determined to keep his place. In contrast, the sharing of the stage space is central to the supportive character relationships of a play such as *And the Soul Shall Dance*.

Chapter 6

The Designers

STAGE DESIGN—THE WORK of the scene designer, the costume designer, the lighting designer, and the sound designer—is an essential part of what makes the audience experience in the theatre a magical one. Stage design, together with the presence of the actor, creates a world apart from the life outside the theatre's boundaries. The designers create a poetry of space, visual and aural, that brings the stage to life with startling images and creates an eloquent foundation for the actor's work.

We begin by considering the design for *Metamorphoses,* a play about transformations, directed and adapted by Mary Zimmerman. Taken from Greek myths about life and death, love and rebirth, the text of *Metamorphoses* offers a collection of beloved stories that distill essences of human experience. To tell these ancient stories in today's theatre, the designers Daniel Ostling (set), Mara Blumenfeld (costumes), and TJ Gerckens (lights) joined images of the past and present to create

a place that seems to float in the imagination. A huge golden door provides the entrance to the playing space; clouds on a panel of blue make a home for the gods; a crystal chandelier hangs above, suggesting the many possibilities of light; and a large pool of water provides the stage for much of the action where humans and gods meet and struggle with life's mysteries. The costumes mingle flowing robes and gowns reminiscent of Greek dress with elements of contemporary style. Modern theatre lights focused from above are augmented by lanterns and candles handled by the actors. Tying all the design elements together is the large pool of water. The water reinforces the movements of the actors, becoming playful or highly dramatic. And the water is full of metaphoric significance as it suggests many of life's passages.

The stage speaks with color and shape, with light and shadow, with music and sound. The flight of an angel, a boardinghouse seen against a city skyline, a rolling piece of tumbleweed, the haunting sound of a shakuhachi flute, the lyrics of a blues song—these images from productions discussed in this book appeal to the senses. The designers engage the audience with sensory information to locate the actor physically and psychologically and to support the ideas of the text.

STAGECRAFT AND THE THEATRE

The actor and the director are artists who are made for the theatre. Their skills and talents are wholly claimed by the theatre itself.

Designers, on the other hand, have skills and talents that they share with other visual artists, sound artists, and craftspeople. Scene designers have drafting and construction skills. Costume designers work with fabrics and have cutting, sewing, and dyeing skills. Many scene and costume designers also have extensive training in drawing, painting, sculpture, or architecture. Lighting designers create with a broad range of electrical instruments and control boards. Sound designers work with music, sound effects, recording equipment, and amplifiers. If designers do not sew or do carpentry or work with electricity themselves, they must clearly understand the properties of the materials they incorporate in their designs.

The final scene of *Metamorphoses* is shown here in the production presented at the Circle in the Square Theatre in New York City in 2002.

Fuerzabruta (Brute Force), currently playing in New York, offers audience members a unique experience. Actors and audience share the same space and audience members stand throughout. There are no seats. With the emphasis on spectacle, audience members continuously need to adjust their positions as large scenic units are propelled through the space by stagehands or descend from overhead. In this photo, a large Mylar pool with water and swimming actors is lowered to within reach of audience members. *Fuerzabruta* demonstrates some of the principles of Antonin Artaud, see page 382, who proposed that the theatre presentation should surround the audience members and fully engage all of their senses. The creator and director is Diqui James.

But no matter how many overlapping abilities designers share with visual artists or craftspeople, like actors and directors they are interpretive artists whose creativity must be used to shape the world of the play or the theatre piece. A designer's work of art does not stand alone onstage as an individual creation but interprets the ideas of the play with materials just as the actors shape ideas with their voices and bodies.

Much of our discussion of the theatre has to do with the serious interpretation of serious subjects. But whether the material is comedy or tragedy, spontaneity and playfulness are crucial to theatre work and part of the theatre's great appeal to its participants. The possibility for creative problem solving, for tackling curious challenges that most people never have the opportunity to take on, is part of the basic work of the stage designers and technicians. The following examples demonstrate some of the intriguing problems designers and technicians are called on to address.

- For the New York production of *Angels in America*, discussed in Chapter 10, the staff faced the problem of flying the angel in such a way that she could perform her aerial gymnastics without catching her wires in her very elaborate costume.

- For *Apollo* (Chapters 4 and 5), the crew needed to stack 3,000 boxes across the stage for each performance, many of which would then be moved by the actors. The boxes needed to be arranged in a precise order because some contained props that had to be accessed by the actors.

- For *Fuerzabruta* the technical staff needed to install a three ton swimming pool that could be lowered over the heads of audience members to such a close distance that audience members could reach up to touch it. The suspended pool with a clear bottom needed to hold one hundred gallons of water and four swimming actors.

- For the Wooster *Hamlet* (Chapter 5), the technical director Boskurt Karusu has to dress in a costume at each performance in case he needs to go onstage and fix malfunctioning media equipment.

- For the production of *Macbeth* discussed in Chapter 5, the costume designer Deborah Dryden needed to find white fabric for the costumes that could be stained with "blood" at each performance and then washed and

Dreya Weber plays the Spiderwoman in this photo-graph from *A Very Old Man With Enormous Wings* by Nilo Cruz, based on a story by Gabriel Garcia Marquéz. The costume designer Allison Leach needed to create a grotesque version of a spider with deformed extra limbs. The actor had to play her part, while suspended, as well as negotiate her web and manage the unusual costume. The play was produced at the Kirk Douglas Theatre in Los Angeles in 2005.

dried for the next performance, sometimes on the same day when there was a matinee as well as an evening show.

Bodies need to disappear and ghosts walk the earth; costumes and sets must be changed in a matter of seconds; ships must sail across the sea; or a mountain must give the appearance of snow and ice. Theatrical design requires continuous imaginative thinking, first to visualize the image in response to the needs of the play and then to come up with the technological solution that will make it possible.

THE THEATRICAL SPACE

The first condition that governs the work of all the designers is the nature of the theatrical space, the relationship between the audience and the stage. The size and atmosphere of theatres in the United States vary widely, from the traditional elegance of Broadway to the modern comfort of large regional theatres such as the Oregon Shake-speare Festival and the Mark Taper Forum to the small and sometimes cramped spaces of equity waiver theatres such as East West Players (Chapter 8) and the Eureka Theatre (Chapter 10).

The common denominator for all theatre spaces is their three-dimensionality. In contrast, movie audiences sit in front of a large flat screen on which filmed images give the impression of dimensional space, but that sense of depth is in fact an illusion created by the camera. In the theatre, the dimensionality of the stage space is actual. For this reason, the audience space and the stage space can be arranged in different configu-rations. The audience relationship to the screen at the movies, however, always remains the same.

The Proscenium Theatre

In many large theatres, such as the Oregon Shakespeare Festival's Bowmer Theatre and Broadway theatres, the audience sits opposite the stage, facing what is called the **proscenium** or end stage. A proscenium theatre is a theatre constructed in a rectangular form with the stage at one end of the rectangle. The stage opening follows the rectangular form of the space as if the audience were looking through one end of a box. The audience's view is shaped by a framing device that defines the rectangular opening called the **proscenium arch.** The proscenium arch is like a picture frame. The stage frame of the proscenium masks the mechanics of the backstage operations and creates a clearly defined theatrical space that

The set shown in this photo of the play *Waiting for Godot* is actually an abandoned house in the Gentilly neighborhood of New Orleans. A group of artists believed that staging a play about people waiting for someone or something that never comes would help to focus attention on the situation of the people of New Orleans following Hurricane Katrina and the tremendous difficulties faced by people waiting for assistance. Paul Chan collaborated with Creative Time and the Classical Theater of Harlem to produce the play and all of the artists involved also worked with neighborhood groups in New Orleans to present educational seminars, theatre workshops, and conversations with the community. Fundraising for New Orleans organizations was also part of the project. The play was produced in the street in two different neighborhoods. The performances were free and were preceded by food and music. Wendell Pierce plays Vladimir and J. Kyle Manzay plays Estragon in the production, directed by Christopher McElroen in 2007. The artists were in part inspired by the production of *Waiting for Godot* in Sarajevo discussed in Chapter 2. Setting the play in an abandoned house and in the street are examples of using found spaces to produce theatre.

is particularly suited to realism. The opening of the proscenium arch can be covered by a curtain, which also functions as a masking device to allow scene changes out of the view of the audience. Today, however, many styles of theatre other than realism are presented on proscenium stages. Rectangular stages that lack a curtain or even a defined frame are referred to as end stages.

Thrust, Arena, and Black Box Stages

In contrast to the seating arrangement in a proscenium theatre, some theatres are designed to allow the audience to sit on three sides of the stage, which may be rectangular or rounded in its shape. The three-sided arrangement is called a **thrust stage.** The thrust stage extends into the audience, and different sections of seating look across to other seating areas. (The space for *Metamorphoses* shown on page 162 is arranged as a thrust stage.) The audience members in a thrust situation are much more aware of the presence of other audience members than they would be in an end stage arrangement and are therefore more likely to be conscious of their own presence in a theatre watching a play. When the audience sits surrounding the entire stage space, the configuration is referred

The proscenium stage began its evolution in the Italian court theatre of the sixteenth century; painted scenery and lavish special effects became an increasingly important part of stage spectacle. A framing device, the proscenium arch, was placed around the scenic spectacle to define the boundaries of the picture and to hide the backstage activity. Eventually, the rectangular proscenium theatre became a home to realism. This production of August Wilson's *Jitney,* directed by Marion McClinton and designed by David Gallo, was staged in a proscenium configuration with the stage at one end of a rectangular theatre space. Such staging allows for a full scenic environment visible to all audience members from the same point of view. The collage influence of Romare Bearden is seen in this set, which is designed in layers with the interior of the taxi station in the foreground, a sloping street with cars parked on it immediately behind, and, in the upstage area farthest from the audience, the shuttered and decaying buildings in Pittsburgh's Hill District. The actors are placed horizontally in the space, taking advantage of the actor–audience relationship shaped by the proscenium stage. From left to right the actors are Stephen McKinley Henderson, Russell Hornsby, Carl Lumbly, and Barry Shabaka Henley.

to as **arena staging,** or **theatre in the round,** whether the stage space is an actual circle or a square with the audience on four distinct sides.

Theatre architecture is frequently permanent; that is, a theatre building is constructed so that the actor–audience relationship always remains the same. Sometimes a theatre plant will have more than one stage, as the Oregon Shakespeare Festival does; this arrangement allows the staging of plays in different kinds of spaces. Sometimes a theatre space will be constructed specifically so that the stage space itself can be flexible. Small theatres and colleges frequently have what are called **black box** spaces that can be arranged differently depending on the needs of the specific production. A found space can also function as a flexible theatre. The Omaha Magic Theatre performed in an old department store. The audience members sat in swivel chairs that allowed them to turn to any part of the space. The store elevator and staircases provided intriguing entrances and additional playing spaces. Factories, garages, churches, train stations, packing plants, and armories have all been turned into theatres.

The Implications of Theatre Architecture for Designers

Thrust and arena stages have neither the masking of the proscenium arch nor curtains that can block the stage from the audience's view. Therefore, all set changes must be done in view of the audience. In the production of *And the Soul Shall Dance* at East West Players, the set changes were performed by costumed actors, kurokos, whose choreographed movements were an integral part of the play and were important for the audience to see. In *Angels in America*, the actors themselves changed the set, but during scene changes they projected a neutral persona rather than portraying one of their characters from the play. In other productions, the lights are dimmed for the

The thrust stage is historically connected to the Greek and Shakespearean theatres, where the audience was placed around three sides of the stage. A thrust stage allows for a close relationship between actors and audience members. Theatre historians speculate that the soliloquies of Shakespearean characters such as Hamlet would have been played in very close proximity to the audience so that overhearing the character's thoughts would have seemed very natural. Actors working on thrust stages frequently make entrances through the auditorium, reinforcing the integration of the audience space and the stage space. For this production of *In the Belly of the Beast* presented in 1985 by Berkeley Repertory Theatre, the scene designer Michael Olich created a very compressed space on a thrust stage to represent the confinement of a death row inmate.

The arena stage is surrounded on all sides by audience seating. The arena stage emerged from performance traditions in which ceremonial plays were performed in community plazas. The morality plays of medieval times, at which audience members sat on the hillsides of a natural amphitheatre, are one of the best-known historical uses of arena staging. Today the arena stage provides an intimate relationship between actors and audience members. Scenic elements must be carefully scaled and arranged to protect the audience's view. The emphasis in the performance is on the actors. The Oregon Shakespeare Festival has recently opened a new theatre with an arena stage, shown here for the production of *Macbeth* in 2002. The pool of blood in the center was the only constant scenic element except for the structure of the stage itself. Two chairs were brought on for the banquet scene to suggest the thrones of the Macbeths.

set changes, which are performed by stagehands in dark clothes who move quickly and quietly across the stage space, changing or rearranging the set as efficiently as possible. In theatres with sophisticated physical plants and large budgets, scenic units may be moved mechanically across the stage or on a revolving platform, or they may be flown in from above. The movement of scenery in musicals is frequently choreographed to the music and becomes part of the visual spectacle.

Each spatial configuration makes different kinds of demands on the designers. In an end stage arrangement, the audience cannot see the back of set pieces, which therefore do not have to be finished; in theatre in the round, however, every object on the stage has to be completely finished because it can be seen from all angles. Towering set pieces or backgrounds can be used on proscenium stages or at the back of a thrust stage, whereas set pieces on an arena stage must be designed not to block the view of anyone in the audience. All kinds of ingenious solutions have been developed for arena stages to allow the audience to look over or through stage objects. Costumes and properties become the design focus in arena or thrust staging. The size of the stage and the size of the audience area are also important factors in determining the scale of the scenery and the detail of the sets and costumes.

Three-Dimensional Space

Although the shape of each stage configuration presents unique problems and opportunities, the basic notion of three-dimensional space remains the same. The director and the designers are composing in space. The costume designer and the lighting designer are particularly concerned with shaping the body of the actor. The costume designer creates a silhouette; the lighting designer molds that silhouette. The scene designer creates the physical environment that contains and defines the figures shaped by the costume designer and the lighting designer. The director creates meaningful relationships between the figures of the actors within the space defined by the set designer. Ultimately, the lighting designer unifies all the stage elements, including the figure of the actor.

MEETINGS AND INTERACTIONS

Once rehearsals begin, the actors and the director become a tight unit and do almost all their work on the play together, developing their ideas about the play as an ensemble. The designers spend as much time in rehearsal as possible to see the blocking; to get a sense of character development and relationships; and to monitor how a costume piece, a prop, or a lighting choice will work. But much of their work is done before the rehearsal process begins, and much is done away from the process going on in the rehearsal hall. To illustrate how theatre design evolves, we

Blackbird, **written and directed** by Adam Rapp, was designed by David Korins to be performed in the Blue Heron Studio Theatre that seats only 33 audience members. Korins created a squalid tenement apartment setting that encompassed the actors and the audience with its life-like environment for the production staged by Edge Theater in 2004. The actors are Paul Sparks and Mandy Siegfried.

examine the unique collaborative processes of two productions: We return to the Oregon Shakespeare Festival's production of *Joe Turner's Come and Gone* and then shift our attention to the Public Theatre's production of the musical *Bring in da Noise, Bring in da Funk* in New York.

Because *Joe Turner's Come and Gone* was to open in Ashland in February, the director, Clinton Turner Davis, began meeting with the designers in October. Conflicting work schedules necessitated design meetings in New York, Los Angeles, and Ashland in restaurants and hotel rooms as well as at the theatre. Usually only two or three of the four central production staff members could be present at any one time. This is typical of the American professional theatre. Most directors and designers work for more than one theatre, and frequent travel is not an unusual part of their lives. Geography becomes part of the design process.

At the design meetings, the discussions shifted back and forth between highly practical matters and more abstract images and feelings. The scene and costume designers brought in examples of their initial research. The scene designer, Mike Fish, studied photographs and engravings of Pittsburgh at the turn of the twentieth century as well as period wallpapers and furniture found in old Sears Roebuck catalogues. He found a very useful book, *Blast Furnaces*, that contained photographs of steel mills from places around the world, including Pittsburgh. The photographs of the steel mills in Pittsburgh eventually were influential in the backdrop that

WORKING IN THE THEATRE •••

Summary of the Designers' Responsibilities

- *Costume and scene designers*—prepare sketches and then color renderings of sets and costumes to provide visual definition of designs; develop complete designs that meet the needs of the production, the theatre, and the budget

- *Lighting designer*—prepare a light plot that indicates the position and angle of all lighting instruments; arrange for any additional instruments or materials for special effects

- *Sound designer*—identify cues and collect or compose sounds or musical pieces

All designers:

- Read the play carefully and research possible sources

- Collaborate with the director and the other designers to arrive at a production concept

- Prepare appropriate breakdown of design elements (blueprints, elevations, hookups) to allow support technicians to construct sets and costumes and to hang lights and prepare cues

- Attend rehearsals to monitor necessary changes in designs

- Maintain a dialogue with other designers and the director

- Supervise the construction of sets and costumes, and where appropriate, execute the most difficult processes such as painting and dyeing

- Work through the period of technical and dress rehearsals to make all necessary adjustments

Mike Fish designed for the space behind the boardinghouse.

Photographs were also a very important research source for the costume designer, Candice Cain, who used the picture collection at the New York City Public Library extensively. She was also able to bring her own collection of photographs to the meetings; these were period pictures of African American families in posed

The scene designer Anna Louizos has created an urban, New York streetscape for the musical production *In the Heights* that opened on Broadway in 2008. To get a feel for the appropriate neighborhood, Louizos and the production's director, Thomas Kail, visited Washington Heights with the show's composer Lin-Manuel Miranda to tour the streets, which inspired Miranda to create this work. Decaying buildings, with the George Washington Bridge behind, clearly specify the actual part of uptown Manhattan represented by the design. The building storefronts pop out to provide for interior scenes. It is interesting to compare this artistic interpretation of a street scene with the found street scene used for *Waiting for Godot* on p. 165. The costume designer for *In the Heights* is Paul Tazewell; the lighting is by Howell Binkley.

groups and at picnics that had been preserved by an African American photographer. The photographs offered valuable details of dress and accessories as well as more intangible evidence of attitude and bearing. Early on in the design meetings, an image was settled upon that had a major impact on all the designers. For Clinton Turner Davis, seeing the play in historical terms was essential, but he saw it as a memory. Consequently, the decision was made to use the idea of

an old sepia photograph as a visual guide for the look of the production.

Other considerations affect the organization of the design work in general at Ashland. Because the company performs in repertory, the scene shop must build several sets at once, and the light plot needs to accommodate four productions at once. The **light plot** designates the placement of all the lighting instruments hung at various positions in the theatre.

Neither the positions nor the angle of the lights can be changed between performances of different plays in Ashland, although some color changes are possible. The intricate scheduling problems generated by a repertory system demand maximum efficiency in organization as well as a fundamental cooperation among all the members of the production staff and the actors. Thus the basic designs for *Joe Turner's Come and Gone* were well under way before rehearsals began.

For the musical *Bring in da Noise, Bring in da Funk*, the design process was quite different from the advanced planning done at Ashland. The idea for the musical grew out of discussions between George C. Wolfe, the director of the Public Theater in New York, and Savion Glover, a young but remarkably experienced choreographer and tap dancer. They began with a concept, not a written script. The show, which took the form of a series of thematically related scenes built around music and dance, developed in an improvisational workshop process at the Public Theater.

A group of dancers and musicians began working with Wolfe at the Public Theater in August 1995. Even without a script, large amounts of research—in American history and black dance—accompanied and supported the explorations of the performers. A month and a half before the opening, the designers put aside any preconceived notions they had about the material and began sitting in on the rehearsals.[1] The scene designer Riccardo Hernandez, the lighting designers Jules Fisher and Peggy Eisenhauer, the projection specialist Robin Silvestri, and the costume designer Paul Tazewell created their designs in response to the evolving musical numbers, the intense rhythm of the drumming and tap dancing, and the emotional content of the scenes. The designers were as inspired as the dancers and the director by the creative freedom of working without a script. The designs continued to grow and change when the production moved from the 299-seat Newman Theatre at the Public to the 1,000-seat Ambassador Theatre on Broadway. We will return to *Bring in da Noise, Bring in da Funk* in Chapter 11.

THE HISTORY OF SCENE DESIGN

The history of scene design moves back and forth between periods featuring open theatre spaces with little scenic definition and periods when the scenic environment was of utmost importance to the presentation of the drama. The Greek theatre in the fifth century B.C.E., the Elizabethan theatre, and the Chinese theatre are all examples of theatres that used neutral playing spaces defined through character action, language, or minimal use of properties. The Roman and the medieval theatres began to show considerable interest in scenic effect. But it was in the court theatres of the Renaissance and Baroque periods throughout Europe that stage design generated great enthusiasm and remarkable ingenuity. Some of the leading inventors and artists of the time—including Leonardo da Vinci—contributed their skills to the theatre.

To imagine the energy and resources that went into the effects of the Renaissance theatre, the contemporary film industry provides a useful comparison. Film studios spend tens of millions of dollars on intergalactic special effects, stunts, models of cities or spaceships, hundreds or thousands of elaborate costumes, and the most advanced technology in cameras and sound. This was the kind of fascination that swept the court theatres and later the public theatres. During the Renaissance not only was perspective scenery painted lavishly with palatial interiors or mythical lands, but stunning special effects were also executed, with dazzling results. Fifty angels at a time could rise to the heavens on cloud units called **glories.** The stage floor could be made to resemble the ocean, with dolphins and whales diving through the waves. Mythical figures flew across the stage on the backs of animals or birds. Buildings

In this scene from *Bring in da Noise, Bring in da Funk* entitled "Chicago Industrial," the dancers and drummers become integrated into the workings of the factory machinery. The scene design by Riccardo Hernandez and lighting design by Jules Fisher and Peggy Eisenhauer place the actors physically and emotionally. The set supports the gymnastic movement of the dancers, as they become machine parts. The structure is also used to create sound that is produced by the dancers and drummers beating on its surfaces. The light creates a sense of a glaring, cold, hard machine-like existence.

collapsed, and actors appeared in the midst of flames. Stupendous costumes matched the scenic invention.

In the nineteenth century, the introduction of scenic realism was a continuation of the Renaissance ideal of an integrated scenic background or environment for the drama. But the realistic stage focused on the limitations of human existence rather than on the fantasies dramatized in earlier centuries. And in the hands of American directors and designers of the late nineteenth century and the early twentieth century, such as Steele MacKaye and David Belasco, realism

turned into a spectacle of its own, with rivers running across the stage and fifteen-minute sunsets.

Design for the contemporary theatre includes the aesthetics of both the open, neutral playing space and some form of elaborate scenic background. Broadway musicals usually use very elaborate scenic effects, as do the productions of Robert Wilson, although with different goals and a different impact on the audience. Contemporary productions of Shakespeare are frequently, although not exclusively, produced on some kind of open stage, relying on the talents of the actors and the language they speak to express the essence of the world of the play. And elements of the two approaches can be combined in different ways. In both types of staging, the work of the costume and lighting designers has a great deal to do with completing the visual statement of the production. On an open stage, however, the costumes and lights take on particular expressive significance.

At the beginning of the twentieth century, when a fusion of realism and spectacular effects dominated the European and American theatres, a quiet Swiss scene designer, Adolphe Appia (1862–1928), proposed a radical change in scene design. Appia was an idealist searching for a way to merge music, acting, scenery, and light into an integrated expression of the drama. Appia's research in the theatre was aimed at finding the most eloquent way to stage the operas of Richard Wagner. His conclusions about the possibilities of the stage space in combination with new uses of lighting had a lasting effect on the development of scenic and lighting practices throughout the twentieth century.

Appia advocated a return to the idea of the open playing space and the elimination of painted scenery and all realistic objects. However, rather than the flat platform of the Elizabethan or Chinese stages, Appia thought that the stage floor should be broken up into various levels that would help shape the movement of the actor. Through a combination of ramps, steps, and playing areas of different heights, Appia designed a **terrain** for the action of the drama that would have rhythmic as well as visual implications.

A multilevel stage provides many expressive possibilities for arranging groups of actors. The stage picture formulated by the director is greatly facilitated when the possible positions for the actors are increased vertically as well as horizontally. Steps and ramps also provide for movement patterns and in fact dictate a rhythm of movement through the number of steps and the distances that may be measured in the actors' movements. Appia was interested in supporting the moving figure of the actor as the focus of the performance. He believed in stripping away unnecessary details of spectacle because they detracted from a focus on the actor.

He encouraged the use of light instead to bring color to the stage and create mood and atmosphere through the creative use of shadows. Foremost in his writings on the theatre were his observations on the way that light can define and reveal the moving figure of the actor. Experimentation with the expressive possibilities of light was in its infancy. Appia understood the potential of light as a transformative element in theatre design that would take on a new partnership with both the drama and the actor.

SCENE DESIGN TODAY
Designing *The Grapes of Wrath*

Scene design today may emphasize an elaborate scenic background or an architectural shaping of space. The scenic elements may be realistic or abstract; they may be constructed of simple or highly finished materials. The design may acknowledge the architectural definitions of the theatre or attempt to disguise or transform the space. To explore some of the concepts of theatre architecture and scene design that have been introduced thus far, we turn to the scene design for a specific production at the Pacific Conservatory of the Performing Arts.[2]

When R. Eric Stone, now teaching at the University of Iowa, was the resident scene designer at the Pacific Conservatory of the Performing Arts in Santa Maria, California, he designed the scenery for a production of *The Grapes of Wrath*, a play by Frank Galati adapted from the novel by John Steinbeck. The play chronicles the geographical and emotional journey of Tom Joad and his family as they search for a new beginning following the loss of their farm to the dust bowl and the Great Depression. In designing *The Grapes of Wrath*, Stone faced a number of challenges—interpretive, logistical, and technological—as he worked to create a visual expression of the conditions governing the characters' lives. The theatre at Santa Maria has a thrust stage, and so the design needed to accommodate the sight lines of an audience seated on three sides of the playing space. Furthermore, the play itself is written as a journey with multiple scenes and locations. The play also calls for several specific scenic effects: a truck capable of movement that carries thirteen characters, a river in which a number of characters immerse themselves, and falling rain.

Stone designed three major scenic units—a barn door, the truck, and a suspended, sculptural construction—that together formed the visual interpretation of the world inhabited by the characters. The set pieces were designed to provide spatial definition for the stage without compromising any audience member's view. All three scenic structures were composed of rough materials.

Together, the three units gave the environment a weathered, fragile, decaying appearance; separately, each unit had a different function in the production. The scenic unit we refer to as the "barn door" was used to indicate the different structures associated with the characters' journey. It was moved to different locations on the stage to suggest new places. In the first scene only one edge was visible, enough to create an impression of the Joads' house; in a later scene it represented a railroad boxcar; in another scene it became an actual barn. As the placement of the door changed, the entire stage was transformed according to the new location implied by this simple piece of scenery. In the tradition of the medieval theatre, a small symbolic scenic unit defined the entire playing space. This device provided the flexibility needed for the multiple scenes of the play within

The model of the set for *The Grapes of Wrath* shows two of the three basic scenic units: the barn door and the abstract sculptural unit rising above it. Such scale models of set designs provide a three-dimensional representation of the stage that is of great value to the director and the actors as well as to the technical staff.

the limitations of a thrust stage. It also provided a physical dwelling or building to frame the characters' actions, and it expressed thematic content through its frayed surface.

The battered old truck was constructed with far more realistic detail than the other set pieces, adding visual texture to the stage. The truck was a concentrated symbol of the journey, a dilapidated, jerry-built mode of transportation, requiring continuous ingenuity to keep it running until it, too, was lost. The truck also functioned in a practical way to carry the actors and to allow staging opportunities through the placement of actors on and around the vehicle.

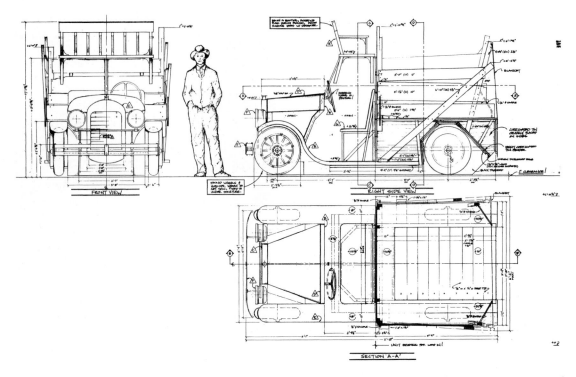

The scene designer provides technical drawings of the scenic elements as blueprints for the construction of each unit.

The sculptural unit at the back of the stage was abstract in comparison with the other scenic pieces. Elevated about ten feet above the stage floor and extending up to a height of twenty-four feet, the vertical construction was made from the same slats of wood as the barn door. It created a looming presence, ominous and oppressive. Streaks of red paint at the top suggested the blood and bitterness of the characters' lives. The appearance of the sculptural unit, however, could be changed dramatically through the contribution of the lighting designer Michael Peterson. Amber light on the weathered wood created a sense of warmth on the stage; blue light created a colder atmosphere. **Gobos,** stenciled cutouts placed inside lighting instruments to produce a patterned effect, were also projected onto the

structure to give additional texture to its surface through slashes of color or through more realistic leaf patterns. The set piece could be lit from behind to outline its shapes in silhouette and cast shadows on the stage floor. When a scene change placed the characters in the desert at night, tiny lights, called "grains of wheat," were used to shine through the open spaces of the structure to create the impression of stars. And finally, by eliminating all light on the structure, the set piece could be made to disappear.

The scene design also included the construction of the stage floor. Traps were built into the floor to allow for fire effects created through light and for the burial of one of the characters who dies on the way. And around the outer edge of the stage a trough was constructed to hold

The truck is the most detailed scenic element in the design for *The Grapes of Wrath*, providing a visual statement of the journey and the condition of the characters' lives.

enough water to make the river. Panels of the stage floor covered the river and could be folded back to reveal the water. The river then formed another level, with the actors in the water fully visible below the actors standing or sitting on the stage. The placement of the river also allowed for the parallel placement of a pipe above the stage that could release rain that would fall into the river, keeping the stage floor dry. For about twelve minutes, the actors were seen through a curtain of rain.

The scene design for *The Grapes of Wrath* demonstrates a combined use of realistic and abstract design elements created for a thrust stage. The design elements for this production shaped the stage space, placed the play geographically and temporally, and reflected the hardships faced by the characters. The design was realized through a minimal amount of scenery in keeping with the imaginative structure of the play and the impoverished lives of the characters.

COSTUME DESIGN

The costume designer creates through fabric, color, and texture. The materials used range from sumptuous brocades and hand-painted fabrics to clothing found in thrift shops, from delicate laces to metal. Hats, wigs, feathers, and jewelry are just some of the many accessories that add detail and style to a character's presentation. Distortion of the actor's body may be achieved through padded costume pieces, masks, or makeup, as illustrated by the spider character on page 164. Costumes may present a dazzling vision of a fairy-tale world or show poverty and deprivation. The costumes may place the characters in terms of time, place, and social status, or the costumes may be symbolic rather than realistic.

The costume designer Angela Wendt begins her work by asking herself questions:

Who are these people and what do the clothes mean to them? How do they decide to put on a particular piece of clothing? What does it say about their attitude toward other people and the world? Even though I do research beforehand, I always leave myself the freedom to wait until I've seen the actors themselves, gotten to know them a little bit, so I can pick costumes that support their artistic choices.[3]

Stylistic Unity

Whatever period and style are established for the costumes in a play, the costume designer must approach the characters as a group. Costumes usually have a coherent sense of style as a unit and clearly express visual relationships between the characters in terms of color, line, shape, and texture. Within the group, individual identities are established through contrast and variations in

The river trough provided a place to collect the rain that fell during the production of *The Grapes of Wrath*. Although the river and the rain could be suggested by light and by the actors' reactions, the use of actual water in the Pacific Conservatory of the Performing Arts production added a degree of realism to the scenic effects. The solution to the problems of creating a functional river and functional rain on a thrust stage exemplify the ingenuity of the scene designer, R. Eric Stone. The costumes draw the characters together as a group and make clear their economic hardships.

the silhouettes, colors, and materials. Together a group of costumes can be "read" to reveal hierarchical relationships based on wealth or power, differences in age and background, and relationships between smaller units of characters, such as families.

The Psychology of Character

The costume designer has a most interesting responsibility in helping the actor to define what could be called the psychology of character. The clothes we wear have a great deal to say about how we see ourselves and about

The costume designer must help with the characterization of two young women who are central characters in *Lydia*, by Octavio Solis. Ceci, played by Onahoua Rodriguez, has suffered an accident leaving her brain damaged. Her costume must allow the actor to portray the character before the accident when she was a vibrant fourteen-year-old looking forward to her fifteenth birthday party and afterwards when she has lost the power of speech and control of her movements. Note the scar on her face, which is a central factor in defining the character. Lydia, play by Stephanie Beatriz, is the family maid, who develops a deep sympathy for Ceci. The costume designer is Christal Weatherly; the director is Juliette Carrillo for the 2009 production at the Mark Taper Forum.

how we wish to be seen or perceived by others. Joe Mantello, who played Louis in *Angels in America*, imagined his character choosing clothes that were too big for him, clothes that the character "could disappear into when things got bad." On the other hand, Molly Cunningham in *Joe Turner's Come and Gone*

is a character who wants to be noticed. The other characters comment on the appeal of her appearance, but she is also careful not to go too far with the impression that it creates. She says of herself, "Molly don't work. And Molly ain't up for sale." The image she presents of herself through the choices the costume designer makes is quite different from the costume image for Mattie Campbell, who is filled with self-doubt, even though the two characters are both young women and come from very similar socioeconomic backgrounds.

There are people who gain security by carefully following social conventions. Dressing "correctly" in the most acceptable manner, therefore, could be an important character statement. For a rebellious character, choosing the way the character breaks the rules in terms of clothing becomes an interesting challenge for the costume designer. For example, Hamlet continues to wear mourning attire out of respect for his father after the rest of the court, particularly his mother and his uncle-stepfather, have returned to their everyday clothes. His solemn clothes become a point of contention between him and his uncle, Claudius; and their disagreement is a very important issue for the costume designer. In consultation with the director, the costume designer must connect the individuation of the characters to internal as well as external considerations.

Deborah Dryden, the resident costume designer for the Oregon Shakespeare Festival, who also designs for many of the other major theatres on the West Coast, points out that a further psychological issue is expressed through clothing chosen by one character for another character. Dryden designed an adaptation of Ibsen's play *A Doll's House*, by Ingmar Bergman, the Swedish film director. In the play, the conservative husband, Torvald, has purchased an "Italian peasant girl dress" for his wife, Nora, to wear as part of a masquerade in which she is to dance the tarantella. The dress is far from

In 2005 *His Girl Friday*, adapted by John Guare, was staged at the Guthrie Theater under the direction of Joe Dowling. In this newsroom scene, we see the way the costumes of the reporters draw them together as a group and offer a startling contrast to the red dress worn by Angela Bassett, playing Hildy. Jess Goldstein designed the costumes; John Lee Beatty designed the set. The other actors include Bill McCallum, Bob Davis, Terry Hempleman, Shawn Hamilton, and Jim Lichtscheidl.

her usual tasteful nineteenth-century Norwegian dress. But the peasant dress is not Nora's choice; it is Torvald's and therefore must be designed from his perspective. Dryden says, first of all, "It is 'costumey' as opposed to 'clothing.'" The dress needs to be "a highly provocative garment that fulfills his fantasy, not hers. At this moment, Nora is at her most doll-like, his sexual toy."[4]

The Costume Designer and the Actor

The character definition expressed through costume must support rather than impede the actor's work. A character grows and changes during the course of a play. The audience should be surprised by revelations as the play progresses. The costume designer must allow room for character development rather than

2. *Light:* Bring notes to class for discussion on the following: (a) Choose an interesting outdoor location. Observe the light at three different times during the day and, if possible, under different weather conditions. (b) Choose three interior locations—such as a store, restaurant, or house—with distinctly different lighting. What kind of lighting is used in each location? Are the light sources natural or artificial? How bright is the light? Is the light soft or harsh? How does the lighting affect the appearance and mood of each space?

3. *Sound:* (a) Over the course of several days, keep a log of sounds that you hear. How many sounds did you hear that you are not normally aware of? How did the various sounds affect your mood? What kinds of qualities do you associate with the different sounds? What sounds are soothing? What sounds are irritating? What emotional characteristics does a specific sound convey? For example, what emotion does a loud automobile horn in a traffic jam convey? Make a list of sounds that seem to have an emotional component. Include some that involve the human voice and some that do not. (b) Creating a soundscape: Work in groups of four or five. Bring interesting soundmakers to class. Using the soundmakers, as well as vocal sounds and hand sounds, compose a "soundscape" that suggests a specific location, such as a harbor, an amusement park, or a bar. Your soundscape may have individual words in it but no descriptive phrases. Think of your composition as a collage in which sounds will be layered. Some will repeat; some will fade in and out. Each soundscape should last thirty seconds. While performing the soundscapes for class members, have them close their eyes. (c) Creating a sound story: After warming up with the soundscape, create a short dramatic story with a beginning, middle, and end, using only sound. The sound stories can be performed live or taped. Use dialogue sparingly or not at all. For example, the subject of a sound story could be a burglary that begins with the sound of cautious footsteps, followed by the rattling of a doorknob, the prying of a lock, and the breaking of glass. Other sounds might include drawers being opened and closed, papers being shuffled, and coins clinking. Breathing and muttered voices might also be used. The story could conclude with a police siren, running footsteps, and shouting. Experiment with different soundmakers to create the most interesting and vivid sounds, keeping in mind that the actual object being represented may not make the most convincing sound effect. The sound story should last from thirty to ninety seconds. Length, however, is not as important as creating an intriguing sequence of sounds.

 For interviews with some of the designers in this chapter and *"Apollo* in Performance," as well as suggested readings and other resources, please visit www.mhhe.com/creativespirit5e.

a turning point in American history. Although our focus at this point is on realism, we must not fail to recognize other stylistic elements in *Joe Turner's Come and Gone*, such as the mythic background that Bynum establishes with his story of the shiny man, and the larger-than-life symbolic struggle that Herald Loomis goes through to gain control of his own destiny.

Realism in Film

Realism has found its most receptive medium in film. A brief discussion of realism and film will help to further define the nature of realism. Film can create the appearance of reality far more completely than most theatre productions can. The camera, in fact, is frequently positioned at what would be the fourth wall. It becomes the silent witness that carries the audience into the most private or intimate of circumstances.

Because a film audience cannot interrupt film actors, cannot alter what is fixed on the screen, the illusion is never broken. During the course of a film, actors cannot forget their lines, because scenes are reshot to achieve a perfection that is neither possible nor even desirable in the theatre. Enormous amounts of money and energy go into building elaborate sets full of intricate, concrete details that simulate "real" spaces, whether they are homes or western towns or space stations. Alternatively, the actors and film crew often go on location and use actual places; they take over houses, public buildings, and city streets to create a realistic effect. A whole city may form the set for a car chase. Real vehicles are blown up to create the effect of car crashes. Mangled bodies and disturbing amounts of stage blood are carefully arranged to create the illusion of death and destruction. Of course, we are also aware that films can overload the senses with such an excess of spectacular realism that they lose any feeling of actuality.

The perfectability of realism in film is one of the reasons theatre practitioners do not try to create completely realistic productions. In the early part of the century, when film was in its infancy,

entire restaurants or rivers with flowing water were created onstage, but rarely do we see this kind of elaborate attempt at realism in today's theatre.

By presenting an accumulation of externally observed details of human action and environment, realism gives us one view of human existence. Other styles of theatrical communication (such as expressionism; see Chapter 9) might move inside the characters' psyches and present a world shaped by distortion and exaggeration, or they might focus on large symbolic actions rather than minute details, or they might emphasize the political context of human action rather than an in-depth exploration of individual characters' lives. Today, theatrical performances are unlikely to follow only one style or another; styles tend to be mixed, reflecting the sense that we experience the world around us in different ways at the same time.

••• ORIGINS OF REALISM

During the nineteenth century the theatre underwent profound changes, in both the subjects that playwrights chose for their plays and the style in which plays were written and performed. Before that time, as we discussed earlier in the book, serious dramas were written about royal or noble families or about religious figures. The histories or conflicts involving kings and gods were considered representative of the concerns of the entire society. Only **comedies** focused on the lives of average citizens or those who were disenfranchised, and then the focus was on human weakness.

In the nineteenth century, however, a movement began that was aimed at making the lives of middle-class and poor characters the focus of serious drama. The world inhabited by these characters was made more tangible by the use of language that seemed to come from overheard daily conversations.

In earlier styles, environment was indicated by suggestion or theatrical conventions, or backgrounds were created for the actors' presentations by a kind of generalized decoration. In the

Greek theatre, for example, the scene building suggested the palace of whatever royal family was the subject of the play, and new characters were indicated by changes in masks. In the Elizabethan theatre, the throne room of the king was indicated by bringing on a chair, or a battlefield was created by the entrance of soldiers carrying banners. The audience's imagination was crucial to completing the stage image.

Decorative backgrounds became popular after the introduction of **perspective** painting by the Italians in the early seventeenth century. They were used in opera, court masques, or pageants, and then in the romantic drama of the eighteenth and early nineteenth centuries. Images of gardens or palaces were painted on flat scenic pieces that were arranged **upstage** (the area of the stage farthest away from the audience) to create a pictorial background for the actors.

But as the drama began to consider the struggles of working people, the theatre shifted in its style of presentation in order to place those struggles in actual three-dimensional environments rather than on bare stages or in front of painted backgrounds. The material environment became a crucial factor in character development. The lives of characters living in harsh circumstances, speaking the informal language of the workplace

Hedda Gabler by Henrik Ibsen offers a psychological study of a nineteenth-century woman who struggles with the restrictions of middle-class society. Played here by Cate Blanchett in a production by the Sydney Theatre Company (2006), Hedda seeks power through manipulating those around her because she is too frightened of scandal to lead an independent life.

and the home, presented in seemingly real environments, also generated the development of a new acting style. Actors and directors sought a more natural style of acting that would make sense of the changes playwrights were bringing to the drama. No longer could actors be expected to stand at the front edge of the stage and declaim their lines with grand gestures directly to the audience. Actors had to move upstage to give the appearance that they lived in the onstage furnishings and speak to each other conversationally as if the audience were not there. This new fusion of subject matter and performance became the basis for the realistic style of theatre. A working definition of *realism* might be theatre that seeks to give the appearance of everyday life.

THE SOCIAL BACKGROUND OF REALISM

Realism occurred at a particular point in human history and served as an artistic crossroads, as a representation of the intersection of various developments in philosophical, social, and scientific thought. It is no coincidence that dramas began to portray the "common" man or woman at the same time democratic governments began to replace kings ruling by "divine right." Nor is it surprising that as advances in science and technology fueled the industrial revolution, the theatre would include more evidence of the material world. The study of human psychology also had its counterpart in the theatre, as playwrights, directors, and actors probed the sources of human behavior and looked to heredity and environment to explain why human beings act as they do. And as social reformers began to consider the inequitable distribution of wealth and the consequences of poverty, the impact of social circumstances on the development of character became an important consideration in the theatre as well.

Realism became a dominant force in the theatre as society became interested in questions of how individuals are defined by or overcome the limitations placed on them by the circumstances of

their history, their environment, their social positions, and their relationships. In examining realism, however, it is always crucial to remember that although realistic plays are constructed to give the appearance of reality, realism is a theatrical style involving artistic choices; it is not life itself.

EUROPEAN REALISM
Henrik Ibsen

The Norwegian playwright Henrik Ibsen (1828–1906) profoundly changed the nature of the European theatre when he wrote a group

Before being recognized as one of the leading playwrights of the late nineteenth century, Henrik Ibsen worked in almost every capacity in the theatre, directing plays, building scenery, and selling tickets. In addition to writing twelve plays that provided the foundation for realism in the theatre, Ibsen wrote verse plays such as *Peer Gynt* and symbolic plays such as *The Wild Duck*.

One of the early realistic plays was *An Enemy of the People* by the Norwegian playwright Henrik Ibsen. Shown here in a production directed by Trevor Nunn in 1998, Ian McKellan portrays Dr. Stockmann, a character trying to persuade his fellow citizens that the mineral baths on which the town depends for revenue must be shut down because the water is polluted.

of plays during the latter part of the nineteenth century that focused on social problems and the struggle of individuals to resist the social, religious, and familial restrictions of a tightly structured, hierarchical society. Writing about surprisingly contemporary subjects such as pollution, venereal disease, and women's rights, Ibsen brought onto the stage problems and concerns that shifted the emphasis of theatrical content. In *An Enemy of the People* (1882), for example, a town furiously turns on the doctor who exposes the pollution in the community water system because the citizens fear that their lucrative spa business will be ruined. In *A Doll's House* (1879), a woman chooses to leave her husband and children rather than go on living the charade of a doll wife in a doll's house.

Ibsen looked at the daily lives of middle-class characters as they dealt with the need to earn a living, to provide properly for their children, to find meaningful work, to establish satisfying relationships. And he placed his characters in the environment of the middle class, replacing flat, painted scenery with the detailed furnishings of three-dimensional houses. The settings became metaphors for the characters' lives: warm but stifling rooms filled with wood stoves, rocking chairs, and needlework; or colder spaces furnished with thick, heavy couches and draperies, the windows looking out on endless rain or withered leaves.

August Strindberg

Whereas Ibsen focused on the struggle between individual self-determination and social restrictions, his fellow Scandinavian August Strindberg (1849–1912), from Sweden, laid bare the highly charged emotions of couples caught in love–hate relationships. Strindberg's characters tear at each other using words as weapons to wound or destroy each other in what frequently becomes a fight to the death. The American critic Ruby Cohn has called these verbal battles "dialogues of cruelty."[1]

In Strindberg's play *The Father* (1887), the Captain is tormented by his own unfounded doubts about his daughter's paternity. A power struggle with his wife, Laura, over the direction of their daughter's education and upbringing turns into a nightmarish conflict of manipulation and attack. Laura's cleverness in outmaneuvering her husband sends him into a violent rage that becomes her proof that he is unfit to remain in the household.

Strindberg's play *Miss Julie* (1888) adds class conflict to sexual conflict. The aristocratic mistress of a wealthy house, Miss Julie, is seduced by the valet, Jean. Their struggle for domination in

August Strindberg's early plays were known for their combination of detailed naturalism and emotional explosiveness. This photo of a production of *Miss Julie* at the Rattlestick Theatre (2006) demonstrates the intensity of a conflicted sexual relationship. Miss Julie (Marin Hinkle) is torn between her desires and the need to maintain her social position as the daughter of a count. She commits suicide rather than face the consequences of her affair with the valet (Reg Rogers).

the relationship results in her suicide. This brief and intense relationship unleashes bitter, insulting denunciations from both characters that alternate with painful admissions of dependency. Strindberg's pessimistic examination of male–female relationships was in part meant to answer Ibsen's apparent championship of women's rights.

Anton Chekhov

The third major playwright in the development of European realism was the Russian Anton Chekhov (1860–1904). Chekhov finished his

medical degree and supported himself and his family as a writer during his student days, before he turned to writing as his primary occupation. He wrote numerous short stories and sketches, and at the end of his career and his short life he wrote the four plays that established his unique place in the theatre.

Chekhov's plays have neither the complicated plots of Ibsen nor the emotional fireworks of Strindberg. In fact, very little seems to happen in Chekhov's plays. The characters barely hear each other, so absorbed are they by their own concerns. In *The Cherry Orchard* (1904), for example, a group of characters gather at the

Anton Chekhov's medical training and his own problems with tuberculosis seemed to make him an especially acute observer of human interactions. He approached his characters with an objectivity that revealed human weakness in all of them. He was sympathetic to his characters yet gently exposed their hypocrisy and vanity.

In *The Three Sisters,* Chekhov presents the gradual wearing away of the characters' hopes and dreams for the future. Shown here is a production at Lewis and Clark College, directed by Stephanie K. Arnold in 1987. In the first act, most of the characters still share an optimism about the future; but Masha (far left) already seems to sense the disappointments to come. Heidi Van Schoonhoven plays Masha; Christine Calfas plays Irina, Mark Woollett plays the doctor.

family estate supposedly to prevent the sale of their beloved cherry trees. But while they gossip and give sad little parties and fret endlessly over their own failures, the cherry orchard slips away, sold to a developer who will cut down the trees for summer cottages. The developer was once a peasant on the very land that he has purchased. As a friend of the family members, he has tried to advise them on ways to save the cherry orchard, but they are incapable of hearing him. Chekhov's characters speak passionately about love, but lasting relationships prove to be as elusive for them as the ability to save the cherry orchard.

Although much in Chekhov's plays is very painful, the plays are actually full of humor. By juxtaposing incongruous incidents and exposing the foolishness of characters who take themselves too seriously, the Chekhovian world shifts constantly between evoking sympathy and evoking laughter. Chekhov concentrated on the small details of his characters' lives and wrote dialogue that frequently goes unanswered because the characters are more interested in what they have to say than in listening to each other. Although Chekhov chose each detail carefully, his plays lack the obvious buildup of increasing tension and the exciting plot development that shape the dramas of Ibsen and Strindberg. But because of the seeming randomness of the actions and dialogue, Chekhov's plays may be the most realistic, the most like life. And yet the construction of the worldview through carefully selected objects and actions gives a heightened sense of life that takes on a poetic quality.

AMERICAN REALISM

Realism was the dominant style of American theatre in the first half of the twentieth century. Lillian Hellman (1905–1984), Arthur Miller (1915–2005), and Tennessee Williams (1911–1983) consolidated and shaped the foundation of American realism during the 1930s and 1940s. Hellman and Miller were particularly concerned with the moral positions of their characters, whereas Williams wrote about highly sensitive characters struggling to reconcile personal longing with the harsh and judgmental society surrounding them. Hellman and Williams also brought issues of gay and lesbian sexuality onto the stage, startling their audiences, given the taboos concerning such subjects at the time.

Lillian Hellman

Lillian Hellman's first major play, *The Children's Hour*, was produced in New York in 1934. The play is the story of two young women teachers whose lives are ruined by a lie told by a restless student looking for attention. In both *The Children's Hour* and *The Little Foxes* (1939), which looks at the greed and exploitation inherent in American capitalism, Hellman was concerned with characters who are aware of a wrong being perpetrated but who do not step forward, thereby leaving a

Liam Neeson plays John Proctor and Laura Linney plays Elizabeth Proctor in the 2002 Broadway revival of Arthur Miller's play *The Crucible* about the Salem witch trials, directed by Richard Eyre. In *The Crucible*, a rigid belief system is easily corrupted by lies when community members are falsely accused of witchcraft. Here the Proctors are separated by judges, acting on false testimony.

void that is quickly filled by slander and manipulation. The kind of realism used by Hellman in her plays is reminiscent of Ibsen, with an emphasis on the concrete details of the characters' lives and a plot in which one incident causes the next.

Poetic Realism: Arthur Miller and Tennessee Williams

Arthur Miller and Tennessee Williams transformed the realism of Hellman's work by focusing on a psychological exploration that places the characters' memories and fantasies onstage. Williams's *A Streetcar Named Desire* (1947) and Miller's *Death of a Salesman* (1949) begin in what seem to be realistic family situations but then change the point of view by moving inside the minds of characters who are beginning to slip away from reality. The plays shift back and forth between the present and the past, and it becomes impossible to know if what the characters remember is truth or illusion.

In *Death of a Salesman* the walls actually dissolve, allowing the space to become as flexible as the title character's mind. In *A Streetcar Named Desire* symbolic characters enter the seemingly realistic stage space. The imagery and structure of Miller's and Williams's plays inspired memorable productions directed by Elia Kazan and designed by Jo Mielziner in a style that came to be known as **poetic realism.** For decades, this style was considered the most eloquent representation of American drama.

Arthur Miller's first play, *All My Sons* (1947), is a traditional, realistic family drama that concerns the corrosive effect of greed on the human spirit and the need for individuals to take responsibility, both for the larger society and for their families. In this play, the father, Joe Keller, has sold flawed aircraft parts to the government during World War II. His partner, a less forceful man, goes to prison when this fraud is exposed. Although Keller continues to proclaim his innocence, his own son, a pilot in the war, disappears in combat, unable to live with the knowledge

Arthur Miller continued to be a force in American theatre and film until shortly before his death in 2005. A highly regarded revival of *Death of a Salesman*, with Brian Dennehy playing Willy Loman, was produced on Broadway in 1999. It was followed by a new production of *The Crucible*, about the Salem witch trials, in 2002 with Liam Neeson and Laura Linney. Miller also participated in the adaptation of his play *A View from the Bridge* into an opera, which premiered in 1999 and continues to be produced at opera houses around the country. And more recently he wrote a new play, *Resurrection Blues*, produced in 2002 at the Guthrie Theater in Minneapolis, which in Miller's words is about "the commercialization of everything."

of his father's crime against all the young pilots destined to fly unsafe equipment.

Miller took the essence of the family drama from *All My Sons*, the conflict between fathers and sons, and expanded its dimensions in his play *Death of a Salesman*. In this play, the father, Willy Loman, is driven to suicide by the fear that he has failed his son, Biff. Biff, who was full of promise until his senior year in high school, has spent his adult life drifting from job to job, and even serving a stint in prison for stealing. Through

Biff (John Malkovich) tries to convince his father Willy (Dustin Hoffman) that neither of them was meant to be a leader of men, in Arthur Miller's most famous play, *Death of a Salesman*, produced here in 1984.

flashbacks we see Willy's obsession with Biff's youth and Willy's attempt to defend the lesson that he repeatedly taught him: to create an image for yourself in a world in which everything is for sale rather than build a base of accomplishment.

Although the play critiques the notion of success in the United States as measured by dollar signs, it also looks again to the theme of responsibility for one's children and the children of the nation. Here Miller presents a character cut off from his roots, cut off from his heritage, who consequently does not know what to teach his own children.

Tennessee Williams came to prominence as a playwright with his play *The Glass Menagerie* (1944). The central character, Tom, ultimately abandons his domineering mother and fragile sister in order to make a life for himself. The mother, Amanda, lives through exaggerated memories of her own youth as a much sought-after southern belle, while the sister, Laura, lives in an imaginary world she shares with her glass figurines. Laura is too mentally unstable to cope with life beyond the shabby family apartment; she is a complete contradiction of her mother's fantasy that a gentleman caller will appear to marry her and transform all their lives.

In *A Streetcar Named Desire*, Williams explores the disintegration of a young woman, Blanche Dubois, who retreats further and further into a world of illusions to block out her own failures and the failures of those around her to live up to a code of gentility from a bygone era. When her reduced circumstances force her to move in with her sister, Stella, and brother-in-law, Stanley, the tensions between the characters explode in Stanley's sexual assault on Blanche and her final collapse.

KONSTANTIN STANISLAVSKY AND REALISTIC ACTING

The new realistic dramas of the nineteenth century prompted actors to rethink the nature of their craft. The most influential figure in the development of a new approach to acting was Konstantin Stanislavsky (1863–1938), an actor who became a prominent stage director and teacher as cofounder and artistic director of the Moscow Art Theatre. Stanislavsky directed the initial productions of all of Chekhov's plays. It was in part from his work with Chekhov that Stanislavsky evolved his approach to acting—one appropriate to the subtlety and introspection of Chekhov's characters. This approach has become a mainstay of realistic theatre and film.

The ideas suggested by Stanislavsky have come to be organized into something of a system that is frequently referred to as **method acting.** In his own time, however, Stanislavsky was continuously reviewing and adjusting his approach. Stanislavsky believed that the actor should look for ways to identify as closely as possible with his or her character, to undergo a transformation in which the actor would disappear and the character would emerge in his or her place. He proposed an internal rather than an external approach to character development.

From Stanislavsky's work has come the idea that one of the major sources for character development should be the life of the actor. That is, the actor should draw on personal experiences and relationships to provide the foundation for the character's inner life. The actor should also study the role closely to discover a network of objectives—motivations that can then carry the

Marlon Brando and Jessica Tandy created the original interpretations of Tennessee Williams's famous characters, Stanley and Blanche, in *A Streetcar Named Desire (1947)*, directed by Elia Kazan.

actor from moment to moment. At all times the actor must know what the character's intention is. The actor may then invent strategies or tactics to achieve the objective. Each objective, together with the actions and words involved in playing that objective, is considered a **beat.** A role is composed of a sequence of beats that together form a coherent **through line** for the character. The character's dominant motive, or the **superobjective,** will make sense of all the smaller objectives that feed into the particular focus of the character.

In developing this internal acting approach, Stanislavsky was particularly concerned with keeping actors in an alert and creative frame of mind to offset the numbness that he believed resulted from the endless repetitions of the same lines and actions in rehearsals and performances. Stanislavsky also looked to maximize actors'

affection, does for his daughter what he cannot do for his wife. He surrounds her with American "luxuries"; he tries to overcome his cultural isolation by creating the appearance that he and Kiyoko are part of America, that they fit in. Emiko will sell her most treasured possessions, her kimonos, before she will give up her dream of recovering the sense of herself that she projects onto Japan.

Another characteristic of realism is that the objects used in the play and the material concerns, such as crop failure and financial worries, not only ground the lives of the characters in a particular time and place and form an integral part of the plot structure but also have symbolic significance. *And the Soul Shall Dance* is dense with objects that communicate layers of meaning. For example, the food and drink—the sake, chiles and tea—that Hana puts on the table are signs of a functioning home, of warmth and nourishment. In contrast, Emiko refuses to make tea. The absence of food at the Okas' house symbolizes the emptiness of the dwelling; the family members fail to nurture each other. The illegal liquor they brew and the cigarettes Emiko smokes are poisonous substitutes for the missing food. The parents' addictions are part of the profound dysfunction of the family. At the same time that the cigarettes indicate a self-destructive attitude, they are also an important symbol of Emiko's rebellion against her husband and the accepted Japanese social structure.

Even the hairstyles of the two daughters have extremely important symbolic value. Kiyoko is transformed by a permanent wave in act 2 of the play. The processed curly hair says a great deal about the father–daughter relationship and the movement of Oka and Kiyoko toward an image of assimilation. The permanent wave suggests the fabrication of a value system to cover the confusion brought on by their dislocation. The permanent wave is also a weapon in the war between husband and wife. Oka revenges himself on Emiko by spending on Kiyoko the money that Emiko has hoarded to return to Japan. Additionally, the permanent wave provides a way of acknowledging the firm foundation of the Murata family. Hana shows her love and regard for her daughter and also her own strength and stability when she says simply to Masako at the end of the play, "Your hair is so black and straight . . . nice."

The use of objects to develop the symbolic meaning of the play leads to one final conclusion about realism. The careful selection of lifelike details highlights the characters' experiences. Realism, in fact, has its own poetic quality. A movement of the spirit is expressed in the precisely chosen actions and objects that contain the essence of the characters' lives. The appearance of reality becomes a concentrated view of a particular way of life. In *And the Soul Shall Dance*, the simplicity of the play's structure, delicately rendered like Japanese brush painting, presents an almost lyrical impression of memory and longing.

And the Soul Shall Dance

WAKAKO YAMAUCHI

CHARACTERS

MURATA, 40, *Issei* farmer
HANA, 35, *Issei* wife of Murata
MASAKO, 11, *Nisei* daughter of the Muratas
OKA, 45, *Issei* farmer
EMIKO, 30, wife of Oka
KIYOKO, 14, Oka's daughter

Kokoro Ga Odoru	*And the Soul Shall Dance*
Akai kuchibiru	Red lips
Kappu ni yosete	Press against a glass
Aoi sake nomya	Drink the green wine
Kokoro ga odoru	And the dreams will dance
Kurai yoru no yume	In the dark night
Setsu nasa yo	Dreams are unbearable
Aoi sake nomya	Drink the green wine
Yume ga odoru	And the soul shall dance
Asa no munashisa	The morning's truth
Yume wo chirasu	Scatter the dreams
Sora to kokoro wa	Sky and soul
Sake shidai	Are suspended by wine
Futari wakare no	In the separation
Samishisa yo	The desolation
Hitori sake nomya	Drink the wine
Kokoro ga odoru	And the soul shall dance

ACT ONE

Scene 1

Summer afternoon, 1935. Interior of the Murata house. The set is spare. There are a kitchen table, four chairs, a bed, and on the wall, a calendar indicating the year and month: June 1935. A doorway leads to the other room. Props are: a bottle of sake, two cups, a dish of chiles, a phonograph, and two towels hanging on pegs on the wall. A wide wooden bench is outside.

The bathhouse has just burned to the ground due to MASAKO's carelessness. Offstage there are sounds of MURATA putting out the fire. Inside, HANA MURATA, in a drab housedress, confronts MASAKO (in summer dress). MASAKO is sullen and defiant.

HANA: How could you be so careless, Masako? You know you should be extra careful with fire. How often have I told you? Now the whole bathhouse is gone. I told you time and again—when you stoke a fire, you must see that everything is swept into the fireplace.

(MURATA enters. He is in old work clothes. He suffers from heat and exhaustion.)

MURATA: (coughing) Shack went up like a matchbox. This kind of weather dries everything . . . just takes a spark to make a bonfire out of that dry timber.

HANA: Did you save any of it?

MURATA: No. Couldn't.

HANA: (to MASAKO) How many times have I told you . . .

(MASAKO moves nervously.)

MURATA: No use crying about it now. *Shikata ga nai.* It's gone now. No more bathhouse. That's all.

HANA: But you've got to tell her. Otherwise she'll make the same mistake. You'll be building a bathhouse every year.

(MURATA removes his shirt and wipes off his face. He throws his shirt on a chair and sits at the table.)

MURATA: *Baka!* Ridiculous!

MASAKO: I didn't do it on purpose.

(MASAKO goes to the bed. She opens a book. HANA follows her.)

HANA: I know that, but you know what this means? It means we bathe in a bucket . . . inside the house. Carry water in from the pond, heat it on the stove . . . we'll use more kerosene.

MURATA: Tub's still there. And the fireplace. We can still build a fire under the tub.

HANA: (shocked) But no walls! Everyone in the country can see us!

MURATA: Wait till dark then. Wait till dark.

HANA: We'll be using a lantern. They'll still see us.

MURATA: Angh! Who? Who'll see us? You think everyone in the country waits to watch us take a bath? Hunh! You know how stupid you sound? Who cares about a couple of farmers taking a bath at night?

HANA: (defensively) It'll be inconvenient.

(HANA is saved by a rap on the door. OKA enters. He is short and stout. He wears faded work clothes.)

OKA: Hello! Hello! *Oi!* What's going on here? Hey! Was there some kind of fire?

(HANA rushes to the door to let OKA in. He stamps the dust from his shoes and enters.)

HANA: Oka-san! You just wouldn't believe . . . We had a terrible thing happen.

OKA: Yeah. Saw the smoke from down the road. Thought it was your house. Came rushing over. Is the fire out?

(MURATA half rises and sits back again. He's exhausted.)

MURATA: (gesturing) *Oi, oi.* Come in. Sit down. No big problem. It was just our bathhouse.

OKA: Just the *furoba,* eh?

MURATA: Just the bath.

HANA: Our Masako was careless, and the *furoba* caught fire. There's nothing left but the tub.

(MASAKO looks up from her book, pained. She makes a small sound.)

OKA: Long as the tub's there, no problem. I'll help you with it.

(He starts to roll up his sleeves.)

MURATA: What . . . now? Now?

OKA: (heh-heh) Long as I'm here.

HANA: Oh, Papa. Aren't we lucky to have such friends?

MURATA: (to HANA) We can't work on it now. The ashes are still hot. I just now put the damned fire out. Let me rest a while. (to OKA) *Oi,* how about a little sake? (gesturing to HANA) Make sake for Oka-san.

(OKA sits at the table. HANA goes to prepare the sake. She heats it, gets out the cups, and pours it for the men.)

MURATA: (continuing) I'm tired . . . I am tired.

HANA: Oka-san has so generously offered his help . . .

(OKA is uncomfortable. He looks around and sees MASAKO sitting on the bed.)

OKA: Hello, there, Masako-chan. You studying?

MASAKO: No, it's summer vacation.

MURATA: (sucking in his breath) Kids nowadays . . . no manners.

HANA: She's sulking because I had to scold her.

(MASAKO makes a small moan.)

MURATA: Drink, Oka-san.

OKA: (sipping) Ahhhh . . . That's good.

MURATA: Eh, you not working today?

OKA: No-no. I took the afternoon off today. I was driving over to Nagata-san's when I saw this big black cloud of smoke coming from your yard.

HANA: It went up so fast.

MURATA: What's up at Nagata-kun's? (to HANA) Get out the chiles. Oka-san loves chiles.

(HANA opens a jar of chiles and puts them on a plate. She serves them and gets out her mending basket and walks to MASAKO. MASAKO makes room for her.)

OKA: (helping himself) Ah, chiles.

(MURATA waits for an answer.)

OKA: (continuing) Well, I want to see him about my horse. I'm thinking of selling my horse.

MURATA: Sell your horse?

OKA: (scratching his head) The fact is, I need some money. Nagata-san's the only one around made money this year, and I'm thinking he might want another horse.

MURATA: Yeah, he made a little this year. And he's talking big . . . big! Says he's leasing twenty more acres this fall.

OKA: Twenty acres?

MURATA: Yeah. He might want another horse.

OKA: Twenty acres, eh?

MURATA: That's what he says. But you know his old woman makes all the decisions at that house.

(OKA scratches his head.)

HANA: They're doing all right.

MURATA: Heh. Nagata-kun's so henpecked, it's pathetic. Peko-peko. (He makes henpecking motions.)

OKA: (feeling the strain) I better get over there.

MURATA: Why the hell you selling your horse?

OKA: Well . . . a . . . I need cash.

MURATA: Oh yeah. I could use some too. Seems like everyone's getting out of the depression but the poor farmers. Nothing changes for us. We go on and on planting our tomatoes and summer squash and eating them. Well, at least it's healthy.

HANA: Papa, do you have lumber?

MURATA: Lumber? For what?

HANA: The bath . . .

MURATA: (impatiently) Don't worry about that. We need more sake now.

(HANA rises wearily.)

OKA: You sure Nagata-kun's working twenty more?

MURATA: Last I heard. What the hell, if you need a few bucks, I can loan (you) . . .

OKA: A few hundred. I need a few hundred dollars.

MURATA: Oh, a few hundred. But what the hell you going to do without a horse? Out here a man's horse is as important as his wife.

OKA: (seriously) I don't think Nagata will buy my wife.

(The men laugh, but HANA doesn't find it so funny. MURATA glances at her. She fills the cups again. OKA makes a half-hearted gesture to stop her. MASAKO watches the pantomime carefully. OKA finishes his drink.)

OKA: (continuing) I better get moving.

MURATA: What's the big hurry?

OKA: Like to get the horse business done.

MURATA: Eh . . . relax. Do it tomorrow. He's not going to die, is he?

OKA: (laughing) Hey, he's a good horse. I want to get it settled today. If Nagata-kun won't buy, I got to find someone else.

OKA: (continuing) You think maybe Kawaguchi-kun . . . ?

MURATA: No-no. Not Kawaguchi. Maybe Yamamoto.

HANA: What is all the money for, Oka-san? Does Emiko-san need an operation?

OKA: No-no. Nothing like that.

HANA: Sounds very mysterious.

OKA: No mystery, Missus. No mystery. No sale, no money, no story.

MURATA: (laughing) That's a good one. "No sale, no money, no . . ." Eh, Mama . . . (He points to the empty cups.)

HANA: (filling the cups, muttering) I see we won't be getting any work done today. (to MASAKO) Are you reading again? Maybe we'd still have a bath if you . . .

MASAKO: I didn't do it on purpose.

MURATA: (loudly) I sure hope you know what you're doing, Oka-kun. What'd you do without a horse?

OKA: I was hoping you'd lend me yours now and then. (He looks at HANA.) I'll pay for some of the feed.

MURATA: Sure! Sure!

OKA: The fact is, I need that money. I got a daughter in Japan, and I just got to send for her this year.

(HANA leaves her mending and sits at the table.)

HANA: A daughter? You have a daughter in Japan? Why, I didn't know you had children. Emiko-san and you . . . I thought you were childless.

OKA: (scratching his head) We are. I was married before.

MURATA: You son-of-a-gun!

HANA: (overlapping) Is that so? How old is your daughter?

OKA: Kiyoko must be . . . fifteen now. Yeah, fifteen.

HANA: Fifteen! Oh, that *would* be too old for Emiko-san's child. Is Kiyoko's-san living with relatives in Japan?

OKA: (reluctantly) With grandparents. Shizue's parents. (pause) Well, the fact is, Shizue—that's my first wife—Shizue and Emiko were sisters. They come from a family with no sons. I was a boy when I went to work for them . . . as an apprentice. They're blacksmiths. Later I married Shizue and took on the family name—you know, *yoshi*—because they had no sons. My real name is Sakakihara.

MURATA: Sakakihara! That's a great name!

HANA: A magnificent name!

OKA: No one knows me by that here.

MURATA: Should have kept that—Sakakihara.

OKA: (muttering) I don't even know myself by that name.

HANA: And Shizue-san passed away and you married Emiko-san?

OKA: Oh. Well, Shizue and I lived with the family for a while, and we had the baby—you know, Kiyoko. (He gets looser with the liquor.) Well, while I was serving apprentice with the family, they always looked down their noses at me. After I married, it got worse.

HANA: (distressed) Worse!

OKA: That old man . . . (unnnnh!) Always pushing me around, making me look bad in front of my wife and kid. That old man was the meanest . . . ugliest . . .

MURATA: Yeah, I heard about that apprentice work—*detchi-boko*. Heard it was damned humiliating.

OKA: That's the God's truth!

MURATA: Never had to do it myself. I came to America instead. They say *detchi-boko* is blood work.

OKA: The work's all right. I'm not afraid of work. It's the humiliation! I hated them! Pushing me around like I was still a boy. Me, a grown man! And married to their daughter!

(MURATA and HANA groan in sympathy.)

OKA: (continuing) Well, Shizue and I talked it over, and we decided the best thing was to get away. We thought if I came to America and made some money . . . you know, send her money until we had enough, and I'd go back and we'd leave the family . . . you know, move to another province . . . start a small business, maybe in the city . . . a noodle shop or something.

MURATA: That's everyone's dream. Make money, go home, and live like a king.

OKA: I worked like a dog. Sent every penny to Shizue. And then she dies. She died on me!

(HANA and MURATA observe a moment of silence in respect for OKA's anguish.)

HANA: And you married Emiko-san.

OKA: I didn't marry her. They married her to me! Right after Shizue died.

HANA: But Oka-san, you were lu(cky) . . .

OKA: Before the body was cold! No respect. By proxy. The old man wrote me that they were arranging a marriage by proxy for me and Emiko. They said she'd grown to be a beautiful woman and would serve me well.

HANA: Emiko-san *is* a beautiful woman.

OKA: And they sent her to me. Took care of everything! Immigration, fare, everything.

HANA: But she's your sister-in-law. Kiyoko's aunt. It's good to keep the family together.

OKA: That's what I thought. But hear this: Emiko was the favored one. Shizue was not so pretty, not so smart. They were grooming Emiko for a rich man—his name was Yamato—lived in a grand house in the village. They sent her to schools; you know, the culture thing: the dance, tea ceremony, you know, all that. They didn't even like me, and suddenly they married her to me.

MURATA: Yeah. You don't need all that formal training to make it over here. Just a strong back.

HANA: And a strong will.

OKA: It was all arranged. I couldn't do anything about it.

HANA: It'll be all right. With Kiyoko-san coming . . .

OKA: (dubiously) I hope so. (pause) I never knew human beings could be so cruel. You know how they mistreated my daughter? After Emiko came here, things got from bad to worse, and I never had enough money to send to Kiyoko and . . .

MURATA: They don't know what it's like here. They think money's picked off the ground here.

OKA: And they treated Kiyoko so bad. They told her I forgot about her. They told her I didn't care . . . said I abandoned her. Well, she knew better. She wrote to me all the time, and I always told her I'd send for her . . . as soon as I got the money. (He shakes his head.) I just got to do something this year.

HANA: She'll be happier here. She'll know her father cares.

OKA: Kids tormented her for being an orphan.

MURATA: Kids are cruel.

HANA: Masako will help her. She'll help her get started at school. She'll make friends. She'll be all right.

OKA: I hope so. She'll need friends. (He tries to convince himself he's making the right decision.) What could I say to her? Stay there? It's not what you think over here? I can't help her? I just have to do this thing. I just have to do this one thing for her.

MURATA: Sure.

HANA: Don't worry. It'll work out fine.

(MURATA gestures to HANA. She gets the sake.)

MURATA: You talk about selling your horse, I thought you were pulling out.

OKA: I wish I could. But there's nothing else I can do.

MURATA: Without money, yeah.

OKA: You can go into some kind of business with money, but a man like me . . . no education . . . there's no kind of job I can do. I'd starve in the city.

MURATA: Dishwashing, maybe. Janitor.

OKA: At least here we can eat. Carrots, maybe, but we can eat.

(They laugh. HANA starts to pour more wine.)

OKA: I better not drink anymore. Got to drive to Nagata-san's yet. (He walks over to MASAKO.) You study hard, don't you? You'll teach Kiyoko English, eh? When she gets here . . . ?

HANA: Oh, yes, she will.

MURATA: Kiyoko-san could probably teach her a thing or two.

OKA: She won't know about American ways.

MASAKO: I'll help her.

HANA: Don't worry, Oka-san. She'll have a good friend in our Masako.

(They move to the door.)

OKA: Well, thanks for the sake. I guess I talk too much when I drink. (He scratches his head and laughs.) Oh. I'm sorry about the fire. By the way, come to my house for your bath . . . until you build yours again.

HANA: Oh, a . . . thank you. I don't know if . . .

MURATA: Good, good! I need a good hot bath tonight.

OKA: Tonight, then.

MURATA: We'll be there.

HANA: (bowing) Thank you very much. *Sayonara*.

OKA: (nodding) See you tonight.

(OKA leaves. HANA faces MURATA as soon as the door closes.)

HANA: Papa, I don't know about going over there.

MURATA: (surprised) Why?

HANA: Well, Emiko-san . . .

MURATA: (irritated) What's the matter with you? We need a bath and Oka's invited us over.

HANA: (to MASAKO) Help me clear the table.

(MASAKO reluctantly leaves her book.)

HANA: (continuing) Papa, you know we've been neighbors already three, four years, and Emiko-san's never been very hospitable.

MURATA: She's shy, that's all.

HANA: Not just shy. She's strange. I feel like she's pushing me off. She makes me feel like—I don't know—like I'm prying or something.

MURATA: Maybe you are.

HANA: And never puts out a cup of tea . . . If she had all that training in the graces . . . why, a cup of tea . . .

MURATA: So if you want tea, ask for it.

HANA: I can't do that, Papa. (pause) She's strange. . . . I don't know . . . (to MASAKO) When we go there, be very careful not to say anything wrong.

MASAKO: I never say anything anyway.

HANA: (thoughtfully) Would you believe the story Oka-san just told? Why, I never knew . . .

MURATA: There're lots of things you don't know. Just because a man don't . . . don't talk about them, don't mean he don't feel . . . don't think about . . .

HANA: (looking around) We'll have to take something. There's nothing to take. Papa, maybe you can dig up some carrots.

MURATA: God, Mama, be sensible. They got carrots. Everybody's got carrots.

HANA: Something . . . Maybe I should make something.

MURATA: Hell, they're not expecting anything.

HANA: It's not good manners to go empty-handed.

MURATA: We'll take the sake.

(HANA grimaces. MASAKO sees the phonograph.)

MASAKO: I know, Mama. We can take the Victrola! We can play records for Mrs. Oka. Then nobody has to talk.

(MURATA laughs.)

Scene 2

That evening. The exterior wall of the Okas' weathered house. There is a workable screen door and a large screened window. Outside there is a wide wooden bench that can accommodate three or four people. There is one separate chair, and a lantern stands against the house.

The last rays of the sun light the area in a soft golden glow. This light grows gray as the scene progresses, and it is quite dark by the end of the scene.

Through the screened window, EMIKO can be seen walking erratically back and forth. She wears drab cotton but her grace and femininity come through. Her hair is bunned back in the style of the Issei women of the era.

OKA sits cross-legged on the bench. He wears a Japanese summer robe (yukata) and fans himself with a round Japanese fan.

The MURATAS enter. MURATA carries towels and a bottle of sake. HANA carries the Victrola, and MASAKO, a package containing their yukata.

OKA: (standing to greet the MURATAS) Oh, you've come. Welcome!

MURATA: *Yah* . . . Good of you to ask us.

HANA: (bowing) Yes, thank you very much. (to MASAKO) Say hello, Masako.

MASAKO: Hello.

HANA: And thank you.

MASAKO: Thank you.

(OKA makes motions of protest. EMIKO stops her pacing and watches from the window.)

HANA: (glancing briefly at the window) And how is Emiko-san this evening?

OKA: (turning to the house) Emi! Emiko!

HANA: That's all right. Don't call her out. She must be busy.

OKA: Emiko!

(EMIKO comes to the door. HANA starts a bow toward the house.)

MURATA: *Konbanwa!?* (Good evening)

HANA: Konbanwa, Emiko-san. I feel so badly about this intrusion. (pause) Your husband has told you our bathhouse was destroyed by fire, and he graciously invited us to come use yours.

(EMIKO shakes her head.)

OKA: I didn't have a chance to . . .

(HANA recovers and nudges MASAKO.)

HANA: Say hello to Mrs. Oka.

MASAKO: Hello, Mrs. Oka.

(HANA lowers the Victrola to the bench.)

OKA: What's this? You brought a phonograph?

MASAKO: It's a Victrola.

HANA: (laughing indulgently) Yes. Masako wanted to bring this over and play some records.

MURATA: (extending the wine) Brought a little sake too.

OKA: (taking the bottle) Ah, now that I like. Emiko, bring out the cups.

(OKA waves at his wife, but she doesn't move. He starts to ask again but decides to get them himself. He enters the house and returns with two cups.)

(EMIKO seats herself on the single chair. The MURATAS unload their paraphernalia; OKA pours the wine, the men drink, HANA chatters and sorts the records. MASAKO stands by helping her.)

HANA: Yes, our Masako loves to play records. I like records too, and Papa, he . . .

MURATA: (watching EMIKO) They take me back home. The only way I can get there. In my mind.

HANA: Do you like music, Emiko-san?

(EMIKO looks vague, but smiles.)

HANA: (continuing) Oka-san, you like them, don't you?

OKA: Yeah. But I don't have a player. No chance to hear them.

MURATA: I had to get this for them. They wouldn't leave me alone until I got it. Well . . . a phonograph . . . what the hell; they got to have *some* fun.

HANA: We don't have to play them, if you'd rather not.

OKA: Play. Play them.

HANA: I thought we could listen to them and relax. (She extends some records to EMIKO.) Would you like to look through these, Emiko-san?

(EMIKO doesn't respond. She pulls out a sack of Bull Durham and begins to roll a cigarette. HANA pushes MASAKO to her.)

HANA: (continuing) Take these to her.

(MASAKO goes to EMIKO with the records. She stands watching her as EMIKO lights a cigarette.)

HANA: (continuing) Some of these are very old. You might know them, Emiko-san. (She sees MASAKO watching EMIKO.) Masako, bring those over here. (She laughs uncomfortably.) You might like this one, Emiko-san. (She starts the player.) Do you know it?

(The record whines out "Kago No Tori." EMIKO listens with her head cocked.)

(She smokes her cigarette. She is wrapped in nostalgia and memories of the past. MASAKO watches her carefully.)

MASAKO: (whispering) Mama, she's crying.

(Startled, HANA and MURATA look toward EMIKO.)

HANA: (pinching MASAKO) Shhh. The smoke is in her eyes.

MURATA: Did you bring the record I like, Mama?

(EMIKO rises abruptly and enters the house.)

MASAKO: They're tears, Mama.

HANA: From yawning, Masako. (regretfully to OKA) I'm afraid we offended her.

OKA: (unaware) Hunh? Aw . . . no . . . pay no attention. No offense.

(MASAKO looks toward the window. EMIKO stands forlornly and slowly drifts into a dance.)

HANA: I'm very sorry. Children, you know . . . they'll say anything. Anything that's on their minds.

(MURATA notices MASAKO looking through the window and tries to divert her attention.)

MURATA: The needles. Masako, where're the needles?

MASAKO: (still watching) I forgot them.

(HANA sees what's going on. OKA is unaware.)

HANA: Masako, go take your bath now. Masako . . .

(MASAKO reluctantly takes her towel and leaves.)

OKA: Yeah, yeah. Take your bath, Masako-chan.

MURATA: (sees EMIKO still dancing) Change the record, Mama.

OKA: (still unaware) That's kind of sad.

MURATA: No use to get sick over a record. We're supposed to enjoy.

(HANA stops the record. EMIKO disappears from the window. HANA selects a lively ondo ["Tokyo Ondo"].)

HANA: We'll find something more fun.

(The three tap to the music.)

HANA: (continuing) Can't you just see the festival? The dancers, the bright kimonos, the paper lanterns bobbing in the wind, the fireflies . . . How nostalgic. Oh, how nostalgic.

(EMIKO appears from the side of the house. Her hair is down; she wears an old straw hat. She dances in front of the MURATAS. They are startled.)

(After the first shock, they watch with frozen smiles. They try to join EMIKO's mood, but something is missing. OKA is grieved. He finally stands as though he's had enough. EMIKO, now close to the door, ducks into the house.)

HANA: That was pretty. Very nice.

(OKA settles down and grunts. MURATA clears his throat, and MASAKO returns from her bath.)

MURATA: You're done already? (He's glad to see her.)

MASAKO: I wasn't very dirty. The water was too hot.

MURATA: Good! Just the way I like it.

HANA: Not dirty?

MURATA: (picking up his towel) Come on, Mama . . . scrub my back.

HANA: (laughing with embarrassment) Oh, oh . . . well . . . (She stops the player.) Masako, now don't forget. Crank the machine and change the needle now and then.

MASAKO: I didn't bring them.

HANA: Oh. Oh . . . all right. I'll be back soon. Don't forget . . . Crank. (She leaves with her husband.)

(OKA and MASAKO are alone. OKA is awkward and falsely hearty.)

OKA: So! So you don't like hot baths, eh?

MASAKO: Not too hot.

OKA: (laughing) I thought you like it real hot. Hot enough to burn the house down.

(MASAKO doesn't laugh.)

OKA: (continuing) That's a little joke.

(MASAKO busies herself to conceal her annoyance.)

OKA: (continuing) I hear you're real good in school. Always top of the class.

MASAKO: It's a small class. Only two of us.

OKA: When Kiyoko comes, you'll help her in school, yeah? You'll take care of her . . . a favor for me, eh?

MASAKO: Okay.

OKA: You'll be her friend, eh?

MASAKO: Okay.

OKA: That's good. That's good. You'll like her. She's a nice girl too.

(OKA stands, yawns, and stretches.)

OKA: (continuing) I'll go for a little walk now. (He touches his crotch to indicate his purpose.)

(MASAKO turns her attention to the records and selects one, "And the Soul Shall Dance," and begins to sway with the music. The song draws EMIKO from the house. She looks out the window, sees MASAKO is alone, and slips into a dance.)

EMIKO: Do you like that song, Masa-chan?

(MASAKO is startled. She remembers her mother's warning. She doesn't know what to do. She nods.)

EMIKO: (continuing) That's one of my favorite songs. I remember in Japan I used to sing it so often. My favorite song. (She sings along with the record.) *Akai kuchibiru / Kappu ni yosete / Aoi sake nomya / Kokoro ga odoru.* Do you know what that means, Masa-chan?

MASAKO: I think so. The soul will dance?

EMIKO: Yes, yes, that's right. The soul shall dance. Red lips against a glass, drink the green . . .

MASAKO: Wine?

EMIKO: (nodding) Drink the green wine . . .

MASAKO: Green? I thought wine was purple.

EMIKO: Wine is purple, but this is a green liqueur.

(EMIKO holds up one of the cups as though it were crystal and looks at the light that would shine through the green liquid.)

EMIKO: (continuing) It's good. It warms your heart.

MASAKO: And the soul dances.

EMIKO: Yes . . .

MASAKO: What does it taste like? The green wine?

EMIKO: Oh, it's like . . . it's like . . .

(The second verse starts: Kurai yoru no yume / Setsu nasa yo / Aoi sake nomya / Yume ga odoru.)

MASAKO: In the dark night . . .

EMIKO: Dreams are unbearable . . .

MASAKO: Drink the . . .

EMIKO: Drink the green wine . . .

MASAKO: And the dreams will dance.

EMIKO: (softly) I'll be going back one day.

MASAKO: Where?

EMIKO: My home. Japan. My real home. I'm going back one day.

MASAKO: By yourself?

EMIKO: Oh, yes. It's a secret. You can keep a secret?

MASAKO: Un-hunh. I have lots of secrets. All my own.

(The music stops. EMIKO sees OKA approaching and disappears into the house. MASAKO attends to the record and does not know EMIKO is gone.)

MASAKO: (continuing) Secrets I never tell anyone . . .

OKA: Secrets? What kind of secrets? What did she say?

MASAKO: (startled) Oh! Nothing.

OKA: What did you talk about?

MASAKO: Nothing. Mrs. Oka was talking about the song. She was telling me what it meant . . . about the soul.

OKA: (scoffing) Heh! What does she know about soul? (calming down) Ehhh . . . Some people don't have them—souls.

MASAKO: (timidly) I thought . . . I thought everyone has a soul. I read in a book . . .

OKA: (Hah!) Now! Go now! Who needs you? Who needs you? You think a man waits ten years for a woman? You think you're some kind of . . . of diamond . . . treasure . . . he's going to wait his life for you? Go to him. He's probably married with ten kids. Go to him. Get out! Goddam *joro*. Go! Go!

(OKA sweeps EMIKO off the bench.)

EMIKO: Ahhh! I . . . I don't have the money. Give me money to . . .

OKA: If I had money I would give it to you ten years ago. You think I been eating this *kuso* for ten years because I like it?

EMIKO: You're selling the horse. Give me the (money) . . .

OKA: (scoffing) That's for Kiyoko. I owe you nothing.

EMIKO: Ten years, you owe me.

OKA: Ten years of what? Misery? You gave me nothing. I give you nothing. You want to go, pack your bag and start walking. Try cross the desert. When you get dry and hungry, think about me.

EMIKO: I'd die out there.

OKA: Die? You think I didn't die here?

EMIKO: I didn't do anything to you.

OKA: No, no, you didn't. All I wanted was a little comfort and you . . . no, you didn't. No. So you die. We all die. Shizue died. If she was here, she wouldn't treat me like this. Ah, I should have brought her with me. She'd be alive now. We'd be poor but happy like . . . like Murata and his wife . . . and the kid.

EMIKO: I wish she were alive too. I'm not to blame for her dying. I didn't know. I was away. I loved her. I didn't want her to die. I . . .

OKA: (softening) I know that. I'm not blaming you for that. And it's not my fault what happened to you either.

(OKA is encouraged by EMIKO's silence which he mistakes for a change of attitude.)

OKA: (continuing) You understand that, eh? I didn't ask for you. It's not my fault you're here in this desert with . . . with me.

(EMIKO weeps. OKA reaches out.)

OKA: (continuing) I know I'm too old for you. It's hard for me too. But this is the way it is. I just ask you be kinder . . . understand it wasn't my fault. Try make it easier for me. For yourself too.

(OKA touches her and she shrinks from his hand.)

EMIKO: Ach!

OKA: (humiliated again) Goddam it! I didn't ask for you! *Aho!* If you was smart, you'da done as your father said . . . cut out that *saru shibai* with the *Etta* . . . married the rich Yamato. Then you'd still be in Japan. Not here to make my life so miserable.

(EMIKO is silent.)

OKA: (continuing) And you can have your *Etta* . . . or anyone else you want. Take them all on.

(OKA is worn out. It's hopeless.)

OKA: (continuing) God, why do we do this all the time? Fighting all the time. There must be a better way to live. There must be another way.

(OKA waits for a response, gives up, and enters the house. EMIKO watches him leave and pours another drink. The storm has passed, the alcohol takes over.)

EMIKO: I must keep the dream alive. The dream is all I live for. I am only in exile now. If I give in, all I've lived before will mean nothing . . . will be for nothing. Nothing. If I let you make me believe this is all there is to my life, the dream would die. I would die.

(She pours another drink and feels warm and good.)

ACT TWO

Scene 1

Mid-September afternoon. Muratas' kitchen. The calendar reads September. MASAKO is at the kitchen table with several books. She thumbs through a Japanese magazine. HANA is with her sewing.

MASAKO: Do they always wear kimonos in Japan, Mama?

HANA: Most of the time.

MASAKO: I wonder if Kiyoko will be wearing a kimono like this.

HANA: (looking at the magazine) They don't dress like that. Not for every day.

MASAKO: I wonder what she's like.

HANA: Probably a lot like you. What do you think she's like?

MASAKO: She's probably taller.

HANA: Mr. Oka isn't tall.

MASAKO: And pretty.

HANA: (laughing) Mr. Oka . . . Well, I don't suppose she'll look like her father.

MASAKO: Mrs. Oka is pretty.

HANA: She isn't Kiyoko-san's real mother, remember?

MASAKO: Oh, that's right.

HANA: But they are related. Well, we'll soon see.

MASAKO: I thought she was coming in September. It's already September.

HANA: Papa said Oka-san went to San Pedro a few days ago. He should be back soon with Kiyoko-san.

MASAKO: Didn't Mrs. Oka go too?

HANA: (glancing toward the Oka house) I don't think so. I see lights in their house at night.

MASAKO: Will they bring Kiyoko over to see us?

HANA: Of course. First thing, probably. You'll be very nice to her, won't you?

(MASAKO finds another book.)

MASAKO: Sure. I'm glad I'm going to have a friend. I hope she likes me.

HANA: She'll like you. Japanese girls are very polite, you know.

MASAKO: We have to be or our mamas get mad at us.

HANA: Then I should be getting mad at you more often.

MASAKO: It's often enough already, Mama. (She opens the book.) Look at this, Mama. I'm going to show her this book.

HANA: She won't be able to read at first.

MASAKO: I love this story. Mama, this is about people like us—settlers—it's about the prairie. We live in a prairie, don't we?

HANA: Prairie? Does that mean desert?

MASAKO: I think so.

HANA: (looking at the bleak landscape) We live in a prairie.

MASAKO: It's about the hardships and the floods and droughts and how they have nothing but each other.

HANA: We have nothing but each other. But these people . . . they're white people.

MASAKO: Sure, Mama. They come from the east. Just like you and Papa came from Japan.

HANA: We come from the far far east. That's different. White people are different from us.

MASAKO: I know that.

HANA: White people among white people . . . that's different from Japanese among white people. You know what I'm saying?

MASAKO: I know that. How come they don't write books about us . . . about Japanese people?

HANA: Because we're nobodies here.

MASAKO: If I didn't read these, there'd be nothing for me.

HANA: Some of the things you read, you're never going to know.

MASAKO: I can dream though.

HANA: (sighing) Sometimes the dreaming makes the living harder. Better to keep your head out of the clouds.

MASAKO: That's not much fun.

HANA: You'll have fun when Kiyoko-san comes. You can study together, you can sew, and sometime you can try some of those fancy American recipes.

MASAKO: Oh, Mama. You have to have chocolate and cream and things like that.

HANA: We'll get them.

(We hear the sound of Oka's old car. MASAKO and HANA pause and listen. MASAKO runs to the window.)

MASAKO: I think it's them!

HANA: Oka-san?

MASAKO: It's them! It's them!

(HANA stands and looks out. She removes her apron and puts away her sewing.)

HANA: Two of them. Emiko-san isn't with them. (pause) Let's go outside.

(OKA and KIYOKO enter. OKA is wearing his going-out clothes: a sweater, white shirt, dark pants, but no tie. KIYOKO walks behind him.)

(KIYOKO is short, broad-chested, and very self-conscious. Her hair is straight and banded into two shucks. She wears a conservative cotton dress, white socks, and two-inch heels.)

(OKA is proud. He struts in, his chest puffed out.)

OKA: Hello, hello! We're here. We made it! (He pushes KIYOKO forward.) This my daughter, Kiyoko. (to KIYOKO) Murata-san. Remember, I was talking about? My friends . . .

KIYOKO: (bowing deeply) *Hajime mashite yoroshiku onegai shimasu.*

HANA: (also bowing deeply) I hope your journey was pleasant.

OKA: (pushing KIYOKO to MASAKO while she still bows) This is Masako-chan; I told you about her.

(MASAKO is shocked at KIYOKO's appearance. The girl she expected is already a woman. She stands with her mouth agape and withdraws noticeably. HANA rushes in to fill the awkwardness.)

HANA: Say hello, Masako. My goodness, where are your manners? (She laughs apologetically.) In this country they don't make much to-do about manners. (She stands back to examine KIYOKO.) My, my, I didn't picture you so grown up. My, my . . . Tell me, how was your trip?

OKA: (proudly) We just drove in from Los Angeles this morning. We spent the night in San Pedro, and the next two days we spent in Los Angeles . . . you know, Japanese town.

HANA: How nice!

OKA: Kiyoko was so excited. Twisting her head this way and that—couldn't see enough with her big eyes. (He imitates her fondly.) She's from the country, you know . . . just a big country girl. Got all excited about the Chinese dinner—we had a Chinese dinner. She never ate it before.

(KIYOKO covers her mouth and giggles.)

HANA: Chinese dinner!

OKA: Oh, yeah. Duck, *pakkai,* chow mein, seaweed soup . . . the works!

HANA: A feast!

OKA: Oh, yeah. Like a holiday. Two holidays. Two holidays in one.

(HANA pushes MASAKO forward.)

HANA: Two holidays in one! Kiyoko-san, our Masako has been looking forward to meeting you.

KIYOKO: (bowing again) *Hajime mashite . . .*

HANA: She's been planning all sorts of things she'll do with you: sewing, cooking . . .

MASAKO: Oh, Mama . . .

(KIYOKO covers her mouth and giggles.)

HANA: It's true, Kiyoko-san. She's been looking forward to having a best friend.

(KIYOKO giggles and MASAKO pulls away.)

OKA: Kiyoko, you shouldn't be so shy. The Muratas are my good friends, and you should feel free with them. Ask anything, say anything. Right?

HANA: Of course, of course. (She is annoyed with MASAKO.) Masako, go in and start the tea.

(MASAKO enters the house.)

HANA: (continuing) I'll call Papa. He's in the yard. Papa! Oka-san is here! (to KIYOKO) Now tell me, how was your trip? Did you get seasick?

KIYOKO: (bowing and nodding) Eh (affirmative). A little.

OKA: Tell her. Tell her how sick you got.

(KIYOKO covers her mouth and giggles.)

HANA: Oh, I know, I know. I was too. That was a long time ago. I'm sure things are improved now. Tell me about Japan. What is it like now? They say it's so changed . . . modern.

OKA: Kiyoko comes from the country . . . backwoods. Nothing changes much there from century to century.

HANA: Ah! That's true. That's why I love Japan. And you wanted to leave. It's unbelievable. To come here!

OKA: She always dreamed about it.

HANA: Well, it's not really that bad.

OKA: No, it's not that bad. Depends on what you make of it.

HANA: That's right. What you make of it. I was just telling Masako today . . .

(MURATA enters. He rubs his hands to remove the soil and comes in grinning. He shakes OKA's hand.)

MURATA: *Oi, oi* . . .

OKA: *Yah* . . . I'm back. This is my daughter.

MURATA: No! She's beautiful!

OKA: Finally made it. Finally got her here.

MURATA: (to KIYOKO) Your father hasn't stopped talking about you all summer.

HANA: And Masako too.

KIYOKO: (bowing) *Hajime mashite* . . .

MURATA: (with a short bow) *Yah.* How'd you like the trip?

OKA: I was just telling your wife . . . had a good time in Los Angeles. Had a couple of great dinners, took in the cinema—Japanese pictures, bought her some American clothes . . .

HANA: Oh, you bought that in Los Angeles.

MURATA: Got a good price for your horse, eh? Lots of money, eh?

OKA: Nagata-kun's a shrewd bargainer. Heh. It don't take much money to make her happy. She's a country girl.

MURATA: That's all right. Country's all right. Country girl's the best.

OKA: Had trouble on the way back.

MURATA: Yeah?

OKA: Fan belt broke.

MURATA: That'll happen with these old cars.

OKA: Lucky I was near a gasoline station. We were in the mountains. Waited in a restaurant while it was getting fixed.

HANA: Oh, that was good.

OKA: Guess they don't see Japanese much. Stare? Terrible! Took them a long time to wait on us. Dumb waitress practically threw the food at us. Kiyoko felt bad.

HANA: Ah! That's too bad . . . too bad. That's why I always pack a lunch when we take trips.

MURATA: They'll spoil the day for you . . . those barbarians!

OKA: Terrible food too. Kiyoko couldn't swallow the dry bread and bologna.

HANA: That's the food they eat!

MURATA: Let's go in . . . have a little wine. Mama, we got wine? This is a celebration.

HANA: I think so. A little.

(They enter the house talking. MASAKO has made tea and HANA serves the wine.)

HANA: (continuing) How is your mother? Was she happy to see you?

KIYOKO: Oh, she . . . yes.

HANA: I just know she was surprised to see you so grown up. Of course, you remember her from Japan, don't you?

KIYOKO: (nodding) *Eh* (affirmative). I can barely remember. I was very young.

HANA: Of course. But you do, don't you?

KIYOKO: She was gone most of the time . . . at school in Tokyo. She was very pretty, I remember that.

HANA: She's still very pretty.

KIYOKO: Yes. She was always laughing. She was much younger then.

HANA: Oh, now, it hasn't been that long ago.

(MASAKO goes outside. The following dialogue continues muted as the light goes dim in the house and focuses on MASAKO. EMIKO enters, is drawn to the Murata window, and listens.)

OKA: We stayed at an inn on East First Street. *Shizuokaya.* Whole inn filled with Shizuoka people . . . talking the old dialect. Thought I was in Japan again.

MURATA: That right?

OKA: Felt good. Like I was in Japan again.

HANA: (to KIYOKO) Did you enjoy Los Angeles?

KIYOKO: Yes.

OKA: That's as close as I'll get to Japan.

MURATA: *Mattakuna!* That's for sure. Not in this life.

(Outside MASAKO is aware of EMIKO.)

MASAKO: Why don't you go in?

EMIKO: Oh. Oh. Why don't you?

MASAKO: They're all grown-ups in there. I'm not grown up.

EMIKO: (softly) All grown-ups. Maybe I'm not either. (Her mood changes.) Masa-chan, do you have a boyfriend?

MASAKO: I don't like boys. They don't like me.

EMIKO: Oh, that will change. You will change. I was like that too.

MASAKO: Besides, there's none around here . . . Japanese boys. There are some at school, but they don't like girls.

HANA: (calling from the kitchen) Masako . . .

(MASAKO doesn't answer.)

EMIKO: Your mother is calling you.

MASAKO: (to her mother) *Nani?* (What?)

HANA: (from the kitchen) Come inside now.

EMIKO: You'll have a boyfriend one day.

MASAKO: Not me.

EMIKO: You'll fall in love one day. Someone will make the inside of you light up, and you'll know you're in love. Your life will change . . . grow beautiful. It's good, Masa-chan. And this feeling you'll remember the rest of your life . . . will come back to you . . . haunt you . . . keep you alive . . . five, ten years . . . no matter what happens. Keep you alive.

HANA: (from the house) Masako . . . Come inside now.

(MASAKO turns aside to answer and EMIKO slips away.)

MASAKO: What, Mama?

(HANA comes out.)

HANA: Come inside. Don't be so unsociable. Kiyoko wants to talk to you.

MASAKO: (watching EMIKO leave) She doesn't want to talk to me. You're only saying that.

HANA: What's the matter with you? Don't you want to make friends with her?

MASAKO: She's not my friend. She's your friend.

HANA: Don't be silly. She's only fourteen.

MASAKO: Fifteen. They said fifteen. She's your friend. She's an old lady.

HANA: Don't say that.

MASAKO: I don't like her.

HANA: Shhh! Don't say that.

MASAKO: She doesn't like me either.

HANA: Ma-chan. Remember your promise to Mr. Oka? You're going to take her to school, teach her the language, teach her the ways of Americans.

MASAKO: She can do it herself. You did.

HANA: That's not nice, Ma-chan.

MASAKO: I don't like the way she laughs. (She imitates KIYOKO holding her hand to her mouth and giggling and bowing.)

HANA: Oh, how awful! Stop that. That's the way the girls do in Japan. Maybe she doesn't like your ways either. That's only a difference in manners. What you're doing now is considered very bad manners. (She changes her tone.) Ma-chan, just wait: when she learns to read and speak, you'll have so much to say to each other. Come on, be a good girl and come inside.

MASAKO: It's just old people in there, Mama. I don't want to go in.

(HANA calls to KIYOKO inside.)

HANA: Kiyoko-san, please come here a minute. Maybe it's better for you to talk to Masako alone.

(KIYOKO dutifully goes outside.)

HANA: (continuing) Masako has a lot of things to tell you . . . about what to expect in school and . . . things.

MURATA: (calling from the table) Mama, put out something . . . chiles—for Oka-san.

(HANA enters the house. KIYOKO and MASAKO stand awkwardly facing each other, KIYOKO glancing shyly at MASAKO.)

MASAKO: Do you like it here?

KIYOKO: (nodding) *Eh* (affirmative).

(There is an uncomfortable pause.)

MASAKO: School will be starting next week.

KIYOKO: (nodding) *Eh*.

MASAKO: Do you want to walk to school with me?

KIYOKO: (nodding) *Hai*.

(MASAKO rolls her eyes and tries again.)

MASAKO: I leave at 7:30.

KIYOKO: *Eh*.

(There's a long pause. MASAKO gives up and moves offstage.)

MASAKO: I have to do something.

(KIYOKO watches her leave and uncertainly moves back to the house. HANA looks up at KIYOKO coming in alone, sighs, and quietly pulls out a chair for her.)

Scene 2

November night. Interior of the Murata home. Lamps are lit. The family is at the kitchen table.

HANA sews, MASAKO does her homework, MURATA reads the paper. They're dressed in warm robes and are having tea.

Outside, thunder rolls in the distance and lightning flashes.

HANA: It'll be *ohigan* (autumn festival) soon.

MURATA: Something to look forward to.

HANA: We'll need sweet rice for *omochi* (rice cakes).

MURATA: I'll order it next time I go to town.

HANA: (to MASAKO) How is school? Getting a little harder?

MASAKO: Not that much. Sometimes the arithmetic is hard.

HANA: How is Kiyoko-san doing? Is she getting along all right?

MASAKO: She's good in arithmetic. She skipped a grade already.

HANA: Already? That's good news. Only November and she skipped a grade! At this rate she'll be through before you.

MASAKO: Well, she's older.

MURATA: Sure, she's older, Mama.

HANA: Has she made any friends?

MASAKO: No. She follows me around all day. She understands okay, but she doesn't talk. She talks like, you know . . . she says "ranchi" for lunch and "ranchi" for ranch too, and like that. Kids laugh and copy behind her back. It's hard to understand her.

HANA: You understand her, don't you?

MASAKO: I'm used to it.

HANA: You should tell the kids not to laugh. After all, she's trying. Maybe you should help her practice those words . . . show her what she's doing wrong.

MASAKO: I already do. Our teacher told me to do that.

MURATA: (looking up from his paper) You ought to help her all you can.

HANA: And remember, when you started school, you couldn't speak English either.

MASAKO: I help her.

(MURATA goes to the window. The night is cold. Lightning flashes and the wind whistles.)

MURATA: Looks like a storm coming up. Hope we don't have a freeze.

HANA: If it freezes, we'll have another bad year. Maybe we ought to start the smudge pots.

MURATA: (listening) It's starting to rain. Nothing to do now but pray.

HANA: If praying is the answer, we'd be in Japan now. Rich.

MURATA: (wryly) We're not dead yet. We still have a chance.

(HANA glares at the small joke.)

MURATA: (continuing) Guess I'll turn in.

HANA: Go to bed, go to bed. I'll sit up and worry.

MURATA: If worrying was the answer, we'd be around the world twice and in Japan. Come on, Mama. Let's go to bed. It's too cold tonight to be mad.

(There's an urgent knock on the door. The MURATAS react.)

MURATA: (continuing) *Dareh da!* (Who is it?)

(MURATA goes to the door and hesitates.)

MURATA: (continuing) Who is it!

KIYOKO: (weakly) It's me . . . help me . . .

(MURATA opens the door and KIYOKO stumbles in. She wears a kimono with a shawl thrown over. Her legs are bare except for a pair of straw zori. Her hair is wet and stringy, and she trembles uncontrollably.)

MURATA: My God! Kiyoko-san! What's the matter?

HANA: (overlapping) Kiyoko-san! What is it?

MURATA: What happened?

KIYOKO: They're fighting, they're fighting!

MURATA: Oh, don't worry. Those things happen. No cause to worry. Mama, make tea for her. Sit down and catch your breath. Don't worry. I'll take you home when you're ready.

HANA: Papa, I'll take care of it.

MURATA: Let me know when you're ready to go home.

HANA: It must be freezing out there. Try to get warm. Try to calm yourself.

MURATA: Kiyoko-san, don't worry. (He puts his robe around her.)

(HANA waves MASAKO and MURATA off. MURATA leaves. MASAKO goes to her bed in the kitchen.)

HANA: Papa, I'll take care of it.

KIYOKO: (looking at MURATA'S retreating form) But I came to ask your help. . . .

HANA: You ran down here without a lantern? You could have fallen and hurt yourself.

KIYOKO: I don't care . . . I don't care . . .

HANA: You don't know, Kiyoko-san. It's treacherous out there—snakes, spiders . . .

KIYOKO: I must go back! I . . . I . . . you . . . please come with me. . . .

HANA: First, first we must get you warm. Drink your tea.

KIYOKO: But they'll kill each other. They're fighting like animals. Help me stop them!

(HANA warms a pot of soup.)

HANA: (calmly) I cannot interfere in a family quarrel.

KIYOKO: It's not a quarrel. It's a . . . a . . .

HANA: That's all it is. A family squabble. You'll see. Tomorrow . . .

(KIYOKO pulls at HANA's arm.)

KIYOKO: Not just a squabble! Please . . . please . . .

(KIYOKO starts toward the door, but HANA stops her.)

HANA: Now listen. Listen to me, Kiyoko-san. I've known your father and mother a little while now. I suspect it's been like this for years. Every family has some kind of trouble.

KIYOKO: Not like this, not like this.

HANA: Some have it better, some worse. When you get married, you'll understand. Don't worry. Nothing will happen. (She takes a towel and dries KIYOKO's hair.) You're chilled to the bone. You'll catch your death.

KIYOKO: I don't care. . . . I want to die.

HANA: Don't be silly. It's not that bad.

KIYOKO: It is! They started drinking early in the afternoon. They make some kind of brew and hide it somewhere in the desert.

HANA: It's illegal to make it. That's why they hide it. That home brew is poison to the body. The mind too.

KIYOKO: It makes them crazy. They drink it all the time and quarrel constantly. I was in the other room studying. I try so hard to keep up with school.

HANA: We were talking about you just this evening. Masako says you're doing so well. You skipped a grade?

KIYOKO: It's hard . . . hard. I'm too old for the class and the children . . .

(She remembers all her problems and starts crying again.)

HANA: It's always hard in a new country.

KIYOKO: They were bickering and quarreling all afternoon. Then something happened. All of a sudden they were on the floor . . . hitting and . . . and . . . He was hitting her in the stomach, the face . . . I tried to stop them, but they were so . . . drunk.

HANA: There, there. It's probably all over now.

KIYOKO: Why does it happen like this? Nothing is right. Everywhere I go. Masa-chan is so lucky. I wish my life was like hers. I can hardly remember my real mother.

HANA: Emiko-san is almost a real mother to you. She's blood kin.

KIYOKO: She hates me. She never speaks to me. She's so cold. I want to love her, but she won't let me. She hates me.

HANA: I don't think so, Kiyoko-san.

KIYOKO: She does! She hates me.

HANA: No. I don't think you have anything to do with it. It's this place. She hates it. This place is so lonely and alien.

KIYOKO: Then why didn't she go back? Why did they stay here?

HANA: You don't know. It's not so simple. Sometimes I think . . .

KIYOKO: Then why don't they make the best of it here? Like you?

HANA: That isn't easy either. Believe me. (She leaves KIYOKO to stir the soup.) Sometimes . . . sometimes the longing for home . . . the longing fills me with despair. Will I never return again? Will I never see my mother, my father, my sisters again? But what can one do? There are responsibilities here . . . children . . . (pause) And another day passes . . . another month . . . another year. (She takes the soup to KIYOKO.) Did you have supper tonight?

KIYOKO: (bowing) Ah. When my . . . my aunt gets like this, she doesn't cook. No one eats. I don't get hungry anymore.

HANA: Cook for yourself. It's important to keep your health.

KIYOKO: I left Japan for a better life.

HANA: It isn't easy for you, is it? But you must remember your filial duty.

KIYOKO: It's so hard.

HANA: But you can make the best of it here, Kiyoko-san. And take care of yourself. You owe that to yourself. Eat. Keep well. It'll be better, you'll see. And sometimes it'll seem worse. But you'll survive. We do, you know.

HANA: (continuing) It's getting late.

KIYOKO: (apprehensively) I don't want to go back.

HANA: You can sleep with Masako tonight. Tomorrow you'll go back. And you'll remember what I told you. (She puts her arm around KIYOKO.) Life is never easy, Kiyoko-san. Endure. Endure. Soon you'll be marrying and going away. Things will not always be this way. And you'll look back on this . . . this night and you'll . . .

(There is a rap on the door. HANA exchanges glances with KIYOKO and opens the door a crack.)

(OKA has come looking for KIYOKO. He wears an overcoat and holds a wet newspaper over his head.)

OKA: Ah! I'm sorry to bother you so late at night—the fact is . . .

HANA: Oka-san.

OKA: (jovially) Good evening, good evening. (He sees KIYOKO.) Oh, there you are. Did you have a nice visit?

HANA: (irritated) Yes, she's here.

OKA: (still cheerful) Thought she might be. Ready to come home now?

HANA: She came in the rain.

OKA: (ignoring HANA's tone) That's foolish of you, Kiyoko. You might catch cold.

HANA: She was frightened by your quarreling. She came for help.

OKA: (laughing with embarrassment) Oh! Kiyoko, that's nothing to worry about. It's just we had some disagreement.

HANA: That's what I told her, but she was frightened just the same.

OKA: Children are . . .

HANA: Not children, Oka-san. Kiyoko. Kiyoko was terrified. I think that was a terrible thing to do to her.

OKA: (rubbing his head) Oh, I . . . I . . .

HANA: If you had seen her a few minutes ago . . . hysterical . . . shaking . . . crying . . . wet and cold to the bone . . . out of her mind with worry.

OKA: (rubbing his head) Oh, I don't know what she was so worried about.

HANA: You. You and Emiko fighting like you were going to kill each other.

OKA: (lowering his head in penitence) Aaaaaaahhhhhhhh . . .

HANA: I know I shouldn't tell you this, but there's one or two things I have to say: You sent for Kiyoko-san, and now she's here. You said yourself she had a bad time in Japan, and now she's having a worse time. It's not easy for her in a strange country; the least you can do is try to keep from worrying her . . . especially about yourselves. I think it's terrible what you're doing to her . . . terrible!

OKA: (bowing in deep humility) I am ashamed.

HANA: I think she deserves better. I think you should think about that.

OKA: (still bowing) I thank you for this reminder. It will never happen again. I promise.

HANA: I don't need that promise. Make it to Kiyoko-san.

OKA: Come with Papa now. He did a bad thing. He'll be a good Papa from now. He won't worry his little girl again. All right?

(They move toward the door. KIYOKO tries to return Murata's robe.)

KIYOKO: Thank you so much.

OKA: Thank you again.

HANA: (to KIYOKO) That's all right. You can bring it back tomorrow. Remember . . . remember what we talked about. (loudly) Good night, Oka-san.

(They leave. HANA goes to MASAKO, who pretends to sleep. She covers her. MURATA appears from the bedroom. He's heard it all. He and HANA exchange a quick glance and together they retire to their room.)

Scene 3

The next morning. The Murata house and yard. HANA and MURATA have already left the house to examine the rain damage in the fields.

MASAKO prepares to go to school. She puts on a coat and gets her books and lunch bag. Meanwhile, KIYOKO slips quietly into the yard. She wears a coat and carries Murata's robe and sets it on the outside bench.

MASAKO walks out and is surprised to see KIYOKO.

MASAKO: Hi. I thought you'd be . . . sick today.

KIYOKO: Oh. I woke up late.

MASAKO: (scrutinizing KIYOKO's face) Your eyes are red.

KIYOKO: (averting her face) Oh. I . . . got . . . sand in it. Yes.

MASAKO: Do you want eye drops? We have eye drops in the house.

KIYOKO: Oh, no. That's all right.

MASAKO: That's what's called bloodshot.

KIYOKO: Oh.

MASAKO: My father gets it a lot. When he drinks too much.

KIYOKO: Oh.

(MASAKO notices KIYOKO doesn't carry a lunch.)

MASAKO: Where's your lunch bag?

KIYOKO: I . . . forgot it.

MASAKO: Did you make your lunch today?

KIYOKO: Yes. Yes, I did. But I forgot it.

MASAKO: Do you want to go back and get it?

KIYOKO: No. (pause) We will be late.

MASAKO: Do you want to practice your words?

KIYOKO: (thoughtfully) Oh . . .

MASAKO: Say, "My."

KIYOKO: My?

MASAKO: Eyes . . .

KIYOKO: Eyes.

MASAKO: Are . . .

KIYOKO: Are.

MASAKO: Red.

KIYOKO: Red.

MASAKO: Your eyes are red.

(KIYOKO will not repeat it.)

MASAKO: (continuing) I . . .

(KIYOKO doesn't cooperate.)

MASAKO: (continuing) Say, "I."

KIYOKO: I.

MASAKO: Got . . .

KIYOKO: Got.

MASAKO: Sand . . .

(KIYOKO balks.)

MASAKO: (continuing) Say, "I."

KIYOKO: (sighing) I.

MASAKO: Reft . . .

KIYOKO: Reft.

MASAKO: My . . .

KIYOKO: My.

MASAKO: Runch.

KIYOKO: Run . . . Lunch. (pause) Masako-san, you are mean. You are hurting me.

MASAKO: It's a joke! I was just trying to make you laugh!

KIYOKO: I cannot laugh today.

MASAKO: Sure you can. You can laugh. Laugh! Like this! (She makes a hearty laugh.)

KIYOKO: I cannot laugh when you make fun of me.

MASAKO: Okay, I'm sorry. We'll practice some other words then, okay?

(KIYOKO doesn't answer.)

MASAKO: (continuing) Say, "Okay."

KIYOKO: (reluctantly) Okay.

MASAKO: Okay, then . . . um . . . um . . . Say . . . um . . . (rapidly) "She sells seashells by the seashore."

(KIYOKO turns away indignantly.)

MASAKO: (continuing) Aw, come on, Kiyoko! It's just a joke. Laugh!

KIYOKO: (sarcastically) Ha-ha-ha. Now you say, "Kono kyaku wa yoku kaki ku kyaku da!"

MASAKO: Sure I can say it. Kono kyaku waki ku kyoku kaku . . .

KIYOKO: That's not right.

MASAKO: Koki kuki kya . . .

KIYOKO: No. No-no-no.

MASAKO: Okay, then. You say, "Sea sells she shells . . . shu . . . sh."

(They both laugh, KIYOKO with her hands over her mouth. MASAKO takes KIYOKO's hands away.)

MASAKO: Not like that. Like this! (She makes a big laugh.)

KIYOKO: Like this? (She imitates MASAKO.)

MASAKO: Yeah, that's right! (pause) You're not mad anymore?

KIYOKO: I'm not mad anymore.

MASAKO: Okay. You can share my lunch because we're . . .

KIYOKO: "Flends?"

(MASAKO looks at KIYOKO. They giggle and move on.)

(HANA and MURATA come in from assessing the storm's damage. They are dressed warmly. HANA is depressed. MURATA tries to be cheerful.)

MURATA: It's not so bad, Mama.

HANA: Half the ranch is flooded. At least half.

MURATA: No-no. Quarter, maybe. It's sunny today. It'll dry.

HANA: The seedlings will rot.

MURATA: No-no. It'll dry. It's all right. Better than I expected.

HANA: If we have another bad year, no one will lend us money for the next crop.

MURATA: Don't worry. If it doesn't drain by tomorrow, I'll replant the worst places. We still have some seed left. Yeah, I'll replant.

HANA: More work.

MURATA: Don't worry, Mama. It'll be all right.

HANA: (quietly) Papa, where will it end? Will we always be like this—always at the mercy of the weather . . . prices . . . always at the mercy of the Gods?

MURATA: (patting HANA's back) Things will change. Wait and see. We'll be back in Japan by . . . in two years. Guarantee. Maybe sooner.

HANA: (dubiously) Two years . . .

MURATA: (finding the robe on the bench) Ah, look, Mama. Kiyoko-san brought back my robe.

HANA: (sighing) Kiyoko-san . . . poor Kiyoko-san. And Emiko-san . . .

MURATA: Ah, Mama. We're lucky. We're lucky, Mama.

Scene 4

The following spring afternoon. Exterior of the Oka house. OKA is dressed to go out. He wears a sweater, long-sleeved white shirt, dark pants, no tie. He puts his foot to the bench to wipe off his shoe with the palm of his hand. He straightens his sleeve, removes a bit of lint, and runs his fingers through his hair. He hums softly.

KIYOKO comes from the house. Her hair is frizzled in a permanent wave, she wears a gaudy new dress and a pair of new shoes. She carries a movie magazine.

OKA: (appreciatively) Pretty. Pretty.

KIYOKO: (turning for him) It's not too *hadeh?* I feel strange in colors.

OKA: Oh, no. Young girls should wear bright colors. Time enough to wear gray when you get old. Old-lady colors.

(KIYOKO giggles.)

OKA: (continuing) Sure you want to go to the picture show? It's such a nice day . . . shame to waste in a dark hall.

KIYOKO: Where else can we go?

OKA: We can go to Murata-san's.

KIYOKO: All dressed up?

OKA: Or Nagata-san's. I'll show him what I got for my horse.

KIYOKO: I love the pictures.

OKA: We don't have many nice spring days like this. Here the season is short. Summer comes in like a dragon . . . right behind . . . breathing fire . . . like a dragon. You don't know the summers here. They'll scare you.

(He tousles KIYOKO's hair and pulls a lock of it. It springs back. He shakes his head in wonder.)

OKA: (continuing) Goddam. Curly hair. Never thought curly hair could make you so happy.

KIYOKO: (giggling) All the American girls have curly hair.

OKA: Your friend Masako like it?

KIYOKO: (nodding) She says her mother will never let her get a permanent wave.

OKA: She said that, eh? Bet she's wanting one.

KIYOKO: I don't know about that.

OKA: Bet she's wanting some of your pretty dresses too.

KIYOKO: Her mother makes all her clothes.

OKA: Buying is just as good. Buying is better. No trouble that way.

KIYOKO: Masako's not interested in clothes. She loves the pictures, but her mother won't let her go. Someday, can we take Masako with us?

OKA: If her mother lets her come. Her mother's got a mind of her own. Stiff back.

KIYOKO: But she's nice.

OKA: (dubiously) Oh, yeah. Can't be perfect, I guess. Kiyoko, after the harvest I'll have money, and I'll buy you the prettiest dress in town. I'm going to be lucky this year. I feel it.

KIYOKO: You're already too good to me . . . dresses, shoes, permanent wave . . . movies . . .

OKA: That's nothing. After the harvest, just wait . . .

KIYOKO: . . . magazines. You do enough. I'm happy already.

OKA: You make me happy too, Kiyoko. You make me feel good . . . like a man again. (That bothers him.) One day you're going to make a young man happy.

(KIYOKO giggles.)

OKA: (continuing) Someday we going to move from here.

KIYOKO: But we have good friends here, Papa.

OKA: Next year our lease will be up and we got to move.

KIYOKO: The ranch is not ours?

OKA: No. In America Japanese cannot own land. We lease and move every two to three years. Next year we going go someplace where there's young fellows. There's none good enough for you here. Yeah. You going to make a good wife. Already a good cook. I like your cooking.

KIYOKO: (a little embarrassed) Shall we go now?

OKA: Yeah. Put the magazine away.

KIYOKO: I want to take it with me.

OKA: Take it with you?

KIYOKO: Last time, after we came back, I found all my magazines torn in half. Even the new ones.

OKA: (looking toward the house) Torn?

KIYOKO: This is the only one I have left.

OKA: All right, all right.

(The two prepare to leave when EMIKO lurches through the door. Her hair is unkempt—she looks wild. She holds an empty can in one hand, the lid in the other.)

EMIKO: Where is it?

(OKA tries to make a hasty departure.)

KIYOKO: Where is what?

(OKA pushes KIYOKO ahead of him, still trying to make a getaway.)

EMIKO: Where is it? Where is it? What did you do with it?

(EMIKO moves toward OKA.)

OKA: (with false unconcern to KIYOKO) Why don't you walk on ahead to Murata-san's.

KIYOKO: We're not going to the pictures?

OKA: We'll go. First you walk to Murata-san's. Show them your new dress. I'll meet you there.

(KIYOKO enters the house, pushing past EMIKO, emerges with a small package, and exits, looking worriedly back at OKA and EMIKO. OKA sighs and shakes his head.)

EMIKO: (shaking the can) Where is it? What did you do with it?

OKA: (feigning surprise) With what?

EMIKO: You know what. You stole it. You stole my money.

OKA: *Your* money?

EMIKO: I've been saving that money.

OKA: Yeah? Well, where'd you get it? Where'd you get it, eh? You stole it from me! Dollar by dollar! You stole it from me! Out of my pocket!

EMIKO: I saved it!

OKA: From *my* pocket!

EMIKO: It's mine! I saved for a long time. Some of it I brought from Japan.

OKA: *Bakayuna!* What'd you bring from Japan? Nothing but some useless kimonos.

... PRODUCING *AND THE SOUL SHALL DANCE*

INTRODUCTION TO EAST WEST PLAYERS

The Oregon Shakespeare Festival, discussed in Chapter 3, is firmly rooted in the English (European) theatre tradition. The next producing company we discuss, East West Players, represents another tradition and community altogether. The primary focus of East West Players is presenting the voices of Asian/Pacific Americans as writers, actors, and producers. The repertoire of East West Players emphasizes American plays that reflect the experiences of Asian/Pacific Americans.

The theatre's early productions most frequently featured plays by Americans of Japanese, Chinese, and Korean heritage; more recently, performances have expanded to include the work of Southeast Asians and Pacific Islanders. Although there is an international influence, that influence is first Asian and then European. And when European plays are performed, they are acted by Asian American or multiracial casts. A production by East West Players of Ibsen's *Hedda Gabler*, for example, was set in Japan rather than Norway, and the roles were played by Asian American actors. The name East West Players reflects this theatre's goal of serving as a cultural bridge between the East and the West.

History of East West Players

In 1965 a group of Japanese American, Chinese American, and Korean American actors came together in Los Angeles to form East West Players, the first Asian American theatre company in the United States. Tired of the demeaning and frequently ridiculous, stereotypical roles they were playing in films and theatre, such as subservient "houseboys," exotic and treacherous women, or sinister villains, these actors were determined to create a theatre in their own image, where they could choose how they were represented on the stage.

As with so many other struggling young theatre groups, the first performances of East West Players took place in a church basement. In 1968, however, they made the triumphant move to their own space. At first the Asian American casts performed plays written by Europeans and non-Asian Americans; actors at long last had the opportunity to play major, complex roles rather than one-dimensional characters.

The group also supported the development of new plays by Asian American playwrights. These plays recorded the experiences of Asian immigrants to the United States and their Asian American children, histories that had not been recorded elsewhere. They were stories of farming California's agricultural valleys in the 1930s, of struggling for survival in the internment camps in the 1940s, of creating new families when American soldiers returned from World War II with Japanese "war brides." They were about dislocation, the clash of cultures, and the struggle for identity. These stories were dramatized for audiences made up largely of Asian Americans who recognized themselves and the stories of their own lives in the plays.

Location and Physical Space

And the Soul Shall Dance was produced by East West Players for the second time in 1996, when they still performed in their long-standing home, a renovated garment factory in a run-down section of Santa Monica Boulevard in Los Angeles. With only ninety-nine seats, East West Players was at that time an Equity waiver theatre—a professional theatre that because of its limited seating was exempt from certain regulations of the Actors Equity union.

To get to the theatre, audiences had to drive past factories and industrial yards cluttered with trucks, pipes, and metal fittings. There were few shops or restaurants within walking distance of the theatre. The external ambience of East West Players was light-years away from the slow pace and charm of Ashland, Oregon, with its quiet streets, cafés, and parks.

In the late 1990s, East West Players moved from the renovated garment factory to a larger and more graceful theatre space housed in the centrally located Union Center for the arts, which is also home to Visual Communication and L.A. Art Core, two other arts organizations. The David Henry Hwang Theatre provides expanded seating, including a balcony and sophisticated technical support for lights, sound, and scenery. Tim Dang is the current producing artistic director of East West Players.

Since the production of *And the Soul Shall Dance* in 1996, East West Players, having more than outgrown its space on Santa Monica Boulevard, moved to the Union Center for the Arts in the Little Tokyo area of downtown Los Angeles. The company now has a 236-seat theatre, expanded rehearsal and classroom spaces, sophisticated technology, and comfortable parking for the staff and audiences. But the creativity that was generated in the cramped old space, the careers that were launched, and the barriers that were broken all reflected a wealth of talent and commitment not dependent on an impressive physical plant. In fact, for many theatre practitioners, the satisfaction is greater in a theatre of limited resources, where gold seems to be spun out of straw.

For our production analysis, we return to the experience of the performance at the garment factory where East West Players spent its first thirty years. Inside the theatre, the audience steps away from the grubby Los Angeles street into a tiny but lively and congenial lobby crowded with photographs and posters from previous productions. The audience is drawn largely from the Asian American community, and for this play,

And the Soul Shall Dance, most noticeably from the Japanese American community. Many audience members know each other and exchange friendly greetings over coffee and cookies. Older members of the audience recall the original production of the play, staged eighteen years ago. Younger members of the audience seeing the play for the first time are prepared to be introduced to one of the classics of the Asian American theatre.

STAGING THE PLAY
The Director's Prologue

The small stage (measuring twenty by thirty feet) of East West Players is completely empty except for a muslin scrim (curtain) that hangs around the upstage perimeter of the playing space. A small

The set design for *And the Soul Shall Dance*, by Yuki Nakamura, featured two small rolling house units that were unfolded ingeniously in view of the audience. The walls were either cut down or covered with transparent material to allow the audience a full view of the interiors.

elevated platform juts out over the audience at one side. On the platform are Japanese wind and percussion instruments, including shakuhachi (bamboo) flutes of various lengths, taiko drums of different sizes, Tibetan cymbals, and Japanese wind chimes. While the house lights are still up, a light comes up on the platform, where a musician (either George Abe or Masakazu Yoshizawa) in a Japanese *yukata* (a loose tunic) and *hakama* (wide-cut pants) appears. He begins to beat the large taiko drum, sending sharp reverberations through the small theatre, announcing the beginning of the play. At the end of the short drum overture, the lights go down on both the audience and the stage space.

The sound of the wind comes over the theatre's speakers, and the musician begins to play long, mournful notes on the largest shakuhachi flute. A dim light illuminates a single shape on the stage. The shape is a piece of tumbleweed. A **kuroko**—a hooded actor dressed completely in black—who seems to blend in with the darkness of the stage, rolls and lifts the tumbleweed through the air as if it is being blown by the wind.

With these simple elements—the sounds of the wind, the haunting notes of the flute, and the single piece of blowing, rolling tumbleweed—the production creates the sense of a vast, open, lonely space. Suddenly a sharp clicking sound is heard, and two more hooded figures dressed in black rush silently onto the stage and sweep aside half of the curtain hanging at the back. Using highly stylized, choreographed movement, the three kurokos roll forward and unfold what will become the walls of the Muratas' house. As the simple frame of the house takes shape, one of the kurokos whirls in first with a table and then with chairs. All of the movement suggests that it is the wind that is blowing the small dwelling and its simple furnishings onto the stage. The walls of the house are suggestive rather than complete. They are cut low to allow the audience to see all the action inside. A table and chairs, a bed, a stove, a sink, and dishes give the sense of a functional but spartan household.

The drumming that has accompanied the scene shift gives way to the sound of fire. The actors playing the Murata family enter, dismayed over the loss of the bathhouse, and the play as it is written in the script begins: the realistic story of a child who has been careless; an anxious, scolding mother; and a weary father. But in the few minutes that precede their entrance, a vivid atmosphere has been created for their story. With a few strokes of sound and stage imagery, like the brushstrokes of Japanese calligraphy, the characters have been placed spatially and emotionally in the emptiness and desolation of the Imperial Valley.

The Influence of Asian Theatre

The presence of the kurokos, in combination with the sounds of the musical instruments, also introduces the cultural background of the characters. They are clearly tied to Asia. The director of the production, Jim Ishida, says, "No matter how long the Issei, first-generation, are here, there is still that connection to their cultural heritage."[6] Through the references to Asian theatre, the director, in collaboration with the scene designer Yuki Nakamura, who has also designed the sound, establishes the production's theatrical style. Realism is combined with a simple, concentrated, poetic expression to take us into the daily lives of the characters and beyond, into their "souls."

> **JIM ISHIDA:** I wanted to incorporate as much of Eastern theatre technique as I possibly could. So therefore we thought of kabuki and the use of kurokos and the cycs (**cyclorama**—cloth that forms the background for the action) rising and everything coming out in a big flurry. I like actors to be very physical. I like the actors to be part of the wind, bringing the tumbleweed in, creating the nothing space into something.
>
> The kurokos are based on figures from the traditional kabuki theatre of Japan. In kabuki the kuroko changes the scenery, helps actors make onstage costume changes, and brings in props. The role of the kuroko has its own history in Japanese theatre tradition. Just as acting certain parts was handed down from father to son, so the position of kuroko was passed down through certain families.

In the production of *And the Soul Shall Dance*, the kurokos serve a double purpose. They serve first to change the scenery and the props. But the movement of the kurokos is also meaningful choreographically. As they whirl about the stage, they suggest the feeling of the wind; and the audience accepts the notion that the kurokos are invisible. The kurokos allow for a certain kind of theatrical magic that does not depend on highly complex or expensive technical equipment. The actors playing the kurokos have prepared for their roles by studying dance and the stylized movement of the Japanese theatre. In contrast, the actors playing Yamauchi's characters must create a physically and psychologically believable rendering of Japanese American life in the 1930s.

Through the stylized movement of the kurokos and the realistic acting of the characters, the production blends the poetic and concrete elements of the play. Another example of blending is the mixture of expressive musical accompaniment with realistic sound effects. The production is a fusion of lyricism and realism.

Staging a Period Play: The Work of the Director and the Actors

In rehearsing the actions of the characters, in constructing the realistic life of poor families struggling with hardship, Jim Ishida finds the starting point in "Japanese behavior." The characters' manners, their posture and gestures, and their speech rhythms must echo the conduct of Japanese immigrants to the United States in the early part of the twentieth century.

> **JIM ISHIDA:** That was the hardest work, the physical work, the dance and the behavior. To eliminate the actors' Western colloquialisms, their Western behavior. They've lived their lives as Westerners. In a short period of time they've had to find Japanese behavior. The way they bow, the way farmers hold their hands, the way they drink.

Acquiring such specialized mannerisms is a highly complex task. The actors, third- and fourth-generation descendents of immigrant families, must learn from the outside what was a way of life for their grandparents and great-grandparents.

> **DENISE IKETANI (EMIKO):** We are so American. The culture has changed. I'm fourth-generation. In terms of how we talk to our parents and how our parents talked to their parents and how their parents talked to their parents, each generation is completely different.

PERIOD STYLE   In the American theatre, specialists typically coach actors in what is called **Period Style,** the deportment, manners, attitudes, and gestures of times past. Frequently, actors take classes in various aspects of period behavior, particularly combat and dance, which are excellent sources of posture and gesture in addition to being useful for their own sake when a fight must be staged or movement sequences choreographed. Dance styles and the martial arts codify physical attitudes in forms that can be passed down through generations. Paintings and, more recently, photographs and films offer additional sources for details of period behavior.

Another essential source for understanding the movement and posture of other eras is period clothing. If a character must wear a garment that binds the body in various ways—a military uniform or a kimono, for example—the garment structure determines to a large degree how the character will stand and walk. Although the period of *And the Soul Shall Dance*, the 1930s, does not seem very long ago, in fact the cultural circumstances of that time pose a geographic and temporal distance that cannot be bridged without assistance.

MOVEMENT AND GESTURE   Ishida and the actors turn to a variety of sources for the period information they need. Ishida draws on his memory of the actions and attitudes of his grandparents, as well as observations made during recent travels to Japan. The actors watch Japanese films and observe the interactions of senior members of the community. In this production Ishida takes responsibility for coaching the men, and Mary Tamaki is invited to join the production staff to coach the women's movement and to choreograph Emiko's dance sequences. Mary Tamaki has spent years studying the classical dance of Japan and is designated *natori*, the level of achievement that the character Emiko had aspired to.

For this production, the director has another special consultant—the playwright, Wakako Yamauchi. Playwrights are frequently unavailable for consultation after the original production of a play, and theatre companies feel honored if the playwrights come to see their particular productions. But in this case, Wakako Yamauchi attends rehearsals and makes suggestions to Ishida. The play, of course, represents her own experience, the times that she lived through as a child.

During the early rehearsals, Jim Ishida and Mary Tamaki coach the actors on the basics of movement and social interaction—how to walk and stand, how to bow, how to greet each other. Although ultimately Ishida will give the actors much freedom to experiment and make choices, this beginning work is all done through imitation and drill, with endless precise corrections.

For example, the male characters—*Murata* and *Oka*— meet twice in the two opening scenes and drink sake. The greeting between them is far from a contemporary American handshake or slap on the back. They make repeated shallow, sharp bows to each other and greet each other heartily, with a guttural, barking kind of laughter. In the first scene they sit together to drink—as if it is understood that the privilege of the sake and the table is theirs—while Hana as dutiful wife waits on them. They drink their sake quickly, with short bursts of energy. When the chiles are called for, Hana serves them, head down, using chopsticks to take them out of the jar. The men punctuate their speech with Japanese rather than American exclamations. After eating the chiles, both men cover their mouths and pick their teeth while continuing their conversation.

The movement work for the women is very difficult. American women have a freedom of movement and a lift in their walk that is incompatible with the style necessary to give authenticity to the production.

MARY TAMAKI: The women must learn to walk with the center of gravity lower, which is the more traditional Japanese style, shuffling the feet. Japanese women do not pick up their feet. They shuffle, wearing the zoris (Japanese sandals). They must be demure. There's no loud laughing, and they must cover their mouths when they want to smile.

Mary Tamaki brings kimonos to rehearsals to facilitate the learning of the necessary body positions and walking style, even though the actors will not wear kimonos in the production.

MARY TAMAKI: These are not natural movements . . . to walk with your knees slightly bent, to shuffle along taking tiny steps. It is a style that you learn. It is not part of our Western nature to be so humble. When you're in kimonos the movements become so much more natural. You are slightly bound in them, so your movements of course are restricted. The way you walk is definitely restricted by the kimono.

DENISE IKETANI (EMIKO): Having to wear the kimono completely changes the way you move. When you put on a kimono it's very tight. It's even hard to breathe sometimes. That just affects what you can and cannot do.

ANNA QUIRINO (MASAKO): When you wear the kimono, it can't flap open at the bottom. Once you see the flap you know you're walking wrong. It has to be like a cylinder walking, so the steps are very small and pigeon-toed.

In rehearsal under Mary Tamaki's guidance, the women practice entering a room, bowing, and greeting each other. They learn the correct way to pour tea and to sit down.

MARY TAMAKI: I walked for them. Then I would remind them to bend their knees more. Don't bounce. Shuffle along. Keep your hands to your side.

DANCE   Mary Tamaki also works separately with Denise Iketani on the dances that come from Emiko's past. Tamaki choreographs a dance of two minutes that is based on five basic movements from the classical Japanese dance. One minute of this dance will be used when Emiko dances inside her house and first captivates Masako. Denise Iketani will use the full two-minute piece as the basis for the improvised movements she does outside at other points in the play. Mary Tamaki and Denise Iketani rehearse the two-minute dance sequence for ten hours during different rehearsals. Tamaki feels the pressure of the time limit. In her own dance studies, a ten-minute dance would be rehearsed for over a year. However, in the theatre, time is always measured. In a concentrated period of time, choreography that serves the needs of the production must be created and learned.

The period movement that Jim Ishida, Mary Tamaki, and the actors have worked hard to achieve gives the play a certain authenticity, a texture of the times. It establishes the cultural background that makes clear the standards of propriety, what is expected of or acceptable for men and for women.

MARY TAMAKI: As far as the women's role at that time, the women were second to the men. They had no large gestures. They were not usually able to express themselves in public in front of the men. The wife was able to express herself inside the home but not outside of the home.

But most important, the period movement provides the starting point for the development of character. In Jim Ishida's words, "emotionality must come out of the Japanese behavior." What begin as general standards of deportment and social interaction evolve into highly individuated characters.

SPEECH RHYTHMS   Another element Yamauchi uses to create a realistic atmosphere for her play is the suggestion that the adult characters are

Oka (Benjamin Lum) and Murata (Nelson Mashita) share painful memories as Hana (Sharon Omi) and Masako (Anna Quirino) look on.

all speaking Japanese. She includes a number of Japanese words in the text, but it is the rhythm of the speeches that is most important and that also poses another significant task for the actors. They must learn their lines in English, of course, but with Japanese inflection and intonation. In addition to the physical work they must do to develop the characters' behavior, they must study and acquire Japanese speech rhythms. Speech and dialect coaching plays a regular part in the American theatre, preparing actors to speak with foreign or regional accents.

Only the actor playing Masako speaks an Americanized English. The Americanization of Masako's speech rhythms and the freedom of her movement obviously set her apart from the other characters. She is of a new generation, without her parents' ties to Japan. Whereas her parents maintain their identities through observing Japanese traditions and long to return to Japan,

Masako looks to the future. She seeks a wider view of the world and her place in it.

Building Character Relationships

To further examine the way realism and lyricism are combined to shape character and to establish crucial character relationships, we consider now the staging of act 1, scene 2 of *And the Soul Shall Dance* at East West Players. Following scene 1, the kurokos roll away the Murata house, and the other half of the curtain is pulled back to allow the unfolding of a second small house on the right side of the stage. The shakuhachi flute is heard again as the Oka house appears.

The sweeping aside of the curtains to reveal each little house is an actual and figurative expression of the opening of memory. What the audience sees is what Masako remembers. When the curtain is brushed aside and the Murata house appears in scene 1, we go back with Masako to the day she burned down the

Denise Iketani (Emiko) and Anna Quirino (Masako) rehearse a sequence that uses choreography developed by Mary Tamaki. Quirino uses a kimono for rehearsal although she will not wear one in the play.

bathhouse. The significance of the burning of the bathhouse becomes clear as the curtain draws back on scene 2, the memory of the Oka house. It is through this small catastrophe that Masako encounters the elusive, withdrawn Emiko.

As act 1, scene 2 begins, Oka, Murata, and Hana sit amicably together on a bench by the door to the Oka house while Masako kneels in front of them with the Victrola. At Oka's insistence, Emiko finally, but reluctantly, comes outside and moves to the other side of the door, where she sits in a chair with her face turned partly away. As the script is written, Emiko does not speak until she is alone with Masako. This means that in the first part of the scene, everything that Emiko communicates must be expressed physically.

As the other characters uneasily make cheerful but forced small talk about the records and the Victrola, Emiko begins to roll herself a cigarette. The rolling of the cigarette is clearly called for in the stage directions: "She pulls out a sack of Bull Durham and begins to roll a cigarette." The playwright has chosen this detail very carefully. Emiko does not speak. She does not greet her guests or offer to serve them tea. But she does roll herself a cigarette. This single action speaks volumes about Emiko's attitude. She is rebellious and defiant; she does not care to be seen as a proper, traditional Japanese woman.

Hana attempts to break the tension of this moment by sending Masako to Emiko with a stack of records. As Masako timidly approaches

Emiko with her arms folded around the record albums, Emiko finishes rolling her cigarette. Then, holding the cigarette in one hand and the pouch of tobacco in the other, Emiko inclines her head and pulls the string to close the bag of tobacco sharply with her teeth. This tough, masculine gesture secures Masako's attention. Emiko then turns her head to look at Masako for the first time. She has the cigarette in her mouth and a defiant look on her face, an attitude that makes a large impression on an eleven-year-old girl raised by a very proper mother.

ANNA QUIRINO (MASAKO): When she pulls out the cigarette . . . that's the big thing for me. Wow! Who is this woman? Because my mother is so traditional. She wants me to be polite. Hana would never do this. She's very strong, especially against my father. She can speak up. But here is Emiko who is very quiet

The attitude of Masako (Emily Keiko Pruiksma) contrasts with that of her parents, Murata and Hana (Ken Chin and Kathy Hsieh) in the production of *And the Soul Shall Dance* at Northwest Asian American Theatre in Seattle, directed by Judi Nihei.

of a Japanese woman who drinks and smokes and is also trained in classical movement.

Masako's relationship to Emiko continues to grow when the other adults exit and Masako is left alone on the stage. She puts "And the Soul Shall Dance" on the Victrola and becomes lost in the music. When Emiko returns and sees Masako with a distant expression on her face, she recognizes some kinship between them.

DENISE IKETANI (EMIKO): The song, of course. "And the Soul Shall Dance" *Kokoro ga odoru.* The fact that Masako plays this song that was Emiko's favorite song and that she understands—that's the instant connection. The whole world that she lives in right now is just so horrible. This one little thing that Masako does—it amazes her that Masako does understand. She knows that she's found some sort of bonding, a kinship, with this person even though she is a child. She sees this child who understands what it is about your soul dancing.

Emiko begins to sing with the voice on the record, and after a moment Masako sings too. With warmth growing between them, Emiko crosses to Masako, and the two seem bound in the same spell. They kneel together by the Victrola, and Emiko speaks for the first time: "Do you like that song, Masa-chan?" Their intimacy deepens, and Emiko rises to dance again, now easily and fluidly. The woman and the child speak the words of the song together while Emiko dances. She seems to be dancing out the feeling of the green wine as Masako watches, enchanted.

EMIKO: Drink the green wine . . .

MASAKO: Green? I thought wine was purple.

EMIKO: Wine is purple, but this is a green liqueur. It's good. It warms your heart.

MASAKO: And the soul dances.

EMIKO: Yes . . .

MASAKO: What does it taste like? The green wine?

in her corner. But what she's doing! My character is so fascinated by her, scared too in the beginning. At first I just don't want to be there. But the taking out of the cigarette. I've never seen a woman do that before.

The second sequence of actions that draws Masako to Emiko begins when Emiko reenters the house after they begin to play the Japanese records on the Victrola. Emiko dances by herself inside the house, and the audience can see her because the walls are partially cut away or constructed in places with transparent mesh. The adult characters outside are unaware of the dancing, but Masako, on her way to the bath, stops at the window and stares in at Emiko dancing. She is now captivated by the strangeness and wonder

In the Northwest Asian American Theatre production, Emiko (Sherryl Ray) attracts Masako's attention with her cigarette and her mysterious attitude.

EMIKO: Oh, it's like . . . it's like . . .

MASAKO: In the dark night . . .

EMIKO: Dreams are unbearable . . .

MASAKO: Drink the . . .

EMIKO: Drink the green wine . . .

MASAKO: And the dreams will dance. (act 1, scene 2)

The two actors speak the words as if together they understand a special language that lifts them out of the present. The song provides a vocabulary, a rhythm, a melody, and an atmosphere that allow for a shift in consciousness. Emiko's soul emerges through the grace of the dance, and Masako's spirit seems to join in the dance of the soul with her. It is a transcendent moment.

All too quickly the moment is interrupted by Oka's return. In this scene Masako is exposed to abuse, the battery of Emiko by her husband, and she sees a drunk Japanese woman smoking a cigarette. But she also experiences Emiko's passion for music and dance. She catches a glimpse of a way of life not limited by the unending cycle of protecting seedlings from freezes, irrigating fragile crops, and paying bills.

ANNA QUIRINO (MASAKO): Masako has dreams that go way beyond the ranch. That's why her books are so important to her. And Masako has a rebellious streak. Watching Emiko being able to break away from tradition. She's almost a hero. She sees in Emiko this whole other world.

CONTRASTING PRODUCTIONS: EAST WEST PLAYERS AND NORTHWEST ASIAN AMERICAN THEATRE

To deepen our understanding of *And the Soul Shall Dance*, we examine now three points of contrast between the production by East West Players in 1996 and a production by Northwest Asian American Theatre in Seattle in 1994. Different productions of the same play may offer strikingly different interpretations of the playwright's material, or through more subtle distinctions they may turn the audience's attention to one idea instead of another.

Scene Design and the Physical Space

A tangible difference that is relatively easy to assess is the arrangement of the physical space. Northwest Asian American Theatre was located in the basement space under the Wing Luke Asian Museum in the International District of Seattle. Like East West Players when they were located in the renovated factory, Northwest Asian American Theatre had a small stage space and little technical support for elaborate scenic effects. But given similar stage limitations, the two productions take entirely different approaches to staging.

In the play the two small houses are isolated and set apart in the desert landscape. The script simply calls for an alternation between the Murata kitchen and yard and the Oka yard. At East West Players, a design was created by Yuki Nakamura to keep the space as open and empty as possible through the use of the rolling and unfolding house units. Only one house appears on the stage at a time, suggesting that each exists in a completely separate space.

In the design of the Seattle production by Jan Tominaga, both houses are permanent structures on the stage, placed immediately next to each other. To suggest the distance between the two locations, the actors move though the aisles of the audience area. This approach to staging highlights certain meanings in the play. The proximity of the houses reinforces the contrast between the responses of the two families to the hostile environment in which they find themselves. The Muratas create a home that will sustain them and nurture Masako's aspirations. The Okas engage in a mutually destructive relationship fed by alcohol and despair. One house is a home that may be entered; the other features only a window that reveals fragments of the misery inside. The physical presentation of the houses symbolizes the life of those within.

There are two key differences in the visual images presented by these companies. First, in contrast to the Seattle production, the Los Angeles production emphasizes the sense of isolation, of two tiny houses in the vast, dusty Imperial Valley, widely separated from neighbors and community. The physical isolation speaks eloquently of the spiritual isolation. The windblown effect of the scene shifts heightens the idea of lives at the mercy of the elements. Second, in contrast to the Los Angeles production, the Seattle production features dissimilar

house exteriors to comment on the health or dysfunction of the families. In the Los Angeles production, each family has essentially the same physical environment; the difference is the response to that environment.

Interpreting Family Relationships

In addition to the differences in scene design, the two productions approach relationship issues differently. For example, after Emiko exits with her kimonos, the play describes a moment of closeness between Hana and Masako.

Masako and Hana watch as Emiko leaves. The light grows dim as though a cloud passed over. Hana strokes Masako's hair.

HANA: Your hair is so black and straight . . . nice.

They stand close. The wind chimes tinkle; light grows dim. Light returns to normal. Murata enters. He sees the tableau of mother and child and is puzzled. (act 2, scene 5)

Hana's line is an understated way of expressing her love for her daughter. At this painful moment when she recognizes Emiko's desperation and Masako's longing, Hana pulls Masako to her with this gentle remark about straight hair, which so obviously contrasts with the loss of identity represented by Kiyoko's curly permanent. Hana underlines the health of their relationship and her determination to protect her daughter's childhood and her heritage. The stage directions imply that the father, Murata, is outside this intimacy between mother and daughter and that he is "puzzled" by it, although he recognizes the growing bond between them.

The production at Northwest Asian American Theatre accentuates the father's distance at this particular moment. However, the East West Players' production opens up this moment to reinforce the family bond. The stage directions indicate that "the wind chimes tinkle." At

East West Players, it is Murata who sounds the chimes. As he enters, the actor playing Murata responds with delight to the newly hung *furin* (wind chimes) and brushes his hand across them, sharing his obvious pleasure at their sound with Masako. The smile that the father and daughter share creates a sense of family that builds on the moment shared by Hana and Masako. The director, Jim Ishida, said he saw the foundation for his interpretation of the play in the short story: "the beautiful little thing . . . the Murata family . . . this combination of people makes life bearable." The emphasis at the end of the play is on the shared responsibility of the parents and the strength that both share with their daughter.

The production at Northwest Asian American Theatre focuses instead on the inner lives of Emiko and Hana and on their isolation. The director, Judi Nihei, looks for moments where that isolation might be broken. For example, Nihei sees in Hana and Masako a reinvention of the mother–daughter relationship that responds to their unique environment and the difficulties and opportunities that it presents.

JUDI NIHEI: Masako gets away with murder. If I had spoken to my mother the way Masako speaks to her mother, I wouldn't be sitting here today. I always take the writer at their word. So if this is who Wakako Yamauchi was writing about, then there is obviously something more going on here than what we might assume to be a typical mother–daughter relationship. So that says something to me about Hana and how she sees her daughter in her life.

The director and the actor playing Hana, Kathy Hsieh, together develop an approach to this character that depends not on the certainty of an experienced mother who is confident of what is best for her child but on a continuous process of discovery. Kathy Hsieh is actually younger than her character; her youth

In the **Northwest Asian American Theatre** production of *And the Soul Shall Dance,* Hana holds the kimonos that she knows she cannot accept for her daughter. She recognizes Emiko's desperation and Masako's longing. The kimonos also bring back her own memories of life in Japan.

immediately reminds the audience of the enormous difficulty of facing life in a hostile country without the benefit of family and social structure. She has no mother or sisters to turn to for advice. Her only support comes from the women she knows at church.

Hsieh's age and performance choices clarify the struggle of the character to invent solutions to the challenges of dislocation and racism. There is no ready-made wisdom that can be transferred easily from her Japanese background to the circumstances of raising a Japanese American daughter caught between cultures. Each challenge from her daughter leads to introspection and experimentation. We see her puzzling out each decision. The answers come not from the past but from an attempt to imagine the future. Although there is a very special bond between mother and daughter, the very spirit of openness and shared discovery that distinguishes the relationship will eventually lead to separation.

> **KATHY HSIEH (HANA):** She wants her daughter to have those dreams, but she doesn't want her to be disappointed at things that don't come true. She wants her daughter to study and learn, but the things that she is learning and the language that she is studying are all about American people, white people, and English, not Japanese. There are more and more things that her daughter is learning about that Hana will never be able to understand, because she doesn't read English. She knows Masako is learning a whole different world than the world Hana knows. And she realizes that that is creating distance between her and her daughter.

Nihei and Hsieh also look for connections between Hana and Emiko that may be discovered in the subtext rather than in their guarded conversations.

> **JUDI NIHEI:** I really wanted to make more of a relationship between Emiko and Hana even though they don't really have one scene seriously together. To have Hana not be judgmental of Emiko but have much more sympathy for her, just not have a venue in which to express it. And that's a cultural conflict and a cultural imposition on a woman that even if you'd want to align yourself with your sex in support, you may not have that opportunity.

Sexuality and Gender

An aspect of Emiko's character that receives considerable attention in the Seattle production is her sexuality. More powerful than her memory of dancing and singing in her kimonos is her immersion in her memory of desire. When Emiko is alone, the actress playing the role touches herself as her lover may have touched her. She expresses herself as a sensual woman who defines herself at least in part through her own sexual response. What she seeks is control of her own body. All her acts of defiance are related to this claiming of herself.

By contrast, in the Los Angeles production, Emiko's character is built through withdrawal, defiance, and escape into a dreamworld of dance and music. But her state of mind does not lead to overt expression of sexual desire. In fact, her life with Oka seems to have robbed her of connections to the world around her and even to herself. The dancing of Denise Iketani (East West Players) is ethereal and leads the character away from earthly or bodily concerns. For Sherryl Ray (Northwest Asian American Theatre), her own body and the comfort of sexual response are a primary focus of the characterization.

In Japan, Emiko's point of contention with her parents was her sexuality and ownership of her body. They saw her as a commodity to be traded to the "rich Yamato." Yamato is the name of the older, wealthy merchant to whom Emiko's parents had expected to marry her, but it is also a name that refers to all of Japan. Thus, it contains a suggestion of the position of women in the social hierarchy of Japan. In the eyes of Emiko's father, when she had engaged in a sexual relationship of her own choosing, she had become damaged goods, no longer of value in the marriage market. For this reason, Emiko was married by proxy to Oka against her wishes and sent to the United States.

Oka has been dispossessed by both the Japanese and the American economic and social structures. In Japan he gave up his name and self-respect as an apprentice to his father-in-law. In the United States he is an alien ineligible for citizenship, unable to purchase land and make a home for his family. But he is still in a position to regard Emiko as his property.

The confrontation between Emiko and Oka in act 1, scene 3 results largely from her challenge to his authority. He sees her drunkenness as a personal affront to him: "You made a fool of *me!*" Infuriated that she will not speak to him, he attacks her physically. When Emiko asserts her autonomy—"Don't touch me. Don't touch me"—he is outraged: "Who the hell you think you are? . . . Too good for me?" And when Emiko answers his accusations of promiscuity by assuming ownership of her body—"Just because I let . . . let you . . ."—he responds, "Let me (obscene gesture)? I can do what I want with you. Your father palmed you off on me—like a dog or cat—animal." While Oka struggles to maintain the patriarchal view of a woman as property, Emiko, for all of her self-destructive actions, is set on self-determination. Emiko's rebellion against the traditional social structures is all the more striking when possession of her own sexuality is joined with her sense of herself as an artist.

Theatre production is an interpretive art. The three points of contrast identified here—the design of the houses and the arrangement of the physical space, the handling of the wind chimes scene, and the treatment of Emiko's sexuality—underscore the kinds of choices that may be made in different productions of the same play. The directors, actors, and designers all add layers of meaning to the words written by the playwright.

Summary

In *And the Soul Shall Dance*, the playwright presents the harsh lives of immigrant farmers eking out a living in the Imperial Valley in the 1930s. The past, the characters' Japanese background, is an important factor in shaping the present, as is the hostile attitude of Americans toward Asian immigrants. The playwright tells her story through small domestic incidents such as the bathhouse burning down. Although the details seem to come from ordinary circumstances, they are selected to express the characters' spirits. Emiko's longing to return to Japan is bound up in her kimonos. Masako's search for inspiration draws her to Emiko's music and dance.

In the East West Players' performance of *And the Soul Shall Dance*, realistic style was mixed with the more abstract style of the kabuki theatre. Scenes were performed with attention to period authenticity in speech, in characters' attitudes and manners, and in dress. But the scenery was made up of unfolding houses that were whirled around by dancing figures dressed in black, and Japanese percussion and wind instruments were used to create a musical background for the characters' lives. Realism is frequently modified by more abstract elements.

Another production of *And the Soul Shall Dance* at Northwest Asian American Theatre in Seattle demonstrates how two productions of the same play may differ. The scene design in Seattle focused on the contrast between the homes of the Okas and the Muratas, whereas the scene design of the Los Angeles production emphasized the isolation of all the characters. The Seattle production explored gender conflict, whereas the Los Angeles production was concerned with family connections that are sustaining.

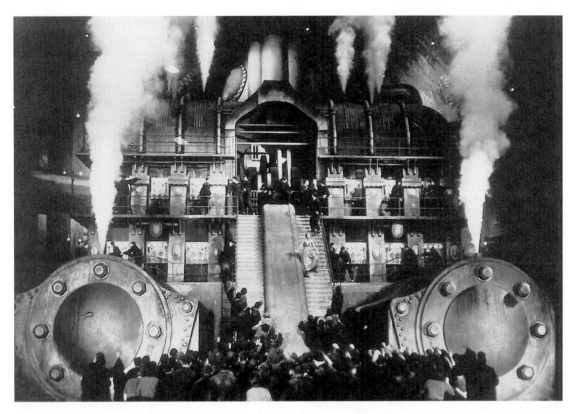

The film *Metropolis* (1927), by Fritz Lang, drew on many of the techniques developed in the German expressionist theatre to create the bitter mechanical world inhabited by oppressed workers. The style and scale of the images have been influential ever since the film was made.

for the later expressionists. Early in his career, Bertolt Brecht was part of the German expressionist movement. The innovations and concerns of the expressionists can still be seen in a play such as *Angels in America*.

German Expressionism

German expressionist theatre was infused with a sense of anguish. It has even been called the theatre of the shriek or the cry; its aim was to put into theatrical terms the feeling that was expressed in Edvard Munch's then highly influential painting *The Scream*. The German expressionists were horrified by the arms buildup in Germany and the militarization of their country. Their theatre

performances were a cry for humanitarianism to replace the brutality they saw around them. The expressionists, of course, proved to be prophetic. Many of them fled Germany during Hitler's rise in the 1930s, but those who didn't died in the concentration camps.

The silent film *Metropolis*, by the great German filmmaker Fritz Lang, uses many of the techniques developed in the German expressionist theatre. At this point we briefly examine the techniques used in *Metropolis* because this classic film is readily accessible on video and provides an excellent opportunity to experience the fundamental principles and themes of the German expressionist movement.

The plot of *Metropolis* focuses on the attempt of an industrialist's son to stop the manufacture of poison gas in his father's chemical plant. The film is dominated by striking visual images of the gleaming modern city above ground, inhabited by the unthinking rich; and the brutal factory below, where the workers live out their hopeless days. The workers have become dehumanized cogs in the operation of the vast factory. Almost lifeless, dressed in identical clothes like prisoners, they go through choreographed sequences that integrate their stylized, repetitive, robotlike movements with the workings of the wheels and pulleys of the machinery and the giant hands of a huge, regulatory clock. The enormous scenic images of the factory below and the skyscrapers above dwarf the tiny human characters, who have become insignificant in the world of relentless machines.

The scenes are presented as a sequence of episodes enacted by characters without names who are meant to be types rather than individuals and who speak (in subtitles) in abbreviated bursts of dialogue. The actors' stylized movements and the visual images are as important as the spoken language—or even more important. Although some of the acting is humorous by today's standards because of the exaggerated facial expressions and body language, the power of the workers' segments is undiminished by time.

American Expressionism: Eugene O'Neill

Early in the twentieth century, a number of American playwrights were drawn to expressionism as a style suited to exploring the contradictions and anxieties of American life. Elmer Rice wrote about the dehumanization of the machine world in *The Adding Machine*; Sophie Treadwell explored gender conflicts in *Machinal* (1927); and Eugene O'Neill used expressionistic elements in a number of his plays. Of these playwrights O'Neill has had the most lasting influence.

Eugene O'Neill (1888–1953) grew up in an Irish American family dominated by his father, James O'Neill, a well-known actor. James O'Neill played the lead in *The Count of Monte Cristo* for years, unable to give up the role for fear of financial failure. Thus Eugene O'Neill's youth was steeped in nineteenth-century melodrama. O'Neill remains a seminal figure in the American theatre because of his attempt to lift the level of the medium above nineteenth-century melodrama and spectacle and find an authentic American voice in playwriting that would approach the eloquence of the Europeans Ibsen and Strindberg.

No established form of serious American drama existed when O'Neill began writing one-act plays for the Provincetown Players in 1915. O'Neill's career as a playwright was marked by his experimentation with form, as he searched for the language and dramatic structures that would express his understanding of the American experience. He was concerned with the way human beings deceive themselves with illusions of success or love and then become paralyzed when those illusions are shattered.

Early in his career, in his plays *The Emperor Jones* (1920) and *The Hairy Ape* (1922), O'Neill used expressionism to present the distorted, nightmarish worlds of his characters. Borrowing a convention of the ancient Greek theatre, O'Neill used masks in *The Great God Brown* (1925). And in *Strange Interlude* (1928), which took many hours to perform, he had the characters speak their **inner monologues** and **subtext** aloud. He turned in yet another direction when he wrote *Mourning Becomes Electra* (1931), a trilogy modeled on Greek tragedy. Set during and after the Civil War, the three plays explore the destructive passions of the Mannon family.

O'Neill finally came to a bitter kind of realism in his last and most successful plays, *The Iceman Cometh* (produced posthumously in 1956), *Hughie* (produced posthumously in 1958), *A Moon for the Misbegotten* (1947), and *Long Day's Journey into Night* (produced posthumously in

Willem Dafoe and Kate Valk appeared in a new production (1997) of Eugene O'Neill's *The Hairy Ape,* produced by the Wooster Group and directed by Elizabeth LeCompte.

1957). The Irish American personages of his youth figure prominently in O'Neill's work, and in the last two plays, he turns to the searing history of his own family, destroyed by alcoholism and drug addiction. These four late plays continue to draw the participation of America's finest actors on Broadway and in regional theatre.

EPIC THEATRE: BERTOLT BRECHT

Bertolt Brecht (1898–1956) was a prolific playwright and director who began his work in the theatre as part of the German expressionist movement. Brecht envisioned a new theatre experience to replace what he perceived as the failings of the realistic theatre. Brecht's

epic theatre has achieved an influence on the development of the modern theatre equal to the influence of Stanislavsky's system on the development of contemporary psychological acting. Following World War II, Brecht moved to East Berlin. There he founded the famous Berliner Ensemble theatre, where he directed highly regarded performances of his plays. We investigate Brecht's theories of theatre here at some length because of their continuing importance to the modern theatre and because of their influence on the major playwright we study in Chapter 10, Tony Kushner.

Brecht believed that there was a danger in the audience becoming too deeply engrossed or

Bertolt Brecht, who began his theatre work in Germany, became an exile in the United States during World War II. The repressive political climate in the United States following the war encouraged Brecht to return to East Germany, where he founded the Berliner Ensemble, which became one of the most distinguished theatres of the century.

lost in the story of a play. For Brecht, the goal of realism—to make the audience members forget that they were in the theatre—made the theatre into a kind of anesthetic. He wanted to find ways to make the audience step back from the drama in order to encourage analysis rather than empathy or identification. He wanted to provoke questioning so that audiences would maintain an active, internal dialogue with the performance. From Brecht comes the idea, then, of interruption, of breaking the narrative to snap the audience out of what Brecht saw as a hypnotic state.

Brecht also did not want the experience of the play to be completed within the time and space of the performance. Rather, he saw theatre as a call to action. He hoped the performance would be a beginning point or part of a process in which audience members and actors would become engaged in social action. Therefore, Brecht did not look to provide the audience with the kind of experience that involves empathy and then the emotional release often referred to as **catharsis.** Brecht wrote:

> The spectator was no longer in any way allowed to submit to an experience uncritically (and without practical consequences) by means of simple empathy with the characters in a play. . . .
>
> The dramatic [realist] theatre's spectator says: Yes, I have felt like that too—Just like me—It's only natural—It'll never change—The sufferings of this man appall me, because they are inescapable—That's great art; it all seems the most obvious thing in the world—I weep when they weep, I laugh when they laugh.
>
> The epic theatre's spectator says: I'd never have thought it—That's not the way—That's extraordinary, hardly believable—It's got to stop—The sufferings of this man appall me, because they are unnecessary—That's great art: nothing obvious in it—I laugh when they weep, I weep when they laugh.[1]

Brecht's Concept of Alienation

To bring the audience to this receptive or alert mental state, Brecht employed techniques to achieve an **alienation effect,** or, in German, the *Verfremdungseffekt (V-effekt).* In Brecht's vocabulary, *alienation* did not mean "withdrawal;" rather, it meant "to make strange." He saw this strangeness as a way of interrupting the audience's involvement in the fiction created onstage.

As a director and a playwright, Brecht used a number of theatrical devices to create the alienation effect. The mechanics of the theatre were exposed to destroy any sense of magic or illusion.

In this 2007 production of Brecht's *Mother Courage* at the Berkeley Repertory Theatre, the action of the play is broken with cabaret-style singing. Here Yvette, played by Katie Barrett, sings one of the songs composed by Gina Leishman, with Mark Danisovszky at the piano, in the production directed by Lisa Peterson.

do in British and American musicals, songs in Brecht's plays change the mood and demand the audience's attention. Brecht's goal was to separate the music from the other elements of the drama, whereas in musical or lyrical theatre the goal is to integrate the music into the drama. According to Tony Kushner, the music in Brecht's plays provokes thought rather than provides a mental break:

> When it's good, [Brecht's music is] harder to listen to than the dialogue. It's more upsetting and more difficult. Which sort of reverses the traditional notion of musical theatre, at least American musical theatre, where the music is sort of your rest from thinking. And I think that really great composers for Brecht respond to the lyrics by writing something ugly and hard and difficult.[2]

Set pieces and props were simple and suggestive. Titles posted at the beginning of each new scene told the audience in advance what would happen to interrupt the development of suspense. Slide projections and films were introduced to provide information that clarified or contradicted the situations of the characters. In Brecht's conception, epic theatre encourages spectators to question why the characters make the choices that they do.

Brecht also used music to interrupt the action and to comment on the situation. Rather than heighten the emotional mood of scenes as songs

Brecht's Approach to Acting

Brecht's approach to acting was one of his most intriguing and challenging ideas about changing the nature of the theatre. Brecht was opposed to Stanislavsky's idea of complete identification with the character. Brecht suggested a new approach to performance in which the actor would comment on the character, that is, stand both inside and outside the character—as if the actor were describing his or her conduct and in some way engaging in a dialogue with the

Lynn Nottage has written a new play, inspired in part by *Mother Courage,* entitled *Ruined,* which won the Pulitzer Prize for drama in 2009. Nottage moves the location of the play to the Congo, where an ongoing war currently brutalizes that country. In fact, the playwright interviewed Congolese women in preparing to write the play. In Brecht's version of the play, the character Mother Courage is a peddler who sells food and other goods to the warring armies. Lynn Nottage sets the action in a brothel, where Mama, the Mother Courage figure, played here by Saidah Arrika Ekulona, prepares Sophie, Condola Rashad, to sing for their customers. The play's premiere shown here is a co-production by the Goodman Theatre of Chicago and the Manhattan Theater Club, directed by Kate Whoriskey in 2009.

audience about the character. This technique is sometimes referred to as **acting in quotes.** In Brecht's words:

> The actor does not allow himself to become completely transformed on the stage into the character he is portraying. He is not Lear, Harpagon, Schweik; he shows them.[3]

Brecht is very clear in his writings that he did not mean that the actor should not be emotionally invested in the characterization or that the emotions of the audience should remain disengaged.

Instead, he wanted both the actor and the audience to bring a critical attitude to their participation in the theatre event so that they could consider what was possible under the circumstances:

> Human behavior is shown as alterable; man himself as dependent on certain political and economic factors and at the same time as capable of altering them. . . . The idea is that the spectator should be put in a position where he can make comparisons about everything that influences the way in which human beings behave.[4]

Brecht focused his plays on characters forced to make difficult choices. The plays are written in long sequences of short scenes that reveal the various forces affecting the characters' decision-making process. Brecht also presented a comprehensive history of the situation rather than entering the story line at a late point, as did Ibsen, whose plays begin just before the characters' major crises. For example, *Mother Courage*, which Brecht wrote in collaboration with Margarete Steffin, takes place during the Thirty Years' War of the seventeenth century. Concerned with the devastation of war, Brecht and Steffin created some historical distance so that the audience could consider the effect of all wars. The central character is a peddler who crosses back and forth over the battlefields, selling her wares to both sides in the conflict. She is a pragmatist who is committed to her own survival. But during the many years of the war, she ends up losing her own children because of decisions she makes about the family's economic welfare. Brecht's play *Galileo* demonstrates the influences on the central character Galileo as he first proposes his notion that the earth revolves around the sun and then recants his position after being threatened by the Catholic Church.

THEATRE OF THE ABSURD

In the 1950s another dramatic style evolved in response to the devastation of modern warfare, this time World War II. Based more on philosophical or metaphysical explorations than was the overtly political German expressionist theatre, the **theatre of the absurd** was created by a group of international playwrights who all lived and wrote in Paris: the Irish Samuel Beckett; the Romanian Eugène Ionesco; the Russian Arthur Adamov; and the French Jean Genet, who began writing in a prison cell.

In the face of the horrendous slaughter of World War II and the complicity of various segments of European society in the extermination of huge groups of innocent people, the playwrights of the absurd found traditional value systems bankrupt. They wrote about the meaninglessness of human existence and the inability of language to communicate in an effective way. The ultimate isolation of human beings shaped the images of futility that emerged from the absurdist movement. In his definitional study on absurdism, Martin Esslin writes:

> The Theatre of the Absurd . . . tends toward a radical devaluation of language, toward a poetry that is to emerge from the concrete and objectified images of the stage itself. The element of language still plays an important part in this conception, but what happens on the stage transcends and often contradicts the words spoken by the characters.[5]

The most famous play of the theatre of the absurd is Samuel Beckett's *Waiting for Godot*. Two tramps wait by the side of the road, essentially a physical "void" interrupted only by the presence of a shriveled tree. In the play the two characters wait for another character, named Godot, who never comes. While they wait, they struggle to fill the empty time with patter and activity reminiscent of clowning routines from vaudeville. But each attempt at interaction is more futile than the last. Long silences surround and break their speeches. The tree is the only visual detail that breaks the bleakness of the physical space, just as their meaningless chatter may be seen as only a brief interruption of the vast silence of the universe.

Although the two characters speak of parting from each other, they don't. They speak of leaving, yet they are unable to exit from the stage. They simply go on waiting. The nature of Godot is never defined; he is a puzzle that has led to intense speculation about what he may represent. Interpreted simply, Godot represents a reason for the characters to go on waiting, and that must suffice. In his play, Beckett constructs a powerful and disturbing image of life itself: Life

***Endgame* is another major play** by Samuel Beckett that, like *Waiting for Godot,* explores the futility of human existence and the trivial activities which people concoct to pass the time. And like *Godot,* the vivid language of the characters presents the bleakness of their situation at the same time that it offers biting humor and opportunities for theatrical brilliance. Here Alvin Epstein plays Nag and Elaine Stritch plays Nell, two characters confined to garbage cans for the entire play, in a 2008 production directed by Andrei Belgrader at the Brooklyn Academy of Music.

is reduced to the act of waiting for something that never comes. Beckett's plays are extremely dark in spite of their humor.

Eugène Ionesco also wrote about the uselessness of human activity, but sometimes in a more playful way than Beckett. Ionesco delighted in creating situations in plays, such as *The Bald Soprano,* in which characters speak to each other at length in various forms of nonsense. Ionesco was particularly concerned with the failure of language to provide us with a means of reaching one another, as is Tony Kushner, whose *Angels in America* includes a scene in which an assembly of angels blather empty phrases simultaneously.

A REVOLUTION IN MOVEMENT: MARTHA GRAHAM

The expressionists and the absurdists made major changes in the use of language, in plot structure, in characterization, and in the nature of stage action. It would require an artist of a different sensibility to contribute a way of approaching stage movement to match the other innovations of expressionism and absurdism. Martha Graham (1893–1991) stands out as one of the most innovative and influential artists of the twentieth century, comparable to Picasso in visual art and James Joyce in literature. Her work has changed the way we understand the expressive possibilities of the human figure in space and the interactions of the figure with objects and costumes. Although Graham's contributions are most evident in modern dance and theatre, her influence, like that of other seminal artists and thinkers, spreads across many disciplines.

Martha Graham was a dancer, choreographer, actress, and playwright. Dance was her language, but her compositions took the form of drama. Graham was an actor who communicated through her body her own versions of Greek and American myths. She began her independent work as a choreographer in the early 1930s and continued to compose dramatic dance works until her death in 1991. The enormous output of this visionary artist spanned the twentieth century.

A New Dance Vocabulary

All the innovators of modern theatre in the West, from the realists to the expressionists to Brecht to the absurdists, sought new styles of acting that would fully engage the body of the actor as well as the voice, to make performance more

Early in her career, Martha Graham choreographed and performed *Lamentation,* a dance of grief that recalls images of the German expressionists.

than posed figures declaiming speeches. Many of these theatre practitioners were inspired by the brilliance of the moving actor in the Asian theatre but frustrated by the lack of a comparable movement tradition in the West. Graham revolutionized what was possible in movement on the stage. Strongly influenced by Asian forms, Graham developed a movement system that contributed to both the technique and the climate that would enable Western experimentation with Eastern forms.

Until the early part of the twentieth century, the available dance vocabulary came from the ballet. In Graham's work, the bare, flexed foot replaced the pointed foot in ballet toe shoes. Angular, asymmetrical movement contrasted sharply with the symmetrical elegance of ballet. The pelvis and abdomen became a primary center for movement so the body could contract and then release rather than always maintain a vertical line. And fundamental to the movement of both women and men was the expression of the body's weight. The floor became a partner in this exploration of the substance of the human body rather than a springboard. The fall, the pull of gravity, was central to Graham's movement system; dancers pressed up from the floor, using their visible power to oppose gravity. Graham herself was a virtuoso performer with an astounding technique and a riveting dramatic presence. She opened the way for much of what would follow in the twentieth-century experimental theatre.

Costume and Set as Partners in Dance

Graham also approached scenic and costume elements as partners to the dancers rather than as decorations or representations of period, although they also served both of these functions. Sewing her own costumes and working with designers such as Isamu Noguchi, who created sculptures for her settings, Graham used design elements to give further definition to the

dancing figure and to provide for the development of character through movement. In an early piece entitled *Lamentation*, the dancer is cloaked and hooded by a piece of draped fabric. In this dance of grief, the dancer pushes with angular, stretching gestures against the fabric that surrounds her. The tension of the dance and its emotional content are generated by the way the fabric resists the efforts of the dancer to displace or break through its binding force.

An example of a sculptural set piece by Noguchi is a free-form metal frame bed that he created for a dance about Jocasta, the mother and wife of Oedipus, in Graham's work *Night Journey*. The bed has a strong symbolic presence. It serves first as the place where Jocasta gave birth to Oedipus, second as the site of their incestuous relationship, and third as the funeral bier that carries Jocasta's body to her grave. The bed has physical importance as well. It is central to the movement of Jocasta and Oedipus as they dance out their relationship on its slanted surface. The hard metal frame supports the dancers' bodies and sets in relief the strength and the vulnerability of their characters: Oedipus, who will lose his eyes; and Jocasta, who will lose her life.

TOTAL THEATRE: ROBERT WILSON

Another American theatre artist, Robert Wilson (1941–), has become one of the dominant figures shaping today's theatre of images. Wilson's theatrical style is connected to a movement called **total theatre,** a form that stretches back to the mid-nineteenth century and the operas of Richard Wagner. Since Wagner's time, many theatre artists have been drawn to a vision of theatre that fuses music, dance, language, scenic image, and light; this is exactly what Wilson aims at. He creates works on a very large scale in terms of (1) the numbers of performers and collaborators involved, sometimes more than 150; (2) the duration of the performances, which can last up to twelve hours; and (3) the size and complexity of the images he constructs. Wilson begins his theatre pieces with scenic images and with music and dance. Language is frequently used, but text is neither the starting point nor the foundation of what is communicated.

Wilson's expectation of the audience experience is very different from that of most of the other theatre artists we have discussed so far. Wilson is not attempting to build a visible and coherent structure of ideas or to interpret character psychology; nor is he offering a social critique. He seeks to trigger associations in the minds of audience members. Rather than consciously constructing work that interprets themes, Wilson and his collaborators present loosely related images that the audience members must then organize and interpret according to their individual responses. Wilson creates stage images that seem to come from the world of dreams and hallucinations.

Wilson's Experience

Robert Wilson brings to his work a unique combination of training and personal experience. A brief consideration of his background is helpful in understanding his point of view and his approaches to his theatre pieces. Wilson studied painting in Paris before he returned to the United States to earn an undergraduate degree in architecture. He experimented with various visual art forms, including large outdoor installations. His first involvement in the New York theatre was as a scene designer. Wilson is a visual thinker; he develops scenes through long sequences of drawings rather than dialogue.

Another profound influence on Wilson's life is dance. As a child Wilson had a pronounced stutter, which inhibited his ability to communicate verbally. At seventeen he began to study dance with a remarkable seventy-year-old teacher, Bird Hoffman. Through controlled movement and relaxation, Wilson was able to overcome his stutter. His studies with Hoffman inspired Wilson's work with children and adults with disabilities, in which he encouraged creative responses, in part through the use of slow, controlled repetitions of patterned movement. Eventually he incorporated this approach to movement into his theatre performances. He also invited the participation of some of the children he worked with, and he used their contributions onstage. Wilson frequently communicates nonverbally with the performers in his pieces as he works with them on stylized gestures and abstract movements. There is none of the discussion of character or motivation that is so important to the realistic theatre.

The Interior Landscape

Wilson's work includes *The Life and Times of Joseph Stalin*, *A Letter to Queen Victoria*, *Einstein on the Beach*, and *The Life and Times of Sigmund Freud*. As the titles suggest, Wilson uses large subjects that can be interpreted in many ways. He frequently focuses on a major historical figure whose influence has been felt across generations and continents; he builds collages of images in response to the impact of the central figure. The images relate to each other thematically, often in a very loose sense. The critic John Rockwell summarizes Wilson's approach to these subjects:

> What Wilson really is concerned with is deeper questions of authority, terror, fear and hope and the smaller (deeper?) human quirks of such seemingly overpowering figures.[6]

In Wilson's work one image slowly dissolves to the next: immense architectural backgrounds; enormous figures; characters in elaborate costumes from different periods; dancers; animals such as bears, elephants, and fish; suspended objects and people; burning houses. Various pieces of text are read or spoken, sometimes in several different languages. Exploratory work that was done for a production of *King Lear* involved a complete reordering of Shakespeare's text, spoken sometimes in English and sometimes in German, with an early Russian film version of *King Lear* playing in the background. Music also

Time Rocker, designed and directed by Robert Wilson with music by Lou Reed and based on H. G. Wells's *Time Machine*, is the last piece of a trilogy of rock operas. Wilson produces his work more frequently in Europe than in the United States, and *Time Rocker* was created in Hamburg, Germany, before being produced at the Théâtre de L'Odeon in Paris.

A NEW MEETING OF EAST AND WEST: SHEN WEI

Both Martha Graham and Bertolt Brecht were deeply influenced by Asian performance styles. Graham's movement vocabulary and Brecht's approach to playwriting and acting reflect their contact with dancers and actors from India, Japan, and China. As Western theatre practitioners adopted ideas from Asian sources, Western performance traditions also have had a major impact on Asian culture. The Japanese perform Shakespeare in the kabuki style, and the Chinese have been exploring realistic spoken drama through performance of plays, like Arthur Miller's *Death of a Salesman*, translated into Chinese or new plays written by Chinese playwrights that use Western-style spoken dialogue instead of dialogue sung in the style of Chinese opera. Most recently, the fusion of Eastern and Western traditions has achieved a striking new direction in the work of Shen Wei.

From Opera to Modern Dance

Shen Wei (1968–) is a Chinese-born dance theatre artist now working in the United States. His father, an actor and a director; and his mother, a producer, both worked in the Chinese opera company in Xianying and were displaced by the Cultural Revolution. Some of Shen's early childhood was spent in harsh circumstances while his parents were forced to do agricultural work in the countryside. He says, "After the Cultural Revolution, the government tried to get back all that had been lost" and some of the Chinese opera schools and companies were reopened.[7] At the age of nine, Shen Wei left his family to study at the Hunan Arts School and prepare for his own career as an opera performer. Classes began at 5:30 in the morning and continued until 8:00 at night. They included movement, acrobatics, martial arts, acting, speech, singing, and learning the roles of different characters. "It was difficult as a young child to get up at 5:30 in the morning, to do your own laundry by hand with

takes a prominent role in Wilson's work. Some of his work has featured the compositions of the **avant-garde** musicians Philip Glass and Laurie Anderson and the voice of the opera singer Jessye Norman. Through the intersection of abstract scenic imagery, hauntingly strange music, hypnotic dance, and pedestrian and poetic fragments of text, Wilson pushes back the boundaries of theatrical expression to reveal, in Martha Graham's words, "the interior landscape."

Shen Wei created *Folding* on a visit to China in 2000 and then re-created it for his company Shen Wei Dance Arts in the United States. Taking his inspiration from the action of folding paper or fabric or any other item, he choreographed a work in which the dancers engage in slow folding and unfolding of their bodies. Dressed in long, draped costumes of red and black and wearing shaped headdresses to extend their height, the dancers have a sculptural quality as they move across a white floor and in front of a huge painting of fish swimming through a mysterious sea. Shen Wei is responsible for the choreography and the set, costume, and makeup design. The lighting is by David Ferri.

no hot water. I saw my parents twice a year. You had to be independent very early. It was really, really hard."

In 1984, at the age of sixteen, Shen started his professional career in the theatre. For the next five years he performed with the Hunan State Opera Company, where he specialized in the roles of the acrobatic warrior hero. By this time, not only was Shen an accomplished actor and singer, he was also skilled in music, calligraphy, poetry, and painting. He explains that he was raised in a tradition where an educated person was expected to develop multiple artistic abilities

in order "to achieve spiritual development." And in addition to his mastery of traditional Chinese art forms, he began to teach himself to paint in the Western style that was becoming visible as Chinese society became more open. Just when his interest in painting had become the focus of his creative energies, on a trip to Beijing in 1987, Shen was exposed to yet another art form, Western modern dance. The restless young artist had found the basis of his future work.

The first Chinese modern dance company, Guangdong Modern Dance Company, was established in 1989. Shen Wei was the only

In contrast to the slow meditative movement of *Folding*, *Rite of Spring* demands the dancers to move with lightning speed while they execute complicated sequences of turns and falls. Choreographed to music by Stravinsky, the movement draws on vocabulary from both the Chinese opera and contemporary dance. The costumes and set including the floor are realized in colors of black, white, and gray as the dancers perform abstract sequences of movement connected to Stravinsky's phrases and rhythms.

member of the new company who did not have a firm background in ballet or classical Chinese dance forms. "I was the only one from Chinese opera. But the director saw my paintings and recognized that I had an open mind, so even though I lacked classical dance training, I was accepted." Studying with visiting teachers from the Martha Graham, José Limón, and Paul Taylor companies, Shen quickly became as interested in choreography as he was in dancing.

The evolution of Shen Wei's artistic journey reflects the rapidity of change in China in the last twenty-five years and the way that change is transforming its culture. However, in 1995 Shen Wei decided to leave China for the United States in search of more opportunities and greater artistic freedom. Drawing on his training in both modern dance and Chinese opera; his skills as a painter; and his knowledge of music, makeup, and costuming, Shen formed his own company in 2000 and began to create new theatre works that merge East and West, performing arts and visual arts.

Choreographer and Designer

In creating his theatre works, Shen is like Martha Graham in the way he choreographs and dances in the pieces and then also designs the makeup and costumes, which are very important to shaping the movement. And like Robert Wilson, he designs his own sets. However, as a choreographer, Shen Wei is unique in an important way. Rather than defining himself through a signature movement style that forms an identifiable foundation for his pieces as a group, he attempts to develop a new dance vocabulary for each new work he undertakes. So the rehearsal process always begins with training the dancers in the new movement he has invented or is exploring. He is known for some works that use very slow, repetitive, meditative movement passages in which stillness is an essential part of the composition. In these works, the dancers seem to inhabit a dreamlike world in which their bodies change shape and have the ability to move in entirely new ways. In other pieces, the movement is lightning-fast and percussive, with the dancers leaping or rolling on the floor with breathtaking speed. Uniting the different pieces is a sense that the dancers' bodies and movement patterns are clearly connected to the world of painting and sculpture. In *Connect Transfer*, a canvas covers the entire stage floor and the dancers have paint on their bodies, with which they color the floor in the patterns of their movements. In *Folding* and *Deep Resonance*, the dancers' bodies themselves seem to be the evolving sculptural forms. A more recent work, *Second Visit to the Empress* (2005), offers a restaging of a prominent opera from the Chinese repertoire in which Shen Wei returns to his roots. But now the traditionally costumed singing characters share the stage with contemporary dancers, an interplay between forms of East and West and the past and the present. In 2008 Shen Wei brought his talents and international perspective to the world stage as the principal choreographer for the spectacular opening ceremonies of the Beijing Olympics.

Summary

In response to what many saw as realism's failure to completely reveal the human condition, new theatre styles arose in the early twentieth century. These theatrical forms communicated through overtly theatrical images, through stylized movement and poetic language, through the abstract rather than the concrete, through a concentration of expression rather than through the accumulation of detail. Although these theatre styles are often grouped under the category of nonrealism, or theatricalism, no single term adequately defines the many forms of theatre that seek to express the inner life of human beings.

Since the beginning of the twentieth century, many playwrights, choreographers, and directors have taken various approaches to theatrical expression. In the theatre of the German expressionists, plays often took the form of protest against war, industrialization, and inhumanity. Characters and language were reduced to their essence and supported by stylized movement and distorted scenic images to produce an effect of anguish. The American playwright Eugene O'Neill used expressionism in much of his early work. Bertolt Brecht sought an alienation effect to interrupt the audience's emotional involvement in the drama in order to encourage analysis of the dramatic event. Absurdist playwrights such as Samuel Beckett and Eugène Ionesco used theatrical imagery to explore philosophical rather than social issues.

Other theatre artists have created unique styles through the use of movement, music, and scenic image rather than language. Martha Graham invented a movement vocabulary to explore the passions of archetypal characters engaged in mythic dramas. Robert Wilson creates a dreamlike total theatre in which enormous scenic images, evocative music, and dancing figures suggest mysterious relationships. Shen Wei draws together theatre, dance, and visual art traditions of China and the West.

Topics for Discussion and Writing

1. Research the works of such artists as Edvard Munch, Pablo Picasso, Salvador Dalí, and Käthe Kollwitz that distort and fracture the represented figures, landscapes, or environments. What kinds of commentary about the human condition do these paintings make? How do they diverge from more realistic image making?

2. What changes in the nature of the actor–audience relationship were proposed by Bertolt Brecht? How do Brecht's ideas about acting contrast with those of Stanislavsky outlined in Chapter 7? We frequently see evidence of Stanislavsky's approach to acting in theatre and film today. Cite some examples of Brecht's approach to acting, in which actors call attention to themselves as actors.

3. Compare the plot of *Waiting for Godot* with that of *Joe Turner's Come and Gone* or *And the Soul Shall Dance*. What is the difference in the kinds of actions performed by the characters, and what is the significance of those actions? What is the difference in the endings and what we imagine will happen to the characters after the plays have ended?

 For suggested readings and other resources related to this chapter, please visit www.mhhe.com/creativespirit5e.

Chapter 10

Expressing a Worldview through Theatricalism

Looking at *Angels in America:*
Millennium Approaches
by Tony Kushner

TONY KUSHNER WAS BORN IN New York in 1956 but grew up in Lake Charles, Louisiana. Both of his parents were professional musicians, and Kushner was raised in an artistic world rich with music and theatre. Although he was raised in a close-knit and supportive Jewish family, life was a struggle for a politically concerned teenager coming to terms with his identity as a gay man. Kushner chose to attend Columbia University in the hope that New York City would provide a more hospitable social and political environment than he had found in Louisiana. At Columbia, Kushner discovered that his interests in political activism and theatre complemented each other. Through his studies of Bertolt Brecht, Kushner began to envision an idea of theatre that would address the social inequities that he saw damaging the fabric of American life. Kushner pursued his theatre studies further at New York University, where he received a master of fine arts in directing, before turning his energies to playwriting.

Kushner had completed only one major play, *A Bright Room Called Day,* before he began work on *Angels in America,* which would become one of the most celebrated plays of the 1990s and, for some, one of the most important American plays of the twentieth century. Since writing *Angels in America,* Kushner has written *Slavs!*—a play set against the experience of Soviet repression— as well as adaptations of major works from different historical periods, including *Stella,* by the German romantic playwright Johann Wolfgang von Goethe; *The Illusion,* by the seventeenth-century playwright Pierre Corneille; *The Good Woman of Sezuan,* by Bertolt Brecht; and *The Dybbuk,* a play from the Yiddish theatre early in the twentieth century by Solomon Ansky. Recent work includes two plays: *Homebody/Kabul* (2001), about the political turmoil in Afghanistan; and *Caroline, or Change* (2003), an autobiographical musical with a score by Jeanine Tesori. Kushner also wrote the screenplay for the film *Munich* (2005).

In May 2009, Kushner's play entitled *The Intelligent Homosexual's Guide to Capitalism and Socialism with a Key to the Scriptures* premiered at the Guthrie Theatre in Minneapolis as part of a festival dedicated to Kushner's works. This new work has a more realistic structure than *Angels in America* but continues to focus on themes of identity, politics, and the nature of philosophical conflicts in contemporary America.

Angels in America is a brilliant example of the kind of experimentation with form that is characteristic of the nonrealistic theatre. In constructing his play, Tony Kushner draws on elements of expressionism, absurdism, and epic theatre, as well as realism. *Angels in America*, in fact, is not one play but two: *Millennium Approaches* and *Perestroika*. Each play lasts about three and a half hours; the two plays are sometimes presented on alternate days or in marathon sessions beginning in the afternoon, breaking for dinner, and

then going on until late into the night. The presentation of *Angels in America* was considered a major theatrical event because of the scale of the undertaking, the sheer theatricality of the work, and the themes and issues that the two plays address.

Our study focuses on the first play, *Millennium Approaches*, with a more limited discussion of *Perestroika*. In the production analysis following the playscript, we examine the development of the play itself in relation to its production at the Eureka Theatre, a small theatre in San Francisco; and at the Mark Taper Forum in Los Angeles. In both the introduction to the play and the production analysis, we consider how Kushner juxtaposes realistic and theatricalized elements to create his vision of life in the United States in the late twentieth century.

EXPLORING THE TEXT
••• OF *ANGELS IN AMERICA: MILLENNIUM APPROACHES*

Angels in America comprises a complicated mix of characters, plot incidents, and ideas. The playwright, Tony Kushner, tells a broad sweep of a story that involves love and betrayal, politics and religion. Subtitled "A Gay Fantasia on National Themes," *Angels in America* examines American life in the 1980s from a gay male point of view that is heavily influenced by the AIDS epidemic.

PLOT AND CHARACTERS: A WORLD IN SPIRITUAL COLLAPSE

The plot of *Angels in America: Millennium Approaches* focuses on two troubled couples living in New York City. Louis and Prior are gay lovers who have been together for four years when Prior is diagnosed with AIDS. Unable to cope with the grim realities of the disease and the ever-present threat of death, Louis abandons

Louis (Michael Ornstein, *left*) and Joe (Michael Scott Ryan) begin their friendship in *Angels in America: Millennium Approaches,* produced at the Eureka Theatre under the direction of David Esbjornson in 1991.

Tony Kushner

I believe that the playwright should be a kind of public intellectual, even if only a crackpot public intellectual: someone who asks her or his thoughts to get up before crowds, on platforms, and entertain, challenge, instruct, annoy, provoke, appall. I'm amused and horrified when I realize that, on occasion, I'm being taken seriously. But of course being taken seriously is my ambition, semisecretly-and-very-ambivalently held. I enjoy the tension between responsibility and frivolity; it's where my best work comes from.[1]

—*Tony Kushner*

[1]This photo of Tony Kushner was taken at the 12th annual BAFTA/LA Tea Party in 2006 in Century City, California.

Prior. Harper and Joe Pitt are a young, married Mormon couple who have moved from Utah so that Joe, an ambitious lawyer, can take a job clerking for a federal judge. Joe is struggling with his own closeted homosexuality or bisexuality and eventually abandons Harper, having been absent emotionally for some time already. Harper is a frightened young woman, addicted to Valium, who hallucinates about a man attacking her with knives and despairs about the depletion of the earth's ozone layer. Louis, a passionately liberal Jew; and Joe, a conservative Republican, become lovers in spite of the apparent conflicts in their political and religious backgrounds.

This personal drama of abandonment and self-gratification is intricately connected to Kushner's larger social and political concerns. The play takes place in the 1980s during Ronald Reagan's presidency. Both Louis and Joe work for the federal government, and their personal behavior clearly mirrors Kushner's interpretation of the Reagan administration's attitude toward those in need. Louis and Joe both have strong political and religious affiliations, yet neither traditional politics nor religion provides a moral or spiritual guide for the times in which they find themselves. They have become, as Louis says, "Reagan's children. Selfish and greedy and loveless and blind."[2]

The two characters whom Louis and Joe abandon each embody the cancers of the body and soul spreading through the country. Prior struggles with the ravages brought on by HIV infection. Harper is obsessed with the damage to the earth's atmosphere. The health crisis of the gay community links to the environmental crisis of the planet.

The Role of Roy Cohn

Kushner introduces one more major character who also serves to expand the play's frame of reference beyond the domestic drama of the two couples. This character, the lawyer Roy Cohn, is an extreme representative of the moral decay of the country. The character of Cohn is based on a real person who, in fact, moved in the upper echelons of Republican power and died of AIDS in 1986, never having publicly acknowledged his homosexuality.

In the play, Joe Pitt, the ambitious young lawyer, turns to Roy Cohn as a kind of mentor, and Cohn eagerly looks to exploit the younger man in his own illegal schemes and power struggles. With the obscene and self-serving character of Cohn serving as background to the rest of the action, Kushner presents us with a nation in physical, moral, and spiritual collapse. Under such circumstances, Kushner asks, how do we restore compassion to our lives? Faced with such enormous obstacles, where do we find the will to change?

The Shifting Point of View

Like August Wilson and Wakako Yamauchi, Kushner is concerned with the impact of historical and sociological issues on his characters' lives. For Wilson and Yamauchi, social and economic injustices—racism, prejudice, slavery, anti-immigration policies—are a basic part of the environment, the fabric against which we see the characters' lives take shape. Kushner also addresses social and economic issues—the deeply ingrained homophobia of American society and the greed and lack of compassion that he perceives were represented by national policies in the 1980s.

But Kushner's approach to his material is different in essential ways from that of Wilson and Yamauchi. Wilson and Yamauchi focus on the interior movement of the characters' psyches, a progression of struggle, recognition, and awareness. As members of the audience, we are aware of the social background, but our principal concern is the story of the characters. Kushner changes this focus; he asks the audience for analysis as much as for empathy.

Wilson and Yamauchi draw us deeper and deeper into a created world that remains constant. We see their characters from a consistent point of view. Kushner, however, keeps shifting the perspective, alternating between domestic intimacy and spectacle, between a realistic representation of relationships and a surrealistic presentation of dreams and hallucinations. The nature of the created world changes abruptly, going through wild swings of imagery and point of view. Sometimes we see the characters objectively from the outside; sometimes we see them subjectively from the inside. We move inside the characters' minds and see distorted views of experience that have been brought on by illness or addiction. Sometimes the characters enter each other's dreams, and the view of reality seems to

be objective and subjective at the same time. And sometimes the play becomes fantasy, with the entrance of historical characters into the present or the appearance of supernatural characters.

INFLUENCES ON KUSHNER AS PLAYWRIGHT: BERTOLT BRECHT AND CARYL CHURCHILL

As we discussed in Chapter 9, the work of Bertolt Brecht has had a significant influence on Tony Kushner. Epic theatre, whose ideas come largely from Brecht's plays and productions as they evolved from the 1930s to the 1950s, has also shaped the playwriting of another source of inspiration for Kushner: the British playwright Caryl Churchill (1938–). Churchill has refined the Brechtian approach to respond to such contemporary concerns as race, gender, class, and economics. She has developed her own vocabulary of alienation devices. For example, in her play *Cloud 9*, Churchill uses **cross-gender casting** and **nontraditional casting;** that is, some of the female roles are played by men, some of the male roles are played by women, and a white actor plays the role of a black character. The purpose of such casting is to raise questions about how attitudes toward gender and race have originated. This casting calls attention to the idea that much human behavior is a result of social conditioning—that the way we perceive other people is the result of social expectations. These theatrical strategies challenge stereotypical thinking and ask us to question the social values regarding race and gender that limit human potential. In *Angels in America*, Tony Kushner employs this particular strategy of Churchill's by specifying in the script that some of the male roles be played by women actors.

Churchill develops her Brechtian approach further by creating a panorama that juxtaposes contemporary characters with historical figures who comment on the situations of the contemporary characters. She essentially widens the

Mr. Lies emerges from Harper's hallucinations to help her escape when the reality of living with Joe Pitt becomes overwhelming, as seen in the New York production of *Angels in America* directed by George C. Wolfe in 1993. Jeffrey Wright plays Mr. Lies; Marsha Gay Harden plays Harper.

respective times. Much of the political theatre that exploded in the United States in the 1960s and afterward was heavily influenced by Brecht. And Caryl Churchill has had a similar impact on American theatrical expression since the 1980s. Although Tony Kushner is generally associated with the Brechtian tradition, his dramatic structure is very specifically shaped by Churchill's influence. She has provided him with a method of bringing together the private and public aspects of his vision and then of placing the contemporary situation in a historical framework.

THE HISTORICAL FRAMEWORK OF *ANGELS IN AMERICA*

frame surrounding her characters to expose more than their daily lives and their physical and psychological environments. In the frame she places historical figures whose presence connects the characters' situations to larger economic and political concerns. In her play *Top Girls*, the difficult lives of ordinary, contemporary Englishwomen and their children are placed against a background of remarkable women from different periods in history. Dialogues occur between characters from different centuries and between historical and fictional characters.

Brecht and Churchill are among the most influential theatre practitioners of their

An obvious example of a historical framework in *Millennium Approaches* is the appearance of two ghostlike characters, both named Prior Walter, in act 3, scene 1. Prior Walter is also the name of the central character of *Angels in America*, who becomes a representative of the gay community and the larger American community through his suffering with AIDS and then his transcendence of both illness and despair. Prior 1 and Prior 2 are the English ancestors of the twentieth-century Prior: Prior 1 from the thirteenth century and Prior 2 from the seventeenth century. Prior 1 and Prior 2 visit the contemporary Prior while he is

Caryl Churchill's *Top Girls* begins with a scene in which a contemporary business executive, Marlene (Deborah Kassner), meets extraordinary women from earlier centuries. This scene from a production at Lewis and Clark College, directed by Stephanie Arnold, shows Lady Nijo (Sakiko Taoka), a thirteenth-century Buddhist nun; Dull Gret (Christine Calfas), a figure from a Breughel painting; and Pope Joan (Heidi Van Schoonhoven), a pope from the eighth century who was discovered to be a woman when she gave birth to a child.

in bed one night to warn him of the coming of the Angel (a character who makes a spectacular appearance at the end of *Millennium Approaches*), much like the ghosts who appear to Scrooge in Dickens's *Christmas Carol*. Prior 1 and Prior 2 were both victims of the plague, the thirteenth century's "spotty monster" and the seventeenth century's "Black Jack." The presence of these plague victims puts the AIDS epidemic in historical perspective; the Prior ancestors place the twentieth-century Prior in a long line of descendents that can be seen as the human family. We

see outbreaks of plague as illnesses that affected entire societies, not as historically unique events or as punishments visited on any one group of people for their sins.

The Character Roy Cohn as a Historical Figure

Kushner's most complex and original development of Churchill's historical framework comes in the character Roy Cohn. Cohn is central to Kushner's dramatic vision and his commentary on history and politics.

Roy Cohn (John Bellucci, *center*) seeks to persuade Joe Pitt (Michael Scott Ryan) to become a "Royboy" in the premiere production of *Angels in America* at the Eureka Theatre. The part of Martin Heller (*left*) is played by a woman, Anne Darragh.

Born in 1927, Roy Cohn first achieved national prominence during the cold war of the late 1940s and 1950s. He served as an assistant to the prosecutor in the trial of Julius and Ethel Rosenberg, who in 1951 were found guilty of selling atomic secrets to the Soviet Union and in 1953 were executed in the electric chair. Cohn claimed that he personally influenced the judge to sentence the Rosenbergs to death. Cohn then became counsel and sidekick to Senator Joseph McCarthy, who launched the anticommunist "witch hunts" of the early 1950s that destroyed the lives and careers of many American writers, artists, and intellectuals. McCarthy died in 1957, discredited and censured, but Cohn lived

on, finding new allies in right-wing politics and new opportunities as a lawyer to the wealthy. He died of AIDS in 1986.

Because of Roy Cohn's position in U.S. history, the character Roy Cohn brings onstage with him a long trail of historical baggage. His appearance evokes the excesses of the cold war and especially the execution of the Rosenbergs. But he is also a contemporary reference, with his connections to the Reagan administration and his death from AIDS.

A study in contradictions, Cohn is a homophobic homosexual; a Jew whose harshest judgments were made against other Jews; a lawyer who twisted the law for his own

••• IN CONTEXT

The Life and Times of Roy Cohn

Date	Event
1927	Birth of Roy Cohn.
1938	Formation of the House Committee on Un-American Activities (HUAC). The committee focuses on subversive, communist activity, contributing to the climate of suspicion that would prepare the way for the unfounded accusations of Joe McCarthy and Roy Cohn.
1946	Joseph McCarthy is elected to the U.S. Senate as a Republican from Wisconsin.
1947	Bertolt Brecht is called to testify before the HUAC. Scrutiny of artists and intellectuals expands.
1951	Espionage trial of Julius and Ethel Rosenberg begins. Roy Cohn is appointed assistant to the prosecutor, Irving Saypol. The Rosenbergs are convicted of stealing atomic secrets for the Soviet Union, although the case against Ethel Rosenberg indicates minimal involvement. Judge Irving Kaufman sentences both Rosenbergs to die in the electric chair against even the recommendation of the FBI. Roy Cohn claims that he personally influenced the judge on the sentencing.
1952	Joseph McCarthy is reelected to the U.S. Senate in a campaign that focuses on the communist menace. He accuses the Democratic administrations of Franklin Roosevelt and Harry Truman of "twenty years of treason." McCarthy receives the chairmanship of the Senate's Government Operations Committee, which gives him a platform for attacking individuals in the Eisenhower administration, in public life, and in the Senate. Eisenhower tolerates such attacks no matter how outrageous and damaging to individuals and to the atmosphere in the nation as long as they seem to benefit the Republican Party.
1953	Following Roy Cohn's successful participation in the Rosenberg trial, McCarthy appoints him as the chief counsel for his Senate committee.
1953	Execution of Julius and Ethel Rosenberg.
1954	Army-McCarthy hearings, in which the tactics and "above the law" attitude of McCarthy and Cohn are exposed on television.
1954	Cohn resigns as McCarthy's chief counsel. McCarthy is "condemned" by the Senate. Cohn begins his career as lawyer to the wealthy. He cultivates connections and trades favors with the powerful in business and government.
1956	Arthur Miller is called to testify before the HUAC.
1957	McCarthy dies, apparently of acute alcoholism.
1986	Roy Cohn dies of AIDS. He never publicly acknowledges his homosexuality.

enrichment, self-gratification, and aggrandizement. Condensed in the character of Cohn is a large share of the contradictions in American life that are the subjects of Kushner's play. Cohn, real and fictionalized, historical and contemporary, is placed in the center of Kushner's plot structure as a background to the rest of the action.

Roy Cohn is shown here (*right*) as assistant to Joseph McCarthy during the Army-McCarthy hearings in 1954.

Belize. Of course, these tangled interactions at crucial points are calculated. There is no pretense here that all of these characters' paths would intersect in such convenient ways in the natural course of events, as there would be in a realistic play. Kushner wants us to see these lives in contrast with each other; he cleverly and boldly arranges the circumstances to enable such encounters.

Roy Cohn and the Plot of *Angels in America*

Kushner brings Cohn into the construction of *Angels in America: Millennium Approaches* through two subplots. In the first subplot, Cohn faces disbarment proceedings because of his shady dealings as a lawyer. He is therefore searching for an attractive, loyal, young Republican man to place in the Justice Department in a desperate attempt to outmaneuver the disbarment. The young lawyer on whom Cohn fixes his attention and hopes for salvation is Joe Pitt, the Mormon husband at a crossroads in his own life.

The second subplot develops when Cohn's health deteriorates and he becomes part of the AIDS community inhabited by Prior and Prior's close friend and nurse,

Roy Cohn and Ethel Rosenberg

Toward the end of *Millennium Approaches*, Kushner expands the focus on Cohn as a historical figure by providing him with a disturbing companion. He creates a fictional version of Ethel Rosenberg as she might have appeared had she lived to be an older woman. The association of Cohn with the execution of Ethel Rosenberg

Prior (Stephen Spinella) is comforted by Belize (Harry Waters, Jr.) in the Eureka Theatre production of *Angels in America* in 1991.

The political activists Julius and Ethel Rosenberg were convicted of stealing atomic secrets for the Soviet Union in 1951 and executed for treason in 1953.

(1953) is the most heinous of the various crimes against humanity that Kushner draws on in his construction of the Cohn character.

Although few historians continue to argue that Julius Rosenberg was framed by the government, the degree of Ethel Rosenberg's involvement as a spy is uncertain. Some conclude that she provided her husband a minimal amount of support; others maintain that her only crime was knowledge of Julius Rosenberg's treason. Government documents released in 1980 make clear that the execution of this young mother of two children was a ploy to gain information from her husband. It was also part of the government's anticommunist propaganda campaign. Above all, the execution of Ethel Rosenberg was far in excess of any reasonable sentence for her limited participation in espionage. For people who

lived through the repressive climate of the 1950s in the United States, the appearance of Ethel Rosenberg on the stage in *Angels in America* is shocking.

The character that Kushner creates for Ethel Rosenberg bears little resemblance to the historical woman, at least as she has been interpreted by historians. A young woman when she died, she now appears as a comfortable Jewish grandmother with a toughness beneath the recognizable stereotypical role. In keeping with Kushner's outrageous approach to his material, Cohn and Rosenberg banter and bicker as if they are old friends rather than mortal enemies.

Like the figure of Cohn, the character of Ethel Rosenberg is loaded with complex significance. She seems to represent the angel of death, coming for Cohn at the end of his

Ethel Rosenberg (Kathleen Chalfant) approaches the bedside of the dying Roy Cohn (Ron Liebman) in *Angels in America: Perestroika*, produced at the Mark Taper Forum under the direction of Oskar Eustis and Tony Taccone in 1992.

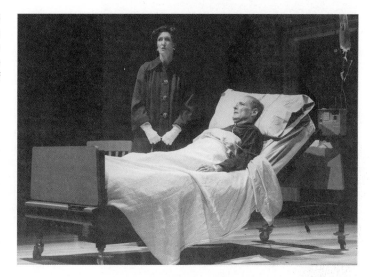

life. She is an accusation and a reminder. But perhaps most startling, there is also forgiveness in this character, a character who would have less reason than anyone in the United States to forgive Roy Cohn and his colleagues for their transgressions.

Angels in America: Millennium Approaches

TONY KUSHNER

CHARACTERS

ROY M. COHN, a successful New York lawyer and unofficial power broker.

JOSEPH PORTER PITT, chief clerk for Justice Theodore Wilson of the Federal Court of Appeals, Second Circuit.

HARPER AMATY PITT, Joe's wife, an agoraphobic with a mild Valium addiction.

LOUIS IRONSON, a word processor working for the Second Circuit Court of Appeals.

PRIOR WALTER, Louis's boyfriend. Occasionally works as a club designer or caterer, otherwise lives very modestly but with great style off a small trust fund.

HANNAH PORTER PITT, Joe's mother, currently residing in Salt Lake City, living off her deceased husband's army pension.

BELIZE, a former drag queen and former lover of Prior's. A registered nurse. Belize's name was originally Norman Arriaga; Belize is a drag name that stuck.

THE ANGEL, four divine emanations, Fluor, Phosphor, Lumen, and Candle; manifest in One: the Continental Principality of America. She has magnificent steel-gray wings.

Other Characters in Part One

RABBI ISIDOR CHEMELWITZ, an orthodox Jewish rabbi, played by the actor playing Hannah.

MR. LIES, Harper's imaginary friend, a travel agent, who in style of dress and speech suggests a jazz musician; he always wears a large lapel badge emblazoned "IOTA" (The International Order of Travel Agents). He is played by the actor playing Belize.

THE MAN IN THE PARK, played by the actor playing Prior.

THE VOICE, the voice of The Angel.

HENRY, Roy's doctor, played by the actor playing Hannah.

EMILY, a nurse, played by the actor playing The Angel.

MARTIN HELLER, a Reagan Administration Justice Department flackman, played by the actor playing Harper.

SISTER ELLA CHAPTER, a Salt Lake City real-estate saleswoman, played by the actor playing The Angel.

PRIOR 1, the ghost of a dead Prior Walter from the 13th century, played by the actor playing Joe. He is a blunt, gloomy medieval farmer with a guttural Yorkshire accent.

PRIOR 2, the ghost of a dead Prior Walter from the 17th century, played by the actor playing Roy. He is a Londoner, sophisticated, with a High British accent.

THE ESKIMO, played by the actor playing Joe.

THE WOMAN IN THE SOUTH BRONX, played by the actor playing The Angel.

ETHEL ROSENBERG, played by the actor playing Hannah.

PLAYWRIGHT'S NOTES

A Disclaimer

Roy M. Cohn, the character, is based on the late Roy M. Cohn (1927–1986), who was all too real; for the most part the acts attributed to the character Roy, such as his illegal conferences with Judge Kaufmann during the trial of Ethel Rosenberg, are to be found in the historical record. But this Roy is a work of dramatic fiction; his words are my invention, and liberties have been taken.

A Note about the Staging

The play benefits from a pared-down style of presentation, with minimal scenery and scene shifts done rapidly (no blackouts!), employing the cast as well as stagehands—which makes for an actor-driven event, as this must be. The moments of magic—the appearance and disappearance of Mr. Lies and the ghosts, the Book hallucination, and the ending—are to be fully realized, as bits of wonderful *theatrical* illusion—which means it's OK if the wires show, and maybe it's good that they do, but the magic should at the same time be thoroughly amazing.

> In a murderous time
> the heart breaks and breaks
> and lives by breaking.
> —Stanley Kunitz
> "The Testing-Tree"

ACT ONE

Bad News

October–November 1985

Scene 1

The last days of October. Rabbi Isidor Chemelwitz alone onstage with a small coffin. It is a rough pine box with two wooden pegs, one at the foot and one at the head, holding the lid in place. A prayer shawl embroidered with a Star of David is draped over the lid, and by the head a yarzheit candle is burning.

RABBI ISIDOR CHEMELWITZ (He speaks sonorously, with a heavy Eastern European accent, unapologetically consulting a sheet of notes for the family names): Hello and good morning. I am Rabbi Isidor Chemelwitz of the Bronx Home for Aged Hebrews. We are here this morning to pay respects at the passing of Sarah Ironson, devoted wife of Benjamin Ironson, also deceased, loving and caring mother of her sons Morris, Abraham, and Samuel, and her daughters Esther and Rachel; beloved grandmother of Max, Mark, Louis, Lisa, Maria . . . uh . . . Lesley, Angela, Doris, Luke and Eric. (Looks more closely at paper) Eric? This is a Jewish name? (Shrugs) Eric. A large and loving family. We assemble that we may mourn collectively this good and righteous woman.

(He looks at the coffin)

This woman. I did not know this woman. I cannot accurately describe her attributes, nor do justice to her dimensions. She was. . . . Well, in the Bronx Home of Aged Hebrews are many like this, the old, and to many I speak but not to be frank with this one. She preferred silence. So I do not know her and yet I know her. She was . . .

(He touches the coffin)

. . . not a person but a whole kind of person, the ones who crossed the ocean, who brought with us to America the villages of Russia and Lithuania—and how we struggled, and how we fought, for the family, for the Jewish home, so that you would not grow up *here,* in this strange place, in the melting pot where nothing melted. Descendants of this immigrant woman, you do not grow up in America, you and your children and their children with the goyische names. You do not live in America. No such place exists. Your clay is the clay of some Litvak shtetl, your air the air of the steppes—because she carried the old world on her back across the ocean, in a boat, and she put it down on Grand Concourse Avenue, or in Flatbush, and she worked that earth into your bones, and you pass it to your children, this ancient, ancient culture and home.

(Little pause)

You can never make that crossing that she made, for such Great Voyages in this world do not any more exist. But every day of your lives the miles that voyage between that place and this one you cross. Every day. You understand me? In you that journey is.

So . . .

She was the last of the Mohicans, this one was. Pretty soon . . . all the old will be dead.

Scene 2

Same day. Roy and Joe in Roy's office. Roy at an impressive desk, bare except for a very elaborate phone system, rows and rows of flashing buttons which bleep and beep and whistle incessantly, making chaotic music underneath Roy's conversations. Joe is sitting, waiting. Roy conducts business with great energy, impatience and sensual abandon: gesticulating, shouting, cajoling, crooning, playing the phone, receiver and hold button with virtuosity and love.

ROY (Hitting a button): Hold. (To Joe) I wish I was an octopus, a fucking octopus. Eight loving arms and all those suckers. Know what I mean?

JOE: No, I . . .

ROY (Gesturing to a deli platter of little sandwiches on his desk): You want lunch?

JOE: No, that's OK really I just . . .

ROY (Hitting a button): Ailene? Roy Cohn. Now what kind of a greeting is. . . . I thought we were friends, Ai. . . . Look Mrs. Soffer you don't have to get. . . . You're upset. You're yelling. You'll aggravate your condition, you shouldn't yell, you'll pop little blood vessels in your face if you yell. . . . No that was a joke, Mrs. Soffer, I was joking. . . . I already apologized sixteen times for that, Mrs. Soffer, you . . . (While she's fulminating, Roy covers the mouthpiece with his hand and talks to Joe) This'll take a minute, eat already, what is this tasty sandwich here it's—(He takes a bite of a sandwich) Mmmmm, liver or some. . . . Here.

(He pitches the sandwich to Joe, who catches it and returns it to the platter.)

ROY (Back to Mrs. Soffer): Uh huh, uh, huh. . . . No, I already told you, it wasn't a vacation, it was business, Mrs. Soffer, I have clients in Haiti, Mrs. Soffer, I. . . . Listen, Ailene, YOU THINK I'M THE ONLY GODDAM LAWYER IN HISTORY EVER MISSED A COURT DATE? Don't make such a big fucking. . . . Hold. (He hits the hold button) You HAG!

JOE: If this is a bad time . . .

ROY: *Bad* time? This is a *good* time! (Button) Baby doll, get me. . . . Oh fuck, wait . . . (Button, button) Hello? Yah. Sorry to keep you holding, Judge Hollins, I. . . . Oh Mrs. Hollins, sorry dear deep voice you got. Enjoying your visit? (Hand over mouthpiece again, to Joe) She sounds like a truckdriver and he sounds like Kate Smith, very confusing. Nixon appointed him, all the geeks are Nixon appointees . . . (To Mrs. Hollins) Yeah yeah right good so how many tickets dear? Seven. For what, *Cats, 42nd Street,* what? No you wouldn't like *La Cage,* trust me, I know. Oh for godsake. . . . Hold. (Button, button) Baby doll, seven for *Cats* or something, anything hard to get, I don't give a fuck what and neither will they. (Button; to Joe) You see *La Cage?*

JOE: No, I . . .

ROY: Fabulous. Best thing on Broadway. Maybe ever. (Button) Who? Aw, Jesus H. Christ, Harry, *no,* Harry, Judge John Francis Grimes, Manhattan Family Court. Do I have to do every goddam thing myself? *Touch* the bastard, Harry, and don't call me on this line again, I told you not to . . .

JOE (Starting to get up): Roy, uh, should I wait outside or . . .

ROY (To Joe): Oh sit. (To Harry) You hold. I pay you to hold fuck you Harry you jerk. (Button) Half-wit dick-brain. (Instantly philosophical) I see the universe, Joe, as a kind of sandstorm in outer space with winds of mega-hurricane velocity, but instead of grains of sand it's shards and splinters of glass. You ever feel that way? Ever have one of those days?

JOE: I'm not sure I . . .

ROY: So how's life in Appeals? How's the Judge?

JOE: He sends his best.

ROY: He's a good man. Loyal. Not the brightest man on the bench, but he has manners. And a nice head of silver hair.

JOE: He gives me a lot of responsibility.

ROY: Yeah, like writing his decisions and signing his name.

JOE: Well . . .

ROY: He's a nice guy. And you cover admirably.

JOE: Well, thanks, Roy, I . . .

ROY (Button): Yah? Who is *this?* Well who the fuck are you? Hold—(Button) Harry? Eighty-seven grand, something like that. Fuck him. Eat me. New Jersey, chain of porno film stores in, uh, Weehawken. That's—Harry, that's the beauty of the law. (Button) So, baby doll, what? *Cats?* Bleah. (Button) *Cats!* It's about cats. Singing cats, you'll love it. Eight o'clock, the theatre's always at eight. (Button) Fucking tourists. (Button, then to Joe) Oh live a little, Joe, *eat* something for Christ sake—

JOE: Um, Roy, could you . . .

ROY: What? (To Harry) Hold a minute. (Button) Mrs. Soffer? Mrs. . . . (Button) God-fucking-dammit to hell, where is . . .

JOE (Overlapping): Roy, I'd really appreciate it if . . .

ROY (Overlapping): Well she was here a minute ago, baby doll, see if . . .

(The phone starts making three different beeping sounds, all at once.)

ROY (Smashing buttons): Jesus fuck this goddam thing . . .

JOE (Overlapping): I really wish you wouldn't . . .

ROY (Overlapping): Baby doll? Ring the *Post* get me Suzy see if . . .

(The phone starts whistling loudly.)

ROY: CHRIST!

JOE: *Roy.*

ROY (Into receiver): Hold. (Button; to Joe) What?

JOE: Could you please not take the Lord's name in vain?

(Pause)

I'm sorry. But please. At least while I'm . . .

ROY (Laughs, then): Right. Sorry. Fuck. Only in America. (Punches a button) Baby doll, tell 'em all to fuck off. Tell 'em I died. You handle Mrs. Soffer. Tell her it's on the way. Tell her I'm schtupping the judge. I'll call her back. I *will* call her. I *know* how much I borrowed. She's got four hundred times that stuffed up her. . . . Yeah, tell her I said that. (Button. The phone is silent) So, Joe.

JOE: I'm sorry Roy, I just . . .

ROY: No no no no no, principles count, I respect principles, I'm not religious but I like God and God likes me. Baptist, Catholic?

JOE: Mormon.

ROY: Mormon. Delectable. Absolutely. Only in America. So, Joe. Whattya think?

JOE: It's . . . well . . .

ROY: Crazy life.

JOE: Chaotic.

ROY: Well but God bless chaos. Right?

JOE: Ummm . . .

ROY: Huh. Mormons. I knew Mormons, in, um, Nevada.

JOE: Utah, mostly.

ROY: No, these Mormons were in Vegas. So. So, how'd you like to go to Washington and work for the Justice Department?

JOE: Sorry?

ROY: How'd you like to go to Washington and work for the Justice Department? All I gotta do is pick up the phone, talk to Ed, and you're in.

JOE: In . . . what, exactly?

ROY: Associate Assistant Something Big. Internal Affairs, heart of the woods, something nice with clout.

JOE: Ed . . . ?

ROY: Meese. The Attorney General.

JOE: Oh.

ROY: I just have to pick up the phone . . .

JOE: I have to think.

ROY: Of course.

(Pause)

It's a great time to be in Washington, Joe.

JOE: Roy, it's incredibly exciting . . .

ROY: And it would mean something to me. You understand?

(Little pause.)

JOE: I . . . can't say how much I appreciate this Roy, I'm sort of . . . well, stunned, I mean. . . . Thanks, Roy. But I have to give it some thought. I have to ask my wife.

ROY: Your wife. Of course.

JOE: But I really appreciate . . .

ROY: Of course. Talk to your wife.

Scene 3

Later that day. Harper at home, alone. She is listening to the radio and talking to herself, as she often does. She speaks to the audience.

HARPER: People who are lonely, people left alone, sit talking nonsense to the air, imagining . . . beautiful systems dying, old fixed orders spiraling apart . . .

When you look at the ozone layer, from outside, from a spaceship, it looks like a pale blue halo, a gentle, shimmering aureole encircling the atmosphere encircling the earth. Thirty miles above our heads, a thin layer of three-atom oxygen molecules, product of photosynthesis, which explains the fussy vegetable preference for visible light, its rejection of darker rays and emanations. Danger from without. It's a kind of gift, from God, the crowning touch to the creation of the world: guardian angels, hands linked, make a spherical net, a blue-green nesting orb, a shell of safety for life itself. But everywhere, things are collapsing, lies surfacing, systems of defense giving way. . . . This is why, Joe, this is why I shouldn't be left alone.

(Little pause)

I'd like to go traveling. Leave you behind to worry. I'll send postcards with strange stamps and tantalizing messages on the back. "Later maybe." "Nevermore . . ."

(Mr. Lies, a travel agent, appears.)

HARPER: Oh! You startled me!

MR. LIES: Cash, check or credit card?

HARPER: I remember you. You're from Salt Lake. You sold us the plane tickets when we flew here. What are you doing in Brooklyn?

MR. LIES: You said you wanted to travel . . .

HARPER: And here you are. How thoughtful.

MR. LIES: Mr. Lies. Of the International Order of Travel Agents. We mobilize the globe, we set people adrift, we stir the populace and send nomads eddying across the planet. We are adepts of motion, acolytes of the flux. Cash, check or credit card. Name your destination.

HARPER: Antarctica, maybe. I want to see the hole in the ozone. I heard on the radio . . .

MR. LIES (He has a computer terminal in his briefcase): I can arrange a guided tour. Now?

HARPER: Soon. Maybe soon. I'm not safe here you see. Things aren't right with me. Weird stuff happens . . .

MR. LIES: Like?

HARPER: Well, like you, for instance. Just appearing. Or last week . . . well never mind.

People are like planets, you need a thick skin. Things get to me, Joe stays away and now. . . . Well look. My dreams are talking back to me.

MR. LIES: It's the price of rootlessness. Motion sickness. The only cure: to keep moving.

HARPER: I'm undecided. I feel . . . that something's going to give. It's 1985. Fifteen years till the third millennium. Maybe Christ will come again. Maybe seeds will be planted, maybe there'll be harvests then, maybe early figs to eat, maybe new life, maybe fresh blood, maybe companionship and love and protection, safety from what's outside, maybe the door will hold, or maybe . . . maybe the troubles will come, and the end will come, and the sky will collapse and there will be terrible rains and showers of poison light, or maybe my life is really fine, maybe Joe loves me and I'm only crazy thinking otherwise, or maybe not, maybe it's even worse than I know, maybe . . . I want to know, maybe I don't. The suspense, Mr. Lies, it's killing me.

MR. LIES: I suggest a vacation.

HARPER (Hearing something): That was the elevator. Oh God, I should fix myself up, I. . . . You have to go, you shouldn't be here . . . you aren't even real.

MR. LIES: Call me when you decide . . .

HARPER: Go!

(The Travel Agent vanishes as Joe enters.)

JOE: Buddy?

Buddy? Sorry I'm late. I was just . . . out. Walking. Are you mad?

HARPER: I got a little anxious.

JOE: Buddy kiss.

(They kiss.)

JOE: Nothing to get anxious about.

So. So how'd you like to move to Washington?

Scene 4

Same day. Louis and Prior outside the funeral home, sitting on a bench, both dressed in funeral finery, talking. The funeral service for Sarah Ironson has just concluded and Louis is about to leave for the cemetery.

LOUIS: My grandmother actually saw Emma Goldman speak. In Yiddish. But all Grandma could remember was that she spoke well and wore a hat.

What a weird service. That rabbi . . .

PRIOR: A definite find. Get his number when you go to the graveyard. I want him to bury me.

LOUIS: Better head out there. Everyone gets to put dirt on the coffin once it's lowered in.

PRIOR: Oooh. Cemetery fun. Don't want to miss that.

LOUIS: It's an old Jewish custom to express love. Here, Grandma, have a shovelful. Latecomers run the risk of finding the grave completely filled.

She was pretty crazy. She was up there in that home for ten years, talking to herself. I never visited. She looked too much like my mother.

PRIOR (Hugs him): Poor Louis. I'm sorry your grandma is dead.

LOUIS: Tiny little coffin, huh?

Sorry I didn't introduce you to. . . . I always get so closety at these family things.

PRIOR: Butch. You get butch. (Imitating) "Hi Cousin Doris, you don't remember me I'm Lou, Rachel's boy." Lou not Louis, because if you say Louis they'll hear the sibilant S.

LOUIS: I don't have a . . .

PRIOR: I don't blame you, hiding. Bloodlines. Jewish curses are the worst. I personally would dissolve if anyone ever looked me in the eye and said "Feh." Fortunately WASPs don't say "Feh." Oh and by the way, darling, cousin Doris is a dyke.

LOUIS: No.

Really?

PRIOR: You don't notice anything. If I hadn't spent the last four years fellating you I'd swear you were straight.

LOUIS: You're in a pissy mood. Cat still missing?

(Little pause.)

PRIOR: Not a furball in sight. It's your fault.

LOUIS: It is?

PRIOR: I warned you, Louis. Names are important. Call an animal "Little Sheba" and you can't expect it to stick around. Besides, it's a dog's name.

LOUIS: I wanted a dog in the first place, not a cat. He sprayed my books.

PRIOR: He was a female cat.

LOUIS: Cats are stupid, high-strung predators. Babylonians sealed them up in bricks. Dogs have brains.

PRIOR: Cats have intuition.

LOUIS: A sharp dog is as smart as a really dull two-year-old child.

PRIOR: Cats know when something's wrong.

LOUIS: Only if you stop feeding them.

PRIOR: They know. That's why Sheba left, because she knew.

LOUIS: Knew what?

(Pause.)

PRIOR: I did my best Shirley Booth this morning, floppy slippers, housecoat, curlers, can of Little Friskies; "Come back, Little Sheba, come back. . . . " To no avail. Le chat, elle ne reviendra jamais, jamais . . .

(He removes his jacket, rolls up his sleeve, shows Louis a dark-purple spot on the underside of his arm near the shoulder)

See.

LOUIS: That's just a burst blood vessel.

PRIOR: Not according to the best medical authorities.

LOUIS: What?

(Pause)

   Tell me.

PRIOR: K.S., baby. Lesion number one. Lookit. The wine-dark kiss of the angel of death.

LOUIS (Very softly, holding Prior's arm): Oh please . . .

PRIOR: I'm a lesionnaire. The Foreign Lesion. The American Lesion. Lesionnaire's disease.

LOUIS: Stop.

PRIOR: My troubles are lesion.

LOUIS: Will you *stop*.

PRIOR: Don't you think I'm handling this well?
   I'm going to die.

LOUIS: Bullshit.

PRIOR: Let go of my arm.

LOUIS: No.

PRIOR: Let go.

LOUIS (Grabbing Prior, embracing him ferociously): No.

PRIOR: I can't find a way to spare you baby. No wall like the wall of hard scientific fact. K.S. Wham. Bang your head on that.

LOUIS: Fuck you. (Letting go) Fuck you fuck you fuck you.

PRIOR: Now that's what I like to hear. A mature reaction.
   Let's go see if the cat's come home.
   Louis?

LOUIS: When did you find this?

PRIOR: I couldn't tell you.

LOUIS: Why?

PRIOR: I was scared, Lou.

LOUIS: Of what?

PRIOR: That you'll leave me.

LOUIS: Oh.

(Little pause.)

PRIOR: Bad timing, funeral and all, but I figured as long as we're on the subject of death . . .

LOUIS: I have to go bury my grandma.

PRIOR: Lou?

(Pause)

   Then you'll come home?

LOUIS: Then I'll come home.

Scene 5

Same day, later on. Split scene: Joe and Harper at home; Louis at the cemetery with Rabbi Isidor Chemelwitz and the little coffin.

HARPER: Washington?

JOE: It's an incredible honor, buddy, and . . .

HARPER: I have to think.

JOE: Of course.

HARPER: Say no.

JOE: You said you were going to think about it.

HARPER: I don't want to move to Washington.

JOE: Well I do.

HARPER: It's a giant cemetery, huge white graves and mausoleums everywhere.

JOE: We could live in Maryland. Or Georgetown.

HARPER: We're happy here.

JOE: That's not really true, buddy, we . . .

HARPER: Well happy enough! Pretend-happy. That's better than nothing.

JOE: It's time to make some changes, Harper.

HARPER: No changes. Why?

JOE: I've been chief clerk for four years. I make twenty-nine thousand dollars a year. That's ridiculous. I graduated fourth in my class and I make less than anyone I know. And I'm . . . I'm tired of being a clerk, I want to go where something good is happening.

HARPER: Nothing good happens in Washington. We'll forget church teachings and buy furniture at . . . at *Conran's* and become yuppies. I have too much to do here.

JOE: Like what?

HARPER: I *do* have things . . .

JOE: What things?

HARPER: I have to finish painting the bedroom.

JOE: You've been painting in there for over a year.

HARPER: I know, I. . . . It just isn't done because I never get time to finish it.

JOE: Oh that's . . . that doesn't make sense. You have all the time in the world. You could finish it when I'm at work.

HARPER: I'm afraid to go in there alone.

JOE: Afraid of what?

HARPER: I heard someone in there. Metal scraping on the wall. A man with a knife, maybe.

JOE: There's no one in the bedroom, Harper.

HARPER: Not now.

JOE: Not this morning either.

HARPER: How do you know? You were at work this morning. There's something creepy about this place. Remember *Rosemary's Baby?*

JOE: *Rosemary's Baby?*

HARPER: Our apartment looks like that one. Wasn't that apartment in Brooklyn?

JOE: No, it was . . .

HARPER: Well, it looked like this. It did.

JOE: Then let's move.

HARPER: Georgetown's worse. The *Exorcist* was in Georgetown.

JOE: The devil, everywhere you turn, huh, buddy.

HARPER: Yeah. Everywhere.

JOE: How many pills today, buddy?

HARPER: None. One. Three. Only three.

LOUIS (Pointing at the coffin): Why are there just two little wooden pegs holding the lid down?

RABBI ISIDOR CHEMELWITZ: So she can get out easier if she wants to.

LOUIS: I hope she stays put.

I pretended for years that she was already dead. When they called to say she had died it was a surprise. I abandoned her.

RABBI ISIDOR CHEMELWITZ: "Sharfer vi di tson fun a shlang iz an umdankbar kind!"

LOUIS: I don't speak Yiddish.

RABBI ISIDOR CHEMELWITZ: Sharper than the serpent's tooth is the ingratitude of children. Shakespeare. *Kenig Lear.*

LOUIS: Rabbi, what does the Holy Writ say about someone who abandons someone he loves at a time of great need?

RABBI ISIDOR CHEMELWITZ: Why would a person do such a thing?

LOUIS: Because he has to.

Maybe because this person's sense of the world, that it will change for the better with struggle, maybe a person who has this neo-Hegelian positivist sense of constant historical progress towards happiness or perfection or something, who feels very powerful because he feels connected to these forces, moving uphill all the time . . . maybe that person can't, um, incorporate sickness into his sense of how things are supposed to go. Maybe vomit . . . and sores and disease . . . really frighten him, maybe . . . he isn't so good with death.

RABBI ISIDOR CHEMELWITZ: The Holy Scriptures have nothing to say about such a person.

LOUIS: Rabbi, I'm afraid of the crimes I may commit.

RABBI ISIDOR CHEMELWITZ: Please, mister. I'm a sick old rabbi facing a long drive home to the Bronx. You want to confess, better you should find a priest.

LOUIS: But I'm not a Catholic, I'm a Jew.

RABBI ISIDOR CHEMELWITZ: Worse luck for you, bubbulah. Catholics believe in forgiveness. Jews believe in Guilt. (He pats the coffin tenderly)

LOUIS: You just make sure those pegs are in good and tight.

RABBI ISIDOR CHEMELWITZ: Don't worry, mister. The life she had, she'll stay put. She's better off.

JOE: Look, I know this is scary for you. But try to understand what it means to me. Will you try?

HARPER: Yes.

JOE: Good. Really try.

I think things are starting to change in the world.

HARPER: But I don't want . . .

JOE: Wait. For the good. Change for the good. America has rediscovered itself. Its sacred position among nations. And people aren't ashamed of that like they used to be. This is a great thing. The truth restored. Law restored. That's what President Reagan's done, Harper. He says "Truth exists and can be spoken proudly." And the country responds to him. We become better. More good. I need to be a part of that, I need something big to lift me up. I mean, six years ago the world seemed in decline, horrible, hopeless, full of unsolvable problems and crime and confusion and hunger and . . .

HARPER: But it still seems that way. More now than before. They say the ozone layer is . . .

JOE: Harper . . .

HARPER: And today out the window on Atlantic Avenue there was a schizophrenic traffic cop who was making these . . .

JOE: Stop it! I'm trying to make a point.

HARPER: So am I.

JOE: You aren't even making sense, you . . .

HARPER: My point is the world seems just as . . .

JOE: It only seems that way to you because you never go out in the world, Harper, and you have emotional problems.

HARPER: I do so get out in the world.

JOE: You don't. You stay in all day, fretting about imaginary . . .

HARPER: I get out. I do. You don't know what I do.

JOE: You don't stay in all day.

HARPER: No.

JOE: Well. . . . Yes you do.

HARPER: That's what you think.

JOE: Where do you go?

HARPER: Where do you go? When you walk. (Pause, then angrily) And I DO NOT have emotional problems.

JOE: I'm sorry.

HARPER: And if I do have emotional problems it's from living with you. Or . . .

JOE: I'm sorry buddy, I didn't mean to . . .

HARPER: Or if you do think I do then you should never have married me. You have all these secrets and lies.

JOE: I want to be married to you, Harper.

HARPER: You shouldn't. You never should.

(Pause)

Hey buddy. Hey buddy.

JOE: Buddy kiss . . .

(They kiss.)

HARPER: I heard on the radio how to give a blowjob.

JOE: What?

HARPER: You want to try?

JOE: You really shouldn't listen to stuff like that.

HARPER: Mormons can give blowjobs.

JOE: Harper.

302

HARPER (Imitating his tone): Joe.

 It was a little Jewish lady with a German accent.

 This is a good time. For me to make a baby.

(Little pause. Joe turns away.)

HARPER: Then they went on to a program about holes in the ozone layer. Over Antarctica. Skin burns, birds go blind, icebergs melt. The world's coming to an end.

Scene 6

First week of November. In the men's room of the offices of the Brooklyn Federal Court of Appeals; Louis is crying over the sink; Joe enters.

JOE: Oh, um. . . . Morning.

LOUIS: Good morning, counselor.

JOE (He watches Louis cry): Sorry, I . . . I don't know your name.

LOUIS: Don't bother. Word processor. The lowest of the low.

JOE (Holding out hand): Joe Pitt. I'm with Justice Wilson . . .

LOUIS: Oh, I know that. Counselor Pitt. Chief Clerk.

JOE: Were you . . . are you OK?

LOUIS: Oh, yeah. Thanks. What a nice man.

JOE: Not so nice.

LOUIS: What?

JOE: Not so nice. Nothing. You sure you're . . .

LOUIS: Life sucks shit. Life . . . just sucks shit.

JOE: What's wrong?

LOUIS: Run in my nylons.

JOE: Sorry . . .?

LOUIS: Forget it. Look, thanks for asking.

JOE: Well . . .

LOUIS: I mean it really is nice of you.

(He starts crying again)

 Sorry, sorry, sick friend . . .

JOE: Oh, I'm sorry.

LOUIS: Yeah, yeah, well, that's sweet.

Three of your colleagues have preceded you to this baleful sight and you're the first one to ask. The others just opened the door, saw me, and fled. I hope they had to pee real bad.

JOE (Handing him a wad of toilet paper): They just didn't want to intrude.

LOUIS: Hah. Reaganite heartless macho asshole lawyers.

JOE: Oh, that's unfair.

LOUIS: What is? Heartless? Macho? Reaganite? Lawyer?

JOE: I voted for Reagan.

LOUIS: You did?

JOE: Twice.

LOUIS: Twice? Well, oh boy. A Gay Republican.

JOE: Excuse me?

LOUIS: Nothing.

JOE: I'm not . . .

 Forget it.

LOUIS: Republican? Not Republican? Or . . .

JOE: What?

LOUIS: What?

JOE: Not gay. I'm not gay.

LOUIS: Oh. Sorry.

 (Blows his nose loudly) It's just . . .

JOE: Yes?

LOUIS: Well, sometimes you can tell from the way a person sounds that . . . I mean you *sound* like a . . .

JOE: No I don't. Like what?

LOUIS: Like a Republican.

(Little pause. Joe knows he's being teased; Louis knows he knows. Joe decides to be a little brave.)

JOE (Making sure no one else is around): Do I? Sound like a . . .?

LOUIS: What? Like a . . .? Republican, or . . .? Do *I*?

JOE: Do you what?

LOUIS: Sound like a . . .?

JOE Like a . . .?

I'm . . . confused.

LOUIS: Yes.

My name is Louis. But all my friends call me Louise. I work in Word Processing. Thanks for the toilet paper.

(Louis offers Joe his hand, Joe reaches, Louis feints and pecks Joe on the cheek, then exits.)

Scene 7

A week later. Mutual dream scene. Prior is at a fantastic makeup table, having a dream, applying the face. Harper is having a pill-induced hallucination. She has these from time to time. For some reason, Prior has appeared in this one. Or Harper has appeared in Prior's dream. It is bewildering.

PRIOR (Alone, putting on makeup, then examining the results in the mirror; to the audience): "I'm ready for my closeup, Mr. DeMille."

One wants to move through life with elegance and grace, blossoming infrequently but with exquisite taste, and perfect timing, like a rare bloom, a zebra orchid. . . . One wants. . . . But one so seldom gets what one wants, does one? No. One does not. One gets fucked. Over. One . . . dies at thirty, robbed of . . . decades of majesty.

Fuck this shit. Fuck this shit.

(He almost crumbles; he pulls himself together; he studies his handiwork in the mirror)

I look like a corpse. A corpsette. Oh my queen; you know you've hit rock-bottom when even drag is a drag.

(Harper appears.)

HARPER: Are you. . . . Who are you?

PRIOR: Who are you?

HARPER: What are you doing in my hallucination?

PRIOR: I'm not in your hallucination. You're in my dream.

HARPER: You're wearing makeup.

PRIOR: So are you.

HARPER: But you're a man.

PRIOR (Feigning dismay, shock, he mimes slashing his throat with his lipstick and dies, fabulously tragic. Then): The hands and feet give it away.

HARPER: There must be some mistake here. I don't recognize you. You're not. . . . Are you my . . . some sort of imaginary friend?

PRIOR: No. Aren't you too old to have imaginary friends?

HARPER: I have emotional problems. I took too many pills. Why are you wearing makeup?

PRIOR: I was in the process of applying the face, trying to make myself feel better—I swiped the new fall colors at the Clinique counter at Macy's. (Showing her)

HARPER: You stole these?

PRIOR: I was out of cash; it was an emotional emergency!

HARPER: Joe will be so angry. I promised him. No more pills.

PRIOR: These pills you keep alluding to?

HARPER: Valium. I take Valium. Lots of Valium.

PRIOR: And you're dancing as fast as you can.

HARPER: I'm not *addicted.* I don't believe in addiction, and I never . . . well, I *never* drink. And I *never* take drugs.

PRIOR: Well, smell *you,* Nancy Drew.

HARPER: Except Valium.

PRIOR: Except Valium; in wee fistfuls.

HARPER: It's terrible. Mormons are not supposed to be addicted to anything. I'm a Mormon.

PRIOR: I'm a homosexual.

HARPER: Oh! In my church we don't believe in homosexuals.

PRIOR: In my church we don't believe in Mormons.

HARPER: What church do . . . oh! (She laughs) I get it.

I don't understand this. If I didn't ever see you before and I don't think I did then I don't think you should be here, in this hallucination, because in my experience the mind, which is where hallucinations come from, shouldn't be able to make up anything that wasn't there to start with, that didn't enter it from experience, from the real world. Imagination can't create anything new, can it? It only recycles bits and pieces from the world and reassembles them into visions. . . . Am I making sense right now?

PRIOR: Given the circumstances, yes.

HARPER: So when we think we've escaped the unbearable ordinariness and, well, untruthfulness of our lives, it's really only the same old ordinariness and falseness rearranged into the appearance of novelty and truth. Nothing unknown is knowable. Don't you think it's depressing?

PRIOR: The limitations of the imagination?

HARPER: Yes.

PRIOR: It's something you learn after your second theme party: It's All Been Done Before.

HARPER: The world. Finite. Terribly, terribly. . . . Well . . .

This is the most depressing hallucination I've ever had.

PRIOR: Apologies. I do try to be amusing.

HARPER: Oh, well, don't apologize, you. . . . I can't expect someone who's really sick to entertain me.

PRIOR: How on earth did you know . . .

HARPER: Oh that happens. This is the very threshhold of revelation sometimes. You can see things . . . how sick you are. Do you see anything about me?

PRIOR: Yes.

HARPER: What?

PRIOR: You are amazingly unhappy.

HARPER: Oh big deal. You meet a Valium addict and you figure out she's unhappy. That doesn't count. Of course I. . . . Something else. Something surprising.

PRIOR: Something surprising.

HARPER: Yes.

PRIOR: Your husband's a homo.

(Pause.)

HARPER: Oh, ridiculous.

(Pause, then very quietly)

Really?

PRIOR (Shrugs): Threshhold of revelation.

HARPER: Well I don't like your revelations. I don't think you intuit well at all. Joe's a very normal man, he . . .

Oh God. Oh God. He. . . . Do homos take, like, lots of long walks?

PRIOR: Yes. We do. In stretch pants with lavender coifs. I just looked at you, and there was . . .

HARPER: A sort of blue streak of recognition.

PRIOR: Yes.

HARPER: Like you knew me incredibly well.

PRIOR: Yes.

HARPER: Yes.

I have to go now, get back, something just . . . fell apart.

Oh God, I feel so sad . . .

PRIOR: I . . . I'm sorry. I usually say, "Fuck the truth," but mostly, the truth fucks you.

HARPER: I see something else about you . . .

PRIOR: Oh?

HARPER: Deep inside you, there's a part of you, the most inner part, entirely free of disease. I can see that.

PRIOR: Is that. . . . That isn't true.

HARPER: Threshhold of revelation.

Home . . .

(She vanishes.)

PRIOR: People come and go so quickly here . . .

(To himself in the mirror) I don't think there's any uninfected part of me. My heart is pumping polluted blood. I feel dirty.

(He begins to wipe makeup off with his hands, smearing it around. A large gray feather falls from up above. Prior stops smearing the makeup and looks at the feather. He goes to it and picks it up.)

A Voice (It is an incredibly beautiful voice): Look up!

PRIOR (Looking up, not seeing anyone): Hello?

A Voice: Look up!

PRIOR: Who is that?

A Voice: Prepare the way!

PRIOR: I don't see any . . .

(There is a dramatic change in lighting, from above.)

A Voice:

> Look up, look up,
> prepare the way
> the infinite descent
> A breath in air
> floating down
> Glory to . . .

(Silence.)

PRIOR: Hello? Is that it? Helloooo!

What the fuck . . .? (He holds himself)

Poor me. Poor poor me. Why me? Why poor poor me? Oh I don't feel good right now. I really don't.

Scene 8

That night. Split scene: Harper and Joe at home; Prior and Louis in bed.

HARPER: Where were you?

JOE: Out.

HARPER: Where?

JOE: Just out. Thinking.

HARPER: It's late.

JOE: I had a lot to think about.

HARPER: I burned dinner.

JOE: Sorry.

HARPER: Not my dinner. My dinner was fine. Your dinner. I put it back in the oven and turned everything up as high as it could go and I watched till it burned black. It's still hot. Very hot. Want it?

JOE: You didn't have to do that.

HARPER: I know. It just seemed like the kind of thing a mentally deranged sex-starved pill-popping housewife would do.

JOE: Uh huh.

HARPER: So I did it. Who knows anymore what I have to do?

JOE: How many pills?

HARPER: A bunch. Don't change the subject.

JOE: I won't talk to you when you . . .

HARPER: No. No. Don't do that! I'm . . . I'm fine, pills are not the problem, not our problem, I WANT TO KNOW WHERE YOU'VE BEEN! I WANT TO KNOW WHAT'S GOING ON!

JOE: Going on with what? The job?

HARPER: Not the job.

JOE: I said I need more time.

HARPER: Not the job!

JOE: Mr. Cohn, I talked to him on the phone, he said I had to hurry . . .

HARPER: Not the . . .

JOE: But I can't get you to talk sensibly about anything so . . .

HARPER: SHUT UP!

JOE: Then what?

HARPER: Stick to the subject.

JOE: I don't know what that is. You have something you want to ask me? Ask me. Go.

HARPER: I . . . can't. I'm scared of you.

JOE: I'm tired, I'm going to bed.

HARPER: Tell me without making me ask. Please.

JOE: This is crazy, I'm not . . .

HARPER: When you come through the door at night your face is never exactly the way I remembered it. I get surprised by something . . . mean and hard about the way you look. Even the weight of you in the bed at night, the way you breathe in your sleep seems unfamiliar.

You terrify me.

JOE (Cold): I know who you are.

heavily, Joe not at all. Louis and the Man are eyeing each other, each alternating interest and indifference.

JOE: The pills were something she started when she miscarried or . . . no, she took some before that. She had a really bad time at home, when she was a kid, her home was really bad. I think a lot of drinking and physical stuff. She doesn't talk about that, instead she talks about . . . the sky falling down, people with knives hiding under sofas. Monsters. Mormons. Everyone thinks Mormons don't come from homes like that, we aren't supposed to behave that way, but we do. It's not lying, or being two-faced. Everyone tries very hard to live up to God's strictures, which are very . . . um . . .

ROY: Strict.

JOE: I shouldn't be bothering you with this.

ROY: No, please. Heart to heart. Want another. . . . What is that, seltzer?

JOE: The failure to measure up hits people very hard. From such a strong desire to be good they feel very far from goodness when they fail.

What scares me is that maybe what I really love in her is the part of her that's farthest from the light, from God's love; maybe I was drawn to that in the first place. And I'm keeping it alive because I need it.

ROY: Why would you need it?

JOE: There are things. . . . I don't know how well we know ourselves. I mean, what if? I know I married her because she . . . because I loved it that she was always wrong, always doing something wrong, like one step out of step. In Salt Lake City that stands out. I never stood out, on the outside, but inside, it was hard for me. To pass.

ROY: Pass?

JOE: Yeah.

ROY: Pass as what?

JOE: Oh. Well. . . . As someone cheerful and strong. Those who love God with an open heart unclouded by secrets and struggles are cheerful; God's easy simple love for them shows in how strong and happy they are. The saints.

ROY: But you had secrets? Secret struggles . . .

JOE: I wanted to be one of the elect, one of the Blessed. You feel you ought to be, that the blemishes are yours by choice, which of course they aren't. Harper's sorrow, that really deep sorrow, she didn't choose that. But it's there.

ROY: You didn't put it there.

JOE: No.

ROY: You sound like you think you did.

JOE: I am responsible for her.

ROY: Because she's your wife.

JOE: That. And I do love her.

ROY: Whatever. She's your wife. And so there are obligations. To her. But also to yourself.

JOE: She'd fall apart in Washington.

ROY: Then let her stay here.

JOE: She'll fall apart if I leave her.

ROY: Then bring her to Washington.

JOE: I just can't, Roy. She needs me.

ROY: Listen, Joe. I'm the best divorce lawyer in the business.

(Little pause.)

JOE: Can't Washington wait?

ROY: You do what you need to do, Joe. What *you* need. *You.* Let her life go where it wants to go. You'll both be better for that. *Somebody* should get what they want.

MAN: What do you want?

LOUIS: I want you to fuck me, hurt me, make me bleed.

MAN: I want to.

LOUIS: Yeah?

MAN: I want to hurt you.

LOUIS: Fuck me.

MAN: Yeah?

LOUIS: Hard.

MAN: Yeah? You been a bad boy?

(Pause. Louis laughs, softly.)

LOUIS: Very bad. Very bad.

MAN: You need to be punished, boy?

LOUIS: Yes. I do.

MAN: Yes what?

(Little pause.)

LOUIS: Um, I . . .

MAN: Yes *what,* boy?

LOUIS: Oh. Yes sir.

MAN: I want you to take me to your place, boy.

LOUIS: No, I can't do that.

MAN: No *what?*

LOUIS: No sir, I can't, I . . .
I don't live alone, sir.

MAN: Your lover know you're out with a man tonight, boy?

LOUIS: No sir, he . . .
My lover doesn't know.

MAN: Your lover know you . . .

LOUIS: Let's change the subject, OK? Can we go to your place?

MAN: I live with my parents.

LOUIS: Oh.

ROY: Everyone who makes it in this world makes it because somebody older and more power-ful takes an interest. The most precious asset in life, I think, is the ability to be a good son. You have that, Joe. Somebody who can be a good son to a father who pushes them far-ther than they would otherwise go. I've had many fathers, I owe my life to them, power-ful, powerful men. Walter Winchell, Edgar Hoover. Joe McCarthy most of all. He valued me because I am a good lawyer, but he loved me because I was and am a good son. He was a very difficult man, very guarded and cagey; I brought out something tender in him. He would have died for me. And me for him. Does this embarrass you?

JOE: I had a hard time with my father.

ROY: Well sometimes that's the way. Then you have to find other fathers, substitutes, I don't know. The father-son relationship is central to life. Women are for birth, beginning, but the father is continuance. The son offers the father his life as a vessel for carrying forth his father's dream. Your father's living?

JOE: Um, dead.

ROY: He was . . . what? A difficult man?

JOE: He was in the military. He could be very unfair. And cold.

ROY: But he loved you.

JOE: I don't know.

ROY: No, no, Joe, he did, I know this. Sometimes a father's love has to be very, very hard, unfair even, cold to make his son grow strong in a world like this. This isn't a good world.

MAN: Here, then.

LOUIS: I. . . . Do you have a rubber?

MAN: I don't use rubbers.

LOUIS: You should. (He takes one from his coat pocket) Here.

MAN: I don't use them.

LOUIS: Forget it, then. (He starts to leave)

MAN: No, wait.
Put it on me. Boy.

LOUIS: Forget it, I have to get back. Home. I must be going crazy.

MAN: Oh come on please he won't find out.

LOUIS: It's cold. Too cold.

MAN: It's never too cold, let me warm you up. Please?

(They begin to fuck.)

MAN: Relax.

LOUIS (A small laugh): Not a chance.

MAN: It . . .

LOUIS: What?

MAN: I think it broke. The rubber. You want me to keep going? (Little pause) Pull out? Should I . . .

LOUIS: Keep going.

Infect me.

I don't care. I don't care.

(Pause. The Man pulls out.)

MAN: I . . . um, look, I'm sorry, but I think I want to go.

LOUIS: Yeah.

Give my best to mom and dad.

(The Man slaps him.)

LOUIS: Ow!

(They stare at each other.)

LOUIS: It was a joke.

(The Man leaves.)

ROY: How long have we known each other?

JOE: Since 1980.

ROY: Right. A long time. I feel close to you, Joe. Do I advise you well?

JOE: You've been an incredible friend, Roy, I . . .

ROY: I want to be family. Familia, as my Italian friends call it. La Familia. A lovely word. It's important for me to help you, like I was helped.

JOE: I owe practically everything to you, Roy.

ROY: I'm dying, Joe. Cancer.

JOE: Oh my God.

ROY: Please. Let me finish.

Few people know this and I'm telling you this only because. . . . I'm not afraid of death. What can death bring that I haven't faced? I've lived; life is the worst. (Gently mocking himself) Listen to me, I'm a philosopher.

Joe. You must do this. You must must must. Love; that's a trap. Responsibility; that's a trap too. Like a father to a son I tell you this: Life is full of horror; nobody escapes, nobody; save yourself. Whatever pulls on you, whatever needs from you, threatens you. Don't be afraid; people are so afraid; don't be afraid to live in the raw wind, naked, alone. . . . Learn at least this: What you are capable of. Let nothing stand in your way.

Scene 5

Three days later. Prior and Belize in Prior's hospital room. Prior is very sick but improving. Belize has just arrived.

PRIOR: Miss Thing.

BELIZE: Ma cherie bichette.

PRIOR: Stella.

BELIZE: Stella for star. Let me see. (Scrutinizing Prior) You look like shit, why yes indeed you do, comme la merde!

PRIOR: Merci.

BELIZE (Taking little plastic bottles from his bag, handing them to Prior): Not to despair, Belle Reeve. Lookie! Magic goop!

PRIOR (Opening a bottle, sniffing): Pooh! What kinda crap is that?

BELIZE: Beats me. Let's rub it on your poor blistered body and see what it does.

PRIOR: This is not Western medicine, these bottles . . .

BELIZE: Voodoo cream. From the botanica 'round the block.

PRIOR: And you a registered nurse.

BELIZE (Sniffing it): Beeswax and cheap perfume. Cut with Jergen's Lotion. Full of good vibes and love from some little black Cubana witch in Miami.

PRIOR: Get that trash away from me, I am immune-suppressed.

BELIZE: I *am* a health professional. I *know* what I'm doing.

PRIOR: It stinks. Any word from Louis?

(Pause. Belize starts giving Prior a gentle massage.)

PRIOR: Gone.

BELIZE: He'll be back. I know the type. Likes to keep a girl on edge.

PRIOR: It's been . . .

(Pause.)

BELIZE (Trying to jog his memory): How long?

PRIOR: I don't remember.

BELIZE: How long have you been here?

PRIOR (Getting suddenly upset): I don't remember, I don't give a fuck. I want Louis. I want my fucking boyfriend, where the fuck is he? I'm dying, I'm dying, where's Louis?

BELIZE: Shhhh, shhh . . .

PRIOR: This is a very strange drug, this drug. Emotional lability, for starters.

BELIZE: Save a tab or two for me.

PRIOR: Oh no, not this drug, ce n'est pas pour la joyeux noël et la bonne année, this drug she is serious poisonous chemistry, ma pauvre bichette.

And not just disorienting. I hear things. Voices.

BELIZE: Voices.

PRIOR: A voice.

BELIZE: Saying what?

(Pause.)

PRIOR: I'm not supposed to tell.

BELIZE: You better tell the doctor. Or I will.

PRIOR: No no don't. Please. I want the voice; it's wonderful. It's all that's keeping me alive. I don't want to talk to some intern about it.

You know what happens? When I hear it, I get hard.

BELIZE: Oh my.

PRIOR: Comme ça. (He uses his arm to demonstrate) And you know I am slow to rise.

BELIZE: My jaw aches at the memory.

PRIOR: And would you deny me this little solace—betray my concupiscence to Florence Nightingale's storm troopers?

BELIZE: Perish the thought, ma bébé.

PRIOR: They'd change the drug just to spoil the fun.

BELIZE: You and your boner can depend on me.

PRIOR: Je t'adore, ma belle nègre.

BELIZE: All this girl-talk shit is politically incorrect, you know. We should have dropped it back when we gave up drag.

PRIOR: I'm sick, I get to be politically incorrect if it makes me feel better. You sound like Lou.

(Little pause)

Well, at least I have the satisfaction of knowing he's in anguish somewhere. I loved his anguish. Watching him stick his head up his asshole and eat his guts out over some relatively minor moral conundrum—it was the best show in town. But Mother warned me: if they get overwhelmed by the little things . . .

BELIZE: They'll be belly-up bustville when something big comes along.

PRIOR: Mother warned me.

BELIZE: And they do come along.

PRIOR: But I didn't listen.

BELIZE: No. (Doing Hepburn) Men are beasts.

PRIOR (Also Hepburn): The absolute lowest.

BELIZE: I have to go. If I want to spend my whole lonely life looking after white people I can get underpaid to do it.

PRIOR: You're just a Christian martyr.

BELIZE: Whatever happens, baby, I will be here for you.

PRIOR: Je t'aime.

BELIZE: Je t'aime. Don't go crazy on me, girlfriend, I already got enough crazy queens for one lifetime. For two. I can't be bothering with dementia.

PRIOR: I promise.

BELIZE (Touching him; softly): Ouch.

PRIOR: Ouch. Indeed.

BELIZE: Why'd they have to pick on you?

And eat more, girlfriend, you really do look like shit.

(Belize leaves.)

PRIOR (After waiting a beat): He's gone.

Are you still . . .

VOICE: I can't stay. I will return.

PRIOR: Are you one of those "Follow me to the other side" voices?

(Louis turns, looks at him. Joe searches for something to say.)

JOE: Yesterday was Sunday but I've been a little unfocused recently and I thought it was Monday. So I came here like I was going to work. And the whole place was empty. And at first I couldn't figure out why, and I had this moment of incredible . . . fear and also. . . . It just flashed through my mind: The whole Hall of Justice, it's empty, it's deserted, it's gone out of business. Forever. The people that make it run have up and abandoned it.

LOUIS (Looking at the building): Creepy.

JOE: Well yes but. I felt that I was going to scream. Not because it was creepy, but because the emptiness felt so *fast.*

And . . . well, good. A . . . happy scream.

I just wondered what a thing it would be . . . if overnight everything you owe anything to, justice, or love, had really gone away. Free.

It would be . . . heartless terror. Yes. Terrible, and . . .

Very great. To shed your skin, every old skin, one by one and then walk away, unencumbered, into the morning.

(Little pause. He looks at the building)

I can't go in there today.

LOUIS: Then don't.

JOE (Not really hearing Louis): I can't go in, I need . . .

(He looks for what he needs. He takes a swig of Pepto-Bismol)

I can't be this anymore. I need . . . a change, I should just . . .

LOUIS (Not a come-on, necessarily; he doesn't want to be alone): Want some company? For whatever?

(Pause. Joe looks at Louis and looks away, afraid. Louis shrugs.)

LOUIS: Sometimes, even if it scares you to death, you have to be willing to break the law. Know what I mean?

(Another little pause.)

JOE: Yes.

(Another little pause.)

LOUIS: I moved out. I moved out on my . . . I haven't been sleeping well.

JOE: Me neither.

(Louis goes up to Joe, licks his napkin and dabs at Joe's mouth.)

LOUIS: Antacid moustache.

(Points to the building) Maybe the court won't convene. Ever again. Maybe we are free. To do whatever.

Children of the new morning, criminal minds. Selfish and greedy and loveless and blind. Reagan's children.

You're scared. So am I. Everybody is in the land of the free. God help us all.

Scene 8

Late that night. Joe at a payphone phoning Hannah at home in Salt Lake City.

JOE: Mom?

HANNAH: Joe?

JOE: Hi.

HANNAH: You're calling from the street. It's . . . it must be four in the morning. What's happened?

JOE: Nothing, nothing, I . . .

HANNAH: It's Harper. Is Harper. . . . Joe? Joe?

JOE: Yeah, hi. No, Harper's fine. Well, no, she's . . . not fine. How are you, Mom?

HANNAH: What's happened?

JOE: I just wanted to talk to you. I, uh, wanted to try something out on you.

HANNAH: Joe, you haven't . . . have you been drinking, Joe?

JOE: Yes ma'am. I'm drunk.

HANNAH: That isn't like you.

JOE: No. I mean, who's to say?

HANNAH: Why are you out on the street at four A.M.? In that crazy city. It's dangerous.

JOE: Actually, Mom, I'm not on the street. I'm near the boathouse in the park.

HANNAH: What park?

JOE: Central Park.

HANNAH: CENTRAL PARK! Oh my Lord. What on earth are you doing in Central Park at this time of night? Are you . . .

Joe, I think you ought to go home right now. Call me from home.

(Little pause)

Joe?

JOE: I come here to watch, Mom. Sometimes. Just to watch.

HANNAH: Watch what? What's there to watch at four in the . . .

JOE: Mom, did Dad love me?

HANNAH: What?

JOE: Did he?

HANNAH: You ought to go home and call from there.

JOE: Answer.

HANNAH: Oh now really. This is maudlin. I don't like this conversation.

JOE: Yeah, well, it gets worse from here on.

(Pause.)

HANNAH: Joe?

JOE: Mom. Momma. I'm a homosexual, Momma.

Boy, did that come out awkward.

(Pause)

Hello? Hello?

I'm a homosexual.

(Pause)

Please, Momma. Say something.

HANNAH: You're old enough to understand that your father didn't love you without being ridiculous about it.

JOE: What?

HANNAH: You're ridiculous. You're being ridiculous.

JOE: I'm . . .

What?

HANNAH: You really ought to go home now to your wife. I need to go to bed. This phone call. . . . We will just forget this phone call.

JOE: Mom.

HANNAH: No more talk. Tonight. This . . . (Suddenly very angry) Drinking is a sin! A sin! I raised you better than that. (She hangs up)

Scene 9

The following morning, early. Split scene: Harper and Joe at home; Louis and Prior in Prior's hospital room. Joe and Louis have just entered. This should be fast and obviously furious; overlapping is fine; the proceedings may be a little confusing but not the final results.

HARPER: Oh God. Home. The moment of truth has arrived.

JOE: Harper.

LOUIS: I'm going to move out.

PRIOR: The fuck you are.

JOE: Harper. Please listen. I still love you very much. You're still my best buddy; I'm not going to leave you.

HARPER: No, I don't like the sound of this. I'm leaving.

LOUIS: I'm leaving.

I already have.

JOE: Please listen. Stay. This is really hard. We have to talk.

HARPER: We are talking. Aren't we? Now please shut up. OK?

PRIOR: Bastard. Sneaking off while I'm flat out here, that's low. If I could get up now I'd beat the holy shit out of you.

JOE: Did you take pills? How many?

HARPER: No pills. Bad for the . . . (Pats stomach)

JOE: You aren't pregnant. I called your gynecologist.

HARPER: I'm seeing a new gynecologist.

PRIOR: You have no right to do this.

LOUIS: Oh, that's ridiculous.

PRIOR: No right. It's criminal.

JOE: Forget about that. Just listen. You want the truth. This is the truth.

BELIZE (Continuing over Louis): . . . and girl-friend it is truly an *awesome* spectacle but I got better things to do with my time than sit here listening to this racist bullshit just because I feel sorry for you that . . .

LOUIS: I am not a racist!

BELIZE: Oh come on . . .

LOUIS: So maybe I am a racist but . . .

BELIZE: Oh I really hate that! It's no fun picking on you Louis; you're so guilty, it's like throwing darts at a glob of jello, there's no satisfying hits, just quivering, the darts just blop in and vanish.

LOUIS: I just think when you are discussing lines of oppression it gets very complicated and . . .

BELIZE: Oh is that a fact? You know, we black drag queens have a rather intimate knowledge of the complexity of the lines of . . .

LOUIS: *Ex*-black drag queen.

BELIZE: Actually ex-ex.

LOUIS: You're doing drag again?

BELIZE: I don't. . . . Maybe. I don't have to tell you. Maybe.

LOUIS: I think it's sexist.

BELIZE: I didn't ask you.

LOUIS: Well it is. The gay community, I think, has to adopt the same attitude towards drag as black women have to take towards black women blues singers.

BELIZE: Oh my we *are* walking dangerous tonight.

LOUIS: Well, it's all internalized oppression, right, I mean the masochism, the stereotypes, the . . .

BELIZE: Louis, are you deliberately trying to make me hate you?

LOUIS: No, I . . .

BELIZE: I mean, are you deliberately transforming yourself into an arrogant, sexual-political Stalinist-slash-racist flag-waving thug for my benefit?

(Pause.)

LOUIS: You know what I think?

BELIZE: What?

LOUIS: You hate me because I'm a Jew.

BELIZE: I'm leaving.

LOUIS: It's true.

BELIZE: You have no basis except your . . .

Louis, it's good to know you haven't changed; you are still an honorary citizen of the Twilight Zone, and after your pale, pale white polemics on behalf of racial insensitivity you have a flaming *fuck* of a lot of nerve calling me an anti-Semite. Now I really gotta go.

LOUIS: You called me Lou the Jew.

BELIZE: That was a joke.

LOUIS: I didn't think it was funny. It was hostile.

BELIZE: It was three years ago.

LOUIS: So?

BELIZE: You just called yourself Sid the Yid.

LOUIS: That's not the same thing.

BELIZE: Sid the Yid is different from Lou the Jew.

LOUIS: Yes.

BELIZE: Someday you'll have to explain that to me, but right now . . .

You hate me because you hate black people.

LOUIS: I do not. But I do think most black people are anti-Semitic.

BELIZE: "Most black people." *That's* racist, Louis, and *I* think most Jews . . .

LOUIS: Louis Farrakhan.

BELIZE: Ed Koch.

LOUIS: Jesse Jackson.

BELIZE: Jackson. Oh really, Louis, this is . . .

LOUIS: Hymietown! Hymietown!

BELIZE: Louis, you voted for Jesse Jackson. You send checks to the Rainbow Coalition.

LOUIS: I'm ambivalent. The checks bounced.

BELIZE: All your checks bounce, Louis; you're ambivalent about everything.

LOUIS: What's that supposed to mean?

BELIZE: You may be dumber than shit but I refuse to believe you can't figure it out. Try.

LOUIS: I was never ambivalent about Prior. I love him. I do. I really do.

BELIZE: Nobody said different.

LOUIS: Love and ambivalence are. . . . Real love isn't ambivalent.

BELIZE: "Real love isn't ambivalent." I'd swear that's a line from my favorite bestselling paperback novel, *In Love with the Night Mysterious,* except I don't think you ever read it.

(Pause.)

LOUIS: I never read it, no.

BELIZE: You ought to. Instead of spending the rest of your life trying to get through *Democracy in America.* It's about this white woman whose Daddy owns a plantation in the Deep South in the years before the Civil War—the American one—and her name is Margaret, and she's in love with her Daddy's number-one slave, and his name is Thaddeus, and she's married but her white slave-owner husband has AIDS: Antebellum Insufficiently Developed Sexorgans. And there's a lot of hot stuff going down when Margaret and Thaddeus can catch a spare torrid ten under the cotton-picking moon, and then of course the Yankees come, and they set the slaves free, and the slaves string up old Daddy, and so on. Historical fiction. Somewhere in there I recall Margaret and Thaddeus find the time to discuss the nature of love; her face is reflecting the flames of the burning plantation—you know, the way white people do—and his black face is dark in the night and she says to him, "Thaddeus, real love isn't ever ambivalent."

(Little pause. Emily enters and turns off IV drip.)

BELIZE: Thaddeus looks at her; he's contemplating her thesis; and he isn't sure he agrees.

EMILY (Removing IV drip from Prior's arm): Treatment number . . . (Consulting chart) four.

PRIOR: Pharmaceutical miracle. Lazarus breathes again.

LOUIS: Is he. . . . How bad is he?

BELIZE: You want the laundry list?

EMILY: Shirt off, let's check the . . .

(Prior takes his shirt off. She examines his lesions.)

BELIZE: There's the weight problem and the shit problem and the morale problem.

EMILY: Only six. That's good. Pants.

(He drops his pants. He's naked. She examines.)

BELIZE: And. He thinks he's going crazy.

EMILY: Looking good. What else?

PRIOR: Ankles sore and swollen, but the leg's better. The nausea's mostly gone with the little orange pills. BM's pure liquid but not bloody anymore, for now, my eye doctor says everything's OK, for now, my dentist says "Yuck!" when he sees my fuzzy tongue, and now he wears little condoms on his thumb and forefinger. And a mask. So what? My dermatologist is in Hawaii and my mother . . . well leave my mother out of it. Which is usually where my mother is, out of it. My glands are like walnuts, my weight's holding steady for week two, and a friend died two days ago of bird tuberculosis; bird tuberculosis; that scared me and I didn't go to the funeral today because he was an Irish Catholic and it's probably open casket and I'm afraid of . . . something, the bird TB or seeing him or. . . . So I guess I'm doing OK. Except for of course I'm going nuts.

EMILY: We ran the toxoplasmosis series and there's no indication . . .

PRIOR: I know, I know, but I feel like something terrifying is on its way, you know, like a missile from outer space, and it's plummeting down towards the earth, and I'm ground zero, and . . . I am generally known where I am known as one cool, collected queen. And I am ruffled.

EMILY: There's really nothing to worry about. I think that shochen bamromim hamtzeh menucho nechono al kanfey haschino.

PRIOR: What?

EMILY: Everything's fine. Bemaalos k'doshim ut'horim kezohar horokeea mazhirim . . .

PRIOR: Oh I don't understand what you're . . .

EMILY: Es nishmas Prior sheholoch leolomoh, baavur shenodvoo z'dokoh b'ad hazkoras nishmosoh.

PRIOR: Why are you doing that? Stop it! Stop it!

EMILY: Stop what?

PRIOR: You were just . . . weren't you just speaking in Hebrew or something.

EMILY: *Hebrew?* (Laughs) I'm basically Italian-American. No. I didn't speak in Hebrew.

PRIOR: Oh no, oh God please I really think I . . .

EMILY: Look, I'm sorry, I have a waiting room full of. . . . I think you're one of the lucky ones, you'll live for years, probably—you're pretty healthy for someone with no immune system. Are you seeing someone? Loneliness is a danger. A therapist?

PRIOR: No, I don't need to see anyone, I just . . .

EMILY: Well think about it. You aren't going crazy. You're just under a lot of stress. No wonder . . . (She starts to write in his chart)

(Suddenly there is an astonishing blaze of light, a huge chord sounded by a gigantic choir, and a great book with steel pages mounted atop a molten-red pillar pops up from the stage floor. The book opens; there is a large Aleph inscribed on its pages, which bursts into flames. Immediately the book slams shut and disappears instantly under the floor as the lights become normal again. Emily notices none of this, writing. Prior is agog.)

EMILY (Laughing, exiting): Hebrew . . .

(Prior flees.)

LOUIS: Help me.

BELIZE: I beg your pardon?

LOUIS: You're a nurse, give me something, I . . . don't know what to do anymore, I. . . . Last week at work I screwed up the Xerox machine like permanently and so I . . . then I tripped on the subway steps and my glasses broke and I cut my forehead, here, see, and now I can't see much and my forehead . . . it's like the Mark of Cain, stupid, right, but it won't heal and every morning I see it and I think, Biblical things, Mark of Cain, Judas Iscariot and his silver and his noose, people who . . . in betraying what they love betray what's truest in themselves, I feel . . . nothing but cold for myself, just cold, and every night I miss him, I miss him so much but then . . . those sores, and the smell and . . . where I thought it was going. . . . I could be . . . I could be sick too, maybe I'm sick too. I don't know.

Belize. Tell him I love him. Can you do that?

BELIZE: I've thought about it for a very long time, and I still don't understand what love is. Justice is simple. Democracy is simple. Those things are unambivalent. But love is very hard. And it goes bad for you if you violate the hard law of love.

LOUIS: I'm dying.

BELIZE: He's dying. You just wish you were.

Oh cheer up, Louis. Look at that heavy sky out there.

LOUIS: Purple.

BELIZE: *Purple?* Boy, what kind of a homosexual are you, anyway? That's not purple, Mary, that color up there is (Very grand) *mauve.*

All day today it's felt like Thanksgiving. Soon, this . . . ruination will be blanketed white. You can smell it—can you smell it?

LOUIS: Smell what?

BELIZE: Softness, compliance, forgiveness, grace.

LOUIS: No . . .

BELIZE: I can't help you learn that. I can't help you, Louis. You're not my business. (He exits)

(Louis puts his head in his hands, inadvertently touching his cut forehead.)

LOUIS: Ow FUCK! (He stands slowly, looks towards where Belize exited) Smell what?

(He looks both ways to be sure no one is watching, then inhales deeply, and is surprised) Huh. Snow.

Scene 3

Same day. Harper in a very white, cold place, with a brilliant blue sky above; a delicate snowfall. She is dressed in a beautiful snowsuit. The sound of the sea, faint.

HARPER: Snow! Ice! Mountains of ice! Where am I? I . . .

I feel better, I do, I . . . feel better. There are ice crystals in my lungs, wonderful and sharp. And the snow smells like cold, crushed peaches. And there's something . . . some current of blood in the wind, how strange, it has that iron taste.

MR. LIES: Ozone.

HARPER: Ozone! Wow! Where am I?

MR. LIES: The Kingdom of Ice, the bottommost part of the world.

HARPER (Looking around, then realizing): Antarctica. This is Antarctica!

MR. LIES: Cold shelter for the shattered. No sorrow here, tears freeze.

HARPER: Antarctica, Antarctica, oh boy oh boy, LOOK at this, I. . . . Wow, I must've really snapped the tether, huh?

MR. LIES: Apparently . . .

HARPER: That's great. I want to stay here forever. Set up camp. Build things. Build a city, an enormous city made up of frontier forts, dark wood and green roofs and high gates made of pointed logs and bonfires burning on every street corner. I should build by a river. Where are the forests?

MR. LIES: No timber here. Too cold. Ice, no trees.

HARPER: Oh details! I'm sick of details! I'll plant them and grow them. I'll live off caribou fat, I'll melt it over the bonfires and drink it from long, curved goat-horn cups. It'll be great. I want to make a new world here. So that I never have to go home again.

MR. LIES: As long as it lasts. Ice has a way of melting . . .

HARPER: No. Forever. I can have anything I want here—maybe even companionship, someone who has . . . desire for me. You, maybe.

MR. LIES: It's against the by-laws of the International Order of Travel Agents to get involved with clients. Rules are rules. Anyway, I'm not the one you really want.

HARPER: There isn't anyone . . . maybe an Eskimo. Who could ice-fish for food. And help me build a nest for when the baby comes.

MR. LIES: There are no Eskimo in Antarctica. And you're not really pregnant. You made that up.

HARPER: Well all of this is made up. So if the snow feels cold I'm pregnant. Right? Here, I can be pregnant. And I can have any kind of a baby I want.

MR. LIES: This is a retreat, a vacuum, its virtue is that it lacks everything; deep-freeze for feelings. You can be numb and safe here, that's what you came for. Respect the delicate ecology of your delusions.

HARPER: You mean like no Eskimo in Antarctica.

MR. LIES: Correcto. Ice and snow, no Eskimo. Even hallucinations have laws.

HARPER: Well then who's that?

(The Eskimo appears.)

MR. LIES: An Eskimo.

HARPER: An antarctic Eskimo. A fisher of the polar deep.

MR. LIES: There's something wrong with this picture.

(The Eskimo beckons.)

HARPER: I'm going to like this place. It's my own National Geographic Special! Oh! Oh! (She holds her stomach) I think . . . I think I felt her kicking. Maybe I'll give birth to a baby covered with thick white fur, and that way she won't be cold. My breasts will be full of hot cocoa so she doesn't get chilly. And if it gets really cold, she'll have a pouch I can crawl into. Like a marsupial. We'll mend together. That's what we'll do; we'll mend.

Scene 4

Same day. An abandoned lot in the South Bronx. A homeless Woman is standing near an oil drum in which a fire is burning. Snowfall.

Trash around. Hannah enters dragging two heavy suitcases.

HANNAH: Excuse me? I said excuse me? Can you tell me where I am? Is this Brooklyn? Do you know a Pineapple Street? Is there some sort of bus or train or . . .?

I'm lost, I just arrived from Salt Lake. City. Utah? I took the bus that I was told to take and I got off—well it was the very last stop, so I had to get off, and I *asked* the driver was this Brooklyn, and he nodded yes but he was from one of those foreign countries where they think it's good manners to nod at everything even if you have no idea what it is you're nodding at, and in truth I think he spoke no English at all, which I think would make him ineligible for employment on public transportation. The public being English-speaking, mostly. Do you speak English?

(The Woman nods.)

HANNAH: I was supposed to be met at the airport by my son. He didn't show and I don't wait more than three and three-quarters hours for *anyone.* I should have been patient, I guess, I. . . . Is this . . .

WOMAN: Bronx.

HANNAH: Is that. . . . The *Bronx?* Well how in the name of Heaven did I get to the Bronx when the bus driver said . . .

WOMAN (Talking to herself): Slurp slurp slurp will you STOP that disgusting slurping! YOU DISGUSTING SLURPING FEEDING ANIMAL! Feeding yourself, just feeding yourself, what would it matter, to you or to ANYONE, if you just stopped. Feeding. And DIED?

(Pause.)

HANNAH: Can you just tell me where I . . .

WOMAN: Why was the Kosciusko Bridge named after a Polack?

HANNAH: I don't know what you're . . .

WOMAN: That was a joke.

HANNAH: Well what's the punchline?

WOMAN: I don't know.

HANNAH (Looking around desperately): Oh for pete's sake, is there anyone else who . . .

WOMAN (Again, to herself): Stand further off you fat loathsome whore, you can't have any more of this soup, slurp slurp slurp you animal, and the—I know you'll just go pee it all away and where will you do that? Behind what bush? It's FUCKING COLD out here and I . . .

Oh that's right, because it was supposed to have been a tunnel!

That's not very funny.

Have you read the prophecies of Nostradamus?

HANNAH: Who?

WOMAN: Some guy I went out with once somewhere, Nostradamus. Prophet, outcast, eyes like. . . . Scary shit, he . . .

HANNAH: Shut up. Please. Now I want you to stop jabbering for a minute and pull your wits together and tell me how to get to Brooklyn. Because you know! And you are going to tell me! Because there is no one else around to tell me and I am wet and cold and I am very angry! So I am sorry you're psychotic but just make the effort—take a deep breath—DO IT!

(Hannah and the Woman breathe together.)

HANNAH: That's good. Now exhale.

(They do.)

HANNAH: Good. Now how do I get to Brooklyn?

WOMAN: Don't know. Never been. Sorry. Want some soup?

HANNAH: Manhattan? Maybe you know . . . I don't suppose you know the location of the Mormon Visitor's . . .

WOMAN: 65th and Broadway.

HANNAH: How do you . . .

WOMAN: Go there all the time. Free movies. Boring, but you can stay all day.

HANNAH: Well. . . . So how do I . . .

WOMAN: Take the D Train. Next block make a right.

HANNAH: Thank you.

WOMAN: Oh yeah. In the new century I think we will all be insane.

Scene 5

Same day. Joe and Roy in the study of Roy's brownstone. Roy is wearing an elegant bathrobe. He has made a considerable effort to look well. He isn't well, and he hasn't succeeded much in looking it.

JOE: I can't. The answer's no. I'm sorry.

ROY: Oh, well, apologies . . .

I can't see that there's anyone asking for apologies.

(Pause.)

JOE: I'm sorry, Roy.

ROY: Oh, well, apologies.

JOE: My wife is missing, Roy. My mother's coming from Salt Lake to . . . to help look, I guess. I'm supposed to be at the airport now, picking her up but. . . . I just spent two days in a hospital, Roy, with a bleeding ulcer, I was spitting up blood.

ROY: Blood, huh? Look, I'm very busy here and . . .

JOE: It's just a job.

ROY: A job? A *job? Washington!* Dumb Utah Mormon hick shit!

JOE: Roy . . .

ROY: *WASHINGTON!* When Washington called me I was younger than you, you think I said "Aw fuck no I can't go I got two fingers up my asshole and a little moral nosebleed to boot!" When Washington calls you my pretty young punk friend you go or you can go fuck yourself sideways 'cause the train has pulled out of the station, and you are *out,* nowhere, out in the cold. Fuck you, Mary Jane, get outta here.

JOE: Just let me . . .

ROY: Explain? Ephemera. You broke my heart. Explain that. Explain that.

JOE: I love you. Roy.

There's so much that I want, to be . . . what you see in me, I want to be a participant in the world, in your world, Roy, I want to be capable of that, I've tried, really I have

but . . . I can't do this. Not because I don't believe in you, but because I believe in you so much, in what you stand for, at heart, the order, the decency. I would give anything to protect you, but. . . . There are laws I can't break. It's too ingrained. It's not me. There's enough damage I've already done.

Maybe you were right, maybe I'm dead.

ROY: You're not dead, boy, you're a sissy.

You love me; that's moving, I'm moved. It's nice to be loved. I warned you about her, didn't I, Joe? But you don't listen to me, why, because you say Roy is smart and Roy's a friend but Roy . . . well, he isn't nice, and you wanna be nice. Right? A nice, nice man!

(Little pause)

You know what my greatest accomplishment was, Joe, in my life, what I am able to look back on and be proudest of? And I have helped make Presidents and unmake them and mayors and more goddam judges than anyone in NYC ever—AND several million dollars, tax-free—and what do you think means the most to me?

You ever hear of Ethel Rosenberg? Huh, Joe, huh?

JOE: Well, yeah, I guess I . . . . Yes.

ROY: Yes. Yes. You have heard of Ethel Rosenberg. Yes. Maybe you even read about her in the history books.

If it wasn't for me, Joe, Ethel Rosenberg would be alive today, writing some personal-advice column for *Ms.* magazine. She isn't. Because during the trial, Joe, I was on the phone every day, talking with the judge . . .

JOE: Roy . . .

ROY: Every day, doing what I do best, talking on the telephone, making sure that timid Yid nebbish on the bench did his duty to America, to history. That sweet unprepossessing woman, two kids, boo-hoo-hoo, reminded us all of our little Jewish mamas— she came this close to getting life; I pleaded till I wept to put her in the chair. Me. I did that. I would have fucking pulled the switch if they'd have let me. Why? Because I fucking hate traitors. Because I fucking hate communists. Was it legal? Fuck legal. Am I a nice man? Fuck nice. They say terrible things about me in the *Nation.* Fuck the *Nation.* You want to be Nice, or you want to be Effective? Make the law, or subject to it. Choose. Your wife chose. A week from today, she'll be back. SHE knows how to get what SHE wants. Maybe I ought to send *her* to Washington.

JOE: I don't believe you.

ROY: Gospel.

JOE: You can't possibly mean what you're saying.

Roy, you were the Assistant United States Attorney on the Rosenberg case, ex-parte communication with the judge during the trial would be . . . censurable, at least, probably conspiracy and . . . in a case that resulted in execution, it's . . .

ROY: What? Murder?

JOE: You're not well is all.

ROY: What do you mean, not well? Who's not well?

(Pause.)

JOE: You said . . .

ROY: No I didn't. I said what?

JOE: Roy, you have cancer.

ROY: No I don't.

(Pause.)

JOE: You told me you were dying.

ROY: What the fuck are you talking about, Joe? I never said that. I'm in perfect health. There's not a goddam thing wrong with me.
(He smiles)

Shake?

(Joe hesitates. He holds out his hand to Roy. Roy pulls Joe into a close, strong clinch.)

ROY (More to himself than to Joe): It's OK that you hurt me because I love you, baby Joe. That's why I'm so rough on you.

(Roy releases Joe. Joe backs away a step or two.)

ROY: Prodigal son. The world will wipe its dirty hands all over you.

JOE: It already has, Roy.

ROY: Now go.

(Roy shoves Joe, hard. Joe turns to leave. Roy stops him, turns him around.)

ROY (Smoothing Joe's lapels, tenderly): I'll always be here, waiting for you . . .
(Then again, with sudden violence, he pulls Joe close, violently)

What did you want from me, what was all this, what do you want, treacherous ungrateful little . . .

(Joe, very close to belting Roy, grabs him by the front of his robe, and propels him across the length of the room. He holds Roy at arm's length, the other arm ready to hit.)

ROY (Laughing softly, almost pleading to be hit): Transgress a little, Joseph.

(Joe releases Roy.)

ROY: There are so many laws; find one you can break.

(Joe hesitates, then leaves, backing out. When Joe has gone, Roy doubles over in great pain, which he's been hiding throughout the scene with Joe.)

ROY: Ah, Christ . . .

Andy! Andy! Get in here! Andy!
(The door opens, but it isn't Andy. A small Jewish Woman dressed modestly in a fifties hat and coat stands in the doorway. The room darkens.)

ROY: Who the fuck are you? The new nurse?

(The figure in the doorway says nothing. She stares at Roy. A pause. Roy looks at her carefully, gets up, crosses to her. He crosses back to the chair, sits heavily.)

ROY: Aw, fuck. Ethel.

ETHEL ROSENBERG (Her manner is friendly, her voice is ice-cold): You don't look good, Roy.

ROY: Well, Ethel. I don't feel good.

ETHEL ROSENBERG: But you lost a lot of weight. That suits you. You were heavy back then. Zaftig, mit hips.

ROY: I haven't been that heavy since 1960. We were all heavier back then, before the body thing started. Now I look like a skeleton. They stare.

ETHEL ROSENBERG: The shit's really hit the fan, huh, Roy?

(Little pause. Roy nods.)

ETHEL ROSENBERG: Well the fun's just started.

ROY: What is this, Ethel, Halloween? You trying to scare me?

(Ethel says nothing.)

ROY: Well you're wasting your time! I'm scarier than you any day of the week! So beat it, Ethel! BOOO! BETTER DEAD THAN RED! Somebody trying to shake me up? HAH HAH! From the throne of God in heaven to the belly of hell, you can all fuck yourselves and then go jump in the lake because I'M NOT AFRAID OF YOU OR DEATH OR HELL OR ANYTHING!

ETHEL ROSENBERG: Be seeing you soon, Roy. Julius sends his regards.

ROY: Yeah, well send this to Julius!

(He flips the bird in her direction, stands and moves towards her. Halfway across the room he slumps to the floor, breathing laboriously, in pain.)

ETHEL ROSENBERG: You're a very sick man, Roy.

ROY: Oh God . . . ANDY!

ETHEL ROSENBERG: Hmmm. He doesn't hear you, I guess. We should call the ambulance.

(She goes to the phone)

Hah! Buttons! Such things they got now. What do I dial, Roy?

(Pause. Roy looks at her, then:)

ROY: 911.

ETHEL ROSENBERG (Dials the phone): It sings! (Imitating dial tones) La la la . . .

Huh.

Yes, you should please send an ambulance to the home of Mister Roy Cohn, the famous lawyer.

What's the address, Roy?

ROY (A beat, then): 244 East 87th.

ETHEL ROSENBERG: 244 East 87th Street. No apartment number, he's got the whole building.

My name? (A beat) Ethel Greenglass Rosenberg.

(Small smile) Me? No I'm not related to Mr. Cohn. An old friend.

(She hangs up)

They said a minute.

ROY: I have all the time in the world.

ETHEL ROSENBERG: You're immortal.

ROY: I'm immortal. Ethel. (He forces himself to stand)

I have *forced* my way into history. I ain't never gonna die.

ETHEL ROSENBERG (A little laugh, then): History is about to crack wide open. Millennium approaches.

Scene 6

Late that night. Prior's bedroom. Prior 1 watching Prior in bed, who is staring back at him, terrified. Tonight Prior 1 is dressed in weird alchemical robes and hat over his historical clothing and he carries a long palm-leaf bundle.

PRIOR 1: Tonight's the night! Aren't you excited? Tonight she arrives! Right through the roof! Ha-adam, Ha-gadol . . .

PRIOR 2 (Appearing, similarly attired): Lumen! Phosphor! Fluor! Candle! An unending billowing of scarlet and . . .

PRIOR: Look. Garlic. A mirror. Holy water. A crucifix. FUCK OFF! Get the fuck out of my room! GO!

PRIOR 1 (To Prior 2): Hard as a hickory knob, I'll bet.

PRIOR 2: We all tumesce when they approach. We wax full, like moons.

PRIOR 1: Dance.

PRIOR: Dance?

PRIOR 1: Stand up, dammit, give us your hands, dance!

PRIOR 2: Listen . . .

(A lone oboe begins to play a little dance tune.)

PRIOR 2: Delightful sound. Care to dance?

PRIOR: Please leave me alone, please just let me sleep . . .

PRIOR 2: Ah, he wants someone familiar. A partner who knows his steps. (To Prior) Close your eyes. Imagine . . .

PRIOR: I don't . . .

PRIOR 2: Hush. Close your eyes.

(Prior does.)

PRIOR 2: Now open them.

(Prior does. Louis appears. He looks gorgeous. The music builds gradually into a full-blooded, romantic dance tune.)

PRIOR: Lou.

LOUIS: Dance with me.

PRIOR: I can't, my leg, it hurts at night . . .
     Are you a ghost, Lou?

LOUIS: No. Just spectral. Lost to myself. Sitting all day on cold park benches. Wishing I could be with you. Dance with me, babe . . .

(Prior stands up. The leg stops hurting. They begin to dance. The music is beautiful.)

PRIOR 1 (To Prior 2): Hah. Now I see why he's got no children. He's a sodomite.

PRIOR 2: Oh be quiet, you medieval gnome, and let them dance.

PRIOR 1: I'm not interfering, I've done my bit. Hooray, hooray, the messenger's come, now I'm blowing off. I don't like it here.

(Prior 1 vanishes.)

PRIOR 2: The twentieth century. Oh dear, the world has gotten so terribly, terribly old. (Prior 2 vanishes. Louis and Prior waltz happily. Lights fade back to normal. Louis vanishes. Prior dances alone.
Then suddenly, the sound of wings fills the room.)

Scene 7

Split scene: Prior alone in his apartment; Louis alone in the park.

Again, a sound of beating wings.

PRIOR: Oh don't come in here don't come in . . .
     LOUIS!!

     No. My name is Prior Walter, I am . . . the scion of an ancient line, I am . . . abandoned

I . . . no, my name is . . . is . . . Prior and I live . . . *here and now,* and . . . in the dark, in the dark, the Recording Angel opens its hundred eyes and snaps the spine of the Book of Life and . . . hush! Hush!

I'm talking nonsense, I . . .

No more mad scene, hush, hush . . .

(Louis in the park on a bench. Joe approaches, stands at a distance. They stare at each other, then Louis turns away.)

LOUIS: Do you know the story of Lazarus?

JOE: Lazarus?

LOUIS: Lazarus. I can't remember what happens, exactly.

JOE: I don't. . . . Well, he was dead, Lazarus, and Jesus breathed life into him. He brought him back from death.

LOUIS: Come here often?

JOE: No. Yes. Yes.

LOUIS: Back from the dead. You believe that really happened?

JOE: I don't know anymore what I believe.

LOUIS: This is quite a coincidence. Us meeting.

JOE: I followed you.

     From work. I . . . followed you here.
(Pause.)

LOUIS: You followed me.

     You probably saw me that day in the washroom and thought: there's a sweet guy, sensitive, cries for friends in trouble.

JOE: Yes.

LOUIS: You thought maybe I'll cry for you.

JOE: Yes.

LOUIS: Well I fooled you. Crocodile tears. Nothing . . . (He touches his heart, shrugs)

(Joe reaches tentatively to touch Louis's face.)

LOUIS (Pulling back): What are you doing? Don't do that.

JOE (Withdrawing his hand): Sorry. I'm sorry.

LOUIS: I'm . . . just not . . . I think, if you touch me, your hand might fall off or something. Worse things have happened to people who have touched me.

JOE: Please.

Oh, boy . . .

Can I . . .

I . . . want . . . to touch you. Can I please just touch you . . . um, here?

(He puts his hand on one side of Louis's face. He holds it there)

I'm going to hell for doing this.

LOUIS: Big deal. You think it could be any worse than New York City?

(He puts his hand on Joe's hand. He takes Joe's hand away from his face, holds it for a moment, then) Come on.

JOE: Where?

LOUIS: Home. With me.

JOE: This makes no sense. I mean I don't know you.

LOUIS: Likewise.

JOE: And what you do know about me you don't like.

LOUIS: The Republican stuff.

JOE: Yeah, well for starters.

LOUIS: I don't not like that. I hate that.

JOE: So why on earth should we . . .

(Louis goes to Joe and kisses him.)

LOUIS: Strange bedfellows. I don't know. I never made it with one of the damned before.

I would really rather not have to spend tonight alone.

JOE: I'm a pretty terrible person, Louis.

LOUIS: Lou.

JOE: No, I really really am. I don't think I deserve being loved.

LOUIS: There? See? We already have a lot in common.

(Louis stands, begins to walk away. He turns, looks back at Joe. Joe follows. They exit.)

(Prior listens. At first no sound, then once again, the sound of beating wings, frighteningly near.)

PRIOR: That sound, that sound, it. . . . What is that, like birds or something, like a really big

bird, I'm frightened, I . . . no, no fear, find the anger, find the . . . anger, my blood is clean, my brain is fine, I can handle pressure, I am a gay man and I am used to pressure, to trouble, I am tough and strong and. . . . Oh. Oh my goodness. I . . . (He is washed over by an intense sexual feeling) Ooohhhh. . . . I'm hot, I'm . . . so . . . aw Jeez what is going on here I . . . must have a fever I . . .

(The bedside lamp flickers wildly as the bed begins to roll forward and back. There is a deep bass creaking and groaning from the bedroom ceiling, like the timbers of a ship under immense stress, and from above a fine rain of plaster dust.)

PRIOR: OH!

PLEASE, OH PLEASE! Something's coming in here, I'm scared, I don't like this at all, something's approaching and I. . . . OH!

(There is a great blaze of triumphal music, heralding. The light turns an extraordinary harsh, cold, pale blue, then a rich, brilliant warm golden color, then a hot, bilious green, and then finally a spectacular royal purple. Then silence.)

PRIOR (An awestruck whisper): God almighty . . .

Very Steven Spielberg.

(A sound, like a plummeting meteor, tears down from very, very far above the earth, hurtling at an incredible velocity towards the bedroom; the light seems to be sucked out of the room as the projectile approaches; as the room reaches darkness, we hear a terrifying CRASH as something immense strikes earth; the whole building shudders and a part of the bedroom ceiling, lots of plaster and lathe and wiring, crashes to the floor. And then in a shower of unearthly white light, spreading great opalescent gray-silver wings, the Angel descends into the room and floats above the bed.)

ANGEL:

Greetings, Prophet;
The Great Work begins:
The Messenger has arrived.

(Blackout.)

··· PRODUCING *ANGELS IN AMERICA*

The productions we have studied so far—*And the Soul Shall Dance* at East West Players and at Northwest Asian American Theatre and *Joe Turner's Come and Gone* at the Oregon Shakespeare Festival—began with completed scripts. Each play had already had a number of successful productions and had achieved national recognition. For *Angels in America* we begin at a much earlier time in the life of the play. We examine the development of the play itself and the relationship between a new play and the performance process.

THE EUREKA THEATRE AND THE PLAYWRIGHT

More and more, American theatre companies are directly involved in the development of new plays. Sometimes playwrights work on their own and submit a new play to a theatre only after it has been completed. But there are also playwrights who are members of theatre companies or are invited or commissioned to write a play for a particular company. A commission involves payment that supports the actual writing of the play. In 1987, a small theatre company in San Francisco, the Eureka Theatre, used a grant from the National Endowment for the Arts to commission Tony Kushner to write a play. That play would become *Angels in America.*

The production history of *Angels in America* begins with Oskar Eustis, the Eureka's artistic director and **dramaturg**; and Tony Taccone, the theatre's producing director at that time. In this case, the development of the play itself was highly dependent on the production process. In the late 1980s, the Eureka Theatre was a small but active theatre committed to a "politically progressive aesthetic" and the production of plays that would be responsive to social issues.[3] Together, the artistic leaders of the theatre—Taccone and Eustis—sought out new plays or commissioned new work to create a vital and forward-looking repertoire for their theatre and the politically conscious San Francisco audience that it attracted.

Oskar Eustis had just directed Kushner's first play, *A Bright Room Called Day*, and was inspired by the originality of Kushner's presentation of political ideas. In the capacity of dramaturg, Eustis began a dialogue with Kushner about what kind of play he might write for the Eureka Theatre. Kushner says of the origins of the new work, "I began *Angels* as a conversation, real and imaginary, between Oskar and myself."[4]

The Role of the Dramaturg

For years, European theatres have employed dramaturgs, whose role is to work with the playwrights in the shaping of their plays and to advise directors on questions of history, analysis, and interpretation. The position of dramaturg is a fairly recent addition to the production staffs of American theatres. The critic and producer Martin Esslin sees the role of the dramaturg as crucial to expanding the intellectual and cultural foundation of the American theatre: "The American dramaturg not only has to do the basic job of finding and nurturing scripts, but has also to work hard on helping to create that basic cultural atmosphere in which a healthy theatre can operate."[5] Robert Brustein, the founding director of the Yale Repertory Theatre and American Repertory Theatre, calls the dramaturg "the conscience of the theatre."[6] In this sense the dramaturg is concerned with developing a repertoire of plays that will challenge the audience as well as working with playwrights and directors to make sure that ideas are substantial and clearly articulated.

Oskar Eustis had been working in Germany and Switzerland as a director and dramaturg before he returned to the United States and joined the staff of the Eureka Theatre. He explains his original goals in assuming the role of dramaturg at the Eureka Theatre:

OSKAR EUSTIS: Being a dramaturg is an art form, not a science. What I felt needed to be done was to help work with playwrights to create a theatre that was more accessible, more political, more audience-friendly, and therefore more narratively based than the theatre I had done before.[7]

Eustis describes the starting point in the development of two plays he commissioned for the Eureka that eventually went on to larger theatres, including some on Broadway—*Execution of Justice* by Emily Mann and *Angels in America* by Tony Kushner.

OSKAR EUSTIS: In both instances, I took a playwright who the Eureka had already produced and that we had had an exciting relationship with. With Emily Mann we had produced her play *Still Life* and had an amazing experience with it. Emily had loved the production. With Tony I had produced the professional premiere of *A Bright Room Called Day.* They were writers with whom I felt deep affinities, aesthetically, theatrically, and politically.

Eustis wanted to merge the interests of the Eureka Theatre with the concerns of the playwrights. He asked each playwright, "What play does it make sense for you to write for the Eureka Theatre?"

OSKAR EUSTIS: And both of them, for different reasons, ended up focusing on things that had to do with the gay community in San Francisco, with subjects that seemed to speak very directly to the audience that was there for us in San Francisco.

••• IN CONTEXT

Production History of *Angels in America*

Date	Event
1987	Oskar Eustis commissions Tony Kushner to write a play for the Eureka Theatre.
1990	*Millennium Approaches* is staged in a workshop production at the Mark Taper Forum in Los Angeles, directed by Oskar Eustis.
1991	*Millennium Approaches* premieres at the Eureka Theatre in San Francisco, directed by David Esbjornson. *Perestroika* is given a staged reading but remains unfinished.
1992	*Millennium Approaches* opens at the Royal National Theatre's small black-box theatre, the Cottesloe, in London, directed by Declan Donnellan. *Perestroika* would be added to the production in 1993.
1992	*Millennium Approaches* and *Perestroika* are produced together for the first time at the Mark Taper Forum in Los Angeles, codirected by Oskar Eustis and Tony Taccone.
1993	*Millennium Approaches* and *Perestroika* are produced together at the Walter Kerr Theatre on Broadway, directed by George C. Wolfe.

Emily Mann turned to a true story about San Francisco itself. She wrote a courtroom drama based on the trial of Dan White, the city supervisor who shot and killed two city officials: another city supervisor, Harvey Milk, the first openly gay elected official in America; and George Moscone, the mayor of San Francisco. When Tony Kushner was invited to work with the Eureka Theatre, he knew that somehow he wanted to write a play that concerned Roy Cohn, AIDS in the gay community, and Mormons. How those subjects were to be connected, what form the play was to take, was still in the future.

One of the remarkable anecdotes about the evolution of *Angels in America* has to do with the company of the Eureka Theatre. The mate[rial] that Kushner wanted to pursue had to do [with] gay men, but the core acting company o[f] Eureka Theatre was made up of three w[omen] and one man. The three women would [play] parts in whatever Kushner wrote.

OSKAR EUSTIS: The play was modele[d ...] the company members of the Eurek[a ...] reason those parts exist in *Angels* is [...] that was the company of the Eureka T[heatre]. We spent a number of sleepless nig[hts ...] Tony tried to figure out how to p[ut ...] straight women into a show that [...] the experience of gay men. But p[art of the] reason why the show is so great is [...] had to continually expand the ran[ge of] subject matter in order to get thos[e ...] into the play. The play ended up taking on a [...] scope that none of us suspected it was going to when we started.

The Developmental Process

Angels in America went through a long and difficult developmental process that lasted six years until both plays were actually completed. Before the official premiere of *Millennium Approaches* at the Eureka Theatre in 1991, there were six workshop productions in San Francisco, in Los Angeles, and at the Sundance Institute; about a dozen readings; endless informal discussions; and many revised drafts of the play. *Perestroika* was given an abbreviated staged reading when *Millennium Approaches* was being performed at the Eureka Theatre. Kushner did not finish the second play until just before its premiere in Los Angeles. *Perestroika* would be rewritten yet one more time before the entire piece opened on Broadway.

The developmental process was affected both by changes in personnel and by financial complications. After beginning the work on *Angels in America* at the Eureka Theatre, Tony

Taccone became the associate artistic director of the Berkeley Repertory Theatre and Oskar [...] became associate artistic director of the [...] Angeles. David Esb[...] [p]lay at [...]duction [...]ccone [...]th the [...]e Pub[...] on the [...] opened [...]les, the [...] Oskar

[...]erent for[...]hem were [...]re. There [...]ing on the [...]es we were [...] of the different scenes o[...] There were times when we were trying to finish the story. And at times we were very much trying to figure out how to produce the thing as a whole, what our production method might be.

Tony Kushner readily acknowledges the help of a variety of dramaturgs, theatre practitioners, and colleagues in the evolution of *Angels in America*. Some people were involved in the development of characters, scenes, and language; others gave crucial advice on cutting the script; and some were engaged with Kushner in dialogues and arguments about the ideas expressed by the play. Each reading or production made a major contribution to the writing process.

TONY KUSHNER: It's deeply suspect that writers—especially male writers—feel that they have to produce everything completely on their own and that the act of writing becomes in part an act of denying that one is in any way reliant on other people. I've thought that maybe other writers simply don't need other people's help as much as I do, or maybe I'm just a bad writer. I suspect that some people are more solitary and really dredge it all out of their own souls. But even there, there may be ways in which people are feeding them about which they're not aware. . . . I haven't been diminished by admitting that other people have participated.[8]

Although Kushner received input from many sources during the six-year gestation of *Angels in America*, the writing and rewriting were his work. Kushner is a playwright who makes continuous adjustments in his material, and *Angels* involved a legendary number of rewrites. Some of the actors who began the production in San Francisco were also part of the cast in Los Angeles and eventually went on to New York, a rather unusual casting history. Ellen McLaughlin, who played the Angel, memorized as many as twenty versions of a crucial scene in *Perestroika* before Kushner was satisfied. The rewrites continued on *Perestroika* throughout most of the rehearsal period in Los Angeles. The directors and actors who were staging two full plays that would run a total of seven hours had only ten weeks to do their preparatory work and had to contend with changes in the script up until days before the production opened.

TONY TACCONE: There were lots of rewrites, and that was both thrilling and scary—thrilling because the writing was fantastic and scary because you have to constantly assess how many changes you can try to incorporate without driving everybody completely insane.

IMPACT OF THE THEATRE SPACE   Just as the writing of the play went through many stages, so the production of the play changed from theatre to theatre, and these changes had an enormous impact on the final shape of the play. The home of the Eureka Theatre was a converted warehouse off Market Street in San Francisco. With a stage that measured twenty-five feet by twenty-five feet and an audience space of 200 seats, the theatre was only a little larger than East West Players or Northwest Asian American Theatre. Old wooden bleachers were used to form ten rows of seating accommodating twenty people per row. The existing pipes were exposed across the ceiling, lowering the height of the performance space and increasing the "rough" atmosphere of the interior of the building. The Brechtian idea of exposing the mechanics of the theatre meshed conveniently with the theatre space.

TONY TACCONE: It had a kind of raw but exciting feel. It was always a little too hot or too cold, but it had a lot of energy. Everything was exposed at the Eureka. You could never hide anything.

The limitations of the stage space and the financial resources of the Eureka Theatre encouraged the development of a play that focused on the resources of the actors. For example, in writing the play for the Eureka Theatre, Kushner ended up creating a play with twenty-one characters for a total of eight actors—five men and three women. The range of characters grew out of the needs of the original Eureka company with the addition of four men who were invited to join the group.

And yet as Kushner expanded the scope of the play in response to the company, he found he needed many more characters than there were actors. Kushner's intention was for the actors to play more than one part. The actors then had the responsibility of shifting between characters who existed in the present and characters who came out of the past or between realistic characters and fantasy characters.

Kathleen Chalfant, who played Hannah Pitt, Joe's Mormon mother from Salt Lake City, also played three other roles in *Millennium Approaches*—Ethel Rosenberg; the rabbi who conducts the funeral service for Louis's grandmother at the beginning of the play; and the doctor, Henry, who tells Roy Cohn that he has AIDS. The development of each character was helped by costume changes, varying hairstyles, and, for the rabbi, a long beard. But the emphasis was on Chalfant's creativity in drawing distinct characters and on her skill in quickly moving from character to character in performance. The double casting had stylistic and philosophical implications. Chalfant observed, "Not only did Tony want women to play men, but he wanted women to play male authority figures, which is rare."[9]

The double casting at the Eureka challenged the ingenuity of the actors and kept the audience from identifying each actor with only one role. The audience became more conscious of the actors as actors rather than only as certain characters. There was an awareness of an ensemble of actors working closely together to tell Kushner's complicated story. The actors also did most of the scene changes, reinforcing the audience's perception of the actors as arrangers of the event as well as inhabitants of the play. The necessities of the Eureka Theatre production—the double casting and having the actors change the sets—were subsequently written into the script to be used even at larger theatres with more substantial resources.

REFINING THE BALANCE BETWEEN INTIMACY AND SPECTACLE The Eureka production emphasized the intimate nature of the character relationships. Most of the scenes in *Angels in America* are between two characters and focus on personal details. In performance at the Eureka, the energy of the work went into the intensity and immediacy of the characters' needs and revelations.

Ellen McLaughlin appears in her first incarnation as the Angel in the original production of *Angels in America* at the Eureka Theatre.

TONY TACCONE: The simplicity of the show when it was done at the Eureka was brilliant. It was really straightforward and wonderfully clear. The play was in the lap of the audience, and that created an intimacy and urgency that made for a fantastic theatre experience.

When the play moved to larger theatres, the spectacle became increasingly important, enlarging the background against which individual lives were seen.

Refining the balance between intimacy and spectacle—expanding Kushner's idea of a "fantasia"—became of primary importance in productions subsequent to the performances at the Eureka. For example, the presence of the Angel took on much larger dimensions at the Mark Taper Forum and then at the Walter Kerr Theatre in New York. The Angel's entrance from eighteen inches at the Eureka Theatre became an entrance from thirty feet above the stage at the Mark Taper Forum.

By the time *Angels in America* was staged in New York, the Angel, still played by Ellen McLaughlin, had become a stupendous creation that symbolized the entire work. Here, the Angel overwhelms Prior in the second play, *Perestroika*. Prior and the Angel battle for his soul.

TONY TACCONE: The Angel was flown in from high above with a halogen light behind her bright enough to light up the city of New York. There was a terrific amount of smoke and a very full sound track. It was spectacular.

The much greater stage height at the Mark Taper and the more sophisticated flying apparatus allowed the producers to build the image of the Angel as a force of majestic power. This possibility contributed to Kushner's development of the emerging relationship between Prior and the Angel in *Perestroika*.

Act 2, scene 2 of *Perestroika*, a ferocious confrontation between Prior and the Angel, is at the heart of Kushner's vision for the play. This is the scene that Ellen McLaughlin memorized in twenty different versions. It becomes a heroic and symbolic or allegorical battle for Prior's soul. The Angel turns out to be a conservative force who demands that human beings stop moving, that they stop trying to change.

ANGEL:

Forsake the Open Road:

Neither Mix nor Intermarry: Let Deep Roots
    Grow:

If you do not Mingle you will Cease to
    Progress:

Seek Not to Fathom the World and its
    Delicate Particle Logic:

You cannot Understand, You can only
    Destroy, . . .

Turn back. Undo.[10]

Prior comes to understand that if he accepts the Angel's message of "stasis," it becomes his death sentence. He rejects the Angel's vision because he realizes that change is the only course of human action that can lead to "more life." Taccone describes the scene as a "wild landscape of evocative images that are all designed to create this huge conflict between a dying gay man, struggling to save his life, and an Angel who is not the miracle he is seeking."

In staging this confrontation in Los Angeles, the directors used the technology of the flying apparatus to create what Taccone calls a "fantastic, surreal wrestling match with an angel flying and leaping around the room and an actor who was both stunned and terrified." The scene became a theatricalized encounter between larger-than-life characters playing out a spiritual crisis. The choreographed battle—part dance, part high-wire gymnastics—merged with Kushner's poetic, dreamlike language to create a defining image for the play.

EXPANDING OPPORTUNITIES FOR THE DEVELOPMENT OF NEW PLAYS

Many of the most interesting plays come out of small theatres that do not have a commercial focus. Some of these plays may go on to larger regional theatres and to New York. The hallmark of a successful American play used to be its success on Broadway, but Broadway is no longer the final judge of a play's merit. At one time most major American plays originated in New York and then toured the country or moved on to regional theatres. Clearly, the course of many successful plays is now reversed. Like *Angels in America*, a play may originate in a regional theatre and work its way to Broadway. New York still has a remarkable concentration of talent and venues that can generate cutting-edge work and support long-running productions. But exciting theatre can emerge from any part of the country where theatres and audiences meet to consider questions about human existence from a new perspective.

In over twenty years of producing plays, the Eureka Theatre supported the development of more than sixty new plays. Many other theatres also attempt to establish opportunities for new playwrights. In developing new work, theatres understand that they may provide only the starting point for new plays that will become part of the larger American theatre.

Angels in America outgrew the boundaries of the Eureka Theatre. It became an event that took on a life of its own.

> **TONY TACCONE:** It felt like an avalanche. It started out as a snowball and ended up coursing down the mountainside at a speed that none of us could possibly keep up with or predict.

The original producers could have tried to contain the play, to keep it within the limits of the Eureka's production capabilities. No one had bargained for a six-year effort that would lead to a marathon extravaganza. But a good part of the energy that comes out of theatre work has to do with the unpredictable nature of whatever may evolve.

OSKAR EUSTIS: We came to a crisis point where we said, the Eureka cannot produce this play; it's not manageable. The play had taken on a scope that none of us had suspected when we started. It became apparent that it was going to be two evenings long, and that was catastrophic for my poor little theatre company, which had no way of believing that it could work or afford to pay for it.

The work was telling us it had to be this thing that was larger than we could afford, and I really had two choices: to try to cut the ambition and scope of the piece to fit the Eureka or to say, let's go on this ride and see what happens. My decision was

obvious. We went on the ride, and it led to extraordinary results. I think it's a perfect little model for what you have to do in this kind of process.

No previous paradigm is sufficient for creating important new work, because the whole point of it, the whole thing that makes it an art form, is that it is being invented and new. Otherwise, what you're doing is trying to fit new wine into old bottles. You might come up with something that sort of works. But you'll never come up with something that has the kind of galvanic effect that *Angels* has, an artwork that is so uniquely, precisely itself. To produce *Angels in America* took years and years. You just have to be willing to get in the trenches and work for as long as it takes. I can't think of anything else that would be more worth doing with your time.

Summary

A play such as *Angels in America* that draws on many sources of theatrical expression reminds us to be wary of trying to define plays according to rigid categories. *Angels in America* tells a sweeping story of American life that functions on political and personal levels at the same time. Among the styles used by the playwright Tony Kushner are realism, epic theatre, expressionism, and absurdism. The rapid shifts between kinds of characters and styles of language are in part influenced by the theatre of Bertolt Brecht. Kushner is also influenced by the plays of Caryl Churchill, who brings together characters from the past and characters from the present to create a historical perspective for contemporary issues. This device

is seen in *Angels in America* in the character Ethel Rosenberg, the ancestor Priors, and most of all the character Roy Cohn. The flamboyant presentation of the Angel demonstrates how a theatrical image can be central to a play's expression.

The dramaturg is a relatively new position in the American theatre. In developing *Angels in America* at the Eureka Theatre, the playwright was assisted by Oskar Eustis, who originally commissioned the play and then worked closely on its development. The responsibilities of the dramaturg include new play development as well as research and analysis to help other theatre practitioners in the production of challenging plays.

The cast of *Rent* sings and dances "La Vie Bohème" on the tables of the Life Café with choreography by Marlies Yearby. In "La Vie Bohème" the characters sing of their social rebellion. Unlike the more structured choreography of *West Side Story* and *A Chorus Line,* the dancing in *Rent* has an informal, improvisational quality.

and performers but had the very experienced and well-connected hand of George C. Wolfe guiding the process. *Rent* was sustained by the energy and commitment of its creator, Jonathan Larson.

Larson studied acting and musical composition in college; and with encouragement from Stephen Sondheim, he committed himself to a career of writing for the musical theatre. It took fifteen years of living the life represented by the characters in *Rent* to bring his vision of a new musical to the stage. Larson sought to merge the tradition of the musical theatre with music of the 1990s and the sensibility of young people raised

with MTV, film technology, and rapidly changing social values. He wanted to place the heart of rock-and-roll culture on the musical stage in order to tell the story of young people struggling to make sense of life in the midst of poverty and the AIDS epidemic.

Larson found the starting point for what would become *Rent* in a nineteenth-century opera, *La Bohème* (1895), by Puccini; and in the novel *Scenes de la Vie Bohème,* by Henri Murger, on which *La Bohème* was based. From *La Bohème* he took the situation of a group of artists struggling with poverty and illness but sustaining themselves through their friendships and their faith in life. Many of the plot incidents and the characters are suggested by the opera; an example is Mimi, who in the opera dies of tuberculosis and in *Rent* is dying of drug addiction and AIDS.

But *Rent* is definitely a late-twentieth-century creation: a rock band is placed on the stage; the characters all wear head mikes; one of the characters records everything on a video camera; and drug addiction underscores the troubled lives of the characters. The music reflects the mix of pop music culture, all with a rock-and-roll beat. Instead of the slickness and polished finish of most musical theatre productions, Larson sought a roughness and rawness in the performance, in terms of both the singing and the visual presentation. The set appears to be made from found pieces of junk; the costumes are a grungy compilation of worn and frayed cast-off garments or the cheapest of the new. The staging has an improvisational feel. Where there is choreography, there is a sense of looseness and invention in the moment rather than the highly crafted dance structures of Jerome Robbins, Michael Bennett, or Savion Glover.

The story behind the creation of *Rent* is as dramatic as what occurs on the stage. The night before the production's final dress rehearsal, thirty-five-year-old Jonathan Larson died suddenly of an aortic aneurysm. The grief-stricken cast "went on with the show," which met with great success. But the success was mixed with sadness for the young playwright and composer who didn't live to see his music and lyrics lighting up Broadway.

Julie Taymor and *The Lion King*

In 1997 a new musical opened on Broadway that once again took the form in a major new direction. *The Lion King* was adapted from the extraordinarily popular Walt Disney film of the same name and followed the Disney recreation of *Beauty and the Beast* as a stage musical. The stage version of *Beauty and the Beast* was guided by the cartoon imagery of the film, but the stage production of *The Lion King* broke new ground

in the musical theatre. The avant-garde director and designer Julie Taymor was invited by Walt Disney Theatrical Productions to interpret the story of *The Lion King* in her own way. Impressed by Taymor's previous intercultural work using astounding sculpted puppets and cinematic design effects, the Disney organization provided the opportunity for highly imaginative exploration in a commercial context. *The Lion King* continues the tradition of Broadway musicals that rely on lavish sets and costumes but integrates these elements into the telling of a story in a significantly new way. The designer-director becomes the driving force behind the expressive elements of the production.

Taymor became a serious student of theatre as a child and expanded her awareness of non-Western theatre traditions when she traveled to India and Sri Lanka during high school. During college she was part of the same experimental theatre company as Bill Irwin at Oberlin College. She also studied mime in Paris, improvisational acting in New York, and puppetry with the Bread and Puppet Theatre. Taymor was always concerned with the anthropological origins of theatre and with mythical subjects. She also showed talent early on as a painter and sculptor as well as a performer, talents that she continued to nurture as she apprenticed with different theatre companies and traditions.

After graduating from college, Taymor spent four years in Indonesia studying its brilliant movement theatre and observing the cultural conditions out of which it emerged. In Indonesia she became part of the Bengkel Theatre, which encouraged her to create a production with the company actors. Her first major work, *Way of Snow*, began her lifelong experimentation with theatre expressed through masks, puppets, live actors, and startling visual effects drawing on myth and ritual to probe the human condition. And she continued to build her design and construction skills in the areas of scene, costume, and puppet design at the same time that she refined her vision as a director. Taymor worked for twenty years directing

Tsidii Le Loka is seen here as the shaman Rafiki in *The Lion King.* Her costume and makeup were designed to suggest the physical characteristics of a baboon.

and designing original works, Shakespeare, and opera before being invited to bring her imaginative approach to *The Lion King.*

Taymor first worked with the original screenwriters of the film to expand and strengthen the narrative of the young lion, Simba, who must undertake a complicated journey to earn his place as king. She became a collaborator on the script itself at the same time that she began to envision the form that the characters should be given and a staging concept that would allow for the extremely adventurous nature of the action. The music from the film also required considerable augmentation, with particular attention paid to its African sources. Elton John and Tim Rice, the original composers who had worked with the South African performer Lebo M, wrote two additional pop-style character songs; Lebo M, Hans Zimmer, and Mark Mancina filled out the score, drawing on Zulu chanting and African rhythms and musical instruments. Just as Taymor's production style would draw on international sources and performance traditions, so the score would be an eclectic blend of American, European, and African styles. But as important as the music and the script were to the production, the greatest excitement would come from the visual presentation.

Taymor determined that various forms of puppets inhabited by actors would bring the animal characters to life and give her the flexibility to create magical action sequences, such as stampeding wildebeests or characters who could fly. The actors were not to be hidden by the puppet forms but rather to exist in puppet form and human form at the same time. The faces of the actors would always be seen. The actors playing lions would wear large masks placed above their own faces and be dressed in gowns of African-inspired fabrics rather than animal bodies. The hippopotamus was designed in full animal form for two actors whose bodies would be inside the large animal but whose heads would appear above the huge puppet. The character of Zazu, the comic bird, was designed as a fully realized rod puppet to be worn on the head of the actor who would sing and dance the role but who would be dressed in a suit that suggested the attitude of the bird character rather than in any kind of costume representing a bird. Human figures were designed into costumes representing plants, vines, and grass. Contraptions were invented such as the Gazelle Wheel, which would allow an actor to push across stage a wheeled vehicle that provided the momentum for the seven leaping figures of gazelle that were attached to it. Other "corporate" puppet forms were designed to enable one actor to present other groups of animals such as a flock of birds. Taymor explains her reasons for keeping the actor-puppeteers visible:

> When we see a person actually manipulating an inanimate object like a puppet and making it come alive, the duality moves us. Hidden special effects lack humanity, but when the human spirit visibly animates an object, we experience a special, almost life giving connection. We become engaged by both the method of story telling as well as by the story itself.[6]

Taymor also conceptualized a method of changing scale that would help develop the sense of movement across vast spaces. Characters would be represented by small puppets when they were meant to be seen at a distance, what she calls a "long shot," and then would be played by human actors when they had traveled far enough to be seen in a "close-up." For the wildebeest stampede, the first image seen by the audience is created by painted figures on cloth being turned on rollers at the back of the stage. As the stampede approaches the audience, larger and larger masks are used to create the sense that the animals are coming closer and closer.

Developing this visually stupendous musical involved the creative collaboration of many theatre artists. Michael Curry codesigned the puppets and was responsible for engineering and constructing them; and Taymor was responsible for sculpture and aesthetics. Richard Hudson created the actual scene design after Taymor developed the basic staging concept. Seven of the actors who ultimately appeared in the production were involved in experimentation with puppets and masks throughout the development process to see what would work and what would communicate effectively. In fact, Taymor incorporated puppets in the audition process:

> I also brought puppets to auditions to see how performers would look in relation to specific puppets and how they would respond when asked to animate an inanimate object. And though performers would not be totally immersed within the puppets nor hidden behind the masks, they would have to be willing to accept that the audience is not going to be looking at them alone. Attitude is a very important part of my casting decision. I want an actor who is going to enjoy the challenge and not view it as a burden. Rather than expressly hiring puppeteers, I look for inventive actors who move well. A strong actor gives an idiosyncratic performance, because he infuses the puppet characters with his own personality instead of relying on generic puppetry technique. The thrill of working with a good actor who is new to this medium, is that he will take the form further than I ever imagined.[7]

Designers have frequently created spectacular environments for musicals in the past with astonishing special effects. However, in *The Lion King*, Julie Taymor has investigated ways in which the work of the actor may be extended through her puppet and mask creations. She has returned to ancient theatre traditions and brought them into contemporary performance to challenge the imaginations of both actors and audiences.

Susan Stroman and *Contact*

Susan Stroman called her theatre piece *Contact* (1999) a "dance play" because the essential medium for storytelling in this work was choreographic. Despite the facts that there was no actual singing in *Contact* and that the music for the dancing was recorded rather than played live, the Broadway community chose to extend the term *musical* to include this performance of three loosely related stories, each in its own way based on the central human need for emotional and physical connection to other people. In *Contact* the work of the choreographer, which had become a major force in earlier American musicals such as *West Side Story*, *A Chorus Line*, and *Bring in da Noise, Bring in da Funk*, replaced the work of both the playwright-librettist and the lyricist. Although John Weidman collaborated with Stroman to provide the actor-dancers with small

segments of spoken dialogue, it was dance that shaped the characters, the characters' relationships, and the actions of their stories.

In 1997 Andre Bishop, who was the artistic director of Lincoln Center Theater, invited Susan Stroman to create an original piece for his theatre because he admired the excitement and energy her choreography had brought to more traditional musicals such as *Crazy for You* (1992) and the revival of *Show Boat* (1994). Bishop provided rehearsal space and resources to enable Stroman to develop material of her own choosing. *Contact* was inspired by Stroman's own experience in a late-night swing club in which she

Deborah Yates, the girl in the yellow dress, confident and flirtatious, dances with two of her many admirers while Boyd Gaines looks on from the background, unable to join the dance. *Contact* was choreographed and directed by Susan Stroman with costume design by William Ivey Long.

observed the magnetism of a stunning dancer in a yellow dress. From this seductive image evolved a story of a man who has lost the will to live until he dances with the woman in the yellow dress. The writer John Weidman explains that dance became salvation for a man betrayed by the failure of words: "The character came from a world that was all about language and language was something that failed him. He was going to have to escape from language to get saved."[8]

The story is danced out in the man's lonely apartment, which, in a dreamlike way, keeps changing into the swing club where he first watches from a distance and then finally, overcoming his inhibitions, dances with the woman in the yellow dress. Much of the piece consists of high-voltage swing dancing by characters who have discovered a world of dance that the alienated man is unable to enter. Because the story is set in a dance club, Stroman chose to use recorded jazz and swing music to reinforce the atmosphere of being in a club. When the work was expanded to include two additional stories, Stroman decided to use recorded music for all three vignettes.

The choreography of Susan Stroman is distinguished by invention and by the way dance movement creates character. For example, the first vignette of *Contact*, entitled "Swinging," consists of a playful and exuberant romantic encounter between lovers on a swing. The young man first pushes the woman on the swing and then joins her, sometimes sharing the seat and sometimes doing gymnastics on the ropes holding the swing. As the swing sails back and forth suspended high above the stage, the lovers find numerous ways of using the swing as part of their romance.

Stroman's ability to develop character through dance is exemplified by the second of the three *Contact* pieces, "Did You Move?" The essence of composing dance drama depends on conceptualizing the needs of the characters and the conflicts between them as physical problems. In this piece the central conflict is between a man trying to control his wife by imprisoning her in stillness while she tries to take back her freedom through movement. The woman begins the short story seated opposite her surly, gangsterlike husband in an Italian restaurant. Hunched over his food, he discourages her attempts at conversation, and when he leaves the table to get more food from the buffet, he barks at her, "don't move." The woman overcomes the paralyzing effect of his threats, and during each of her husband's absences she dances out her fantasies with increasing abandon. Gradually she engages all the other people in the restaurant, diners and waiters, in a wild celebration of human connection. Full of humor, the dance evolves into a broad conspiracy involving actor-dancers and food and serving trays to confuse and outwit the joyless, thuggish husband.

Since the success of *Contact*, Susan Stroman has gone on to work as the director-choreographer first of a revival of *The Music Man* and then most notably of *The Producers* (2001). Starring Nathan Lane and Matthew Broderick, *The Producers* was adapted by the comedian Mel Brooks from his film of the same name and is a comedy about the theatre itself. *The Producers* tells a simple story of a down-on-his-luck theatre producer who hits on an outrageous scheme to make money. He persuades a large number of older women, foolishly susceptible to his charms, to invest in his next show, selling each of them a half interest or more, percentages that are clearly too large to be paid back. Then he guarantees that the show will be a catastrophic failure by choosing the most offensive and tasteless material possible, a cheerful musical about Nazi Germany. He is certain the show will close after one night, and he will be able to keep his elderly investors' money. However, audiences believe the show must be a satire and find it so amusing that it becomes a huge success. This success, of course, means that the producer, Max Bialystock, is exposed as a fraud, dashing his fortunes but not his survival instincts. *The Producers* enjoyed a notable success in the months after September 11, 2001, providing audiences with the much needed release of laughter during disturbing times.

Summary

Works of musical theatre integrate singing, spoken text, and dance to communicate the drama. The musical theatre is a unique development of the American theatre that has had widespread influence throughout the world. The musical theatre grew out of the minstrel shows, revues, and vaudeville of the nineteenth century, which drew heavily on the various immigrant groups that made up the U.S. population.

Oklahoma! made major advances in drawing together the expressive elements of musical theatre. All the songs in *Oklahoma!* were necessary to the development of plot or character, and dance was also used in a new way to further the ideas of the work. In *West Side Story*, based on William Shakespeare's *Romeo and Juliet*, Jerome Robbins made the choreography equal in importance to the singing. *My Fair Lady* drew on its source, *Pygmalion*, by George Bernard Shaw, to bring brilliant language to the musical stage. *Cabaret* turned the musical theatre away from the carefully plotted book musicals represented by *Oklahoma!*, *West Side Story*, and *My Fair Lady* to a new form, the concept musical, in which theme expressed through scenic and performance elements is of greater importance than the plot. Stephen Sondheim contributed major innovations in subject matter and dramatic construction and set new standards for the writing of lyrics. *A Chorus Line* continued the evolution of the concept musical with its prominent use of dance to tell the stories of actors auditioning for a musical. New directions in theme and style have been provided by recent musicals such as *Bring in da Noise, Bring in da Funk*; *Rent*; *The Lion King*; and *Contact*.

The use of popular music to convey dramatic ideas and to build character and the centrality of dance in telling a story distinguish the musical theatre form. The popular music of each era has been embraced by the musical theatre, including, most recently, hip-hop and rock and roll. The choreographer-director has emerged as a new theatre creator, as exemplified by Jerome Robbins, Michael Bennett, and Susan Stroman. In *The Lion King*, it was the designer-director, Julie Taymor, who contributed a startling new vision for musical theatre by extending the actors' expressive possibilities through puppets and masks.

Topics for Discussion and Writing

1. Discuss the ways that music is an integral part of student life today. What kinds of music do you listen to or participate in creating? In addition to concerts, where music is the focus of the event, what events that are significant to you have some kind of musical association? What experiences in your life involve some kind of musical expression?

2. How does experiencing musical theatre differ from experiencing the spoken text of a nonmusical play? Draw on the musicals seen by members of the class, whether on the stage or on film, to discuss the way music changes the nature of theatrical expression and the audience's response. What kinds of material is music especially suited to?

3. What subject material and style of music in a musical production would appeal to an audience of your peers?

 For suggested readings and other resources related to this chapter, please visit www.mhhe.com/creativespirit5e.

Othello and Desdemona, played here by John Douglas Thompson and Juliet Rylance, are characters caught in a catastrophe of jealousy spiraling out of control. Their passionate love for each other is poisoned by the ruinous actions of Iago, who poses as Othello's friend and counselor. Iago is a character formed by maliciousness and spite, whose satisfaction lies in the wanton destruction of others. These three characters are among Shakespeare's most vivid creations. Arin Arbus directed this 2009 production of *Othello* for the Theatre for a New Audience.

that make up their vocabularies, and their reactions and responses to other characters. We learn more about them through what they say about themselves, what others say about them, and the physical descriptions provided by the playwright. For example, in *Angels in America*, the character of Roy Cohn is first defined through his relationship to the telephone. The playwright's description for act 1, scene 2 of the play, in which the character of Roy Cohn first appears, is as follows:

> Roy and Joe in Roy's office. Roy at an impressive desk, bare except for a very elaborate phone system, rows and rows of flashing buttons which bleep and beep and whistle incessantly, making chaotic music underneath Roy's conversations. Joe is sitting, waiting. Roy conducts business with great energy, impatience and sensual abandon: gesticulating, shouting, cajoling, crooning, playing the phone, receiver and hold button with virtuosity and love. (*Angels in America: Millennium Approaches*, act 1, scene 2)

The intensity and sensuality of the interaction with the telephone provide a vivid physicalization of the character's nature. Here is one of the great manipulators in American history, the power player par excellence, lovingly plying the tool of his trade. The telephone is his link to the other power players, and the joy of modern technology allows Cohn to expand his influence according to the number of lines he can control. Cohn's opening line is vulgarly exuberant: "I wish I was an octopus, a fucking octopus. Eight loving arms and all those suckers. Know what I mean?" And while he plays the telephone as he would a musical instrument or a lover, he is acutely aware of being watched. Cohn is always "on." He is always dramatizing himself for effect.

Plot

Character action and plot are closely intertwined. The plot is the spine of the play and is made up of all the essential actions or incidents. The significant events, the sequence and pace of character entrances, the confrontations between characters, the changes in the situation, and the outcome of the various actions contribute to the development of the plot. In *Joe Turner's Come and Gone*, the plot revolves around the arrivals of the different characters at the boardinghouse and the interactions between them. Although the actions of all of the characters are important, the most important plot incidents have to do with the arrival of Herald Loomis, his search for his wife, his conflict with Seth, and his exchanges with Bynum.

A plot structure can be very simple, as is the plot of *And the Soul Shall Dance*; or it can be tremendously complicated, as is the plot of *Angels in America: Millennium Approaches*, with its thirty-five scenes. It is through what happens in the drama that playwrights shape their ideas and their worldviews. To illustrate, let's compare the two plays by Yamauchi and Kushner.

In a realistic play, such as *And the Soul Shall Dance*, causality is extremely important to plot structure. The incidents are all closely linked in terms of both time and logic. One action leads directly to another: The characters are brought together because the bathhouse has burned down; because Oka has stolen Emiko's money, Emiko is driven to sell her kimonos. In contrast, the plot structure of *Angels in America* is more arbitrary; Kushner organizes a sequence of events that lack

the organic connections of a realistic drama. His jump-cut style juxtaposes snippets of different stories. It is only once the various plot threads begin to intertwine that we see an external logic at work.

A further example of causality in *And the Soul Shall Dance* is the inclusion of two contradictory characters, Emiko and Oka, who are married by proxy and come to live in hostile and isolated circumstances. Disaster thus becomes inevitable. The characters are set on a collision course from the outset. In contrast, there is no causal logic for the appearance of Prior 1 and Prior 2 in *Angels in America*; nor is there anything inevitable about the arrival of the Angel.

In her play, Yamauchi presents the closely interwoven details of a small domestic drama as a way of illuminating what turns out to be a moment of great significance for all the characters, and particularly for the child, Masako. In contrast, Kushner presents a cosmic drama to comment on the relationship between individual conduct and national priorities.

Language

Although language is not present in all forms of drama and although many modern theatre practitioners have modified the centrality of words in the theatre, language is one of the great sources of vitality in the theatre. Language defines the characters and gives them authenticity and credibility. The speech rhythms and vocabulary of the characters in *And the Soul Shall Dance* and *Joe Turner's Come and Gone* are critical to the audience's perception of time, place, and character history. In *Angels in America*, Tony Kushner has a number of political arguments to make. What gives the play vitality is the gutsy language of the individual characters that makes them resonate as human beings, not as puppets of the playwright delivering prepared speeches. Dramatic language must somehow appeal to the audience's imagination and contribute to the sensory appeal of the play.

The vitality of Tony Kushner's language comes from the wit and biting sarcasm of his characters. The play is energized by its brashness

The language spoken by the playwright Sarah Ruhl's characters in plays such as *Eurydice,* shown here, or *The Clean House,* is playful and poetic. Ruhl gives her characters surprising and unusual ways of expressing the difficulties of negotiating the different kinds of love in our lives. In *Eurydice,* drawn from the Orpheus myth, the character Eurydice leaves her husband on her wedding day and goes to the Underworld to seek her dead father. In this image, Eurydice (Maria Dizzia) and her father (Charles Shaw Robinson) share family memories in the 2004 production directed by Les Waters at the Berkeley Repertory Theatre.

and its humor. *Angels in America* uses a range of verbal approaches to match the odd and explosive mix of plot devices and characters. Much of the language is the intimate, domestic language of characters who share their lives, and this intimate language is at the heart of the play, the language with which the characters reveal themselves to each other. Frequently this language is sexually charged in an earthy and graphic way. At other times the language incorporates a sexual vocabulary that is hostile and manipulative; in Roy Cohn's mouth, language becomes abuse. Some of the characters also use a kind of **camp** that is associated with the gay community—lines quoted from *The Wizard of Oz, A Streetcar Named Desire,* and *Come Back, Little Sheba.* The Angel speaks in heightened, mystic poetry; Hebrew words and phrases are used to imply the Angel's ancient biblical origins. Yiddish brings a sense of Jewish tradition and history to Ethel Rosenberg and Louis. And of great importance is the intellectual quality of the language as the characters struggle with ideas and arguments:

VOICE: I can't stay. I will return.

PRIOR: Are you one of those "Follow me to the other side" voices?

Playwright David Mamet interprets American life through harsh and repetitive language. Vocabulary is reduced to essential phrases to give a concentrated sense of character and situation. In *Glengarry Glen Ross,* cutthroat real estate salesmen viciously compete for sales opportunities. Alan Alda and Liev Schreiber appear here in a 2005 revival of Mamet's play at the Royale Theatre in New York City directed by Joe Mantello.

VOICE: No. I am no nightbird. I am a messenger . . .

PRIOR: You have a beautiful voice, it sounds . . . like a viola, like a perfectly tuned, tight string, balanced, the truth. . . . Stay with me.

VOICE: Not now. Soon I will return, I will reveal myself to you; I am glorious, glorious; my heart, my countenance and my message. You must prepare.

PRIOR: For what? I don't want to . . .

VOICE: No death, no:
A marvelous work and a wonder we undertake, an edifice awry we sink plumb and straighten, a great Lie we abolish, a great

error correct, with the rule, sword and broom of Truth!

PRIOR: What are you talking about, I . . .

VOICE: I am on my way; when I am manifest, our Work begins:
Prepare for the parting of the air,
The breath, the ascent, Glory to . . .
(act 2, scene 5)

The language of Wakako Yamauchi's play is marked by poetic concentration and restraint. Within the framework of Japanese speech rhythms, the characters speak with economy and understatement. The language has none of the over-the-top verbal fireworks of *Angels*

***Spring Awakening* is a play about teenagers** struggling with issues of identity, particularly related to sexuality, and was written by Frank Wedekind in 1891. A recent production by the Atlantic Theatre of New York City in 2006 updated the play with a rock music score to create a rhythmic expression of the characters' tensions and frustrations. The music is by Duncan Sheik and the book and lyrics by Steven Sater with direction by Michael Mayer.

in America. It operates as if within a different musical scale. Because the characters function in a culture of public reserve, nuance and subtext become very important:

KIYOKO: She does! She hates me.

HANA: No. I don't think you have anything to do with it. It's this place. She hates it. This place is so lonely and alien.

KIYOKO: Then why didn't she go back? Why did they stay here?

HANA: You don't know. It's not so simple. Sometimes I think . . .

KIYOKO: Then why don't they make the best of it here? Like you?

HANA: That isn't easy either. Believe me. Sometimes . . . sometimes the longing for home . . . the longing fills me with despair. Will I never return again? Will I never see my mother, my father, my sisters again? But what can one do? There are responsibilities here . . . children . . . (pause) And another day passes . . . another month . . . another year. (act 2, scene 2)

August Wilson also brings to the theatre unique dialogue that reflects his many years of writing poetry before becoming a playwright. Individual characters are defined by their own speech patterns, and yet a strong contrapuntal structure that blends the many rhythms and patterns connects all the speeches to make an almost musical whole. Repetition is one of the devices that Wilson uses in creating these poetic rhythms. A character may repeat himself, or a phrase may be passed from character to character:

BYNUM: You a farming man, Herald Loomis? You look like you done some farming.

LOOMIS: Same as everybody. I done farmed some, yeah.

BYNUM: I used to work at farming . . . picking cotton. I reckon everybody done picked some cotton.

SETH: I ain't! I ain't never picked no cotton. I was born up here in the North. My daddy was a freedman. I ain't never even seen no cotton!

BYNUM: Mr. Loomis done picked some cotton. Ain't you, Herald Loomis? You done picked a bunch of cotton.

LOOMIS: How you know so much about me? How you know what I done? How much cotton I picked? (act 2, scene 2)

The short, probing exchanges that drive the play forward pause sometimes and open out into the storytelling of first one character and then another. As in a jazz solo improvisation, the storyteller lingers over his subject before the momentum of the play resumes.

Music

When Aristotle included music as one of the basic elements of the drama, he was referring to the musical accompaniment for the choruses and to the chorus members themselves, who chanted parts of their text in the Greek tragedies. Almost all forms of theatre use music in one way or another. In opera all of the text is sung, as it is in most forms of Asian theatre. The modern musical alternates between spoken and sung text. In the Asian theatre, musicians almost always appear onstage and are visible throughout the entire performance. Inspired by the Chinese theatre,

Bertolt Brecht saw songs as a fundamental way of commenting on the characters' situations and choices. For Robert Wilson music is essential to his strange and elusive images (see Chapter 9). Even plays that don't incorporate music in the dramatic structure use music at various points throughout the production—before the play begins, between scenes, and often during the scenes as a kind of atmospheric background or underscoring of the action. This use of music as underscoring has an enormously important function in film.

For both Wakako Yamauchi and August Wilson, music makes a significant contribution to the rhythms of their plays and the feelings that the characters try to express. Yamauchi uses Japanese folk songs to highlight the texture of the characters' lives. The songs provide a certain nostalgia and connection to a distant homeland; but—more important—they provide the characters with a kind of special text that goes beyond the accepted language of polite social interaction. So the song "And the Soul Shall Dance" provides Emiko and Masako with a basis for communicating their mutual understanding of the life of the spirit. In *Joe Turner's Come and Gone*, folk songs and blues songs are interwoven into the text. Finding one's song is a major metaphor throughout the play. The Juba is a song and dance that all the characters share. The "Joe Turner Blues" has major thematic significance and is also sung by Bynum as a way of approaching Herald Loomis. And the child, Zonia, sings a children's song about tomorrow that develops her relationship to her father's journey.

Spectacle

Spectacle comes at the end of Aristotle's discussion of dramatic structure, and he all but dismisses it as the least important and least artistic element of the drama. Needless to say, there are many who would disagree. **Spectacle** encompasses everything from acting style and the blocking or movement of the actors to the

Moliere's seventeenth century play *The Miser* is a comedy about the central character Harpagon's grotesque obsession with money. In this 2004 production, Stephen Epp, playing Harpagon, is seen at the center of the stage, driving away both his family and his servants with his rages and demands. Riccardo Hernandez has designed the set of an enormous but almost barren room, emptied out of furniture and comfort. What appears to have been a grand home is now drafty and crumbling with holes in the walls, windows without glass, a leaking roof, and broken flooring. The set directly reflects the grasping stinginess of Harpagon, who forces all the other characters to join him in his impoverished existence in spite of the fortune he keeps hidden away. Theatre de la Jeune Lune collaborated on the production of *The Miser* with the American Repertory Theater and Actors Theatre of Louisville.

most breathtaking scenic and special effects. As we have already observed, the playwright may include descriptions of the proposed spectacle, but the interpretation of a play through spectacle is in the hands of the director, the actors, the designers, and the technicians.

The playwright Henrik Ibsen (see Chapter 7) took great care in detailing the scenic elements of his plays. Particularly because individualized, realistic settings were not the norm at the time he wrote his plays, Ibsen's descriptions of the settings contributed greatly to the developing style of realism as well as made clear the metaphoric significance of each play's environment. Following is his opening description of the scene for *A Doll House*, in which the environment is very inviting but ultimately stifling:

> A comfortable room, tastefully, but not expensively furnished. A door to the right in the back wall leads to the entryway; another to the left leads to Helmer's study. Between these doors, a piano. Midway in the left-hand wall a door, and further back a window. Near the window a round table with an armchair and a

small sofa. In the right-hand wall, toward the rear, a door, and nearer the foreground a porcelain stove with two armchairs and a rocking chair beside it. Between the stove and the side door, a small table. Engravings on the walls. An etagère with china figures and other small art objects; a small bookcase with richly bound books; the floor carpeted; a fire burning in the stove. It is a winter day.[1]

In *And the Soul Shall Dance*, the playwright suggests simple settings in keeping with a realistic presentation of the material. The East West Players' production of the play with the kabuki-inspired unfolding houses and the rolling tumbleweed added a layer to the cultural context of the play by placing the Japanese theatre as a backdrop to the Japanese American experience.

For a theatre artist such as Robert Wilson, spectacle is the soul of the drama. Wilson conceptualizes with images rather than with words. His initial plan for a theatre piece consists of sequences of sketches that outline a progression of evolving images. Verbal text plays a part in his dramas, but it is a subsidiary part rather than the foundation.

The twentieth-century theatre philosopher Antonin Artaud wrote in his visionary book *The Theatre and Its Double* that the theatre is a three-dimensional space, which must be filled with a concrete poetry of its own.

> I say that the stage is a concrete physical place which asks to be filled, and to be given its own concrete language to speak.
>
>   I say that this concrete language, intended for the senses and independent of speech, has first to satisfy the senses, that there is a poetry of the senses as there is a poetry of language, and that this concrete physical language to which I refer is truly theatrical only to the degree that the thoughts it expresses are beyond the reach of the spoken language.[2]
>
>   The problem is to make space speak, to feed and furnish it; like mines laid in a wall of rock which all of a sudden turns into geysers and bouquets of stone.[3]

When Aristotle suggested a diminished place for spectacle in the drama, he may have been deferring to his teacher, the philosopher Plato, who would have eliminated the theatre altogether because of its illusionary nature. But whatever the reason for Aristotle's dismissal of spectacle, the Greek theatre set on a hillside overlooking the sea, with its masked choruses dancing and gods descending from above, had much more in common with the primacy of spatial poetry of which Artaud writes than Aristotle's evaluation admits.

THE ORGANIZATION OF THE DRAMA IN SPACE AND TIME

Some playwrights believe that a credible theatre event depends on not stretching events across too much time or too much space. In certain historical periods of the drama, place was restricted to a single setting and time to a single day. Nevertheless, most playwrights have great faith in the ability of the audience's imagination to keep up with their leaps through the calendar and around the globe. For these dramatists, space and time are organized according to the needs of their material. The plays of Shakespeare are prime examples, with their scenes that shift quickly between castle and battleground or even from nation to nation and with their events that chronicle a span of months or even years.

In *Joe Turner's Come and Gone*, August Wilson creates an action that takes place in Seth and Bertha's boardinghouse over a period of two weeks. The action of *And the Soul Shall Dance* shifts back and forth between two small houses in the Imperial Valley during a time span of about nine months. The time covered by the action of *Angels in America: Millennium Approaches* extends from October 1985 to January 1986 (although *Perestroika* takes the play all the way to 1990). And the thirty-five scenes of the play move between a multiplicity of locations within New York and even to Salt Lake City, as well as into the nightmares and hallucinations of the characters. The time is the late twentieth century, but characters emerge from the past to create a distorted sense of time just as we move in and out of realistic and expressionistic spaces. And although there seems to be a much more concentrated and realistic approach to time in *And the Soul Shall Dance* and *Joe Turner's Come and Gone* than in *Angels in America*, both of these largely realistic plays offer variations on the sequential progression of time. Because *And the Soul Shall Dance* represents Masako's memory, the play may be said to move backward in time as well as forward. And in *Joe Turner's Come and Gone*, the telling of stories interrupts a sequential, realistic sense of time and opens out moments of consciousness into an almost mythical time frame in which large, symbolic actions and legendary figures replace the everyday goings-on of the boardinghouse kitchen.

The Duration of the Performance

In addition to the fictional time created by the stage action, another factor of great importance to the shaping of the drama is the actual time or duration of the theatre event. In Western society, going to the theatre is usually considered an afternoon or evening event. We think of the theatre as providing a concentrated experience that will last from two to three hours; *And the Soul Shall Dance* and *Joe Turner's Come and Gone* fulfill this expectation. But there are also many one-act plays that may range in time from a few minutes to one hour. One-acts are frequently grouped together to form one program or one evening of theatre. Festivals of one-act plays by different playwrights have been popularized by such theatres as Actors Theatre of Louisville, which sponsors the annual Humana Festival. And in recent years various theatres have experimented with very long performances such as the combined parts of *Angels in America*, which lasts about seven hours. Other marathon presentations have featured the work of Robert Wilson and dramatizations of novels such as *Nicholas Nickleby*, by Charles Dickens. Long productions allow the audience to experience a shift in consciousness. Time seems to become

suspended as the audience members become immersed in the world of the performance. In the words of Robert Wilson:

> Most theatre deals with speeded-up time, but I use the kind of natural time in which it takes the sun to set, a cloud to change, a day to dawn. I give you time to reflect, to meditate about other things than those happening on stage. I give time and space in which to think.[4]

It is not uncommon in Asia for the audience to spend all day or all night at the theatre, or even several days at a time. For such productions, unwavering concentration is not expected of the audience. In addition to watching the performance, theatregoers socialize, eat, drink, and even nap during the course of the event.

Building the Drama: The Internal Rhythm

Within the plot structures of all dramas, no matter what form they may take, there is an internal rhythm, a relationship between the parts that involves the audience progressively in the theatre experience. As the play or performance changes and develops, the audience's understanding of and commitment to the theatre work increases. Usually this internal rhythm has to do with conflict and rising tension or suspense. What is at stake becomes increasingly important and at the same time more difficult to obtain. Expectations on the verge of fulfillment collapse, and characters must begin again with greater obstacles or change course altogether. Mistaken assumptions lead to disastrous choices that cannot be reversed or that require a more heroic effort yet. Characters' needs are set against each other in such a way that a physical or psychological battle is inevitable. Sometimes the internal rhythm of the drama has to do with the building or layering of image upon image or the accumulation of sensory experiences. The interplay between the areas of information or the incidents in the presentation of an epic story create a tension of its own. In this last section of the chapter we examine the more traditional conflict structure that is responsible for building the drama in most of the plays we have studied thus far.

Conflict, Rising Tension, and Resolution

Conflict can occur between individual characters, between groups of characters, or between characters and institutions such as governments or religion. Conflict may be internal—that is, within an individual character. Most plays have at least several layers of conflicts, and they have some form of rising tension—a series of escalating confrontations that heighten the conflict and raise the stakes. Frequently, through these confrontations, characters discover new information that changes or reverses their expectations and therefore also intensifies the urgency of their needs or motivations.

In *And the Soul Shall Dance*, the conflict between the Okas generates rising tension that draws in all the other characters. Some of the hostility we witness directly in their two violent scenes; some we learn of through Kiyoko's distraught

response when she escapes in the middle of the night to seek the Muratas' assistance. In the final confrontation between Oka and Emiko, Oka reveals that he has spent Emiko's savings on Kiyoko. With this terrible reversal of her situation, the urgency of Emiko's motivation increases dramatically. She must now part with her only real treasures if she is to retain any hope of returning to Japan. Thus we have the climactic scene in which Emiko tries to sell her kimonos to Hana and Masako.

In *Topdog/Underdog* by Suzan-Lori Parks, the Pulitzer Prize–winning play for 2002, two brothers search for their place in America and in their own family. Challenging each other through the street con game three-card monte, the brothers engage in a deadly battle of rising tensions. Here Mos Def and Jeffrey Wright appear in the production at the Public Theater directed by George C. Wolfe in 2002.

In Shakespeare's *All's Well That Ends Well* Helena, Kate Forbes, and Bertram, Lucas Hall, share an uneasy moment in their complicated relationship. *All's Well* is a comedy that has darker undertones of illness, unrequited love, and death, which are brought out in this 2006 production directed by Darko Tresnjak for the Theater for a New Audience in New York.

In contrast to tragedy, comedy looks to the continuation of life rather than to its finality. In spite of all the pitfalls and the setbacks, in spite of the pettiness of human behavior and our foolish self-importance, life goes on. Comedy focuses on the success of generations rather than on the mortality of the individual. Through love and rebirth, there is continuance.

The plot of comedy usually begins with an outrageous idea or a fantastic scheme that disrupts the normal workings of the community.

Incongruous events are frequently complicated by mistaken identity and misunderstandings. Gullibility, greed, egotism, and hypocrisy appear to rule the day. Lovers are separated, fortunes are lost, and chaos seems to reign supreme. But common sense prevails, the misunderstandings are resolved, and the reconciliation of all the separated factions leads to the affirmation of true love. Comedies frequently end in marriage or engagements.

Comedy exists to make us laugh. But the brilliance of comedy lies in its ability to take on the most serious subjects while evoking the deepest laughter. Perhaps we laugh hardest at the exposure of things that concern us the most or, as Bill Irwin has observed, that frighten us the most. War, religion, politics, generational conflict, and sexual relationships are common subjects of comedy.

Origins in Greek Drama

The original designations of tragedy and comedy in the theatre were arrived at simply. In the early Greek theatre, all plays that dealt with lofty and serious subjects were called tragedies. The word *tragedy* is derived from the Greek word that means "goat song"—a song that was sung in honor of Dionysus. Plays that dealt with human weakness and folly were called comedies.

The Greeks were certainly aware of the proximity of tragedy and comedy in describing human experience. Originally, comedies were performed as companion pieces to tragedies to complete the picture of human endeavor. The tragic side looked to the human actor engaged in noble causes. The comic side revealed that underneath the heroic guise, humans are terrified and capable of the most ridiculous posturing and mistakes. In the Greek theatre the genres were maintained as separate but complementary entities. In contrast, contemporary playwrights frequently mix comic and tragic elements in the same play because that approach seems to most effectively reflect their understanding of life's rhythms in today's world.

Aristotle on Tragedy and Comedy

In his series of lectures that were collected under the title *The Poetics* (see Chapter 12), Aristotle described the nature of tragedy. In defining tragedy, he included a few asides on the nature of comedy. Aristotle summarized the distinction between tragedy and comedy in two statements. In the first he wrote:

> Comedy aims at representing men as worse,
> Tragedy as better than in actual life.[2]

We may interpret "better than in actual life" to mean that the characters in tragedy come from noble houses. And Aristotle in fact writes later in *The Poetics* that a tragic character must be "highly renowned and prosperous."[3] Tragic characters, by their royal birth, are distinguished from ordinary citizens. But Aristotle's "better" refers more significantly to character, behavior, and choices. In tragic characters, nobility of conduct corresponds to nobility of position.

In his second statement on comedy Aristotle wrote:

> Comedy is, as we have said, an imitation of characters of a lower type—not, however, in the full sense of the word bad, the Ludicrous being merely a subdivision of the ugly. It consists in some defect or ugliness which is not painful or destructive. To take an obvious example, the comic mask is ugly and distorted, but does not imply pain.[4]

Comedy's "imitation of characters of a lower type" suggests conduct that may make audience members feel superior—or that may make them recognize themselves at their worst. Aristotle uses the word *ludicrous* to further delineate the particular area of behavior comedy addresses. *Ludicrous* implies the contradictions in life that make our efforts ridiculous. When Harpo Marx uses huge scissors to cut off pieces of a formal dinner jacket worn by a pompous diplomat while he is conducting serious business, we are in the realm of the ludicrous. Ludicrous has to do with the loss of control, with the incongruous, with the undermining of whatever we take too seriously.

COMEDY: A WORLD WITHOUT PAIN In his second statement, Aristotle made another simple observation about comedy that has far greater significance than the words communicate at first reading: "It consists in some defect or ugliness which is not painful or destructive. To take an obvious example, the comic mask is ugly and distorted, but does not imply pain." The implication here is that comic characters may do all kinds of ridiculous things and may suffer temporary losses, but they are not in pain. And most particularly, the audience does not respond to them as if they were suffering. When we laugh in the theatre, we laugh at the incongruous, we laugh at the foolish, we laugh at ourselves, but we do not laugh if we believe that people are genuinely in pain.

Tragedy: Catharsis and Awareness

The audience's experience in tragedy is quite different from that in comedy. In tragedy we feel the pain and suffering of the characters intensely. The audience empathizes with the tragic characters and shares in their inner journeys. The identification with the suffering in tragedy brings about an emotional release or cleansing of the spirit that is referred to as catharsis. Catharsis is one of the most discussed and debated concepts in the study of drama. To understand catharsis, imagine that you have witnessed an ordeal and have been caught up in the terrible tensions of the situation. When those conflicts and tensions are finally resolved, you feel both relief and heightened awareness. The same emotional experience occurs in tragedy: the tragic character comes to a new understanding or a greater wisdom through his or her suffering, and we in the audience come to a new awareness of life's meaning. This experience that combines emotional sensitivity with insight into life's most difficult questions brings us a degree of exhilaration at the same time that we are deeply moved by the struggle we have witnessed.

Another famous tragic drama of generational conflict is Sophocles' *Electra*, which tells the story of Electra's determination to revenge herself on her mother, Clytaemnestra, for the death of her father, Agamemnon. The plot of Electra is drawn from the same material as the plot of *The Oresteia* described in this chapter. The contemporary playwright Luis Alfaro has adapted *Electra* in a new version he has titled *Electricidad* and set in the middle of gang warfare in Southern California. In this photograph, the brother of Electricidad, Orestes, played by Maximino Arciniega Jr., considers the murder that his sister is asking him to commit in a 2006 production at the Goodman Theatre in Chicago.

Romeo and Juliet by **William Shakespeare** is a tragedy of young lovers separated by their feuding families. While trying to escape together, misunderstandings bring about both of their deaths. Here a family member Paris, played by Lee Mark Nelson, comes upon the apparently dead body of Juliet, played by Christine Marie Brown, in a 2004 production at the Guthrie Theater in Minneapolis directed by Ethan McSweeney.

Plot Summaries of Selected Tragedies

Today we are surrounded by comedies—on the stage, on television, and in the movies. We have abundant material to draw on in our attempt to identify the distinguishing qualities of comedy. But we have only a generalized sense of the "tragic," which we tend to think of in terms of painful incidents that end in loss, disaster, or death. We do not have a large, well-known body of contemporary theatre works to create a frame of reference for identifying that part of human experience explored by tragedy.

To provide a partial foundation for our discussion of tragedy, we include here brief plot summaries of the plays most frequently cited in discussions of tragedy. To the tragedies listed, written in either the fifth century B.C.E. or Elizabethan England, could be added more plays from either of these periods as well as the

tragedies of Racine, written in seventeenth-century France. But even with these additions, we quickly see that a huge area of literary and dramatic study is based on a very small sample of plays.

OEDIPUS REX (SOPHOCLES)

When Oedipus is a young man, he is told by an oracle that he is fated to kill his father and marry his mother and have children with her. Horrified at such a future, he leaves the home and kingdom of his parents, not knowing that he is, in fact, an adopted child. Unwittingly, he travels to the city of his actual parents, where the prophecy comes true. Oedipus murders his father King Laius and marries his mother Queen Jocasta. Because Laius is dead, the people of Thebes choose Oedipus to be their new king. The play focuses on the day, many years after Oedipus's arrival in Thebes, the true city of his birth, that Oedipus comes to know who he really is.

ANTIGONE (SOPHOCLES)

The sons of Oedipus, Eteocles and Polyneices, have both been killed battling each other for the throne. Their uncle, Creon, declares that one is a hero and will be buried appropriately and that the other is a traitor and will be left unburied with his remains to be destroyed by the elements. Creon, who has become the king on the death of Oedipus's sons, further decrees that anyone attempting to bury the abandoned body will be stoned to death. The young men's sister, Antigone, refuses to obey her uncle's decree and performs burial rites for her brother. Creon has Antigone imprisoned in a cave, where she commits suicide.

THE ORESTEIA (AESCHYLUS)

Agamemnon, the Greek king and general who leads the Greek army against Troy in the ten-year Trojan war, is killed by his wife, Clytaemnestra, on his return from the war. Clytaemnestra is then killed by her son, Orestes, as revenge for his father's death. Orestes is tried for murder in a trial by jury and acquitted.

HAMLET (SHAKESPEARE)

Hamlet's father, King Hamlet, is murdered by his uncle Claudius, who is the dead king's brother. Claudius then marries Hamlet's mother, Gertrude, and takes the throne of Denmark. Young Prince Hamlet fears that his uncle has murdered his father but lacks conclusive proof. In the course of Hamlet's attempt to prove his uncle a murderer and avenge his father's death, violence claims eight lives, including those of Hamlet, Claudius, and Gertrude.

MACBETH (SHAKESPEARE)

Macbeth is presented with visions of future power by three witches whom he meets on the heath. The witches' mysterious prophecies fire his own ambitions. He and his wife Lady Macbeth embark on a course of murder, beginning with the reigning king, that ultimately leads to their downfall.

KING LEAR (SHAKESPEARE)

Seeking to bind his three daughters more closely to him, King Lear divides up his kingdom and bestows what would be his children's inheritance in advance of his death. He announces the division of his kingdom in a public ceremony, in which he expects his daughters to declare their love for him above all else. His treacherous older daughters easily proclaim the adulation they know he awaits. However, Cordelia, his youngest daughter (for whom the ceremony is probably staged), refuses to compromise herself with false flattery to surpass her sisters. Lear banishes Cordelia, opening the way for a vicious power struggle that results in the deaths of both Lear and Cordelia.

Common Themes of Tragedy

A STRUGGLE OVER SUCCESSION As these six plot summaries show, the major tragedies all deal with power struggles over succession. Oedipus unknowingly kills the legitimate king, his father, and then taints his own children and heirs through incest. Creon imprisons his rebellious niece, Antigone, to consolidate his own power as king following the deaths of the two legitimate heirs to the throne. Clytaemnestra kills her husband to avenge the death of their daughter and then assumes the leadership of the state; Orestes, Clytaemnestra's son, kills his mother to reclaim the throne he believes by right should be his. Claudius and Macbeth both scheme for power and murder the legitimate king. By giving up his power prematurely, King Lear unleashes a bloody struggle for control of the kingdom. And in *Medea*, Jason leaves his wife to form a new marital alliance that will make him successor to the throne of the aging king of Corinth.

Although succession is not necessarily the primary focus of tragedy, it is integral to many of the works of the past that we categorize as tragedy. A crisis over succession exposes a society at its most vulnerable. Tragedy explores a breakdown or challenge to a society's system of values. And it is during these times of vulnerability that the moral choices of the characters are the most difficult and significant.

A RUPTURING OF FAMILY AND SOCIETAL BONDS Classical tragedies test the moral foundations of human civilization. Tragedies take place when the bonds that tie human society together are ruptured. The family is almost always at the center of tragedy, and it is a royal family that represents both the larger society and the essential relationships between family members. Tragic characters become engaged in conflict leading to or in response to the transgression of principles deemed sacred by the community. All the major tragedies involve royal or aristocratic characters who kill members of their own families. The health or disruption in the royal family is intricately tied to the social and political health of the community.

The relationship of the tragic characters to this wrenching of fundamental values changes from play to play and playwright to playwright. Some characters—such as Oedipus, unknowingly; and King Lear, knowingly—initiate all

ARTISTIC FOUNDATIONS •••

Characteristics of Tragedy

- Tragedy deals with serious subjects and characters who are confronted with their own mortality.
- Many tragic plots revolve around a crisis over succession to a throne, representing a rupture in the bonds that tie families and society together.
- Murder and death occur frequently in tragedy and usually as a result of the transgression of sacred principles.
- Tragic characters come from aristocratic or royal families and usually exhibit admirable behavior.
- Tragic characters act alone and take responsibility for their choices and actions.
- The audience empathizes with tragic characters, identifies with their suffering, and often experiences catharsis.

the events that lead to catastrophe. Others, such as Hamlet and Antigone, must respond to situations initiated by others. What the characters share is an unwillingness to let other characters or circumstances shape their individual destinies. They are determined, even at the cost of their own lives and sometimes the lives of others, to find a course of action that is true to their own natures and true to a value system as they understand it. Some of them, such as King Lear, Creon, and Macbeth, make enormous errors of judgment or miscalculations. Some, such as Oedipus, are caught in such a tangled web that extrication is impossible. Some, such as Hamlet and Antigone, give their lives to restore justice. For all these tragic characters, great suffering results from the actions they choose, and through that suffering comes not only wisdom but also self-determination. They have defined themselves.

ISOLATION OF THE TRAGIC CHARACTER Whereas comedies look at characters as part of a social unit, tragedies examine characters who stand alone. Hamlet was part of the court of Denmark before the play opens; he had family, friends, a woman who loved him, and the highest regard of the people of Denmark. Part of his tragedy is that he becomes increasingly isolated as he pursues his course of action. His father is dead. He is betrayed by his friends Rosencrantz and Guildenstern, attacked by his uncle Claudius, rejected by Ophelia, and abandoned by his mother. In *Medea* the central character is viewed as an outsider who should be banished.

Isolated, the tragic hero or character struggles with a hideous situation: Hamlet's father has been murdered, and the apparent murderer now wears the crown and has married Hamlet's mother; the body of Antigone's brother lies unburied, to be torn apart by wild dogs and vultures, and the king has decreed that anyone burying the body will be stoned to death; Oedipus's people are dying of plague because an old murder goes unpunished; Medea's husband has left her for another woman and she has become a social outcast. The tragic character determines to follow his or her own conscience in addressing these situations rather than accept the solutions of others or the supposed decrees of fate.

THE ACCEPTANCE OF RESPONSIBILITY Although the circumstances with which they are presented are not always of their own making, tragic characters take full responsibility for their actions. Tragedy is about human potential and our ability to choose for ourselves and take responsibility for the consequences of those choices. It is no coincidence that the great tragedies were written in periods of optimism about the ability of human beings to control their own destinies. The fifth century B.C.E. saw the rise of both Athenian democracy and the Athenian empire. In Shakespeare's time, the English navy defeated the Spanish armada and then pursued Queen Elizabeth's goals of building an empire.

Can Tragedy Exist Today?

Because the drama has changed and our philosophical perspective has changed, we might question whether tragedy can exist today. Certainly, the tragedies that we use as our reference points were written during times when dramatists saw royal characters rather than common characters as the best personages to convey their meaning. These characters were seen as larger than life as they undertook epic struggles with the universe. They spoke a poetic, highly charged language that also lifted them out of the realm of ordinary existence. And they were further enlarged by their relationship to myths or legends. They were characters ready to fight the gods or fate.

Today, much of our drama frames human action in realistic terms and examines the struggles of average people to overcome economic and social problems. Our sense of the universe and our place in it has changed. The vastness of the universe defies comprehension; human beings have become no more than flecks barely registering on the surface of endless space and time. Because so much of our lives seems out of our control, much of today's nonrealistic drama has focused on the absurd, on our inability to give meaning to our brief passage on the planet. The idea of taking responsibility for our actions, which is at the heart of tragedy, may seem impossible or irrelevant.

If indeed tragedy is possible today, it cannot be produced from the models of Greek or Elizabethan tragedy. It will have to take a different course. The very nature of democracy, for example, precludes a tragedy of the aristocracy. In the mid-twentieth century several playwrights, including Arthur Miller and Eugene O'Neill, contributed to an American idea of tragedy. And, as part of his epic cycle on America, the playwright August Wilson provides tantalizing

Medea is so obsessed with revenging herself on Jason for his lack of fidelity that she kills their children. At the end of the play, Medea (Fiona Shaw) cradles the body of one of her dead sons while Jason (Jonathan Cake) denounces her actions. But he is too late to stop the course of events that his duplicity set in motion. The tragedy, *Medea,* was produced by the Abbey Theatre in 2002 and directed by Deborah Warner.

possibilities of a tragic view in *Joe Turner's Come and Gone.* The central figure, Herald Loomis, has a larger-than-life quality that comes from both the intensity of his feelings and the symbolic nature of his character. And he speaks a language that is poetic and charged. His name, Herald Loomis, suggests that he brings redemption; he is the "herald" of the light. He emerges from a background of slavery and the chain gang, a background comparable to the harrowing circumstances of classical tragedy.

Just as the tragic figures of ancient Greece or Elizabethan England represented their communities, so Herald Loomis represents his community—all of the enslaved. He endures terrible suffering, and through that suffering he comes to wisdom. Like Oedipus, he is searching for himself, and he reviews his past and those closest to him as he comes to recognize and take his place in the world. Although, like Hamlet, much of his suffering is not of his own making, the play focuses on his spiritual crisis, for which he *is* responsible. And ultimately he chooses the path of self-determination, acting symbolically when he cuts himself. Freedom is central to classical tragedy, and it is central to Herald Loomis. He is not waiting for someone else to bleed or suffer for him. He will suffer for himself. And in that moment of accepting himself, he discharges the spectral chains of Joe Turner.

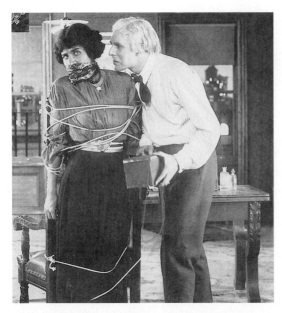

Early film made the most of melodramatic plots in which young women were threatened by villains. The scene depicted here comes from a film of 1919: *Chelsea 7750*. Although such damsel-in-distress scenes are the most vivid representations of melodramatic form, melodrama encompasses a range of plots in which good and evil are clearly opposed.

In its own way, *Joe Turner's Come and Gone* may also deal with the struggle over succession. Herald Loomis may not be a king, but he is a representative of a people enslaved by another people. By throwing off the oppressor and reclaiming himself, Herald Loomis asserts the rights of black people to participate fully in society. His actions help bring change in succession to the rights of the nation. August Wilson places his characters in a world that has meaning and a moral framework.

MELODRAMA

We may see very little tragedy in the theatre and films of today, yet we do see a great deal of another genre, **melodrama.** Melodrama has its origins in very simple conflicts of good and evil. Melodrama externalizes the cause of our problems; there is little internal conflict or probing of moral issues. The nature of good and evil is clear at the outset. The hero may have terrifying obstacles to overcome, but he himself is not one of them; nor does he set in motion the forces that threaten him. The hero is identified as male in this case because in contemporary melodrama, women usually still play supporting roles.

In early melodrama, a helpless young woman would be held hostage in some gruesome way by an obvious villain—only to be rescued at the last possible moment by a courageous and virtuous young man. This was a celebrated formula on the early American stage that has made a transition very easily and happily and largely unchanged into Hollywood movies. Steven Spielberg and George Lucas have based much of their film careers on this formula. A lively version of the damsel in distress takes place in the third film of George Lucas's *Star Wars* trilogy, *Return of the Jedi*. Princess Leia and Han Solo have been taken captive by the evil and disgusting Jabba the Hutt. Solo, weak and blinded from having been imprisoned in ice, is temporarily unable to defend Leia from the vile Jabba, "the slimy piece of worm-ridden filth." Leia, for all her modern courage and independence, is dressed seductively in a bikini with a metal collar and chain about her neck. Jabba holds the chain and uses it to pull Leia closer to his voluminous flesh. It is a particularly gross version of the villain taking advantage of the heroine, a new way of tying her to the railroad tracks. At this point Luke Skywalker, now a Jedi knight, arrives. But he must face more evil before he can win the release of his friends. First he must outwit the horrible Rancor, and then they must all take on the dreaded Sarlac, the vast, pulsing mouth on the desert floor, filled with hundreds of tusk-like teeth. As the battle builds, the well-known *Star Wars* theme music supports the action. Like the early stage melodramas from which the name of this genre is taken, music is an

The Marx Brothers honed their acting skills in vaudeville before turning their special brand of lunacy into films. Animals were frequently featured as part of their performance onstage and in the movies. The French theatre practitioners Antonin Artaud and Samuel Beckett acknowledged the Marx Brothers' influence on their own work well before the comedy team was taken seriously in the United States. Major films of the Marx Brothers include *Duck Soup* and *A Night at the Opera*.

farce would flourish in a nation whose origins are revolutionary and whose goals are democratic. The actors of farce rebel against notions of aristocracy, against the imposition of high culture, against institutions that have lost touch with the people, against all forms of arbitrary rules and hierarchical power structures.

Jim Carrey is an actor known for creating characters who have a wild, anarchic streak. He performs with a highly energized physical abandon that seems to defy the bodily limitations of most humans. In films such as *The Mask* (1994)

and *Liar Liar* (1997) he challenges authority with an attitude of defiance well suited to contemporary farce. His film *The Mask* offers another model of a typical plot in farce. Carrey's character, Stanley Ipkiss, is the little man at the bottom of the ladder at the bank where he works. He is taken advantage of by everyone, abused by his landlady, swindled by his auto mechanics. He wears the ultimate in "geek" ties and pajamas. But by placing a mysterious mask on his face, Carrey breaks through all the social restraint of his "Mr. Nice Guy" role, throws caution to the

Stanley Ipkiss, played by Jim Carrey, re-creates himself as a bizarre, but romantic, hero dancing with Cameron Diaz in *The Mask*. The masked character fulfills the fantasies of the nice guy who always finishes last.

wind, and becomes the embodiment of physical and spiritual anarchy. With a ludicrous green face and an outrageously suave wardrobe, he robs the bank where he works, defeats the town gangsters, and has the police dancing in the streets while he plays the maracas in his persona as "Cuban Pete." With the broadest possible physical humor, sometimes even rendered through cartoon images, he revenges himself on everyone who previously pushed him around. Carrey's character says of the power of the mask, "It brings your innermost desires to life." The same could be said of farce.

WRITING ABOUT THE THEATRE

The unique structural elements of the drama discussed in Chapter 12 and the views of human existence that shape dramatic genres are foundational for the work of the playwright. The study of structure and genre is also essential to the work of two other theatre writers: the dramaturg and the critic. The dramaturg and the critic are particularly concerned with analyzing the work of the playwright in connection with the production of plays. They seek to understand what distinguishes the ideas in the play and what distinguishes the play as a work of art. Frequently dramaturgs and critics have similar backgrounds and interests. They must both be broadly educated in the theatre and be strong and creative writers. In fact, the same individual may work sometimes as a dramaturg and sometimes as a critic. For example, Michael Feingold is a critic for *The Village Voice* and in 2006 he also served as the dramaturg for the production of *All's Well That Ends Well* pictured in this chapter. However, the two roles are distinctly different and demand different points of view.

The dramaturg can be seen as a writer and thinker engaged at the beginning of theatre making, whereas the critic participates at the end. The dramaturg is part of the collaborative process of creating the work; the critic assesses the work when it is performed onstage for an audience. The dramaturg is on the inside, the critic on the outside. But the dramaturg must maintain a certain independence if he or she is to serve the production well. And the critic must be an engaged and respectful member of the larger theatre community in order to be effective, while remaining entirely independent of the production process. Michael Feingold could not review the production for which he was dramaturg. We now consider the contributions of these two important theatre writers who serve both theatre practitioners and theatre audiences.

Passing Strange (2007) is a new musical by the composer and performer Stew, produced at the Public Theater where one of Oskar Eustis's primary goals as artistic director is the development of new work. "On a piece like *Passing Strange* it started with a singer in Joe's Pub to whom we said, 'Have you ever thought of making a theatre piece out of your songs?' and he said, 'I've never been to a piece of theatre.' Now he's opening on Broadway next month. It takes three and a half years to do that. You invest the time and figure out the way for each particular art form."[7]

The Dramaturg

More and more frequently, resident theatre companies—organizations producing a season of plays—employ at least one staff member who works as a dramaturg. The dramaturg is an ongoing member of the company and is involved continuously with the selection of plays and research and writing about those plays. Although the dramaturg is a relatively new position in the American theatre, the idea of the dramaturg is much older; it is usually credited to the German critic G. E. Lessing, who wrote in the late eighteenth century. Stephen Weeks, who is both a dramaturg and a teacher of dramaturgy and playwriting, sees the dramaturg as occupying a unique position in a theatre organization:

> Dramaturgy is a fluid enterprise and dramaturgs wear many hats. Whereas we might think of actors or directors as having specific, well-defined responsibilities, the dramaturg is a theatrical generalist. The dramaturg makes connections, starts conversations, builds bridges.[8]

In Chapter 10, we discussed the work of Oskar Eustis, who served as the dramaturg at the Eureka Theatre in San Francisco and collaborated with the playwright Tony Kushner on the development of *Angels in America*. Eustis is now the artistic director of the Public Theater in New York

City. As dramaturg at the Eureka Theatre, he focused on encouraging the development of new plays and bringing those plays into production. Like Eustis, dramaturgs at other theatre companies provide feedback and assistance to playwrights who are creating new work; and, as Stephen Weeks observes, they must demonstrate great sensitivity to the needs of the play and the needs of the playwright:

> The goal is usually to assist the writer to realize his or her vision for the play. This is a complex task, and the dramaturg might need to serve as a guide, a cheerleader, a surrogate audience member, a critic, or all of these things. A good dramaturg will also know when to leave the playwright to his or her own devices and good judgment.

Tom Bryant, dramaturg for *Apollo*, contrasts the perspective of the dramaturg with that of the director, who is also often concerned with new play development.

> Directors tend to be very pragmatic. They have to focus on immediate production results. Given production demands, directors tend to ask, "What can I do with this text onstage? What kind of actor choices would I make here? What kind of choices would the designers make?" These are all production-oriented choices. The dramaturg looks at the text, beyond the current production choices, and asks, "Does this work as a scene? Does this work as an act? Is there strong momentum here?" They think beyond the current production to the play's future productions. When directors face literary issues in a script they sometimes tend to compensate for the material by production adjustments. They think, "Oh, this isn't working so well. Maybe what I'll do is create a piece of staging that really makes the rhythm faster here." This may solve the problem in the current production but it doesn't necessarily solve the inherent literary problem in terms of the text of the play. So part of what the specialization in dramaturgy becomes is helping the playwright fix those problems on the page.[9]

The dramaturg also works with the artistic director of the theatre to select a provocative and complementary group of plays for the season and must have a wide knowledge of classical as well as recent plays. Another part of the dramaturg's work is to research background materials related to a particular play—first to provide necessary information to the director and the actors, and then to write introductory material for the audience to be presented in the program or possibly in a lobby display. Research that the

---

WORKING IN THE THEATRE •••

Summary of the Dramaturg's Responsibilities

- To keep up with developments in the drama.
- To assist playwrights in the development of new plays.
- To advise the artistic director on selecting plays.
- To study the play text.
- To research appropriate historical materials for the director, designers, and actors.
- To research production history.
- To provide assistance with textual analysis and meaning of words.
- To assist with cuts or adaptation of the text if appropriate.
- To attend rehearsals and provide the director with feedback.
- To write program notes.
- To prepare lobby displays.
- To contribute to public relations materials.
- To lead discussions before or after the show.

Necessary Skills and Talents of the Dramaturg

- Love of dramatic literature.
- Fascination with research.
- Wide knowledge of dramatic literature and theatre history.
- Strong analytical skills.
- Strong writing skills.
- Commitment to collaborative work.
- Teaching skills.
- Ability to clearly articulate observations made in rehearsals.

dramaturg does for the theatre company may be presented through discussion or informally written notes or summaries. Dramaturgs frequently participate in the table work sessions at the beginning of the rehearsal period to explain the historical and philosophical background of the play and to provide resource materials such as photographs, maps, and biographies. They may also be responsible for locating highly specialized information. For example, Nilo Cruz's Pulitzer Prize–winning play *Anna in the Tropics* takes place in a cigar factory, and the actors must learn how to roll cigars. The dramaturg may arrange for a cigar maker to come to one or more rehearsals to demonstrate these skills. The areas of research the dramaturg may be called upon to pursue are limitless.

Once the rehearsal process is under way, the dramaturg must engage in more formal writing for the program and, sometimes, for lobby displays. The lobby display is being used by an increasing number of theatres to expand the amount of contextual information available to audience members. The lobby display also offers the dramaturg an opportunity to use visual materials such as photographs, historical objects, and video clips to support written statements. In the program notes and the lobby display, the dramaturg communicates why the company has chosen to do a particular play and why this play is important for the community that makes up the audience. Background materials are presented to enrich the audience's understanding of the significance of the events in the play. Most of all, the dramaturg shares the excitement that the theatre company feels in undertaking the production, an excitement that should be infectious for the audience.

The Critic

The critic has been in existence almost as long as there has been theatre. Aristotle's writing on drama, which has been part of our discussion of structure and genre, is considered a work of criticism. In *The Poetics*, Aristotle writes about what makes a successful and admirable play. Over the centuries, critics have followed Aristotle with heated arguments about what makes good theatre or art and what place theatre should have in a particular society. Most critics are passionate about their views and recognize something vital and essential in the theatre, although they have strongly divided opinions about what the essence of good theatre is.

Sometimes a critic's ideas are formulated slowly and represent a cumulative process of evaluation. But often criticism is written quickly, particularly when it takes the form of a review composed immediately following a play's opening to be published in a newspaper within a day or two. Some writers and theatre practitioners would separate critics and reviewers into different categories, concluding that the role of the critic is to try to answer larger questions about the significance of a work of theatre than a reviewer can tackle in the sprint to the deadline. But with that reservation in mind, we will examine the role of the contemporary critic in relationship to the theatre.

When the dramaturg writes a program note or prepares a lobby display, it is quite clear who the targeted readers are: the people who have chosen to come to see this particular play. And when the dramaturg provides analysis and research early on in the production process, he or she knows the director and the actors for whom that work is intended and how it is to be used. It is less clear for whom the critic is writing, and so it is profitable to explore who the critic's audience is in order to assess the role the critic plays.

The most immediate source in which a critic may publish an article or review in response to a play is a newspaper, a magazine, or an online site. The readers of this publication may or may not become audience members, and many of them will look to a review to provide guidance about whether a production is worth their time and money. In this regard the review functions as advice for the consumer and there is no doubt that commentary published immediately after a play opens is expected to offer judgment about the production's overall merit. But the critic has a larger obligation to the general reader than merely to indicate thumbs-up or thumbs-down.

Julius Novick, a well-known critic who has spent decades writing about the theatre, sees his responsibility as communicating the experience of the performance as fully as possible to the reader who has not yet seen the play:

> But our obligation and our joy as writers is
> to convey what we have seen and heard and
> thought and felt at the theatre, as truthfully
> and vividly, as gracefully and clearly, and with
> as deep an understanding as we can, and, if
> possible, to refract the truth about the show
> we've just seen through our individual selves
> to a larger truth about the theatre and a still
> larger truth about the world.[10]

WORKING IN THE THEATRE •••

Summary of the Critic's Responsibilities

- To do appropriate preparation before the performance such as reading the play and researching background on the play, playwright, or performance style.
- To attend the performance in an alert and receptive state of mind.
- To write a review that focuses on the particular production, not the preferences or cleverness of the reviewer.
- To provide readers with a vivid sense of the audience's experience and the style and ideas of the play and the production.
- To provide theatre practitioners with constructive feedback about their work.
- To engage in a public dialogue about the significance of work being done in the theatre.

In Novick's judgment the critic must be open and sensitive to the theatre event and then be ready to put that experience into words in order to distill its meaning. There is also a recognition that describing and interpreting one's own experience of an event is not a simple matter. Writing good criticism is itself an art form, requiring creative choices and drawing the significant parts into a coherent whole.

As a way of organizing one's responses to a performance, Novick proposes that the critic answer four questions.

1. What is the work itself trying to do?
2. How well has it done it?
3. Was it worth doing?
4. Why was it or wasn't it worth doing?

And he says of the fourth question, "That's where the bones are buried. That can get us into the relation between the work and the world, the subject to which all the great critics are drawn."[11] In these questions, Novick leads the critic away from judging a theatre work according to personal preference and instead asks the critic to consider the terms of the play itself and the production of that play.

Furthermore, when critics ask Novick's four questions, they are setting up an apparatus to address a second set of readers in addition to potential audience members: the theatre practitioners who have produced the play. A productive review, which serves the theatre profession well, gives the practitioners vital feedback about how successfully they communicated their ideas and how their work was received. Directors, actors, and designers work very hard to craft their storytelling and expressive stage metaphors. A thoughtful response from an insightful critic can be very important to the theatre artists in assessing the impact of their work. The actor Billy Crudup says he hopes that critics will engage in a dialogue with the production by answering important questions for him:

> What was successful? What wasn't successful? Why? Is that interpretation an interesting interpretation?[12]

Of course, all theatre practitioners seek approval of their stage efforts. But the responsible critic contributes far more to the health of the theatre by considering the artistic choices made than by merely announcing which actor was a hit and which one wasn't and whether the scenery and costumes were dazzling.

Although critics are writing most obviously for those who are involved with a production as audience members or producers, they are also participating in a larger conversation about art and culture that extends to many people beyond the immediate radius of a particular production. Criticism is read by those interested in the arts and in the relationship between art and society whether they are other critics, appreciators of art, producers of art, or academics and students of all backgrounds. Frank Rich was for many years the head theatre critic of the *New York Times*. He now writes what may be called cultural criticism that is particularly concerned with the

direction of our country and the various forces that affect political decision making. He draws heavily on his involvement with the theatre to explain contemporary actions through comparisons with characters of great playwrights and by considering political performances in light of the way actors construct stage identities.

Through their writing, critics also address readers of the future by creating a record of the impact of the theatre performance. One of the defining factors of theatre production is its nature as a live event. As we observed at the beginning of the book, the theatre actually exists only during the performance itself with an audience present. Films are by their very nature preserved for future generations. A theatre performance can be documented through video or film, but that documentation does not re-create the actual

---

ARTISTIC FOUNDATIONS •••

The Necessary Skills and Talents of the Critic

- Enthusiasm for the theatre.
- Belief in the importance of the arts in the life of the community.
- Wide knowledge of dramatic literature and theatre history.
- Understanding of the contributions of playwrights, directors, actors, and designers.
- Strong writing skills.
- Ability to communicate the experience of the theatre performance through lively, accessible language.
- Ability to understand symbolic and metaphorical constructs.
- Ability to interpret the meaning of a play in relation to philosophical, cultural, or political concerns of the community.
- Ability to generate interest and excitement about the theatre for readers.

event of the performance. By exploring the visual, aural, kinesthetic, emotional and intellectual experience of being an audience member at a particular performance, the critic leaves a written impression, however imperfect, of the nuances and excitement communicated by the actors' work. This written record of the most eloquent details of the performance offers students of the art of theatre the chance to understand what was meaningful in a given time and place, years after the actors and designers who made the work no longer hold forth on the stage.

••• TWO REVIEWS OF *MEDEA*

Following are two reviews of contemporary productions of the Greek tragedy *Medea*. The first review considers the production done by the Classical Theatre of Harlem; the second evaluates the production done by the Abbey Theatre of Ireland. Both reviews were published in *The New York Times* in 2002. The reviews of *Medea* are included here because they allow us to continue our discussion of this play begun in Chapter 2 in the section on ancient Greek theatre and continued in this chapter's examination of genre and tragedy. The reviews also illustrate the manner in which two different critics approach constructing a review. In each case, the critic creates a vivid sense of the performance by describing the work of the actors and the arrangement of the physical space. Both critics also tell us what distinguishes these productions and how the play's conflicts are interpreted for modern audiences. The reviews demonstrate that the critics have studied the play, its history, and other productions in order to be authoritative in assessing the work of the theatre companies involved.

Passions of *Medea*, Brought up to Date

By D. J. R. Bruckner, *The New York Times*, April 16, 2002

Every performance of "Medea" is an adaptation. Euripides' text is a highly selective commentary on a hugely popular series of legends about this semidivine psychotic, and we can only dimly perceive aspects of what he meant to say about them. We also have far from perfect knowledge of stagecraft in the fifth century B.C. So even those rare performances given in Euripides' own language are adaptations.

That said, the one adapted and directed by Alfred Preisser for the Classical Theatre of Harlem, running until April 28 at the Harlem School of the Arts, is special. Its language is current street talk. Its chorus dances, chants spare lines and occasionally sings to music of striking ingenuity by Kelvyn Fell and David Red Harrington. But this chorus does not carry the burden of the narrative as in Euripides. Here the whole story is told by the three characters: Medea (April Yvette Thompson), Kreon (Arthur French) and Jason (Lawrence Winslow).

This radical personalizing of the lethal conflicts among men and a woman, between different nations, and between mortals and divinities brings out surprising qualities and instabilities in the characters. I suspect that no matter how many versions I see in the future, my perception of them all will be affected by the revelations here.

It is very clear that Kreon, King of Corinth, is not arrogant or unfeeling when he banishes Medea so that Jason will be free to marry the king's daughter; he simply cannot perceive the justice of this barbarian woman's refusal to lose her husband and her sons. And Jason really believes he honors Medea by leaving her and marrying a princess so that Medea's sons will become royal heirs.

Topics for Discussion and Writing

1. What are the fundamental differences between tragedy and comedy? How can they be considered as complementary genres rather than as opposites?

2. How does comedy offer social criticism? Where do you see social criticism in comedies in the theatre or in films? Because we laugh, do we take social criticism less seriously in comedy than in other genres?

3. What is the philosophical perspective expressed by tragicomedy? What view of life is expressed by the situation of the characters in *Waiting for Godot?*

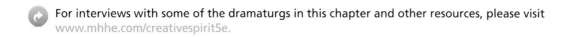 For interviews with some of the dramaturgs in this chapter and other resources, please visit www.mhhe.com/creativespirit5e.

Chapter 14

Choosing a Genre: Comedy

Looking at *Dog Lady*
by Milcha Sanchez-Scott

TO FURTHER OUR STUDY OF GENRE, we examine one more American play through its text and in performance, *Dog Lady* by Milcha Sanchez-Scott. In *Dog Lady* the playwright uses the genre of comedy to reflect on changing family and social relationships. The choice of comedy as the vehicle for her ideas affects the structure of the play itself and the way the play is performed on the stage. Sanchez-Scott's comedy offers a view of life that is resilient and durable even as we see the confusion and foolishness that accompany much of human activity.

become animals, roosters dance, characters walk on water and ascend to the heavens. Characters pray to the spirits, the stars, and the moon as well as to the Catholic hierarchy. And the figure of the *curandera*, whom Sanchez-Scott remembers vividly from *bellarios* (healing ceremonies) witnessed during her childhood in Colombia, appears in one form or another in all four of the early related plays. The *curandera* becomes the connection to the spirit world. The shared action of the older woman, the *curandera*; and the central character, in each play a girl or young woman, makes possible the miraculous transcendence.

Reinterpreting Catholic Imagery: The Virgin of Guadalupe

Sanchez-Scott uses magical realism to explore the cultural collision experienced by her characters, Latina women searching for their identity. The characters challenge traditional ideas of authority and take on activist roles in shaping their own destinies.

One strategy of Latina artists of Mexican and Central American heritage in addressing gender issues is the manipulation of religious imagery important to their communities, particularly the image of the Virgin of Guadalupe, who holds a place of central significance. The Virgin of Guadalupe is the meeting point of European and indigenous cultures, the cross-cultural incarnation of the European Virgin Mary brought by the Spanish to the Americas. The dark Virgin of Guadalupe supposedly first appeared in 1531 to the Indian Juan Diego in Mexico, very close to the shrine of Tonantzin, who was the foremost Aztec goddess, the goddess of corn and regeneration. The connection of Guadalupe to Tonantzin is inescapable and follows the pattern of invaders who build their churches on indigenous religious sites. The Virgin of Guadalupe has become a complex figure who has been seen for centuries as a representation of both faith and liberation. Her image was carried in revolutions

The visual art of Yolanda Lopez is connected in spirit to the plays of Milcha Sanchez-Scott. In the "Portrait of the Artist as the Virgin of Guadalupe," Lopez creates an homage to working-class women. The young woman in the painting exuberantly jumps off the crescent moon that has served as a pedestal in the past, carrying with her the snake that symbolizes the tree of knowledge and sexuality, as well as Aztec concepts of birth, death, and rebirth. The work is an artistic metaphor for women taking control of their lives. The figure in this painting suggests Rosalinda running in *Dog Lady.*

in Mexico and on marches led by César Chávez to organize migrant farmworkers in the 1960s and 1970s in California.

Although Guadalupe historically has an activist component, she became the "traditional role model" promoted by Mexican Catholicism as the ideal for women: "woman as nurturer, protector, and comforter."[7] In a tradition referred to as "marianismo," Guadalupe has also been seen as reinforcing the passivity of Hispanic women. The traditional representation of the Virgin of Guadalupe shows a saintly woman with head bowed and covered by a demure blue cloak. She is a model of submission. By laying claim to this most central image of Hispanic womanhood and recasting the image with ancient and contemporary significance, Latina writers and artists have transformed this religious icon into a repository of lost history and a symbol of power, activism, and liberation.

The artwork of Yolanda Lopez shares the buoyancy and humor of Milcha Sanchez-Scott's approach to gender questions. Yolanda Lopez has created a *triptych*, a work in three parts, that presents images of the Virgin of Guadalupe corresponding to three generations of women. The women that Lopez uses as models for the paintings are her grandmother, her mother, and herself. In a compelling coincidence, Rosalinda, running through the barrio, recalls Lopez's painting of herself, "Portrait of the Artist as the Virgin of Guadalupe." In the painting, Lopez (Guadalupe) is the runner with pink dress flying up over muscular brown legs in white running shoes and with her short black hair on her now bare head blowing free in the wind.

Although there is no mention of the Virgin of Guadalupe in *Dog Lady*, the race in which Rosalinda is running is, of course, Our Lady of a Thousand Sorrows Marathon. The Virgin Mary takes many forms, reflective of different moments of spiritual insight in the many communities worldwide that are part of the Catholic Church. The Virgin of Guadalupe is one of those forms, as is *La Dolorosa*, or Our Lady of Sorrow. Our Lady of a *Thousand* Sorrows is the playwright's magical realist exaggeration of the suffering of women such as Rosalinda's mother, María Pilar.

As the starting point for her comedy, Sanchez-Scott has created a most incongruous situation: Catholic girls running through the streets in honor of the suffering of Catholic women. Just as Yolanda Lopez has liberated the Virgin of Guadalupe from her passivity and sorrow, Milcha Sanchez-Scott does the same. Rosalinda's very existence turns the old imagery upside down. Instead of patiently waiting at home to fulfill her supposed biological destiny, Rosalinda intends to seize the world.

For both Lopez and Sanchez-Scott, a critical issue in the challenge to the traditional image of women is the liberation and physicality of the runner. There is an earth-shaking difference between young women running free through the streets in honor of the Virgin Mary and women on their knees crossing the huge cobblestone courtyard in front of the Basilica of the Virgin of Guadalupe in Mexico City; the latter has been considered one of the ultimate forms of reverence. In both Lopez's painting and Sanchez-Scott's play, the body is active and uncovered, not in an objectified way, but as an expression of female strength. The two characters are doing nothing less than reclaiming the female body. Binding, inhibiting clothing is cast aside, and the strength of the natural world is symbolically associated with women as it has often been associated with men. Yolanda Lopez's runner holds a snake in her hand, the snake that once adorned women's heads until it was incorporated into women's fall from grace and placed under Mary's foot. And Rosalinda is given the strength of the dog.

A Latina Identity

As Rosalinda is reshaping the identity of American Catholic girls from the barrio, Sanchez-Scott is clear about the creation of a Latina identity rather than an "Anglo" one. After Rosalinda has turned into a dog, another neighbor, Mrs. Amador, comes onstage outraged, carrying a broken rosebush. Again, in typical dog fashion, Rosalinda has trampled Mrs. Amador's garden. Growing in that garden are roses named for

••• PRODUCING *DOG LADY*

The production of *Dog Lady* that we consider here was done by an organization called International Arts Relations, or INTAR. INTAR has functioned much like East West Players—in this case as an umbrella organization for the production of new plays and musicals by Hispanic Americans as well as the most prominent work from the Latin American theatre. In addition to the production of her plays at INTAR, Milcha Sanchez-Scott's participation in the INTAR playwrights' laboratory led to the development of her next major play, *Roosters*.

INTAR

INTAR was founded in 1966 by the artistic director Max Ferra to promote Spanish-language theatre for the Spanish-speaking peoples of New York City. INTAR began in a condemned tenement building as an organization committed to providing low-income access to the theatre. It joined a growing movement of Spanish-speaking or interlingual theatres developing on the East and West coasts such as El Teatro Campesino in northern California and the Puerto Rican Traveling Company and Repertorio Español in New York. Today playwrights of Cuban, Mexican, Puerto Rican, and Central and South American heritages are contributing vibrant works to American theatre organizations across the country. As one of the oldest Latino theatres of the period from the 1960s to the present, INTAR has had a significant impact on the careers of many Latino playwrights. This organization is still located in a small off-Broadway theatre where creativity is the most important resource, as it was when Max Ferra directed *Dog Lady* in 1984. The current artistic director of INTAR is the playwright and director Eduardo Machado.

SET DESIGN AND MING CHO LEE

For the production of Milcha Sanchez-Scott's companion one-acts, *Dog Lady* and *The Cuban Swimmer*, Max Ferra invites Ming Cho Lee to do the set design. One of the foremost designers in the United States, Lee is known for his work with the New York Shakespeare Festival, the New York City Opera, the Metropolitan Opera, and the Martha Graham Dance Company, as well as on Broadway and in many of the resident theatre companies in North America. Lee usually works with far larger budgets than the resources of a small not-for-profit off-Broadway theatre will allow.

Max Ferra sees in Sanchez-Scott's one-acts a special quality of lightness and simplicity that he compares to a kite caught up in air currents. He believes that the artistic perspectives of Milcha Sanchez-Scott and Ming Cho Lee are complementary and will make for a productive creative partnership. Ming Cho Lee agrees. He is particularly fascinated by *Dog Lady* and the vivid way it captures the Hispanic world. The INTAR production of *Dog Lady* is shaped by the way Ming Cho Lee physicalizes his imaginative response to the world of the play.

Lee will be working in the INTAR theatre that he describes as a "brownstone, railroad flat of a theatre" because of its long, narrow space, brick interior, and spartan arrangements. The entire space, audience and stage, is 21 feet wide and 59 feet deep. That is divided into a stage space 21 feet wide and 24 feet deep and a seating area 21 feet wide and 35 feet deep for the 99 seats of this Equity waiver theatre. In designing the set for *Dog Lady*, Ming Cho Lee is guided by the nature of the INTAR theatre space as well as the structure, tone, and images of the play.

Pop Art and Forced Perspective

Because Lee sees the play as having a "parable or fairy-tale quality," he has decided to do a "pop art realistic" version of a Los Angeles street scene but with "a very forced perspective."[8] Through painting technique, the street scene appears to continue off into the distance because the houses grow smaller upstage. For *perspective* to work in the theatre, everyone must share the same view of the vanishing point. In theatres with wide audience spaces or audience spaces that wrap around part or all of the stage, creating a forced perspective is not possible. When perspective painting was first introduced into the theatre during the Italian Renaissance in the early sixteenth century, the perspective was drawn essentially from the duke's seat in the center of the palace room that functioned as a theatre. One's importance at court would dictate how close one sat to the royal seat and therefore how much of the perspective effect one was able to enjoy. But because the audience space at INTAR is quite narrow, everyone can, in fact, share the same visual point of view that allows the perspective to work. "The idea was that when people walk in, they think that they are looking at a magical realism re-creation of the Los Angeles barrio." Small stucco houses line the street and are painted brightly in blues, pinks, and yellows, more color than Ming Cho Lee usually uses in his sets. "Seedy looking" palm trees rise above the houses, and off in the distance the freeway can be seen. The sky is a glaring white that suggests a smoggy heat.

The street scene was first suggested by an impressionist painting brought to the planning process by the director, Max Ferra. Ming Cho Lee interpreted the street by turning to his own memories of Los Angeles in the 1950s when he was a student at Occidental College, and to photographs sent by the playwright, Milcha Sanchez-Scott. The set captures a sense of both an actual, recognizable place and a magical place given to the unexpected. The use of perspective is a crucial factor first in establishing the sense of place and then in contributing to the humor in the production.

Breaking the Illusion

When plays were originally done with perspective scenery, the actors performed at the front edge of the stage. Because the painted objects must be made smaller as they are placed farther **upstage** to create the sense of distance or the vanishing point, if actors move upstage and stand next to the smaller objects, the illusion is destroyed. Stories are told of some stage directors even arranging crowd scenes using children or little people upstage to create the effect that, like the painted buildings, the people, too, were getting smaller in the distance.

However, the illusion of the perspective painting in the *Dog Lady* set—with the smaller houses upstage—is created for a purpose other than giving a sense of distance. The actors move upstage deliberately to challenge or break the illusion of the perspective. They appear to become huge because they tower over the tiny houses and the ribbonlike rendering of the freeway. The actors become taller yet because the stage is steeply "raked." That is, the stage floor itself rises on an angle as you move upstage. For example, when Rosalinda does her training runs that seem to take her round the world she moves upstage and runs in exaggerated slow motion. She becomes a giant, circumnavigating what has become an almost toy planet. The relationship of the characters to the physical world keeps changing, and this technique works as a visual surprise to keep the audience off balance as the incidents in the play also continue to startle. Lee gives us a playful, lighthearted image of a Los Angeles barrio and builds into it a shifting perspective that allows the characters to occupy differing levels of reality. When the actors are **downstage,** the houses appear to be normal size. As soon as the actors move upstage, the neighborhood seems to shrink.

STAGING AND ACTING

The staging of *Dog Lady* and the acting style in conjunction with the set make clear to the audience that the characters live in the protected world of comedy. The acting has an exaggerated, cartoonish quality that is both a little flatter than life and at the same time larger than life. There is less internal focus to the acting than in the productions of *And the Soul Shall Dance*

The set for *Dog Lady*, designed by Ming Cho Lee, uses perspective painting to create an image of a Los Angeles barrio street with palm trees and the freeway in the distance. Through the designer's ingenuity, the narrow stage space at INTAR was transformed into a magical setting for Milcha Sanchez-Scott's characters.

and *Joe Turner's Come and Gone*. In those performances each character carries the weight of a difficult and important personal history. The past with its memories is always present. In contrast, in *Dog Lady*, the characters seem to exist only in the present. There is subtext, but not the reference to memory.

Most of the action takes place downstage and has a presentational rather than a representational or realistic quality. The set is less of an environment than a background for the action. The actors do not inhabit the set as they do Bertha's kitchen; rather, the set becomes part of a game

the actors are playing for us, particularly with the visual tricks of the shrinking houses. The actors in *Dog Lady* face out and play to the audience as much as they play to each other. The audience is less the invisible witness of realism; it is more a partner overtly acknowledged by the actors.

The movement of the actors is obviously stylized rather than staged to create the appearance of reality. When Rosalinda runs, she always shifts into slow motion to indicate that she is covering great distances. Her transformation into a dog is indicated suggestively with her hands simply raised and cupped as paws, the infamous Frisbee in her mouth. Before Rosalinda's entrance as a dog, the other characters enter, each with an astonished response to her offstage canine exploits. The characters all stand in a line as if they are too amazed to stand alone, their heads moving precisely together, all the bodies leaning in the same direction.

Sight Gags

Sight gags become important. When María Pilar sends Jesse to find Rosalinda, Jesse is in her pajamas. Jesse pulls a skirt over the pajamas and pulls up the pajama bottoms so that they are out of sight under the skirt. When she returns to tell her story about Manny Argando, the black Impala, and the chopped meat and bones, one pajama leg has slipped down. So the humor of her story is punctuated by her utter disregard for her own appearance. A moment later Orlando, the mailman, enters. It is clear from his appearance that, in the tradition of dogs and mailmen, he has been attacked by Rosalinda and her pack, her newly found comrades in crime. His trousers are badly torn and dangling as if they have been torn by large canine teeth, his hat is askew, and he carries one shoe in his hand. He staggers in and falls onto the step as he says, "La Rosalinda *se freakió*." The costume designer, Connie Singer, is responsible for creating ideas of character and sociological background. But like the work of the scene designer, Ming Cho Lee, her work makes a major contribution to the humor in the performance.

Rosalinda (Jeannette Mirabel) appears as a dog to terrorize Mrs. Amador, who is already furious about her rose garden. The dog character is created through gesture and attitude, not through any change in costume or makeup.

Rosalinda and Jesse (Elizabeth Peña) enjoy Rosalinda's transformation, while the rest of the cast reacts with varying degrees of dismay. The acting style is far more presentational than the more realistic acting in *Joe Turner's Come and Gone* and *And the Soul Shall Dance.*

Vocal Style

The vocal delivery of the actors is also exaggerated. These are not seemingly overheard conversations, but lines delivered for the audience's benefit. The actor playing the mother, María Pilar, has an almost operatic style as she details her various woes with obvious relish and gusto. In her early scene with Luisa Ruiz, the *curandera*, she begins with great pride in her daughter's running and the assistance of Father Estefan. She then becomes very melodramatic over being a "woman alone" who must struggle to provide for her daughters. The self-pity is followed by a scathing commentary on her dead husband's failure to help. Sarcastically, she calls to him

in heaven. She is reduced to tears at his lack of response and then finally unleashes a blast of anger at the *"condenado viejo"* (old sinner). It is almost as if an aria has been made of her shifting moods, and the actor enjoys it as much as the audience.

USING COMEDY TO SHIFT THE WORLDVIEW

In *Dog Lady*, Milcha Sanchez-Scott incorporates many of the traditional expectations of comedy and realigns them. A small community is disrupted by misunderstanding and tangled events. Luisa Ruiz tries to help Rosalinda and seems to create chaos. Love is confused and unrequited.

In the final scene of *Dog Lady* the mood of the play shifts from exaggeration to intimacy. The set becomes more an environment for dreams than the toy planet of earlier scenes. Through acting style, placement of the characters, and lighting, the performance leads to revelation, changing the focus from the physical and verbal humor of the first part of the play.

Raphael loves Rosalinda, who thinks only about running. Jesse loves Raphael, who thinks only about Rosalinda. Like most comedies the play ends with triumph and reconciliation. Rosalinda has won the race and will go to Rome, the first step in her journey out into the world. There is a party of celebration and the outcast, Luisa Ruiz, becomes the honored guest. Jesse is transformed from an awkward adolescent into a radiant young woman. Raphael, who has had eyes only for Rosalinda, is suddenly captivated by Jesse.

The INTAR production deftly underscores the shift in worldview that Sanchez-Scott establishes through her material. In another time Rosalinda (beautiful rose) would be a fairy princess waiting to be rescued by a prince. Now the fair one has become an athlete with her own quest who is helped by a Latina version of the fairy godmother, the *curandera*. Rather than kissing a frog who turns into a prince, Rosalinda moves farther away from the passive, fairy-tale image by becoming an animal herself, unpredictable and even ferocious. The sister living in her shadow dreams not of a beautiful transformation (although she does dream of Rafael) but of roaring away on her own Harley Davidson. The final moment of the play is not a love scene or betrothal involving Raphael and Rosalinda or Raphael and Jesse. The final scene is between the two sisters, both lovely in their fiesta dresses.

Rosalinda is now in a black dress with her hair unbound from the sweatband she has worn throughout the play, and Jesse is in a soft white dress instead of the pajamas under a skirt with one leg rolled up and the other falling down.

In this final scene the pace of the performance slows down and the actors lose the cartoonish, exaggerated quality of the earlier scenes. The sisters sit together on the front step of the Luna house and share the most personal moments of the production. They lean against each other, their faces very close together. When Jesse says, "all the things that will happen to you," she is wistful and sad. There is a clear sense of the unspoken, her sense of loss in feeling that magical things will not happen to her. And Jesse's subsequent "you'll be different" carries a tinge of resentment.

Jesse's subtext, her longing for the world that is opening up to Rosalinda, sets the stage for their focus on the amulet given to Rosalinda by the *curandera*, the apparent source of Rosalinda's

power. Rosalinda shows Jesse the *yu-yu*, holding it reverently as a great treasure, and the amulet seems to emit a magical aura perceived by both young women. The scene is played very deliberately. Jesse reaches to touch the amulet. And then there is a long pause while Rosalinda makes up her mind. She takes the amulet from around her neck and gives it to Jesse. They touch cheeks in the Latina manner. The play and the production suggest that the power to reach, to become, to transcend, is a gift that comes out of the relationships of these women, the *curandera* with her ties to the earth and traditional ways and the sisters with their courage to take on the world.

Jesse stands and Rosalinda exits into the house. Jesse puts on the amulet, and her facial expression changes. The haunted look of vulnerability and longing disappears, replaced by a more knowing expression, an awareness. She gives the audience one last, mysterious look and slowly walks upstage bathed in the moonlight, "*la luna,*" leaving behind her mother's cries of "Jesse, Jesse."

Summary

In *Dog Lady*, Milcha Sanchez-Scott uses comedy to explore questions of gender, religion, and social organization. She takes an outrageous situation in which a young woman becomes a dog to win a race and disrupts the entire community. Tales of Rosalinda's amazing exploits reverse all of the community expectations of female behavior. The play follows the usual pattern in comedy of reconciliation, but in the end Rosalinda and Jesse go their own ways instead of returning to the traditional social structure.

The work of Milcha Sanchez-Scott is influenced by the playwright's childhood in Colombia and her formative years living as part of the Mexican American community in southern California. Other sources include the literary movement of magical realism as well as the feminist movement involving visual artists and writers. The blending of English and Spanish reflects the use of language in the Latino community and contributes to the rhythms of the characters' speeches and the vividness of the play's vocabulary.

The style of the production at INTAR, in terms of both design and acting, was very important to the audience's experience of the comedy. For *Dog Lady*, the set designer Ming Cho Lee created a magical world through perspective painting. The set seemed to grow or shrink, depending on the placement of the actors, and served as a presentational background rather than a realistic environment for the actors. The acting style involved exaggeration and suggestion, with the actors acknowledging the presence of the audience.

Topics for Discussion and Writing

1. Chapter 13, on genre, makes the point that ultimately the world of comedy is a protected one, a world without suffering. *Dog Lady* offers an example of such a protected world. How does the absence of pain contribute to the comedy? Is comedy always without suffering or pain?

2. Usually, associating a girl or woman with a dog would have a negative connotation. What different meanings are suggested by the symbol of the dog in this play?

3. What kinds of changes occur in the characters in *Dog Lady?* What changes do you think the playwright would like to see in our own society?

For suggested readings and other resources related to this chapter, please visit
www.mhhe.com/creativespirit5e.

Chapter 15

The Project

Looking at *Anna in the Tropics*
by Nilo Cruz

IN OUR STUDY OF THEATRE, we have moved from the most basic element of theatre—the impulse in human nature to perform—to the complex development of that performance impulse in the production of plays. In coming to understand the theatre, we have examined the structure of plays, the work of theatre artists, and the relationship between the expression of ideas in performance and the audience. The purpose of this final chapter is to give you an opportunity to integrate the materials presented in the book by participating in the production process. The goal of this culminating project is for groups of students to collaborate on the hypothetical production of a play. You will need to study the play to be produced, consider the ideas of the playwright, and contribute to an interpretation of those ideas in a theatre of your choosing for an audience of your peers.

Several approaches to the production project are possible, depending on the size and organization of your class. The project may be collaborative or individual. It may culminate in the presentation of scenes to your class or in the presentation of a production plan, or both. If the project is done individually, your results may be turned in to the instructor rather than presented to the class. The collaborative project is designed for small classes or large classes that also have discussion sections. Large classes without discussion sections will need to modify the collaborative process or use the individual approach.

PREPARING A PRODUCTION

The collaborative project should be done in groups of approximately five to seven. If possible, groups should include students who are interested in design and students who are interested in performance. After the groups have been organized, each group will meet and decide who will take on the different individual responsibilities as they are described in the "Project Assignments" section of this chapter. One person needs to assume the role of the director. Each group does not need to do all of the possible assignments. Students should choose the area which interests them most and with which they are most comfortable.

After reading the play, each group will hold its first meeting to decide on the distribution of responsibilities. Then each student will begin work on his or her particular assignment. The group should meet for the second time when the members have completed enough preliminary thinking to allow the group to brainstorm and make the group decisions listed on page 446.

Group members will present their production plan to the class, showing the poster design, scene design, and costume designs; outlining the stylistic choices they have made; and explaining how those choices interpret the ideas in the play. The production presentation may also include the presentation of a scene from the play. If time restrictions do not allow a class presentation, the director will write an overview of the stylistic choices. As an alternative presentation plan, each group may display the visual materials its members have developed, and the class time may be used for the presentation of scenes.

If the project is to be completed individually, each student should choose one of the assignments and develop his or her project as described in the "Project Assignments" section. Each student will need to make the decisions listed under "Group Decisions" on an individual basis.

ANNA IN THE TROPICS AND ALTERNATIVE PLAY CHOICES

The play included in this chapter and meant to be used as the subject of the production project is *Anna in the Tropics*, by Nilo Cruz. Although the assignments have been created with *Anna in the Tropics* in mind, they may be adapted to other plays, including the four plays that we have already read. Additional contemporary plays recommended as alternatives for the production project are *Dead Man's Cellphone*, by Sarah Ruhl; and *Rabbit Hole*, by David Lindsay-Abaire. As one further alternative, some classes may wish to explore a play from an earlier period chosen by the instructor.

Introduction to Nilo Cruz

Nilo Cruz was born in Matanzas, Cuba in 1961 and emigrated to the United States when he was nine years old. His sensibility as a playwright was formed in part by a childhood spent in Cuba and a youth spent in Miami, Florida. His plays are set in a variety of geographical locations: *Two Sisters and a Piano* takes place in Cuba, *Night Train to Bolina* takes place in an unnamed but violent Latin American country, *A Bicycle Country* takes place on a raft between Cuba and the United States, and *Anna in the Tropics* is set in Ybor City, a historic district in Tampa, Florida. Thematically, a number of the plays focus on characters trapped by restrictive circumstances, which they try to transcend through acts of imagination and through love. His characters speak a heightened, lyrical language and Cruz has a clear interest in poetic, symbolic writing. He has written a play about the life of the Spanish poet and playwright, Federico García Lorca, entitled *Lorca in a Green Dress*. And he has recently translated and adapted a play for children from a story by Gabriel García Márquez, *A Very Old Man with Enormous Wings* (shown on page 164), and another play based on *Life is a Dream* by Pedro Calderón de la Barca. Cruz also acknowledges that August Wilson is a significant influence on his work.

The lector reads to the workers in the cigar factory in the production of *Anna in the Tropics* at South Coast Repertory Theatre in 2003. Note the interior details of the factory with period apparatus for making cigars, tobacco leaves hanging from above, and a suggestion of palm trees beyond the factory walls. Some productions have brought in an expert to teach the actors cigar-making skills. The actors here include Tony Plana, Geoffrey Ricas, Julian Acosta, Onahoua Rodriguez, Adrian Sevan, and Karmin Murcela. The director is Juliette Carrillo.

Nilo Cruz began his work in the theatre as a student at Miami-Dade Community College. Early on he was encouraged to pursue playwriting and then was invited by María Irene Fornés to participate in her workshop at INTAR. Cruz graduated with an M.F.A. degree in playwriting from Brown University, where he studied with Paula Vogel. Both Fornes and Vogel are known for their own achievements as playwrights and also as mentors to a number of leading younger American playwrights. Nilo Cruz has been supported as a playwright-in-residence at the McCarter Theatre and at the New Theatre of Coral Gables, Florida, where *Anna in the Tropics* was first produced. *Anna in the Tropics* was awarded the Pulitzer Prize

as the outstanding American drama of 2003, the first won by a Latino playwright.

Cruz has said that *Anna in the Tropics* began with his fascination with the lectors who read to workers in cigar factories early in the twentieth century and he decided that a lector would be the subject of his play. Workers, engaged in repetitive manual labor, had the opportunity to listen first to the news and then to stories read to them while they worked. The plot of the play began to take shape after Cruz chose the book for the character of the lector to read, *Anna Karenina*, by Tolstoy. *Anna Karenina* is a story with a passionate, adulterous love affair at its center and Cruz wondered how the characters in his play would react

After writing *Anna in the Tropics* in English, Nilo Cruz wrote a version in Spanish, seen here in a 2004 performance at Repertorio Español, a theatre company in New York. The style of this production contrasts markedly with the production at South Coast Rep. Again, we see the character of the lector, Juan Julian, reading *Anna Karenina*, to the workers. But, this production, directed by René Buch, depends on the imaginations of the actors and the audience members to fill in any of the details of place and occupation. The emphasis is on the language and the inner lives of the characters. By looking at these two photographs of the same moment in the play at different theatres, we see how much latitude there is in making staging choices. Juan Julian is played by Francisco Gattorno. The other actors are Denise Quiñones, Tatiana Vecino, Grettel Trujillo, Raúl Durán, and Gil Ron.

to Tolstoy's story. And so a play evolved in which the lives of the characters in the play are deeply affected by the story they are listening to. The desires, risks, jealousies, quarrels, and betrayals in their own lives are shaped and magnified by the unfolding of the Tolstoy novel and the presence of the romantic figure of the man who reads it.

Cigar making is an important part of the world of *Anna in the Tropics.* It was a major industry in Cuba and became a significant part of the Florida economy in the early twentieth century, when the play takes place. The characters are engaged in cigar making throughout the play and the folding and rolling of tobacco leaves and the smoke of the cigars are part of the sensuous texture of the play. Tobacco is presented from a historical perspective and the playwright does not enter our contemporary debate about the health implications of tobacco.

However, there is no doubt that the staging of *Anna in the Tropics* raises questions about how to stage the party scene in which a new cigar is passed from character to character to be sampled and experienced, to be tried in the same way wine

The lector, Juan Julian, played by Francisco Gattorno, and Marela, played by Denise Quiñones, develop a special bond during the play. Juan Julian takes Marela seriously and she responds by sharing her dreams with him. Theirs is a spiritual bond unlike the relationship Juan Julian has with Marela's sister Conchita. The lector is both a real character in the play and an enigma onto which the other characters project their desires. This photo is from the production of *Ana en el Tropico* at Repertorio Español.

is tasted. In the theatre in general when smoking is called for in a script, some theatre companies have actors smoke herbal products onstage as a substitute for smoking actual tobacco products. Other theatre companies have begun to use cigarettes and cigars as props that are handled by the actors but not lit or smoked, in the same way many other stage actions are presented as indications of actuality rather than actuality itself. There is in fact an important ongoing discussion about the prevalence of tobacco use in some films with questions about why the cigarette has become a signature prop for some actors.

Alternative Plays

DEAD MAN'S CELL PHONE, BY SARAH RUHL
Dramatic Comedy

Four women, two men

Unit set that shifts among multiple locations

A comic play about what happens if you answer someone else's cell phone and enter that person's life. The central character is unable to resist the persistent ring of an unanswered phone and then through half-truths and inventions, she claims a place in the family of the man who had failed to answer his phone because he was dead. The play is a satire about the place of technology in our lives and about human connections, told through bizarre details and slippery, shifting circumstances. Strong two- and three-person scenes with male-female and female-female casting.

RABBIT HOLE, BY DAVID LINDSAY-ABAIRE
Drama

Three women, two men

Realistic interior of family home

The play examines the struggles of family members with their own guilt and with each other after the death of a four-year-old child. The grief of the individual characters is shaded with humor that provides an essential coping mechanism for the characters and the audience. Strong two-person scenes with male-female and female-female casting.

WORKING ON THE PROJECT
Sequence of Work

1. Read the play.

2. *Group Meeting 1.* Begin group discussion topics. Choose individual assignments. Choose a director. Decide *if* you are going to present a scene, and, if so, cast actors.

3. Begin individual research. Begin scene rehearsals.

4. *Group Meeting 2.* Work through group decisions. Establish a calendar for completion of the work. Share initial findings.

5. Complete research and continue rehearsals.

6. Complete design for each area, including set, costumes, music, poster, program note.

7. *Group Meeting 3.* Present designs to other members of the group. Hold a final dress rehearsal with everyone present if you are presenting a scene.

8. Present project to class.

Topics for Group Discussion (Group Meeting 1)

1. What are your initial reactions to the play? What surprises or intrigues you about the characters' relationships? What in the relationships seems familiar to you? What seems strange?

2. *Anna in the Tropics* is a period play set in a specific location and specific time. In what ways does the period affect the style of the play? For help in locating research materials for this play, please see the Appendix, page 483.

3. What does the title of the play, *Anna in the Tropics*, mean? What is the interplay between the Tolstoy novel and the situations of the characters in the play?

4. What is the significance of the lector in the different characters' lives? Is he created with the same degree of reality as the other characters? How is he different from the factory workers?

Group Decisions (Group Meeting 2)

1. What theatre is to be used for your hypothetical production? What would be the most appropriate spatial arrangement (proscenium? thrust? arena?) and actor–audience relationship? How large should the theatre be? How close should the audience be to the action? If possible, choose a theatre on your campus or in your community that you think would be a good space in which to produce the play. Find out the dimensions of the theatre and the number of seats in the auditorium.

2. What style do you think will be appropriate for your production? How realistic should the sets and costumes be? How much detail should they have? Is the setting to be complete with walls and windows, or is the set to be suggestive or expressionistic? Does the environment give the appearance of reality, or is it distorted in some way? What pieces of furniture and architectural features seem essential? Do the costumes seem real, or are they exaggerated?

3. What metaphors or images seem helpful in thinking about the play?

4. What colors best communicate the feelings of the play?

PROJECT ASSIGNMENTS
The Director

The director will lead the discussion on the group topics and questions. The director will develop a written response to questions 8 and 9 in the "Scene Design" section (pages 447–448) and question 6 in the "Costume Design" section (page 448). These issues should be discussed at Group Meeting 2.

The director will write a summary of the ideas for the production based on his or her understanding of the play and the group's responses. If scenes from the same play are to be presented to the class, the directors from the different groups will meet to make sure each group produces a different scene. As part of the director's written project, the director will analyze the content of the scene and its relationship to the play; that is, he or she will identify the important actions or issues in the scene and determine how they contribute to the play's meaning.

Character Analysis

Choose one character. Anyone performing a scene from *Anna in the Tropics* or another play should do the analysis for the character that he or she is playing. If scenes are not to be presented, the character analysis may be done for any character.

1. What does your character say about himself or herself? Make a list quoting all the lines by act and scene.

2. What do the other characters say about your character? Make a list quoting all the lines by act and scene.

3. What are the motives that drive your character? List the things that he or she wants from the other characters in the play. What seems to be the dominant motive for your character?

4. How does your character change during the course of the play? What are the important realizations that your character comes to during the play? What provokes the realizations? Where does the character begin? Where does the character end?

5. What is the history of your character? Put together all the information given by the playwright, your character, and the other characters.

6. What is your character's relationship to other significant characters? How does it change?

7. What does your character look like? Find several pictures that show clothes, physicality, or outlook.

Scene Design

This assignment may be shared by two students.

ASSESSING THE ENVIRONMENT:

1. How does the playwright describe the setting?

2. How many different locations does the setting need to provide for? What is the relative importance of each location to the play? What solutions will allow the play's action to move easily between the different locations?

3. Determine what the play establishes about the time in which the factory would have been built and its location. What kind of a building is it and what is its condition? Find pictures of warehouses or factories built in that approximate time and general area of the country.

4. What seems to be the impact of the factory on the different characters? How important is it in their lives? In what ways does it limit them? What makes it a comfortable environment?

5. Collect exterior and interior pictures of buildings that give the feeling of the factory suggested by the script.

6. What parts of the factory are most important to the play? What parts of the factory need to be seen onstage by the audience? What other parts of the factory or exterior must be indicated in some way during the play? Is some indication of walls necessary to the scenic environment?

7. What pieces of furniture or machinery are referred to by the characters or in the stage directions? Make a list of everything that is necessary to the action of the play. What other furniture pieces seem useful to the characters' actions or to communicating either the period or the atmosphere of the factory? How old and in what condition are the furnishings?

8. What artifacts of the characters' lives might be part of the physical environment? In what ways is the environment personalized? Is one character's point of view more important than another's in determining the details of the physical environment? Does someone seem to own or dominate the space?

9. What are the basic actions of the characters in the play? What are the necessary entrances and exits and the physical actions that the stage space must accommodate and support?

DESIGNING THE SET

1. *Ground plan.* In collaboration with the director, work out a ground plan that will allow for the kind of locations and interactions indicated in the script. What are the necessary pieces of furniture? What would be the most effective placement of entrances, doors, walls, and pieces of furniture? If possible, consult with the scene designer in your theatre department or with a scene design student on the development of your ground plan. The ground plan may be drawn very simply on a diagram of the stage that you are using, with geometric shapes indicating furniture drawn to scale.

    If you do not do a rendering or a model of your set, then use pictures from your research to accompany the ground plan to demonstrate the atmosphere of the factory and the style of architecture and furnishings.

2. *Optional.* Draw or paint a rendering of your set, *or* build a scale model of the set.

Costume Design

1. Make a list of all the references in the stage directions to costuming.

2. Make a list of the references in the dialogue to articles of clothing.

3. What symbols are associated with the costumes?

4. What period or periods do the costumes come from?

5. What is the range of colors expressing the lives of the characters? Are specific colors called for in the script? How would contrasting colors appropriately identify the differences between characters?

6. What qualities of the characters help identify the kind of clothing each character might wear? What clothing pieces seem appropriate, given circumstances such as jobs or activities performed, social status, and the characters' outlook? How do you think the characters feel about what they wear? Do they hide or cover themselves in some way with their clothes? Do any of the characters try to call attention to themselves with their clothing? Are there major costume changes during the play? What do the costume changes signify?

7. Draw or find pictures of costumes that you think would be appropriate for each character. Go to a fabric store and buy small pieces of fabric that you would use to make the costumes for each character. Attach the appropriate fabric swatches to the drawing of each costume.

Music

Music is often a critical factor in setting the mood for a play and in providing transitions between scenes and at the beginning and end of acts. Sometimes the music is chosen by the director, and sometimes it is chosen jointly by the director and the sound designer. Music is typically used more sparingly in the theatre than in films, which often have elaborate scores.

Study the script of *Anna in the Tropics* for mood as well as references to music. What style of music best complements the time period, style, language, and character encounters in the play? How can music be used to bridge scene changes? Are there moments within scenes where music would enhance the action? Are there moments when music is specifically called for? Does the music undergo a change or a progression during the course of the play as the characters change?

Decide on all the places in the script where you think music would be appropriate. Select the music that you think should be played at each cue. Make a CD of the music you would recommend for your production. Make a cue sheet that

CONCHITA: I just want to have a civilized conversation. The same way the characters speak to each other in the novel. I've learned many things from this book.

PALOMO: Such as?

CONCHITA: Jealousy. For Anna's husband jealousy is base and almost animalistic. And he's right. He would never want Anna to think that he's capable of such vile and shameful emotions.

PALOMO: But you can't help being jealous. It's part of your nature.

CONCHITA: Not anymore.

PALOMO: Well, that's a change.

CONCHITA: Oh, I could see the husband so clear in the novel. How the thoughts would take shape in his mind, as they have in my own mind. I mean, not the same . . . No, no . . . Not the same, because he's an educated man, surrounded by culture and wealth, and I'm just a cigar roller in a factory. He is well bred and sophisticated. I barely get by in life.

But with this book I'm seeing everything through new eyes. What is happening in the novel has been happening to us.

No. Don't look at me that way. You might not want to admit it, but Anna and her husband remind me of us. Except I'm more like the husband.

PALOMO: So what does that make me then, Anna Karenina?

CONCHITA: You are the one who has the secret love, not me.

PALOMO: Oh, come on. It's late. Let's go home. I can't work like this.

CONCHITA: That's exactly what Anna said when the husband confronted her about the lover: "It's late. Let's go to sleep."

PALOMO: I think you're taking this a little too far.

CONCHITA: Am I? Have you ever heard the voice of someone who's deaf? The voice is crude and ancient, because it has no sense of direction or place, because it doesn't hear itself and it doesn't know if anybody else in the world

hears it. Sometimes I want to have a long conversation with you, like this. Like a deaf person. As if I couldn't hear you or myself. But I would just talk and talk, and say everything that comes to my mind, like a shell that shouts with the voice of the sea and it doesn't care if anybody ever hears it. That's how I want to speak to you, and ask you things.

PALOMO: And what's the use of talking like this? What sort of things do you want to ask me?

CONCHITA: Things that you wouldn't tell me, afraid that I might not understand.

PALOMO: Like what?

CONCHITA: I'd like to know what she's like. And what does she do to make you happy?

PALOMO: Ah, let's go home.

CONCHITA: Why?

PALOMO (Abruptly): Because I don't want to talk about these things!

(A pause.)

CONCHITA: So what's going to happen to us, Palomo?

PALOMO: I don't know. Do you want a divorce? We could travel to Reno and be divorced in six weeks. But your family will be opposed to it, and the same with mine. So divorce is out of the question.

CONCHITA: And if I tell you that I want to cut my hair, change the way I dress and take on a lover.

PALOMO: Say that again?

CONCHITA: What I just said.

PALOMO: You want to have a lover?

CONCHITA: Yes, like you do.

PALOMO: Ave Maria purissima!

CONCHITA: I have the same right as you do.

PALOMO: This book will be the end of us.

CONCHITA: Don't you think we've already come to the end?

PALOMO: No . . . I . . .

CONCHITA: You don't make love to me like you used to.

PALOMO: Well, we . . . You and I . . . We . . .

CONCHITA: It's all right, Palomo. It's all right. (She touches his arm) There's something that Anna Karenina said and I keep repeating it to myself: "If there are as many minds as there are heads, then there are as many kinds of love as there are hearts." I can try to love you in a different way. I can do that. And you should try to do the same.

(Music plays. Lights change.)

Scene 4

A square of light on the floor suggests the interior of the family's house. Ofelia and Santiago are not on speaking terms. She sits on one side of the room, he sits on the other. Marela stands by Santiago. The dialogue moves fast. Marela runs back and forth as a communicator.

SANTIAGO: Ask your mother for some money to buy me a pack of cigarettes. She's not talking to me.

MARELA: Papá wants money for a pack of cigarettes.

OFELIA: Ask him when is he going back to work.

MARELA: She wants to know when you're going back to work.

SANTIAGO: Tell her as soon as I get money from Camacho to pay Cheché.

MARELA: He says as soon as he gets money from Camacho to pay Cheché.

OFELIA: Tell him to give up smoking till then, that I'm not giving him any money.

SANTIAGO: What did she say?

MARELA: She says—

SANTIAGO: I heard her. (In loud voice, to Ofelia) Tell her that she's insane!

MARELA: He says you're insane.

OFELIA: And tell him he's a drunk, a thief and a-good-for-nothing gambler.

MARELA: She says—

SANTIAGO: I heard.

MARELA: He heard you, Mamá.

OFELIA: Good!

MARELA: Good, she says.

SANTIAGO: You're a crazy woman! Crazy woman!

OFELIA: Tell him I didn't hear that. I told him I don't want him to talk to me.

SANTIAGO: Ah, she heard me!

OFELIA: Tell him I don't want to hear his barbarism.

MARELA: Did you hear that, Papá? She doesn't want to hear your barbarism.

SANTIAGO: Tell her . . .

(Marela starts to walk toward her father.)

OFELIA (Infuriated): Come here, Marela . . .

(Marela walks toward her mother.)

SANTIAGO: Marela, come here . . .

MARELA: Wait! It's not your turn, Mamá.

OFELIA: Marela . . .

MARELA: Stop! I can't be here and there at the same time!

(Silence. Ofelia and Santiago shake their heads as if giving up on the whole thing.)

OFELIA AND SANTIAGO: This is insane!

MARELA: Well, you both heard that.

(Marela tries to put in a word, but they don't give her a chance.)

SANTIAGO: Tell her I'm going to a pawnshop to sell my wedding ring.

OFELIA: Tell him he should've done that a long time ago.

SANTIAGO: She's right, I should've done it a long time ago.

OFELIA: Yes, before his finger got numb.

SANTIAGO: She's right, my finger got numb.

OFELIA: You see, I was right. Numb, like everything else.

SANTIAGO: She's wrong. Not like everything else.

OFELIA: Nothing works on his body. Just his rotten teeth to chew away money.

MARELA: I'm leaving.

OFELIA: Marela!

SANTIAGO: Marela!

MARELA: You can fight without me!

(Marela walks out of the room. Silence. Then, Ofelia and Santiago begin to speak to each other without looking at each other.)

SANTIAGO: I've been listening to the new lector from up here.

OFELIA: You have?

SANTIAGO: He's good. He has a solid voice and I like the novel that he's reading.

OFELIA: Yes, a solid voice he has and I like the novel, too.

SANTIAGO: I 'specially like the character that lives in the countryside.

OFELIA (With delight): Yes.

SANTIAGO: Yes, him.

OFELIA: The one that has the farm?

SANTIAGO: Yes. The one that has the farm. What is his name?

OFELIA: His name is Levin.

SANTIAGO: That's right, Levin.

OFELIA: The one that lives in the forest surrounded by trees.

SANTIAGO: That Levin reminds me of when I was young and my father left me to run the factory. It seems as if Levin has dedicated his whole life to his farm.

OFELIA: Yes, he's a dedicated man.

SANTIAGO: I used to be like him.

OFELIA: Yes, you used to be like him.

SANTIAGO: I like the part of the book when Anna's brother is going to sell the estate next to Levin's property and Levin counsels him not to sell it.

OFELIA: Yes, that's a good part. And I can't believe that you almost gave another share of the factory to Cheché.

SANTIAGO: You're right, I lost my mind. I shouldn't drink.

OFELIA: That's right, drink you shouldn't. That's an idiotic thing to do, give away another share of the business. Cheché doesn't know what he's doing. He's like a scarecrow. He's

been talking about bringing machines and replacing some of the workers. You need to go back to the factory.

SANTIAGO: Yes, you're right. To the factory I need to go back.

(Ofelia looks at him.)

OFELIA: Santiago, what's eating you? You haven't gone to work. You don't eat. You don't sleep well.

SANTIAGO: I've acted like a fool, Ofelia. I'm ashamed of myself and I'm angry and bitter. And I can't shake off this damn agony!

OFELIA: Do you want me to call a doctor?

SANTIAGO: No. I don't need a doctor.

OFELIA: But you can't go on like this. Sooner or later you have to go back and face the workers.

SANTIAGO: I will. When I get the money and I can face Cheché.

OFELIA: And are you going to stay here until then?

SANTIAGO: Yes.

OFELIA: That's silly.

SANTIAGO: That's the way I am.

OFELIA: Well, I'm going to bed.

(Ofelia starts to exit.)

SANTIAGO: Ofelia.

OFELIA: Yes.

SANTIAGO: Stay up a while longer.

OFELIA: I'm tired. You didn't work like I did today.

SANTIAGO: Talk to me about the novel. I can't always hear very well from up here. This fellow, Levin . . . This character that I admire . . . He's the one who is in love with the young girl in the story, isn't he?

OFELIA (A burst of energy): Ah yes! He's in love with Kitty. Levin is in love with Kitty, and Kitty is in love with Vronsky. And Vronsky is in love with Anna Karenina. And Anna Karenina is married, but she's in love with Vronsky. Ay, everybody is in love in this book!

SANTIAGO: But for Levin . . . For Levin there's only one woman.

OFELIA: Yes, for him there's only one woman.

SANTIAGO (Full of love, he looks at her): Ofelia.

OFELIA: Yes.

(Santiago swallows the gulp of love.)

SANTIAGO: No. Nothing.

OFELIA (Fanning herself): Ah, the night breeze is making its way to us again. There's nothing like this Tampa breeze, always a punctual visitor around this time.

SANTIAGO: You know, Ofelia, when I gamble I try to repeat the same motions . . . I try to repeat everything I did the day I won. And when I lose I try to take inventory of what I did wrong. I think to myself, Did I get up from bed with my left foot first? Did I forget to polish my shoes? Did I leave the house in a state of disorder? Was I unkind to someone and that's why luck didn't come my way? Lately, I've been in a fog and I don't know what to do.

Every time I lose, I feel that something has been taken from me. Something bigger than money. And I see a line of little ants carrying breadcrumbs on their backs. But the crumbs they are taking away are my pride and my self-respect. My dignity. (Looks at her again) Have I lost you too, Ofelia? Have I lost you?

OFELIA: If you had lost me, I wouldn't be here. If you had lost me, I wouldn't be by your side. How can you say that you've lost me! (She hugs him)

(Music plays. Lights change.)

Scene 5

Juan Julian, Marela and Conchita at the factory.

JUAN JULIAN: I don't really like cities. In the country one has freedom. When I'm in a city I feel asphyxiated. I feel constriction in my lungs. The air feels thick and dense, as if the buildings breathe and steal away the oxygen. As my father used to say, living in a city is like living inside the mouth of a crocodile, buildings all around you like teeth. The teeth of culture, the mouth and tongue of civilization. It's a silly comparison, but it makes sense to me.

Every time I go to a park, I'm reminded of how we always go back to nature. We build streets and buildings. We work five to six days a week, building and cementing our paths and down come tumbling trees and nests, a whole paradise of insects. And all for what? On Sundays we return to a park where we could still find greenery. The verdure of nature.

CONCHITA: You're right. I don't know what I would do without my walks to the park. Why did you choose to read Tolstoy?

JUAN JULIAN: Because Tolstoy understands humanity like no other writer does.

CONCHITA: That's a good enough reason to read him.

JUAN JULIAN: Someone told me that at the end of his life, when he knew he was going to die, he abandoned his house and he was found dead at a train station. The same as . . .

Oh, perhaps I shouldn't tell you this.

CONCHITA: He was probably on his way to visit God.

JUAN JULIAN: That has always been my suspicion.

MARELA: Pardon me, but I must go. (She exits)

(There is an awkward pause as Juan Julian and Conchita watch Marela leave.)

CONCHITA: How did you become a lector?

JUAN JULIAN: I discovered books one summer. My father owed a lot of money to a creditor and we had to close ourselves up in our house and hide for a while. For my family, keeping up appearances was important. We had to pretend that we had gone away on a trip. We told neighbors that my mother was ill and she had to recuperate somewhere else. We stayed in that closed-up house for more than two months, while my father worked abroad. I remember it was hot and all the windows were kept closed. The heat was unbearable. The maid was the only one

CHECHÉ: As a matter of fact he is. He is distracting you. Some of the cigars you rolled today were faulty, and you're going to get the same dickens that everyone gets.

MARELA: Yes. The new lector is getting to you with *Anna Karenina*.

CHECHÉ: I don't let any book or lector get to me.

MARELA: Sure. You probably remember your wife every time he reads a page.

CHECHÉ: My wife's dead to me.

MARELA: Dead behind your eyes, so everywhere you look you see her.

CHECHÉ: Do you want to see all the cigars you've ruined?

MARELA: Show me. I pride myself in my work. I'm one of the fastest rollers in this whole place.

(Cheché pulls out a bag of cigars.)

CHECHÉ: But fast isn't always good, Marela.

MARELA: Nothing's wrong with it.

CHECHÉ: Here. Feel it. Hollow. A soft spot.

MARELA: Thank you, Chester. Is there anything else? Can I start pasting . . . ?

CHECHÉ: As a matter of fact there's something else . . .

MARELA: What, Chester?

CHECHÉ: Sometimes you get so distracted by the Russian story that I've seen you take shortcuts when you're rolling.

MARELA: What kind of shortcuts?

CHECHÉ: Sometimes you bring a cigar to your mouth and you bite the end of it, instead of reaching for the knife.

MARELA: You've seen me do that?

CHECHÉ: Yes, I've seen you do that and a lot more.

MARELA: Really?

CHECHÉ: Yes. When your mind wanders away from your work and you go far to your own little Russia. You forget the paste jar and you lick the last tobacco leaf, as if you were sealing a letter to a lover or playing with the mustache of a Russian man. Is that what it

is, little Marela, you're playing with some man in your mind and you forget that you're bringing a cigar to your mouth and licking it, instead of pasting it?

MARELA (Laughs): Oh, Chester . . .

CHECHÉ: Do you actually forget that you are working in a little factory where it gets real hot in the summer, and we have to wet the tobacco leaves, because they get dry from the heat and they need moisture, like the wet lick of your tongue.

MARELA: Don't look at me that way, Chester.

CHECHÉ (Touching her hair): And how do you want me to look at you?

MARELA: Don't touch me.

(She moves away. He follows her.)

CHECHÉ: Why not?

MARELA: Because I don't like it.

CHECHÉ: But I do. Every time I listen to that story I do see my wife . . .

(He moves closer to her.)

MARELA: Get away from me!

(He tries to kiss her. She struggles to get away from him.)

CHECHÉ: Marela, please. Come close . . . You don't know . . .

MARELA: Get away from me! Get away from me!

(She pushes him away. He falls to the floor.)

Don't you ever touch me again!

(Marela exits. Cheché remains on the floor. Music plays. Lights change.)

Scene 2

Spotlight on Juan Julian sitting on a chair. He begins to recite a passage from *Anna Karenina*. He remains isolated from the action of the scene.

JUAN JULIAN:

Anna Karenina's husband did not see anything peculiar or improper in his wife's sitting together with Vronsky at a separate table and having a lively conversation with him; but he noticed that the others sitting in the drawing room considered it peculiar and improper, and so it seemed improper to him, too. He decided that he must have a conversation with his wife about it.

(Conchita enters. She goes to her table and begins to roll cigars. Palomo enters. He is like a lost animal. Juan Julian continues to read in silence.)

PALOMO: At what time do you meet your lover?

CONCHITA: At the agreed time.

PALOMO: And what time is that?

CONCHITA: It changes like the moon.

PALOMO: Where do you meet besides this place?

CONCHITA: I can't tell you these things.

PALOMO: Why not?

CONCHITA: Because that's the way it is.

PALOMO: Does he read to you?

CONCHITA: Sometimes when he says that I look sad.

PALOMO: You get sad.

CONCHITA: It's not sadness. Sometimes I feel frightened.

PALOMO: Frightened of what?

CONCHITA: Frightened of something I have never felt or done before.

PALOMO: But isn't this what you wanted?

CONCHITA: Yes. But sometimes I can't help the guilt.

PALOMO: And how does he respond when you tell him this?

CONCHITA: He tells me that we have to make love all over again. That I have to get used to it. To him. To his body.

PALOMO: And what else does he say to you?

CONCHITA: He says things a woman likes to hear.

PALOMO: Like what?

CONCHITA: That I taste sweet and mysterious like the water hidden inside fruits and that our love will be white and pure like tobacco flowers. And it will grow at night, the same way that tobacco plants grow at night.

PALOMO: And what else does he tell you?

CONCHITA: Private things.

PALOMO: Like what?

CONCHITA: Obscenities.

PALOMO: And you like that?

CONCHITA: He knows when and how to say them.

PALOMO: And when does he talk to you this way?

CONCHITA: When we're both deep inside each other and we could almost surrender to death. When he pounds so hard inside me as if to kill me. As if to revive me from that drowning place, from that deep place where he takes me.

PALOMO: I see.

CONCHITA: Why so curious, Palomo?

PALOMO: Because I don't know . . . Because . . . You seem different. You've changed.

CONCHITA: It happens when lovers do what they are supposed to do.

PALOMO: Do you ever talk to him about me?

CONCHITA: Yes. He wanted to know why you stopped loving me.

PALOMO: And what did you tell him?

CONCHITA: I told him that it just happened one day, like everything else in life.

PALOMO: And what was his response?

CONCHITA: He wanted to know what I felt and I told him the truth. I told him that I desire and love you just the same.

PALOMO: And was he fine with that?

CONCHITA: He told me to show him how I love you. To show him on his body.

PALOMO: And what did you do?

CONCHITA: It was terrifying.

PALOMO: What was terrifying?

CONCHITA: I thought it would be impossible. That nobody could occupy that space in me. But he did. He did. And everything seemed so recognizable, as if he had known me all along. His room became a theatre and his bed a stage, and we became like actors in a play. Then I asked him to play my role, to pretend to be me and I dressed him in my clothes. And he was compliant. It was as if I was making love to myself, because he knew what to do, where to go and where to take me.

PALOMO: Show me.

CONCHITA: Show you what?

PALOMO: Show me . . . Show me what he did to you and how he did it.

CONCHITA: You would have to do as actors do.

PALOMO: And what is that?

CONCHITA: Actors surrender. They stop playing themselves and they give in. You would have to let go of yourself and enter the life of another human being, and in this case it would be me.

PALOMO: Teach me then.

CONCHITA: Here, in the factory?

PALOMO: Yes, back there, where you meet him.

(Soft music plays. Conchita traces Palomo's neck and shoulders with her hand. He leads her out of the room. Lights change. Juan Julian closes the book. The soft music fades.)

Scene 3

A danzón plays. It's the inauguration of the new cigar brand. There's a party. The workers start filing in, dressed in their best clothes. Santiago and Ofelia enter with two bottles of rum and glasses.

OFELIA: Did you get enough rum, Santiago?

SANTIAGO: Did I get enough rum? Tell her how much rum I got, Juan Julian.

JUAN JULIAN: He's got enough rum to get an elephant drunk.

OFELIA: Then give me some before anybody gets here, so I can calm my nerves.

SANTIAGO: What are you nervous about?

OFELIA: Oh, I have the heart of a seal and when I get excited it wants to swim out of my chest.

(Santiago gives her a drink.)

SANTIAGO: Let's have a drink, the three of us. We ought to have a private toast before anybody gets here.

(Santiago serves drinks.)

We really haven't done that badly this year. Sales were down last month but we're still staying above water.

OFELIA: We'll do well, Santiago. People need to blow out smoke and vent themselves.

SANTIAGO (Toasting): That's right, salud!

OFELIA: Salud.

JUAN JULIAN: Salud.

OFELIA: Let's bring out the lanterns.

(The three of them exit. Cheché and Palomo, both elegantly dressed, enter with palm leaves to decorate the factory. They are engaged in conversation.)

PALOMO: Sometimes I think . . . I keep wondering if they're still together, if they see each other. I can feel it. Or it's just me. My mind. At night I can't sleep. I lie there awake thinking, imagining the two of them together. I can still smell him on her skin, her clothes and her handkerchief. I can see him on her face and her eyes, and I don't know what to do . . .

CHECHÉ: You should move up North to Trenton and start a new life. Take her away from here. That's what I wanted to do with Mildred. I'd figure we could live up North. The two of us could work in a cigar factory. There are plenty of them in Trenton. And there are no lectors and no good-for-nothing love stories, which put ideas into women's heads and ants inside their pants . . .

(Juan Julian enters with a garland of Chinese lanterns.)

JUAN JULIAN: Would you give me a hand with the lanterns?

PALOMO: Ah, we were just talking about the love stories.

JUAN JULIAN: It's obvious that you don't care much for them. You almost made me lose my job the other day.

PALOMO: Oh, I'm curious as to how the story ends.

CHECHÉ: Yeah! Does the husband ever think of killing the lover? (Laughs) I would've killed the bastard a long time ago.

JUAN JULIAN: The husband would probably choose a duel, instead of killing the lover in cold blood.

CHECHÉ: I would've shot the son of a bitch a long time ago.

JUAN JULIAN: But that's not the way things were done in those days.

CHECHÉ: Then the husband is a coward and a stinker.

PALOMO: Oh, I don't see the husband as a coward. He might be more clever than the three of us. Wouldn't you say so, Juan Julian?

JUAN JULIAN: Well, the husband is acting according to his status. He is a man of power. He has one of the most important positions in the ministry. And we're talking about Saint Petersburg society—everyone knows each other and he doesn't want Anna's affair to turn into a big scandal.

CHECHÉ: The husband is a pansy if you ask me.

PALOMO: So what character do you identify with in the novel?

JUAN JULIAN: I like them all. I learn things from all of them.

PALOMO: And what have you learned from Anna's lover?

JUAN JULIAN: Oh, I don't know . . . I . . .

PALOMO: I'm intrigued as to how he became interested in her.

(Juan Julian knows where Palomo is trying to go with this.)

JUAN JULIAN: Well, it's very obvious in the novel.

PALOMO: And what's your personal opinion?

JUAN JULIAN: She came to him because she thought that he could help her.

PALOMO: Help her how?

JUAN JULIAN: Help her to love again. Help her to recognize herself as a woman all over again. She had probably known only one man and that was the husband. With the lover she learns a new way of loving. And it's this new way of loving that makes her go back to the lover over and over again. But that's my interpretation.

(Santiago and Ofelia enter.)

SANTIAGO: Good! You are all here. We are celebrating the whole day today. Let's have another drink.

OFELIA: Remember you have a speech to make.

SANTIAGO (Lifting the bottle): This will inspire me.

OFELIA: At the rate we're going we'll be drunk before the party gets started.

SANTIAGO (Laughs): Enjoy yourself. Today I'm the happiest man on earth.

(Conchita enters. She's dressed in a chiffon paisley dress.)

CONCHITA: Are you drinking without me?

SANTIAGO: Of course not. Come have a drink with us. Where's your sister? You look beautiful in that dress, my child. I've never seen you wear it.

CONCHITA: Papá, just a month ago I wore it. We were invited to a party. I remember as if it were yesterday. (She looks at her mother) Mamá hates paisleys.

OFELIA: No, I don't, my child.

CONCHITA: You said I looked like an old lady the last time I wore it.

OFELIA: Frankly, I just didn't think much of it when you had it made. But now that you cut your hair and you look so different, it's actually very becoming.

PALOMO: You do look beautiful, my love.

OFELIA: I like paisleys.

CONCHITA: They remind me of gypsies and bohemians.

PALOMO: You actually look very bohemian.

JUAN JULIAN: It's true. Paisleys look dreamy, as if they come from a floating world.

(Palomo looks at Juan Julian. Juan Julian lifts his glass. Palomo brings Conchita close to him and wraps his arm around her.)

Señores, one question. As an outsider, as a foreigner in this country, I have something to ask. Why do Americans prohibit something as divine as whiskey and rum?

SANTIAGO: Because Americans are not socialists when they drink.

(Laughter from the crowd.)

PALOMO: I have another answer to your question. Alcohol is prohibited in this country because alcohol is like literature. Literature brings out the best and the worst part of ourselves. If you're angry it brings out your anger. If you are sad, it brings out your sadness. And some of us are . . . Let's just say, not very happy.

(Ofelia, who is a little tipsy, taps her glass to make a speech.)

OFELIA (Doing a dance step): Ah, but rum brings out your best steps if you are a good dancer. If you have two left feet, it's better if you don't dance at all. So let's face it, señores, Americans are good at making movies, radios and cars, but when it comes to dancing, it's better if . . . With the exception of the colored folks, of course. They've got what it takes to dance up a storm. That's why I think alcohol is prohibited, because most Americans don't know how to dance.

(Grabbing Santiago by the hand) Let's go, I feel like dancing.

SANTIAGO: No. We can't dance yet, because I have an announcement to make. Where's Marela?

OFELIA: She must be putting on her costume.

SANTIAGO: Well, señoras y señores, today we've taken time from work to drink and dance, and to celebrate the new cigar brand we are launching into the market. (He takes out a cigar from his shirt pocket) This well-crafted cigar is wrapped in the finest leaves from Vuelta Abajo in Pinar del Río, the tip of the island of Cuba. The length of this new cigar is six and one-eighth inches. The ring gauge is fifty-two. I truly believe this is our finest toro.

Where's Marela? She should be here.

(Marela enters dressed in an elegant black gown. She is like Anna on the night of the ball.)

MARELA: I'm here, Papá.

SANTIAGO: Let me look at you, my little blue sky.

OFELIA: But my child, you look beautiful.

SANTIAGO: You came just in time . . . I was just about to say that since most cigars are named after women and romantic love stories, today we are baptizing our new cigar with the name Anna Karenina! This cigar will sell for ten cents and we are hoping this new brand will bring us fortune and prosperity. So now that we are all gathered here, I would like to ask my beloved Ofelia to do us the honor of officially lighting the first Anna Karenina.

(Applause from the crowd. The cigar is passed to Ofelia. Santiago lights it with a match. Ofelia takes a puff and blows out a ring of smoke.)

Well?

OFELIA: It's . . . It's . . . Aaaah! It burns like a blue dream.

(The crowd applauds.)

PALOMO: Bravo! Bravo!

(Ofelia passes the cigar to Santiago and he gives it to Marela.)

SANTIAGO: And to the youngest one in the family, our very own Anna.

(Marela takes a puff, coughs a little. She laughs. She passes the cigar to another. This person presents it to Santiago.)

MARELA: Mhm! Lovely!

(Santiago takes a puff.)

SANTIAGO: Ah! It's glorious. Perfecto.

(Applause from the crowd.)

Chester.

(Santiago hands the cigar to someone, who passes it to Cheché. He takes a puff.)

CHECHÉ: Burns well. Pleasant aroma. I detect a little bit of cherry. I think it's our finest horse.

(Applause. The cigar is passed to Palomo. Palomo passes it to Conchita. She takes a puff.)

CONCHITA: Ah! It speaks of forests and orchids.

(Applause. Conchita hands the cigar to Marela. Marela gives it Palomo. He takes a puff.)

PALOMO: Mhm! Magnifico! Definitely like aged rum. Sweet like mangoes.

(Palomo passes it to Santiago.)

SANTIAGO: You forgot Juan Julian.

PALOMO: Ah, yes we can't forget our lector, who brought us the world of *Anna Karenina*.

(Santiago passes the cigar back to Palomo. Palomo takes off his hat and gives Juan Julian the cigar. This is an offense since the cigar should never be handed directly to the person that is supposed to smoke. There has to be a mediator to facilitate communication with the gods. Juan Julian smiles. He smells the cigar, looks up and makes a gesture to the gods.)

JUAN JULIAN: Sweet aroma. (Taking a puff) It sighs like a sunset and it has a little bit of cocoa beans and cedar. I believe we have a cigar, señores!

SANTIAGO: We do have a cigar, señores! We have a champion!

OFELIA (A little tipsy): Indeed we have a champion!

MARELA: Papá, let's go out into the streets and tell the world about our cigar. Let's give our new cigars to the people.

SANTIAGO: And go bankrupt, my child! No, I propose a gunshot!

OFELIA: A gunshot! Santiago, you're drunk. Stop drinking.

SANTIAGO: No inauguration is complete without the breaking of a bottle or a gunshot.

MARELA: I propose two gunshots then!

SANTIAGO: Can't have two gunshots. It's got to be three.

MARELA: Then I'll shoot the third one.

(Laughter.)

SANTIAGO: Let's go. Let's shoot!

OFELIA: Just make sure you aim up high, but don't shoot the moon!

(They all laugh. The workers bring the party outside. As Conchita starts to leave, Palomo grabs her by the arm.)

PALOMO: Where are you going?

CONCHITA: Outside.

PALOMO: You've been looking at him the whole night. You're falling in love with this man.

CONCHITA: Maybe just as much as you are.

PALOMO: I don't like men.

(Sound of a celebratory gunshot. Laughter.)

CONCHITA: Then why do you always want me to tell you what I do with him?

PALOMO: Because it's part of the old habit we have of listening. We are listeners.

CONCHITA: No, there's something else.

PALOMO: You're right there's something else. And it's terrible sometimes.

CONCHITA: Then nothing makes sense to me anymore.

(Another gunshot. More laughter.)

PALOMO: (Grabbing her arm): I want you to go back to him and tell him you want to make love like a knife.

CONCHITA: Why a knife?

PALOMO: Because everything has to be killed.

(Another gunshot. More laughter: Ofelia, Santiago, Marela and Juan Julian reenter.)

OFELIA: Señores, I have a confession to make. When I was seventeen, and that was yesterday, I was chosen to pose for a cigar brand that was called Aida, like the opera. And, of course, just the thought of my face being on a cigar ring and in so many men's hands and lips, my mother was scandalized. You see, we weren't cigar people, we were in the guava jelly business. So when my mother forbid me to pose for the label, I told her that I wanted a picture of my face on a can of guava marmalade. And it was only fair. So, they dressed me up in a red dress and I had a red carnation behind my ear. They had me looking lovely sitting in a hammock and a parrot by my side . . .

(Everyone laughs.)

SANTIAGO: Let's go, my dear. We have smoked, we have fired a gun and you've had too much to drink.

OFELIA: Bah, you just want to take advantage of me because I'm drunk.

MARELA (Embarrassed): Mamá!

(Santiago laughs. He takes Ofelia by the hand. They start to exit.)

SANTIAGO: Good night!

MARELA: Good night!

OFELIA: Marela, are you coming with us?

MARELA: I'll be there in a minute.

OFELIA: Don't be too long. (They exit)

PALOMO (Grabbing Conchita's hand): Let's go home. (To the others) We'll see you tomorrow.

JUAN JULIAN: Adios!

CONCHITA: Adios!

(Conchita and Palomo exit, leaving Marela and Juan Julian alone.)

MARELA: Oh, I don't want this night to end. I could stay up all night. I don't want to sleep. We sleep too much. We spend more than a third of our lives sleeping, sleeping. Darkness descends and everything is a mystery to us. We don't know if trees really walk at night, as I've heard in legends. We don't really know if statues and spirits dance in the squares unbeknown to us. And how would we ever know if we sleep? We sleep and sleep . . .

JUAN JULIAN: Oh, I want to have what you drank. What did you drink?

MARELA: Oh, I didn't drink. I just feel gladness.

Papá was so happy. I like to see him that way. And Mamá was so full of joy. (Laughs) She's the one who drinks a little too much.

JUAN JULIAN: It's good to drink a little once in a while.

(Cheché reenters. He stays at a distance, watching.)

MARELA: Yes, we deserve a little drink. We work hard enough. We deserve all that life offers us, and life is made of little moments. Little moments as small as violet petals. Little moments I could save in a jar and keep forever, like now talking to you.

JUAN JULIAN (Playfully): Ah! So you are a collector. And what sort of things do you like to collect besides a night like this one?

MARELA: The first time you read and the day you walked me to the pharmacy.

JUAN JULIAN: So I'm in one of your jars.

MARELA: In many.

JUAN JULIAN (Smiles): Many. (Beat. Looks at her tenderly) You are clear and fresh as water. Did anybody ever tell you this?

MARELA: No, never.

JUAN JULIAN: Then people are blind.

MARELA: Blind? Do you think so? And how can one teach the blind to see?

JUAN JULIAN: I wouldn't know. I'm not blind.

MARELA: But we are all blind in the eyes of those who can't see.

JUAN JULIAN: You're right.

MARELA: We just have to learn to use our eyes in the dark. We have to learn to see through words and sound, through our hands. (Touches his hand)

JUAN JULIAN: I'm sure those who are blind will see your beauty once they touch your face. (Touches her face tenderly)

I must go now. Sleep well.

MARELA: Adios.

JUAN JULIAN: Adios.

(Just as Juan Julian is about to exit:)

MARELA: Juan Julian . . .

JUAN JULIAN: Yes.

MARELA: Lend me the book.

JUAN JULIAN (Not realizing that he is holding it): What book?

MARELA: The book in your hand.

JUAN JULIAN: Oh!

MARELA: I promise not to get ahead of the story.

JUAN JULIAN: Bring it tomorrow morning or I won't have a book to read.

MARELA: May you dream of angels!

JUAN JULIAN (Kissing her face): You, too.

(As Juan Julian exits, Marela stays looking at him in the distance. She brings the book to her chest, then she opens it and reads, as if to find consolation, the sort one seeks in the lonely hours of the night.)

MARELA:

> *Anna Karenina prepared herself for the journey with joy and willfulness. With small, skillful hands she opened a red bag and took out a little cushion, which she placed on her knees before closing the bag.*

(Cheché emerges from the shadows. He takes a handkerchief from his pocket and dries his face. He looks at Marela. His glance is full of desire. Marela sees him. She closes the book. Cheché grabs her arm. Blackout.)

Scene 4

Palomo enters the factory carrying a couple of heavy boxes. Conchita is clearing up the mess from the night before.

PALOMO: Where's Cheché?

CONCHITA: He hasn't come in yet.

PALOMO: I hope someone gets here with the keys to the safe. The boy who delivered these boxes is out there and he wants to get paid.

CONCHITA: I'll go to the house and ask Mamá for the keys.

PALOMO: No. You got to help me take inventory of all these boxes. (Hands her some papers)

CONCHITA: As soon as I finish with this.

I wonder why Papá isn't here.

PALOMO: He's probably still in bed. He did drink . . .

CONCHITA: Yes you're right. Mamá must be putting cold compresses on his forehead. It always happens.

(Santiago and Ofelia enter. Santiago is trying to get rid of his hangover by rubbing his forehead.)

OFELIA: Morning!

CONCHITA: Morning!

PALOMO: Santiago, I need the key to the safe. I have to pay for this delivery.

SANTIAGO: Ofelia has them.

OFELIA: I just left them at the office on top of the desk.

(Palomo exits. Ofelia sits down and starts rolling cigars.)

SANTIAGO: Where's Cheché?

CONCHITA: He hasn't arrived yet.

SANTIAGO: I don't blame him. I would've stayed in bed myself. But your mother is like a rooster. When she gets up from bed nobody . . .

OFELIA: I didn't wake you up.

SANTIAGO: I didn't say you did. It's those slippers you use to walk around the house. They are louder than a running train. (Makes noise) Shoo . . . Shoo . . . Everywhere . . . One day I'm going to throw them out the window.

OFELIA: You do that and I'll give your Sunday shoes to the chimney cleaner.

SANTIAGO: See, now the pain got worse! This woman, how she likes to bother me! Ay!

CONCHITA: Do you want my bottle of spirits, Papá?

SANTIAGO: Give me anything you have, my child. Your mother doesn't take care of me.

(Conchita gives him the bottle of spirits. He sniffs. Marela enters wearing the long coat. She goes to her table and starts to roll cigars.)

MARELA: Morning!

CONCHITA: Marela, why are you wearing that coat? Aren't you warm? . . .

MARELA: No. Some coats keep winter inside them. You wear them and you find pockets full of December, January and February. All those months that cover the earth with snow and make everything still. That's how I want to be, layered and still.

OFELIA: My child, are you all right?

MARELA: I'm fine, Mamá. Don't worry about me.

(Juan Julian enters.)

JUAN JULIAN: Good morning!

ALL: Good morning!

MARELA: Here's your book. (Hands him the book)

(Juan Julian notices Marela's coat, and that she seems to be in a state of dismay.)

JUAN JULIAN: Thank you.

(Palomo reenters.)

PALOMO: Has Cheché come in yet?

CONCHITA: No. He's just late. Sit down. Juan Julian is going to read to us.

JUAN JULIAN: Today I'll begin by reading Part 3, Chapter 13, of *Anna Karenina*:

In his youth Anna Karenina's husband had been intrigued by the idea of dueling because he was physically a coward and was well aware of this fact. In his youth this terror had often forced him to think about dueling and imagining himself in a situation in which it was necessary to endanger his life.

(Cheché enters unnoticed. His head is heavy with dark thoughts.)

This old ingrained feeling now reasserted itself. Let's suppose I challenge him. Let's suppose someone teaches me how to do it, he went on thinking.

(Cheché pulls out a gun.)

They put us in position, I squeeze the trigger, he said to himself, and it turns out I've killed him. He shook his head to drive away such silly thoughts. What would be the sense of killing a man in order to define one's own relations with a woman . . .

(Cheché shoots Juan Julian. Then shoots again. The sound of the gun echoes and echoes as Juan Julian falls to the floor.

The workers are shocked. Some of them look up to see where the shot came from. The shot still echoes throughout the room as Marela reaches out to touch the dying lector.

The lights fade to black.)

Scene 5

Three days have passed. The factory workers are rolling cigars and organizing the tobacco leaves by their proper size and shape. Marela is still wearing her coat.

OFELIA: What silence! I never knew that silence could have so much weight. Can someone say something? Can someone read? We are listeners! We are oidores! I can't get used to this silence all around us. It's as if a metal blanket has fallen on us.

PALOMO: The same silence we had when our last reader died.

OFELIA: No, this silence is louder. Much louder. Much louder.

SANTIAGO: That's because Juan Julian died before his time, and the shadows of the young are heavier and they linger over the earth like a cloud.

MARELA: I should write his name on a piece of paper and place it in a glass of water with brown sugar, so his spirit knows that he is welcomed in this factory, and he can come here and drink sweet water. And nobody better tell me that it's wrong for me to do this! You hear me, Mamá! (For the first time tears come to her eyes)

SANTIAGO: Your mother hasn't said anything, my child.

MARELA: I know she hasn't. But we must look after the dead, so they can feel part of the world. So they don't forget us and we could count on them when we cross to the other side.

CONCHITA: We should continue reading, Papá!

MARELA: Yes, we should continue reading the story in his honor, so he doesn't feel that he left his job undone. He should know that we're still his faithful listeners.

CONCHITA: If I could, I would read, but I know that if I open that book I'll be weak.

MARELA: We shouldn't cry. Tears are for the weak that mourn the knife and the killer, and the trickle of blood that streams from this factory all the way to the house where he was born.

OFELIA: Could someone read?

(Pause.)

PALOMO: I will read.

OFELIA: That's it, read, so we can get rid of this silence and this heat. And we can pause over a few lines and sigh and be glad that we are alive.

SANTIAGO: But read something else. Read something cheerful.

MARELA: Stories should be finished, Papá. Let him finish the book.

CONCHITA: She's right. Stories should be finished or they suffer the same fate as those who die before their time.

(Palomo opens the book. He looks at Conchita.)

PALOMO: *Anna Karenina.* Part 3, Chapter 14:

> *By the time he arrived in Petersburg, Anna Karenina's husband was not only completely determined to carry out his decision, but he had composed in his head a letter he would write to his wife.*

(He looks up from the book and stares at Conchita.)

> *In his letter he was going to write everything he'd been meaning to tell her.*

(The lights begin to fade.)

END OF PLAY

 For media resources and other materials related to this chapter, please visit www.mhhe.com/creativespirit5e.

Appendix: Guided Writing Assignments

The assignments presented here focus on the analytical and writing skills used by dramaturgs and critics, as discussed in Chapter 13. Three different writing projects ask you to consider the ideas in a play or production while drawing on your own perceptions and creativity. Underlying all three assignments should be a goal articulated by Ben Brantley, the chief theatre critic for *The New York Times:* "to generate excitement about the theatre … [and] open a window for people to look in."

ASSIGNMENT I: WRITE A REVIEW

Write a four-page review of a campus, community, or professional theatre production. Imagine that you will publish the review in your school newspaper, to be read by your college community, students, and faculty. Your readers will also include the participants in the production. The review should explore the content of the play and the stylistic choices made by the director, actors, and designers.

Purpose

The basic goals of writing a review are to come to a greater understanding of the production and to communicate to your readers the experience of being an audience member. A productive review will provide valuable information for potential audience members as well as useful and respectful feedback to the theatre practitioners involved. In order to determine the focus for your review, keep in mind the four questions posed by Julius Novick, a critic for *The Village Voice*, summarized in Chapter 13:

1. What is the work itself trying to do?
2. How well has it done it?
3. Was it worth doing?
4. Why was it worth doing?

A play that offers a hard look at a controversial problem on your campus may be worth doing. But so is a comedy that really makes us laugh or a musical with great music and characters we love. What is important in writing the review is to take the production on its own terms and think about the success of its various elements in building a convincing whole. The question "Was it worth doing?" covers a broad range of theatre experiences that may balance entertainment and ideas in very different ways.

Preparation

Read the play shortly before attending the performance, if possible. Learn what you can about the playwright and the production history of the play. What other plays has the playwright written? Have they been produced in your community? Does the playwright's biography enhance your understanding of the play? What themes or storytelling devices seem most compelling to you when you read the play?

Watching the Play

An essential part of your work as a reviewer takes place during the performance itself. You need to be fully alert and in a receptive state of mind when you go to the play in order to get the most out of the experience and retain what you have seen. Therefore, you should be well rested when you go to the theatre. Arrive at the theatre early enough to comfortably take your seat and read the program. Be sure to take a small notebook and pen.

Your experience of the play and the many observations you make during the performance about staging, design elements, and characterization will be the basis of your review. It is essential that you take notes immediately after the performance while the details of the production are still fresh in your mind. You may take some notes at intermission. However, it is counterproductive to take notes during the performance itself because writing interrupts your own involvement with the performance and may be distracting to the people sitting around you.

Here are some points to consider as you watch the play. How is the performance created for the audience members? What is the layout of the theatre: proscenium? in the round? three sides? Where does the audience sit in relation to the stage, and how close is the audience to the stage? How large is the audience? What do the sets and costumes look like? Are there special effects? What is the sound design? Is there live music? Is the acting realistic and psychologically shaded, or do the actors play to the audience with broad gestures? What are the production's particular strengths? What surprises you? What is particularly moving or disturbing or funny? What do you find yourself thinking about after the performance? Have your own ideas been challenged or changed in some way by this experience?

As you write rough notes after the performance, try to settle on what you think this production was about. What is the central action that drives the different parts of the performance? Is there a theme that ties all the pieces together? What is the story that has been told, and what incidents form the plot?

Writing the Review

The foundation for your introductory paragraph should be a statement summarizing what you think the performance was about. For example, you could say that a production of *Joe Turner's Come and Gone* was about a man's search to find himself, or about the changes that a group of people are going through together as they move from one situation in life to another. What you establish as central to the production in this introductory paragraph will help you decide how to develop the rest of your review in order to explain the development of this major idea or theme.

Some kind of plot summary is important as the next step, but you should not give an overly detailed description of the plot. "First this happened, then that happened" can take up most of your review without providing appropriate interpretation. The plot summary should be approximately one substantial paragraph unless you must explain one aspect of the plot in more detail. The goal of the review is to get underneath the plot to the inner life of the characters and the ramifications of their situation. What you include about the plot should explain how the action of the play develops or should give a summary of the story. What is it that the main characters are trying to accomplish? What are the obstacles they have to overcome to get what they want?

Following the introductory paragraph and the plot summary, explore the production elements of acting and design. Explain how the story was told through acting, sets, costume, lighting, and sound. Here, specific description becomes extremely important for two reasons: (1) You are trying to communicate the experience of being an audience member as vividly as possible; (2) the only way to distinguish effectively between different kinds of plays and interpretations is to evaluate the details and the way they form a whole. Therefore, in writing your review you need to include a good deal of careful description of what you saw and heard.

Ultimately, your review should address one or more of the following questions. What ideas are essential to the play, and how did the production help to shape those ideas? What original interpretations by the producers and actors cast new light on the material? What qualities of the performance captured your imagination and drew you into the world of the play? What performance elements were emphasized, and what did that emphasis mean for the audience? A musical that has an energetic score and exciting choreography offers a different kind of experience from a sad story of lost love or a wild comedy that parodies contemporary politics. What was it like to be an audience member at this event?

The review should focus more on explaining the experience of being an audience member than on judgments about the work of the actors, director, and designers. A useful question to answer in terms of the degree of success of the performance is whether you would recommend it to others. What are the elements that you think are particularly noteworthy? In what ways could the performance be improved in order to be more appealing or compelling? This takes us back to Julius Novick's second question: How well has the work done what it was trying to do? In the end, did the theatre practitioners believe in what they were doing, and did they make you believe?

ASSIGNMENT 2: PREPARE A LOBBY DISPLAY

The instructor will assign a play that has research problems suitable for a lobby display and provide a list of possible topics, issues, or questions that would benefit from investigation. After you have read the play, choose a topic of interest to you and research the history of this subject by consulting books, journals, newspapers, Web sites, or photo archives. Write two pages of text supported by two or three strong visual images that help the audience understand the place of your subject in the play. Arrange the written text and the visual images to make an eye-catching panel for a lobby display.

Purpose

The purpose of a lobby display is to offer the audience important background material on the play in an exciting and inviting presentation that combines text and visual materials. The material should be thought-provoking. It should connect the play to historical issues, contemporary issues, or both. In addition to providing information, the lobby display creates another gathering space for audience members and encourages them to leave their seats at intermission but still stay in touch with the play. Moving around the display may also facilitate interactions between audience members as well as enhance their experience before and after the play. In order to prepare an authoritative and compelling presentation, you must develop your own expertise about the play's background.

Sample Background of a Lobby Display

Let's examine a potential lobby display for the play introduced in Chapter 15: *Anna in the Tropics* by Nilo Cruz. *Anna in the Tropics* is set in a cigar factory in Ybor City, Florida, in 1929. Much of the action of the play is generated by the arrival of a character from Cuba, who is a *lector*, a reader. In actuality, the lectors were major figures in the cigar factories of the early twentieth century who read to the workers from newspapers and novels to educate and entertain them during the workday. Today, most people know little about Cuban immigration to Florida in the late nineteenth century and early twentieth century, or about the cigar industry that provided economic opportunity for many immigrant workers, or about the lectors who read to the workers. However, historians have done a great deal of research in this area, and so there is a variety of excellent books and articles to draw from, including fine photos, that help to illuminate the world of the play. Topics that would contribute to a lively lobby display about *Anna in the Tropics* include the history of Ybor City, particularly in relation to the development of the cigar industry and Cuban immigration to the United States; the nature of work in a cigar factory; and the history of the lector. A map showing the spatial relationship between Ybor City in Florida and Havana in

Cuba would be important, as would a timeline of events in the United States and the world leading up to 1929, which of course is the year the stock market crashed and the Depression began.

ASSIGNMENT 3: INTERVIEW A THEATRE PRACTITIONER AND PRESENT THE INTERVIEW IN WRITING OR IN AN ELECTRONIC FORMAT

Interview a theatre practitioner who is currently engaged in or has just finished working on the production of a specific play on your campus or in your community. You may choose a professional or a student practitioner. A written version of the interview will be three to four pages. An electronic format will be edited to about ten to fifteen minutes.

Purpose

The purpose of an interview is to allow theatre practitioners to express their own insights about their craft and their ideas about or reactions to the play they are working on. For readers, this form of article increases their contact with the art of making theatre through a personal story. The words of an individual bring a subject to life. Anecdotes, emotional responses, examples of the work involved, obstacles to be overcome, and biographical details together weave a story that should capture the reader's attention and illuminate why people are drawn to the theatre and what sustains their efforts. A good interview allows the reader to share in the passion of actors and playwrights for the work they do.

Preparation

Select someone to interview who in your judgment is doing work that merits your attention or from whom you can learn about important issues. At least a week in advance, contact this person to request an interview and arrange for a specific day and time. Determine an appropriate meeting place, and make sure it is available. Although coffee shops and restaurants are popular places for interviews, the noise level at such places can often interfere with your ability to successfully record the conversation.

An interview must be recorded. Otherwise you cannot have an accurate version of your subject's words. You may make an audio recording, or you may use video. Ultimately, the finished presentation of your interview can be in the form of a written article in which you will transcribe parts of the recorded conversation; or you can present the work electronically on a CD or a DVD. Whatever the final form, part of your preparation will involve securing an appropriate recording device, which could be borrowed from your audiovisual department or connected to your own computer. Choose a possible site for the publication or broadcast presentation of the interview, such as your school newspaper, a television station, or a Web site for your class. This will help you determine the audience for the material and the format, whether the interview actually appears at this site or not.

In preparation for the interview, you should read the play in which your subject is involved and, if possible, attend either a rehearsal or a performance. If biographical information about your interviewee is not available, this could become one of the topics for your interview. Consider what is intriguing to you about both the play currently being performed and the work of the artist. What would you like to know about the challenges of this production and the circumstances of personal history, training, or experience that guide artistic decisions? Develop a written list of questions, which you will refer to when you are conducting the interview.

Conducting the Interview

In conducting an interview, the emphasis must be on the person being interviewed, not the person asking the questions. Your job as an interviewer is to encourage your subject to speak while you remain an alert and engaged listener. It is certainly appropriate to briefly explain your background and point of view when you meet with the subject, and in editing the interview material. Observing a time limit of about thirty to forty minutes is appropriate. Avoid the temptation to speak longer. You need to be respectful of your interviewee's schedule, and you will end up with more material than you can use. The time limit does require you to remain focused on your questions and to gently guide your subject back to the point if the conversation begins to wander. Practicing some of your questions with a roommate or friend is a good strategy to help you be more comfortable when you are actually conducting the interview.

Editing the Interview

Select the comments of your subject that are the most vivid and that offer helpful specific examples and details. Eliminate passages or phrases that are redundant, vague, or tangential to the major points you are trying to develop. For a written version of the interview, you should edit out words that meander, whether they fall within a sentence or between sentences that carry clearly focused ideas. For a video or audio presentation, editing out rambling sections will be more practical than trying to tighten up individual sentences. Write a brief introduction that provides the essential background and focus for the interview. The introduction should make two points: why you did the interview, and what may be of greatest interest to the reader. Group statements that are related or contribute to developing the same idea. Choose those questions of yours that successfully introduce and frame the responses you have selected. For example, an interview could be organized around three major topics such as why your subject chose to go into the theatre, what kind of training he or she had, and what was most interesting or challenging about the work on the play you saw.

Notes

Chapter 1

1. The description of this performance draws on details provided in "Postscript: The Treasures of Siwidi," by Judith Ostrowitz and Aldona Jonaitis in Jonaitis, Aldona, *Chiefly Feasts*, New York: American Museum of Natural History, 1991.

2. Bill Irwin, quoted in Bruce Weber, "Just Clowning Around with Intellect," *New York Times*, March 3, 1993, C1.

3. Olga Sanchez interview with the author, December 2005.

4. Dorothy K. Washburn, *Hopi Kachina: Spirit of Life* (San Francisco: California Academy of Sciences, 1980), 40.

5. Washburn, 41.

6. Euripides, *Medea and Other Plays*, translated and edited by James Morwood (Oxford: Oxford University Press, 1998), 32.

7. Jose Luis Valenzuela interview with the author, December 2008.

Chapter 2

1. *Hamlet*, in *The Complete Plays and Poems of William Shakespeare*, ed. William Allen Neilson and Charles Jarvis Hill (Cambridge: Riverside Press, 1942), 1049. (I, i)

2. *King Lear*, in *The Complete Plays*, ed. Neilson and Hill, 1158. (III, ii)

3. *Henry V*, in *The Complete Plays*, ed. Neilson and Hill, 711. (Prologue)

4. *Hamlet*, 1068. (III, ii)

5. *Hamlet*, 1068. (III, ii)

6. A. C. Scott, *The Theatre in Asia* (New York: Macmillan, 1972), 261.

7. Ben Brantley, "Theatre Review, *Black Watch*," *New York Times*, October 24, 2007.

8. Susan Sontag, "Godot Comes to Sarajevo," *New York Review*, October 21, 1993, 52.

9. Sontag, 54.

Chapter 3

1. August Wilson, preface to *Three Plays* (Pittsburgh: University of Pittsburgh Press, 1991), viii.

2. Richard Bernstein, "August Wilson's Voices from the Past," *New York Times*, March 27, 1988, sec. 2, p. 1.

3. Wilson, preface to *Three Plays*, viii.

4. August Wilson, "Aunt Ester's Children: A Century on Stage," American Theatre, Theatre Communications Group, November 2005, p. 30.

5. Wilson, preface to *Three Plays*, ix.

6. Imamu Amira Baraka [LeRoi Jones], *Blues People* (New York: Morrow, 1963), 61.

7. William Barlow, *Looking Up at Down* (Philadelphia: Temple University Press, 1989), 7–8.

8. August Wilson, foreword to Myron Schwartzman, *Romare Bearden: His Life and Art* (New York: Abrams, 1990), 8.

9. Wilson, foreword to *Romare Bearden*, 9.

10. To hear Bessie Smith's version, listen to Bessie Smith, "Nobody Knows You When You're Down and Out," *The Complete Recordings*, Vol. 4, Columbia, 1993.

11. Bernstein, sec. 2, p. 1.

12. August Wilson, *Joe Turner's Come and Gone* (New York: New American Library, 1988), 67.

13. W. C. Handy, *The Father of the Blues* (New York: Collier, 1941), 146.

14. All quotations in the production analysis are from the author's interviews.

15. The early death of LeWan Alexander was a loss to the nation's theatre community.

Chapter 4

1. Billy Crudup quoted in Laurie Stahlbarg, "Brilliant and Brutal Theatre: Interview with Billy Crudup and Michael Stahlbarg," *Scene 4 Magazine*, January 2006.

2. David Warrilow, quoted in Laurie Lassiter, "David Warrilow: Creating Symbol and Cypher," in *Acting (Re)Considered*, ed. Phillip B. Zarrilli (London: Routledge, 1995), 321.

3. BW Gonzalez, interview with the author, July 17, 2002.

4. Anna Deavere Smith, quoted in Stephen Foehr, "Creating Community," *Houston Chronicle*, January 17, 1994, 3.

5. Stephen Spinella, quoted in Janet Sonenberg, *The Actor Speaks* (New York: Random House, 1996), 252.

6. Gonzalez interview.

7. Sean McNall, interview with the author, November 2007.

8. Spinella, quoted in Sonenberg, 278.

9. Heather Robison, interview with the author, November 2008.

10. James Earl Jones, quoted in Holly Hill, *Actors' Lives: On and off the American Stage, Interviews by Holly Hill* (New York: Theatre Communications Group, 1993), 19.

11. Richard Gallegos, interview with the author, January 2009.

12. McNall interview.

13. Gallegos interview.

14. Gordon Davidson, quoted in Gordon Hunt, *How to Audition* (New York: HarperCollins, 1995), 203.

15. Hunt, 184.

16. Jack Bowdan, quoted in Heltie Lynee Hurtes, *The Back Stage Guide to Casting Directors* (New York: Watson-Guptill), 15.

17. Stuart Ostrow, quoted in Hunt, 168.

18. Tamu Gray, interview with the author, March 24, 1993.

19. James Earl Jones, quoted in Hill, 9–10.

20. Kathleen Chalfant, quoted in Sonenberg, 102–103.

21. Robison interview.

22. Joe Mantello, quoted in Sonenberg, 141–42.

23. Gonzalez interview.

24. *King Lear*, in *The Complete Works of Shakespeare*, ed. David Bevington (New York: HarperCollins, 1992), 1173. (I, i)

25. Nancy Keystone, interview with the author, February 2009.

26. Gallegos interview.

27. Valerie Spencer, interview with the author, January 2009.

28. Mary-Louise Parker, quoted in Mervyn Rothstein, "Getting *Proof* to Work is a Delicate Equation," *New York Times*, June 3, 2001, 7.

29. Ray Ford, interview with the author, February 2009.

30. Spencer interview.

31. Cate Blanchett, quoted in Matt Dobkin, "New York Theatre, Hedda Steam," *New York Magazine*, February 27, 2006.

32. Sarah Jessica Parker, quoted in Bruce Weber, "The Starry 'Three Sisters' Cast Reveals a Trend," *New York Times*, February 9, 1997, 31.

33. Spencer interview.

Chapter 5

1. Libby Appel interview with the author, July 17, 2002.

2. Harold Clurman, "In a Different Language," in *Directors on Directing*, ed. Toby Cole and Helen Krich Chinoy (New York: Bobbs-Merrill, 1963), 275.

3. Peter Brook, *There Are No Secrets: Thoughts on Acting and Theatre* (London: Methuen, 1993), 25.

4. Brook, 52–53.

5. Jerzy Grotowski, "Towards a Poor Theatre," in *Towards a Poor Theatre*, ed. Jerzy Grotowski (New York: Simon and Schuster, 1968), 17.

6. Jerzy Grotowski, quoted in Naim Kattan, "Theatre Is an Encounter: An Interview with Jerzy Grotowski," in Grotowski, 58.

7. Ludwik Flaszen, "*Akropolis:* Treatment of the Text," in Grotowski, 62.

8. Grotowski, 164.

9. Ping Chong interview with the author, October 6, 2005.

10. Declan Donnellan, quoted in Maria M. Delgado and Paul Heritage, *In Contact with the Gods? Directors Talk Theatre* (Manchester: Manchester University Press, 1996), 89.

11. Elizabeth LeCompte, quoted in David Savran, *The Wooster Group, 1975–1985: Breaking the Rules* (Ann Arbor, MI: Books on Demand, 1986), 115–116.

12. Adam Rapp interview with the author, November 2007.

13. JoAnne Akalaitis, quoted in Arthur Bartow, *The Director's Voice* (New York: Theatre Communications Group, 1988), 4.

14. Peter Sellars, quoted in Bartow, 276.

15. Lloyd Richards, quoted in April Austin, "Lloyd Richards and August Wilson: A Winning Partnership Plays On," *Christian Science Monitor*, September 18, 1995, 13.

16. Lloyd Richards, quoted in "Theater-Maker at Yale," *Fairpress* (Norwalk, Conn., June 21, 1990), F3.

17. Richards, quoted in "Theater-Maker at Yale," F3.

18. Appel interview.

19. Tisa Chang interview with the author, June 23, 1995.

20. William Ball, *A Sense of Direction* (New York: Drama Book Publishers, 1984), 36.

21. Keystone interview.

22. William Shakespeare, *Macbeth* (New York: Applause, 1996), 46.

23. Bartow, 118.

24. Ford interview.

25. Irene Worth, quoted in Lally Weymouth, "In Order to Achieve Real Wings in Chekhov You Just Live It," *New York Times*, March 6, 1977, 24.

26. Andrei Serban, quoted in Richard Eder, "Andrei Serban," *New York Times*, February 13, 1977, sec. 6, p. 53.

27. Ball, 111.

Chapter 6

1. Elizabeth Kendall, "'Bring in da Noise' Steps Uptown, Feet First," *New York Times*, April 21, 1996, 7.

2. Material on *The Grapes of Wrath* is derived from Eric Stone, interviews with the author, June 1997.

3. Angela Wendt, quoted in Evelyn McDonnell and Katherine Silberger, *Rent: Book, Music, and Lyrics by Jonathan Larson* (New York: Morrow, 1997), 153.

4. Deborah Dryden interview with the author, May 30, 1997.

5. Tharon Musser, quoted in Gary Stevens and Alan George, *The Longest Line: Broadway's Most Singular Sensation—A Chorus Line* (New York: Applause, 1995), 66.

6. Jim Sale interview with the author, April 1994.

7. Justin Townsend interview with the author, January 2009.

8. Joan Arhelger interview with the author, August 5, 2002.

9. Elizabeth LeCompte, quoted in Michael Sommers, "Why Do You Need Sound Anyway?" *Theatre Crafts*, August/September 1991, 36.

10. Tom Mardikes, quoted in Steve Winn, "Tom Mardikes," *Theatre Crafts*, October 1991, 30.

11. Kurt Fischer, quoted in McDonnell and Silberger, 60.

12. Randy Tico interview with the author, January 2009.

Chapter 7

1. Ruby Cohn, *Currents in Contemporary Drama* (Bloomington: Indiana University Press, 1969), 54–55.

2. Jiao Juyin, quoted in program for *The Teahouse*, ed. Meng Shanshan Yang Jing, trans. Wu Zhuhong (Beijing, China: Beijing People's Art Theatre, 2005).

3. Lin Zhaohua interview with the author, November 6, 2005.

Chapter 8

1. Wakako Yamauchi, "And the Soul Shall Dance," in *Songs My Mother Taught Me: Stories, Plays, and Memoir*, ed. Garrett Hongo (New York: Feminist Press, 1994).

2. Sources are Roger Daniels, *The Politics of Prejudice: The Anti-Japanese Movement in California and the Struggle for Japanese Exclusion* (New York: Atheneum, 1977), 63, 88; Ronald Takaki, *Strangers*

from a Different Shore: A History of Asian Americans (Boston: Little, Brown, 1989), 180, 203–209; and the Wing Luke Asian Museum, Seattle.

3. Chiura Obata, quoted in *Chiura Obata's Topaz Moon: Art of the Internment*, ed. Kimi Kodani: Hill (Berkeley: Heyday Books, 2000), 105.

4. Wakako Yamauchi, quoted in preface to *Songs My Mother Taught Me*, vii.

5. Wakako Yamauchi, quoted in Stephanie Arnold, "Dissolving the Half Shadows," in *Making a Spectacle*, ed. Lynda Hart (Ann Arbor: University of Michigan Press, 1988), 181–182.

6. All quotations in the production analysis are from the author's interviews.

Chapter 9

1. Bertolt Brecht, *Brecht on Theatre*, ed. and trans. John Willett (New York: Hill and Wang, 1964), 71.

2. Wendy Arons, "Preaching to the Converted: An Interview with Tony Kushner," *Communications from the International Brecht Society*, 23, no. 2 (1994): 59.

3. Brecht, 137–138.

4. Brecht, 86.

5. Martin Esslin, *The Theatre of the Absurd* (London: Penguin, 1988), 26.

6. John Rockwell, *Robert Wilson: The Theatre of Images* (New York: Harper and Row, 1984), 27.

7. Shen Wei interview with the author, October 6, 2005.

Chapter 10

1. Tony Kushner, *Thinking about the Longstanding Problems of Virtue and Happiness* (New York: Theatre Communications Group, 1995), x.

2. Tony Kushner, *Angels in America: Millennium Approaches* (New York: Theatre Communications Group, 1993), 74.

3. Tony Taccone interviews with the author, June 13 and 16, 1996. All of Taccone's comments in this chapter come from these interviews.

4. Tony Kushner, acknowledgments to *Angels in America: Part Two, Perestroika* (New York: Theatre Communications Group, 1994), xi.

5. Martin Esslin, "Towards an American Dramaturg," in *Dramaturgy in American Theatre*, ed.

Susan Jonas and Geoffrey S. Proehl (Orlando, FL: Harcourt Brace, 1997), 27.

6. Robert Brustein, "From 'The Future of an Un-American Activity," in *Dramaturgy in American Theatre*, ed. Jonas and Proehl, 36.

7. Oskar Eustis interview with the author, June 2, 1996. All of Eustis's remarks in this chapter come from this interview.

8. Susan Jonas, "Tony Kushner's Angels," in *Dramaturgy in American Theatre*, ed. Jonas and Proehl, 473.

9. Kathleen Chalfant, quoted in Eric Grode, "Two Men and a Mormon (and Ethel Rosenberg)," *TheaterWeek*, September 20–26, 1993, 15.

10. Kushner, *Angels: Perestroika*, 52–53.

Chapter 11

1. Richard A. Long, *The Black Tradition in Dance* (New York: Rizzoli, 1990), 11.

2. Walter Kerr, *New York Times*, December 4, 1966, 5.

3. Frank Rich, "A Musical Theatre Breakthrough," *New York Times*, October 21, 1984, sec. 6, 53.

4. Stephen Sondheim quoted in Linda Winer, "Sondheim in His Own Words," *American Theatre*, II, no. 2 (May 1985): 12.

5. Stephen Sondheim and John Weidman, *Pacific Overtures* (New York: Theatre Communications Group, 1991), 20–21.

6. Julie Taymor, *The Lion King: Pride Rock on Broadway* (New York: Hyperion, 1999), 28.

7. Taymor, 136.

8. John Weidman, quoted in Robin Pogrebin, "Making 'Contact' without Conflict," *New York Times*, October 18, 1999, E3.

Chapter 12

1. Henrik Ibsen, *A Doll House*, in *Henrik Ibsen: The Complete Major Prose Plays*, trans. Rolfe Fjelde (New York: New American Library, 1978), 125. Fjelde translates the title as *A Doll House*, though most American productions use the title *A Doll's House*.

2. Antonin Artaud, *The Theatre and Its Double* (New York: Grove, 1958), 37.

3. Artaud, 98.

4. Robert Wilson, quoted in a brochure from UCLA Extension, "Robert Wilson: Artist in Residence," May 1985.

Chapter 13

1. Pindar, quoted in H. D. F. Kitto, *The Greeks* (Baltimore, MD: Penguin, 1962), 10.

2. Aristotle, *The Poetics*, trans. S. H. Butcher (New York: Hill and Wang, 1968), 52.

3. Aristotle, 76.

4. Aristotle, 59.

5. Luigi Pirandello, *Six Characters in Search of an Author*, trans. John Linstrum (London: Methuen, 1986), act 1.

6. Pirandello, act 3.

7. Oskar Eustis interview with the author, November 2007.

8. Stephen Weeks, correspondence with the author, May 10, 2006.

9. Bryant interview.

10. Julius Novick, "Perspectives in Criticism: The Critic as Writer," talk presented at the Friars Club, February 4, 2005.

11. Novick, "Perspectives in Criticism."

12. Billy Crudup, quoted in "The Actor and the Critic," *American Theatre*, May–June 2006, 66.

Chapter 14

1. Milcha Sanchez-Scott interview with the author, June 1, 1994.

2. Sanchez-Scott interview.

3. There continues to be evolution within the communities of Latin American heritage about the words used to identify national ancestry. "Chicano" emerged as a radical term in the 1960s identifying Americans of Mexican heritage who were associated with political activity. At that time, "Hispanic" began to be considered an outdated term originated by "Anglos." But for some the word "Chicano" had other pejorative connotations or limitations because of its reference to Mexican heritage rather than to a wider group of Latin American nations. The more recent "Latino" and (in reference to women) "Latina" were adopted to refer to any Americans of Latin American descent. "Hispanic" has become a more widely used term again and refers to people of Spanish-speaking origins, so that it could also refer to Europeans. Some people use the terms interchangeably; others have strong preferences. The debate is not unlike that within the African American community over the words "black," "African American," "Afro-American," and the rarely used "Negro."

4. M. Elizabeth Osborn, *On New Ground: Contemporary Hispanic-American Plays* (New York: Theatre Communications Group, 1987), 245.

5. Juan Bruce-Novoa, *Retrospace: Collected Essays on Chicano Literature, Theory, and History* (Houston, TX: Arte Publico, 1990), 49–50.

6. Gloria Anzaldúa, *Borderlands: La Frontera* (San Francisco, CA: Aunt Lute, 1987), 55.

7. Erasmo Gamboa and Carolyn M. Buan, *Nosotros: The Hispanic People of Oregon* (Portland: Oregon Council for the Humanities, 1995), 108.

8. Ming Cho Lee interview with the author, May 1996.

Glossary

A

act 1. To play a role on the stage in front of an audience. 2. The basic division of a play. *Joe Turner's Come and Gone* is divided into two acts.

acting in quotes The Brechtian concept of acting in which actors comment on the actions of the characters they are playing rather than maintain continuous identification with the character.

action The movement of the actors and the unfolding of a play's events. Action may be physical or psychological.

actor The central artist of the theatre who creates a dramatic story on the stage through words and gestures. Frequently the actor expresses the language of a playwright; theatre, however, can exist without playwrights, but it cannot exist without actors.

alienation effect The Brechtian idea of distancing the audience from a performance through breaks in the narrative and the suspense to promote critical awareness.

amplification The augmentation of sound through electronic means.

arena stage A round or square stage completely surrounded by the audience.

audition The process through which actors seeking roles in a play or positions with a theatre company present monologues or scene readings for a director.

avant-garde New ideas of drama and performance that push back boundaries and challenge the assumptions of accepted theatre traditions.

B

beat The basic units of an actor's role defined by changes in character motivation.

Beijing Opera A form of Chinese theatre first introduced in 1790 that relies on music, singing, and acrobatics to express dramas based on the traditional Chinese way of life. Domestic relationships and military conquests are frequently the subjects of Beijing Opera, which also uses mythical subjects to reinforce accepted values.

black box A flexible theatre space in which the stage space and the configuration of the audience space can be changed from production to production.

blocking All of the movement of the actors on the stage during a play.

blues Songs that are part of the African American oral tradition. Descended from slave songs, the blues became a major outlet for community concerns and stories.

book The scripted action and dialogue of a musical—as distinguished from the music and lyrics of the songs.

book musical A musical with an integrated plot such as *Oklahoma!* and *My Fair Lady*.

Broadway The long street that runs through the heart of Manhattan, home to the largest concentration of professional theatres in New York City.

C

camp A linguistic form of parody.

catharsis The release of emotion experienced by audience members watching a play. Aristotle understood this emotional release to be one of the essential elements of the experience of watching a tragedy.

character The people in a play. The theatre is distinguished from other forms of storytelling because of the presence of characters onstage who are engaged in action.

chorus In classical Greek theatre, a group of fifteen or more actors who chanted their lines in unison and sometimes functioned as a character in the play and sometimes provided commentary on the dramatic situation. The chorus added to the rhythmic structure of the performances through singing and dancing.

City Dionysia A festival in ancient Athens that became a major event for the presentation of drama. The festival was held in honor of the god Dionysus, who is closely associated with the Greek theatre.

collaborative art The group effort required to produce theatre, as opposed to the separate work of individuals.

comedy The dramatic genre that focuses on human weakness through humor. Comedy celebrates the regeneration of life through love and reconciliation.

community aesthetics The artistic expression formulated over many years that has precise meaning for a particular community; includes accepted traditions and conventions.

concept musical A musical organized around a theme, with the songs or musical numbers functioning as connected episodes; examples include *A Chorus Line* and *Bring in da Noise, Bring in da Funk*.

costume designer The theatre artist responsible for interpreting plays through the costumes created for the actors.

cross-gender casting The casting of actors of the opposite sex in roles written for either men or women. In many early theatres, men played the roles of women characters. In recent productions, cross-gender casting has been used as a strategy to explore issues of gender identity.

cue The line of dialogue, musical moment, or piece of stage action that is the signal for a character entrance or any change in lights or scenery. For a play to run smoothly, every participant must pay scrupulous attention to the cues.

Cultural Revolution The cultural upheaval initiated by Mao Zedong and his wife Jiang Qing in 1966 with the goal of reforming Chinese society. During the Cultural Revolution, traditional forms of theatre were repressed and replaced with model performances that presented an obvious political point of view.

cyclorama A very large piece of light-colored fabric stretched across the back of the stage that serves to create expansive lighting effects and to silhouette actors.

D

dialogue The language spoken by two or more characters in the play.

Dionysus The Greek god of fertility in whose honor plays were performed in ancient Greece.

director The theatre practitioner who has primary responsibility for the interpretation of a play. The director creates the stage action and unifies all the elements of the production.

downstage The front of the stage or area of the stage closest to the audience.

drama The written text of a play as it is constructed by the playwright.

dramatic ritual A ceremony, frequently religious, that expresses community values or beliefs through performance. Participants enact community stories that have been passed down through generations. Dramatic rituals are performed for the welfare of the community and usually involve repetition of the drama in a set form.

dramaturg A theatre practitioner concerned with selecting plays for a theatre company, working with playwrights on the development of new scripts, and working with directors on research issues.

E

ekkyklema The wheeling cart on which the bodies of dead characters were displayed in Greek tragedy. The ekkyklema showed the results of violence that had taken place offstage.

ensemble A group of actors who work closely together and share the responsibility for the performance of a play.

environmental sound Sound effects that may be live or recorded that contribute to the interpretation of the play or are an expressive part of the performance.

epic theatre A theatrical style that emphasizes a historical approach to the subject and uses an episodic structure. Epic theatre also uses devices such as songs and signs to interrupt the action of the play so that emotional distance is created.

episodic art Visual art and theatre that tell a story through a sequence of connected images or episodes. The church-related art of the Middle Ages was particularly known for employing an episodic form.

equity theatre A theatre company or producing organization that performs in a theatre space that seats an audience of one hundred or more patrons and that pays its actors according to a union contract.

equity waiver theatre A professional theatre with ninety-nine or fewer seats that is thereby exempt from certain regulations of the Actors Equity union.

expressionism A theatrical style that uses exaggeration and distortion in both design and acting to reflect the interior world of the characters.

external acting approach An acting approach that begins with text and movement rather than the psychological analysis of character.

F

farce An extreme form of comedy involving challenges to authority that frequently result in anarchy.

G

genre The division of dramas into categories such as tragedy and comedy as they represent different kinds of human experience.

German expressionism An artistic movement in the visual and performing arts that prevailed in Germany from 1905 to 1922; it merged aesthetic and political views.

gestural acting An approach to acting influenced by Bertolt Brecht and Asian performance techniques that relies on distilling the essence of character through concentrated physical gestures.

glory A scenic device used in the Italian court theatre to fly large groups of characters such as angels.

gobo A stencil placed inside a lighting instrument to create a pattern of reflected light on the floor or on a cyclorama or scenic unit.

ground plan The basic diagram for the placement of furniture, walls, doors, and levels such as stairs; evolves through collaboration by the scene designer and the director.

H

HUAC The Congressional committee organized to monitor "un-American activities." From the late 1930s to the 1950s the committee functioned to censor the content of American theatre and film.

I

improvisation The spontaneous invention of actors used to explore text, character, or situation; a tool used by actors to freely create actions and language. Improvisation can be used in either rehearsal or performance.

inner monologue The unspoken thoughts that accompany an actor's lines in method acting. The actor responds to the character's situation with a stream of spontaneous thoughts as if the actor were in the character's place.

internal acting approach An acting approach that is based on a psychological investigation of character and actor identification with character; involves imagining character history and placing oneself in the character's position.

interpretive art Theatre performance that evolves out of the interpretation of the playwright's script. Directors, actors, and designers are interpretive artists.

K

kabuki A popular Japanese theatre form that began in the sixteenth century; highly stylized with elaborate action, exaggerated gestures and speech patterns, and magnificent costumes, makeup, and wigs.

kachina cycle A sequence of ritual ceremonies performed by the Hopi people of the American Southwest that promotes the welfare of their community. The kachinas are the guardian spirits of the Hopi, who believe that the kachinas participate with them in dramatic ceremonies performed to ensure the success of the harvest and to preserve the Hopi way of life.

kathakali A form of dance drama from southern India in which the actors express a story through movement and complex hand gestures accompanied by musicians and singers who communicate the text. The actors play character types as in the Beijing Opera and spend years in intense training to perfect the strenuous and complicated movement skills. The dramas themselves are based on the *Ramayana* and the *Mahabharata*, two epic Sanskrit poems.

kuroko A performer dressed in black (with a hood) in the tradition of the kabuki theatre; changes scenery and props and helps actors with onstage costume changes.

L

language The dialogue of a play written from the multiple points of view of the characters. Dramatic language may be realistic or poetic.

light plot A diagram that shows the position and type of each lighting instrument to be used for a given production. This diagram is used as a tool in discussion between the lighting designer and the director and is also used by the technicians who hang the lights in the theatre.

lighting designer The theatre artist responsible for interpreting plays through the use of light to create atmosphere and imagery and to make the action visible.

M

mask A fundamental device for establishing character that covers the human face and has been used in dramatic presentations throughout the world since the beginning of theatre.

melodrama A dramatic genre that presents the conflict between good and evil.

method acting An internal approach to acting used in the United States that was influenced by the work of Constantin Stanislavsky. Method acting uses a close study of character psychology to determine the character's sequence of intentions or objectives. Method acting also relies on the actor's own life experiences as a major source of material for character creation.

musical theatre A form of theatre in which dialogue, singing, and dance are integrated to communicate character and plot.

mystery cycle A medieval theatre form based on biblical teachings. Episodic in structure, the mystery cycles were composed of many individual playlets.

N

nonrealism A theatrical style that offers a way of interpreting human experience different from the illusion of daily life created by realism. Some nonrealistic theatrical styles are expressionism, symbolism, and surrealism. Nonrealistic styles emphasize bold theatrical imagery and gestural acting.

nontraditional casting The casting of actors of different racial backgrounds in plays that were written for a nonpluralistic society, such as the plays of Shakespeare.

P

pageant wagons Traveling stages drawn by horses or people on which the playlets of the medieval mystery cycles were performed in England.

parody The imitation of a style of writing (for example, songs or plays) for comic effect or ridicule.

perform To engage in the presentation of theatre, dance, or music. In the theatre, performance involves the manipulation of the persona presented by the actor.

performance The live presentation of a play.

period style Presentational elements such as character movement and dress that are determined by the theatrical and social conventions of a particular era.

perspective The painting technique used to create a sense of depth in painted scenery on the stage.

playwright The theatre artist who authors the playscripts that are frequently the starting point for theatrical creation. The playwright uses language to express dramatic action.

poetic realism Realism that is heightened through symbols, the selection of details, and eloquent language.

plot The sequence of actions that determines what happens in a play; the events that make up the play's story.

poor theatre A term used by Polish director Jerzy Grotowski to identify theatre that uses only those materials necessary to extend the expression of the actor. At the Polish Laboratory Theatre, scenery and costumes were made of the simplest, least costly materials, and no scenic elements were used merely to provide background or ornamentation.

potlatch A ceremonial festival observed by Native people of the Northwest coast of the United States and the Southwest coast of Canada. The potlatch includes feasts and elaborate dramatizations, which present community history and important rites of passage. The wealth and status of the host is confirmed through the presentation of valuable gifts to guests.

presentational staging Staging that makes obvious use of the theatre's resources.

preview A performance that is presented to an invited audience or at a reduced ticket price to allow actors to work in front of an audience before the official opening of a play.

progression The sequence of changes that defines character development.

proscenium arch The frame, like a picture frame, defining the opening of a proscenium stage. The proscenium arch creates the sense that the audience is looking into a contained space from which one wall has been removed.

proscenium stage A rectangular theatre with the stage at one end of the rectangle.

R

realism A theatrical style that creates an illusion of daily life through the presentation of a detailed environment, natural actions, and language that sounds as if it were overheard in ordinary circumstances.

rehearsal The process of exploration and repetition used to prepare a play for public presentation.

rehearsal costume A temporary costume worn during rehearsal to give the actor the opportunity to construct character in response to physical costume restrictions and the psychological dimensions of the costume.

rendering A sketch or painting of scenery or costumes that is used as a visual aid by the director, the other designers, and the actors in the development of a production.

repertory The alternating presentation of more than one play at a time practiced by a theatre company such as the Oregon Shakespeare Festival.

representational staging The creation of a complete, realistic illusion on the stage that makes audience members forget that they are in the theatre.

S

scene 1. The smaller units that make up the acts in a play. 2. A particular moment in the performance of a play. 3. The arrangement of the scene design elements.

scene designer The theatre artist responsible for interpreting plays through shaping and defining the stage space.

scenography The work of the scene designer or combined work of the scene designer, costume designer, lighting designer, and sound designer; also known as stage design.

script The dialogue, stage directions, and character descriptions that together constitute the printed text of a play.

sound reinforcement The use of microphones and amplifiers to augment the sound of actors' voices, particularly in the musical theatre.

spectacle The visual elements of a performance, including scenery, lights, costumes, and the movement of actors.

spine According to Constantin Stanislavsky, the through line of a role or the entire play that the director and actors must identify in their preparation for performance.

stage picture The arrangement of actors on the stage to communicate character relationships.

style The combination of expressive choices made by the playwright and the director, designers, and actors that construct the world of the play.

subtext The thoughts and feelings of the character that are unspoken but expressed through gesture, facial expression, and phrasing.

superobjective A term used in method acting to identify the central motivation for a character in a play that brings together in a coherent way all of the character's smaller desires and intentions during the course of the play.

T

table work The reading and discussion of a play done by the cast and the director at the beginning of the rehearsal process.

technical rehearsal A rehearsal dedicated to the integration of scenery, costumes, and lighting cues into the production.

terrain The use of steps, ramps, and levels to reshape the stage floor.

theatre in the round A theatre in which the audience surrounds the stage on all sides.

theatre of the absurd Plays that focus on the lack of meaning in human existence, such as those written by Samuel Beckett, Eugène Ionesco, and Jean Genet.

theatrical conventions Elements of dramatic construction and performance accepted by theatre practitioners and audience members in a given community that facilitate the presentation of plays. Conventions of the Greek theatre include masked actors and offstage violence.

theatricalism A style of playwriting or theatrical production that makes bold use of the resources of the theatre. Theatricalism is nonrealistic and employs vivid imagery and heightened language to express the playwright's meaning. Plays produced in a theatricalist style frequently call attention to the mechanics of the theatre itself.

thespian A term used for "actor" taken from the name of Thespis, the first recognized Greek actor.

through line The arc or progression of an actor's role that ties together all of the character's words and actions.

thrust stage A theatre space in which the audience is placed on three sides of the stage.

total theatre A theatrical style that integrates sound, words, movement, light, music, and color to create a performance that emphasizes gesture and imagery as much as or more than language.

tragedy The dramatic genre initiated by ancient Greek playwrights such as Aeschylus, Sophocles, and Euripides. Tragedy focuses on suffering and loss but celebrates the will of the individual to choose his or her own course of action.

tragicomedy A dramatic genre in which the perspective shifts between serious and comic perspectives.

trilogy Tragedies in ancient Greece were originally written as three interrelated plays called a trilogy.

typecasting A method of choosing actors for roles in a play that relies on generalizations or stereotypical notions of what characters should look like.

U

upstage The area of the stage farthest away from the audience.

Credits

Index

Page numbers in **bold** represent definitions; those in *italics* represent pictures.